German-American Immigration and Ethnicity in Comparative Perspective

Edited by
Wolfgang Helbich and Walter D. Kamphoefner

Max Kade Institute for German-American Studies
University of Wisconsin–Madison

Library of Congress Cataloging-in-Publication Data

German-American immigration and ethnicity in comparative
perspective / edited by Wolfgang Helbich and Walter D. Kamphoefner.
p. cm.
Papers originally presented at a conference at Texas A&M University,
Apr. 1997.
Includes bibliographical references and index.
ISBN 0–924119–18–7
1. German Americans—Social conditions—Congresses. 2.
Immigrants—United States—Social conditions—Congresses.
3. German Americans—Ethnic identity—Congresses. 4. Germany—
Emigration and immigration—History—Congresses. 5. United
States—Emigration and immigration—History—Congresses. 6.
United States—Ethnic relations—Congresses. 7. German Americans—
Politics and government—Congresses. I. Helbich, Wolfgang, 1943– II.
Kamphoefner, Walter D.
E184.G3G295 2004
973'.0431—dc22

2004007238

To the memory of Willi Paul Adams,
contributor, colleague, and friend

Contents

Foreword

We are indebted to the German Historical Institute and Texas A&M University for financial and logistic support of the 1997 College Station conference where these papers originated, and again to the GHI for facilitating the publication of this volume. We also gratefully acknowledge the financial support from the Ministry of Science of the state of North Rhein–Westphalia for part of the editorial work.

Dr. Susan Vogel applied her linguistic talents to going over the English manuscripts written by Germans, and Judith Becker, M.A., spent many months checking, verifying, and coordinating the various manuscripts. Their competent and conscientious work is much appreciated.

At the College Station symposium in April 1997, Willi Paul Adams was still healthy and in good spirits, as most of us had known him for many years, fully participating in the lively discussions and asking his unexpected questions that more often than not yielded worthwhile insights. It was less than three years later that an insidious disease struck and, resisting all kinds of therapy, finally overcame him in October 2002. Our loss was compoinded by the death of his wife Angela Meurer Adams only four months later. Along with being a successful translator in her own right, Angela was a historian and the coeditor of much of Willi's work making classic American texts such as the Declaration of Independence and the Federalist Papers readily accessible for German readers, and a partner in his multifaceted bridge building across the Atlantic.

Willi was one of the very first "genuine" American historians in Germany after World War II. Whereas most of his generation strayed into the field of American history after some work elsewhere, he tackled it with his dissertation and stayed with it ever after. That dissertation on state constitutions in the Revolutionary era was soon to be translated and published in the United States where it won an award from the American Historical Association. It was republished in 2001. He kept working in that period, but added emigration to America and German Americans as a second major research area and also published several surveys and textbooks that were well received and translated into other languages.

But what makes the dedication of this volume resulting from a German-American scholarly conference particularly appropriate is Adams' role as a resourceful, untiring mediator between American historians on both sides of the Atlantic. His dozen or so extended stays at the invitation of prestigious institutions in the United States testify to how fully integrated he was into the profession in America as well as in Germany. In order to facilitate such an integration for other European historians, he actively supported the Organization of American Historians' efforts at internationalization, acting as its liaison in Germany and serving on the editorial board of the *Journal of American History* for almost a decade.

Adams also built bridges between academia and the German general public by writing an important booklet (published at the behest of Berlin's Special Commissioner for Foreigners) depicting the German-American experience and drawing parallels to present-day immigration into Germany with a subtle, but clear appeal for tolerance. One might add that many of the goals we aimed for with the 1997 conference and this resulting volume were also embodied by the scholarship of Willi Paul Adams. It is hard to imagine who could replace him in this role as a knowledgeable, enthusiastic, ever-curious, friendly builder of bridges.

Walter D. Kamphoefner
College Station, Texas

Wolfgang Helbich
Schnepfenthal, Germany

Contributors

Willi Paul Adams (1940–2002) was professor of North American history at the John F. Kennedy Institute for North American Studies of the Free University of Berlin. He published widely in the field of American and German-American history. An expanded edition of his 1980 work, *The First American Constitutions: Republican Ideology and the Making of the State Constitutions in the Revolutionary Era*, appeared in 2001.

Susan Gonzalez Baker was born in La Jolla, California, and was educated at Trinity University; the University of California, Berkeley; and the University of Texas. She served on the faculty of the Department of Sociology at the University of Texas at Austin from 1995 to 2000. Her research interests include Latino immigration and settlement processes in the urban United States, and the relationships among population, environment, and land use characteristics in the nonmetropolitan United States.

Tobias Brinkmann currently works at the Simon Dubnow Institute for Jewish History and Culture at the University of Leipzig. He holds M.A. degrees in history from Indiana University at Bloomington (1992) and the Technical University, Berlin (1994). He has published several articles on modern Jewish history, and his dissertation at the Technical University, Berlin, was recently published as *Von der Gemeinde zur "Community": Jüdische Einwanderer in Chicago, 1840–1900* (2002).

Ingrid Burke is an ecosystem ecologist specializing in soil carbon and nitrogen cycling. Most of her research focuses on semiarid grasslands, shrublands, and croplands. She was born in Richmond, Virginia, and was educated at Middlebury College, Dartmouth College, and the University of Wyoming. She is currently a professor in the Department of Forest Sciences at Colorado State University. Dr. Burke is a National Science Foundation Presidential Faculty Fellow and is the Principal Investigator of the Shortgrass Steppe Long Term Ecological Research Project.

Kathleen Neils Conzen was born in Minneapolis, Minnesota, and received her B.A. from the College of St. Catherine in St. Paul, Minnesota, in 1963. Following a year as a Fulbright scholar in Münster, she completed an M.A. in American history at the University of Delaware in 1966, and received her

Ph.D. in that field from the University of Wisconsin–Madison in 1972. She is now a professor of American history at the University of Chicago, where she has been teaching since 1976. Her main field of interest is nineteenth-century American social history, with special emphases on immigration and ethnicity, urban and rural history, and western history.

Donald DeBats is a professor of American studies and professor of politics at Flinders University in Adelaide, Australia. He was born in upstate Michigan and undertook his higher degrees at the University of Wisconsin–Madison. His major research interests are nineteenth-century politics and the insights into those politics that individual level voting records provide. His major publications include *Elite and Masses* (1990), *Washington County* (1995), and *Degrees of Difference* (1998).

Reinhard R. Doerries was educated in the United States, France, and Germany. He has been a professor of modern history at the University of Hamburg, the University of Kassel, and until 2002 at the Friedrich-Alexander-University Erlangen-Nürnberg, and has taught all aspects of the history of transatlantic relations and American and British history. Besides the history of international relations, his research has concentrated on Germans in the United States, particularly German American Catholicism, as well as the history of Ireland and Irish Americans.

Paul Fessler is an associate professor of history at Dordt College in Sioux Center, Iowa. He was born in New Jersey and received his B.A. from Calvin College in Grand Rapids, Michigan, and his M.A. and Ph.D. from Texas A&M University. His main research interest is in language and education policies, and his doctoral thesis is entitled: "Speaking in Tongues: German-Americans and the Heritage of Bilingual Education."

Jon Gjerde was born in Waterloo, Iowa. He received his Ph.D. at the University of Minnesota in 1982. Since 1985 he has been a professor of history at the University of California, Berkeley. His research interests focus on the history of immigration from Europe to the United States. His present research project is a study of nineteenth-century anti-Catholicism in the United States.

Myron Gutmann was born in Chicago and educated at Columbia and Princeton. He spent twenty-five years at the University of Texas at Austin, most recently as director of the Population Research Center. Since 2001 he has been a professor of history and director of the Inter-University Consortium for Political and Social Research at the University of Michigan. His main research interests are the relationship between population and environment, the history of ethnic group populations in the United States, and the social, demographic, and economic history of early modern Europe.

Wolfgang Helbich was born in Berlin and studied history and English in Berlin, Heidelberg, Paris, and Princeton, where he obtained a B.A. in history. Subsequent to earning his Dr. phil. at Berlin's Free University, he taught North American Civilization at Heidelberg, and from 1974 to 2000 was Professor of North American History at Ruhr-University Bochum. His recent fields of research and publication are German emigration, with an emphasis on immigrant letters and micro-level French-English relations in Québec.

Anne [Aengenvoort] Höndgen received her M.A. (1991) and her Ph.D. (1998) from the University of Bonn. While a visiting fellow at The Ohio State University (1991/1992) she researched her Ph.D. thesis on *Migration, Siedlungsbildung, Akkulturation: Die Auswanderung Nordwestdeutscher nach Ohio, 1830–1914* (1999). Before joining Roland Berger Strategy Consultants in 2000 she worked for five years with the German-American Academic Council Foundation.

Walter D. Kamphoefner was born in 1948 at St. Charles, Missouri, and earned his Ph.D. at the University of Missouri–Columbia in 1978. He is a professor of history at Texas A&M University, where he teaches in the fields of immigration, urbanization, and quantitative methods. Besides his collaborative work with Wolfgang Helbich on immigrant letters, his research interests include immigrant language, bilingual education, and transatlantic social mobility.

Sara Pullum-Pinon was born in Holliston, Massachusetts. She received her Ph.D. in history at the University of Texas at Austin in 2002. Her main field of interest is the cultural history of the United States in the nineteenth century. Her recent research focuses on material culture and comparative regional approaches. Her dissertation is titled "Conspicuous Display and Social Mobility: A Comparison of 1850s Boston and Charleston Elites."

Michael Wala was born in Hamburg, Germany, and received his education at the University of Hamburg (Diplom-Volkswirt), University of Wisconsin-Madison (M.A. in history), University of Hamburg (Ph.D.), and University of Erlangen-Nürnberg (Habilitation). He teaches American History at the University of Bochum. His major research interests are the United States and international relations in the twentieth century, German-American relations, and the history of identity in the eighteenth and nineteenth centuries. His publications cover the Cold War, German-American relations in the twentieth century, gender relations in the eighteenth and nineteenth centuries, and intelligence history.

Introduction

Wolfgang Helbich and Walter D. Kamphoefner

T he historiography of immigration is one entry surprisingly missing from the magisterial and generally very comprehensive *Harvard Encyclopedia of American Ethnic Groups*. But a perusal of the bibliographies of the major entries confirms what scholars in migration or ethnic studies thought they already knew: the bulk of serious studies in those fields appeared in the period after 1960.

The earlier production is not only quantitatively weak, but also suffers from the reputation of over-emphasizing the "contributions" of the respective immigrant nationality or ethnic group (usually with a top-down perspective focusing on atypical elites) and in general indulging in the weakness of "filiopietism," which is frowned upon among modern historians. Most of it deserves its poor reputation, though there are some remarkable exceptions. But even the best of this earlier work is almost always very traditional in its outlook and method.

Reading the bibliographies in the *Harvard Encyclopedia*, however, reveals something else in the context of "filiopietism," something that again most of us have been aware of and taken for granted, even if it might call for some further analysis or interpretation: Though most historians of migration and ethnicity have distanced themselves explicitly or implicitly from the "pietism" part, the "filius" or "filia" component of immigration historiography seems to be very much alive. A very large majority of American scholars, whatever their individual cultural background may be, have names revealing their origin from the same immigrant group they are studying, whereas foreign historians working on minorities in America overwhelmingly tend to choose that of their own nationality. The reasons are fairly obvious: knowledge of language, culture and geography, proximity to sources, and perhaps a fairly complex and elusive syndrome of identification, which may imply all degrees of attraction as well as criticism or even revulsion. Certain of these factors are more prominent among American historians and others among non-Americans, and there are naturally individual differences as well. Yet could it not also be that in our "enlightened" day and age of social history, national history, the mother of all histories, is surviving in a sublimated form?

However that may be, there is nothing wrong or even slightly disreputable with the filii-filiae phenomenon. One might argue, though, that a higher degree of at least detachment, if not objectivity, can be reached if the researcher does not automatically identify with the object of his or her study. Do we not all know that history, especially national history, tends to differ considerably according to whether it has been written by insiders or from the outside? We also know that outsiders may make important contributions precisely because of their foreignness. Thus, we note with great satisfaction that in this volume, three of the seven American authors have names that are not obviously German, which we would like to interpret as indicative of broadness and diversity.

Diversity, not for its own sake but in a similarly meaningful dimension, was also one objective in the selection of the participants in the conference where earlier versions of the chapters in this volume were presented. It took place between April 22–24, 1997, at Texas A&M University in College Station, Texas, under the title "New Approaches to Migration Research: German-Americans in Comparative Perspective." From the very beginning, it was our aim to not only bring together American and German scholars, but also two generations of historians—scholars established in their fields and young academics at the beginning of their careers, who had either just finished their doctoral dissertations or were close to doing so. We extended invitations within this framework of basically one quarter from each of the nationality and generational groups, and though the numerical limitations of participation mandated some difficult choices, the quality of the work presented here seems to justify our selections. Furthermore, we had the great satisfaction that virtually all of those invited accepted, attended, and sent us their papers in revised form.

As the following texts illustrate, there is not one single comparative approach, but a considerable variety of them, even more than are represented here. In three chapters, comparison has an important role but is not the organizing principle. Höndgen describes the development of three German settlements remarkably alike except in religion, but the processes and criteria of acculturation are at the center of her argument, not a systematic point-by-point comparison. Wala's theme underlying his narrative is the difference between Weimar and Nazi policies and German-American responses. Helbich only implicitly compares German-born soldiers and German-American regiments with American ones, except for the explicit confrontation of statements of American and German-born soldiers and officers on "what they were fighting for."

Comparison constitutes the core of several other chapters, though that is not advertised in their titles. Doerries compares German immigrants belonging to different denominations, while Conzen's chapter is based on a three-way comparison, German Catholics with other Germans and with other Catholics. Brinkmann presents a subtle comparative triangle—Jewish, German, American—the major components of German-Jewish identities in mid-nineteenth-century Chicago.

Finally, there are the straight comparative-history chapters. Gjerde's "history of mentalities" approach confronts Anglo-American and immigrant values and their instrumentalization during the nineteenth century, while Gutmann et al., working with an elaborate social scientific apparatus, analyzes which differences from other groups in German-origin farming have been preserved to this day.

DeBats' and Kamphoefner's chapters, both dealing with German and Irish immigrants, offer the most straightforward comparative history. They also have in common a clear-cut objective: proving or disproving the conventional wisdom that Germans were less active and less successful in politics than the Irish. And in what is certainly the most daring comparative enterprise, Fessler juxtaposes nineteenth-century Germans and twentieth-century Hispanics regarding bilingual schooling. At first glance, the differences in time, place, and situation might seem far too great for meaningful comparison, but the narrowing of the question to the best method of bilingual instruction largely overcomes this handicap.

Thus, one might claim that this volume offers a dozen different kinds and several major types of comparative historical work. Of course, that does not exhaust all possibilities, but it does provide an idea of the variety of shapes comparative history can take. It also shows that there is no rigid borderline between fully or genuinely comparative studies and those that employ the instrument of comparison to a greater or lesser degree as one of several tools.

A decade ago, Kathleen Conzen pointed at a multitude of unanswered questions connected with her work on German Americans in Stearns County and concluded: "Only comparison, between Germans within and without settlement concentrations, among various Catholic settlement situations, among German settlements of differing religious orientation, and among different immigrant groups will ultimately sort out these factors. . . ."

If one adds this programmatic list to the empirical examples offered in this volume, the thematic scope of what makes the comparative approach worthwhile in migration and ethnic studies is expanded further. In a more abstract form, one use of comparative history is the testing of beliefs or prejudices about ethnic groups, as here in the chapters by Gutmann et al., DeBats, and Kamphoefner. Comparison within immigrant groups, as suggested by Conzen, may reveal not only commonalities and contrasts, but also their relative weight, such as the religious factor in Höndgen's chapter. And the specific role of German Catholicism and the German Catholic church for settlement patterns and establishing rural traditions could not be elucidated without constant explicit or implicit comparison with Protestant Germans and English-speaking Catholics, as Conzen outlined in 1990 and demonstrates in greater detail in her chapter.

Gjerde does most emphatically what others do in a less direct fashion: compare the majority society with an immigrant group, thereby not only outlining major features of either more distinctly by the contrast, but in Gjerde's case also showing how values or mentalities can be instrumentalized in social conflict. Wala's triple comparison of German policies before World War I, after that war, and after 1933 gives additional depth to his treatment of the middle period, while Helbich's implicit and explicit comparisons between American and German Civil War soldiers put the focus on the differences and show that the comparative method need not be perfectly balanced between differences and similarities in order to be useful.

At least on the basis of the material presented in this volume, we may generalize that a comparative perspective, replacing or at least adding to single-focus work on one ethnic group, can disprove (or confirm) traditional views on immigrant groups, single out unique features, explain the persistence of home-country cultural patterns, sharpen our vision of specific traits, and identify what is part of the cultural baggage, what is environmentally induced, and what must be attributed to other influences.

National history can get by or at least limp along without a comparative dimension; immigration and ethnic history cannot. A group of migrants moving into a foreign country, or an ethnic group residing within a host society, automatically creates a situation of two different entities in contact, and with other migrants following and becoming different ethnic groups, we have several such entities that present-day historians cannot possibly or at least not fruitfully study without at least implicit comparison. Even the most ardent filiopietists in the past (and the few surviving specimens in present-day ethnic studies) cannot operate without comparing—after all, they need a foil to demonstrate the superiority of their stock.

Thus, the comparative approach is a must for serious minority history, though it may be well hidden, and therefore the comparative perspective offered in this volume is as such nothing new. What is new (besides the fairly rare feat of putting chapters between two covers that all have a comparative approach in common) lies in the questions asked, the sources and methods used, and the results.

It is most appropriate that of the four parts into which the twelve chapters have been divided, religion along with politics is represented by four texts each. As Doerries points out movingly and with autobiographic commitment, religious beliefs and institutions have been grievously neglected in our context by a generation of quantifying and economy-oriented social historians. Conzen confirms this emphatically, and focuses on German Catholics, presenting not only a novel interpretative framework, but also a stunning list of what we do not know—and a similar array of topics in need of intensive research. Höndgen highlights the decisive role of religion in a different, most striking way. Settlers in rural Ohio who had the same regional background in Germany, spoke the same dialect, and settled in the same small area founded two villages that maintained very little intercourse and displayed at least latent hostility toward one another, with Catholicism and Protestantism making up the religious curtain between them. For good measure, there was a third village of similar background in the immediate vicinity, similarly segregated, where the third strain of beliefs among German immigrants predominated: Free Thinkers, or radical liberals.

Much smaller in numbers than these three groups, German Jews were in a complicated situation in their attempts to position themselves in various places within the triangle of Jewish, German, and American. Brinkmann manages to disentangle the web of deep-rootedness in the German-Jewish Reform tradition and a typically German disdain for American culture, counterbalanced by distrust of German authorities and leaning toward American liberty.

Agricultural patterns, gender roles, and ethnic identity are all present and intertwined in the next two chapters. Gjerde spins a subtle web around the Yankee accusation that German (and some other) immigrants "make their womenfolk work in the fields." He analyzes the pro and con positions, shows how far into family structure this one phenomenon reaches, and demonstrates how both sides instrumentalized such traditions to attack the other side.

Gutmann and his colleagues are after a different tradition. They ask two important historical questions—did German immigrant farmers in fact employ agricultural methods different from those of the Americans, and if so, is there anything left, that is, presently recognizable, of such differences? In order to find answers, they muster an overwhelming array of meteorological, other scientific, and statistical data aside from the usual census material for a very large territory in the Plains States.

Politics and national identity stand in the foreground in the following four chapters. Two of these—DeBats and Kamphoefner—test the conventional wisdom that Irish immigrants were politically more active, more astute, and more successful than Germans. They do so from the bottom up and from the top down: DeBats interprets the voting behavior—participation levels, block voting and other aspects—of the two ethnicities in three communities in North America on the basis of rare surviving poll books. Kamphoefner counts and comments on the mayors of major American cities during a time span of over a century. Strikingly, their conclusions are almost identical—and contradict the traditional view.

Adams presents two German-born U.S. Congressmen and demonstrates how they represent alternative behavioral patterns: the ethnic politician who also considers the country as a whole, and the one who is almost indistinguishable from his Anglo-American confrères. And Fessler regards the present bilingual education debate about Spanish as a fruitless exercise in view of the fact that we have had all that before, more than a century ago, with German as the contentious language and that—learning from history!—the earlier experience has shown a way that would put the controversy to rest.

War and National Identity is the heading of the final two chapters. In Wala's text, actually two wars figure, World Wars I and II, but his main focus is on the in-between period and the cautious attempts of the Weimar Republic government to revitalize a German America shattered by the war, assiduously trying to avoid the high-handed style of the Empire and in fact having a measure of success until Nazi clumsiness finally scared off all moderate German Americans. Helbich's chapter centers on the problem of the national identity of German-born Union soldiers, elaborating on the "Germanness" of German regiments, analyzing the sharp contrast between the extremely high opinion of German fighting qualities and German generals held by practically all Germans and the abysmally negative judgment on them by Americans, testing the conventional wisdom that fighting and dying together leveled ethnic differences, and complementing James McPherson's studies of Civil War motivation by a parallel analysis of the German-born military men.

Does the mix of generations and nationalities reveal any differences or similarities in topics, sources, or approach? Which dividing line—age or passport—is stronger, if one exists at all? Or is there an academic community that is truly international or at least bi-national?

The question of generations is very hard to answer on the basis of this volume, since one of the German and two of the American junior scholars dropped out for various reasons between conference and publication, and Gutmann's collaborators worked under his guidance. All one can really say about the three that are left is that they wisely and clearly limited the scope of their investigations, whereas the work of the more senior historians is rather open-ended.

Comparing the latter by nationality, again there is no conspicuous difference. One might find some more quantitative work on the American side—DeBats, Kamphoefner, Gutmann et al.—than with the Germans, among whom only Höndgen and Helbich work with figures, and rather marginally at that. There seems to be a certain tendency (not a hard-and-fast rule) for German contributions to reflect the more difficult access to American sources and to the superior resources and logistics of American university libraries, and vice versa. Most certainly the situation of two decades ago, when it was a rare and expensive privilege for Europeans to spend time in the United States, has changed drastically, and the source accessibility gap has narrowed accordingly. But though the expense differential might have shifted, it still makes a considerable difference whether one normally lives in North America or in Europe.

In most areas, however, including theory, methodology, topics, questions asked, approaches, and usually even the language of publication, German and American historians of German immigration and ethnicity are remarkably similar. One might speculate whether this poses a case of assimilation or a transatlantic melting pot of academic cultures. It is debatable which of the two holds true, though all would agree that it is not cultural pluralism. And much speaks for the melting pot scenario.

Perhaps the major reasons for such remarkable homogeneity is the mutual need for information and assistance between two locations and two cultures, but even more so the fact that most of the senior people have crossed the Atlantic many times and have known each other for many years, from conferences as well as visits. And this is no wonder considering that in Germany we have about a dozen senior scholars and about as many junior ones, whereas the number of those American historians who deal not with German history, but mainly with German-American migration and ethnic history, is not much larger. And the conference on which this volume is based was just a way station. Since 1997, some fifteen conferences on related topics, attended by Americans as well as Germans, have taken place both in the United States and Germany.

Immigration and ethnic studies may have been boosted by ethnic revival, directly in the United States and indirectly in Europe. Cultural pluralism or multiculturalism may then have taken over the same function. Multiculturalism, at least where government has not ennobled it into an identity-defining dogma, seems to have lost much of its glamour and its capacity to stimulate, but it is hard to see what, if anything, has replaced it in our context. And yet during the time that has elapsed since the conference where these papers were presented, the production in immigration and ethnic studies, particularly regarding Germans, has not diminished to a trickle but, if anything, has increased substantially. Has it become "self-sustaining?"

By our conservative count, that is, eliminating borderline cases, eighteen scholarly books (several of them former dissertations) have appeared, and eleven dissertations accepted (to be published shortly) on the German side since early 1997, as well as thirteen books and fourteen dissertations here in the United States, each clearly within the area limned by the title of this volume. All of them build solidly on previous work, and most of them are innovative in important respects. Thus, the results presented in the papers published here do not stand alone, but have their place in a living tradition and are constantly being added to in a lively scholarly enterprise.

Part I:

Religious Diversity

1

Immigrants and the Church: German Americans in Comparative Perspective

Reinhard R. Doerries

The linkage of immigration and religion would appear to be an almost natural consequence of the meaning of faith and worship for most men and women. The linkage was reinforced when people who refused to adopt religious procedures and rituals as prescribed by a ruler, a government, or merely an intolerant society were subjected to persecution. Bitter wars were fought in the name of religion and over religious issues, and it is not astonishing that immigrants from most countries brought hatred and prejudice, along with their faith, with them to America. Many of the new Americans even exerted great energy trying to rebuild European structures, in the German case, as we know, to the point of trying to organize a German state in North America.[1]

Religious freedom, in the American sense, had not existed in most regions of Europe, and Germany was no exception. Emigration as an act of self-liberation, that is, breaking with one's own past, might, therefore, also be seen as self-liberation from religious intolerance—that suffered from others and that righteously inflicted by oneself on others. While this was true for many immigrants, even those who, if asked, would have given economic reasons for their migration, it is even more true for those who were actually driven from their homeland by the religious bigotry and violence of their compatriots.

German society, torn asunder by the painful religious and social conflicts connected with the Reformation, may serve as an example of a people beset almost continuously by fierce campaigns of religious intolerance and persecution. The forced union of the Lutherans and the Reformed Church, an unrelenting aggressiveness of the Freethinkers toward organized churches, the ostracizing of all so-called sects by both Lutherans and Catholics, and the *Kulturkampf*, the German chancellor's war against the Catholic Church, all

---

1.   For instance, the Giessener Auswanderungs-Gesellschaft of 1833 wanted a "teutschen Freistaat, ein verjuengtes Teutschland." Reinhard R. Doerries, *Iren und Deutsche in der Neuen Welt* (Stuttgart: Franz Steiner, 1986), 48–49.

illustrate the religious divisiveness apparent in German society throughout much of the nineteenth century. In 1907 Adolf Harnack, a leading German theologian of his time, put it in these words: "Everywhere one meets the colossal prejudice; everywhere one meets the fences, yes, the walls of denominations."[2]

The study of German immigrants to the United States, and, even more so, of their acculturation in American society, would therefore seem to be a futile exercise if faith and religious practice were ignored—as indeed it has been in much of immigration history, not to mention German emigration history. The European churches, with all their inherent structural and doctrinal problems, consciously or unconsciously were brought to America by the immigrants. There, these European churches were confronted by a wide variety of tolerated religious practices, as well as by an older American tradition of the imagination of "religious homogeneity."[3] In that confrontation most European religious institutions, even those brought across the Atlantic by the initially much feared Irish Catholics, underwent considerable alterations and in time came to be considered American. Surely, German immigrants, like most others and in some cases more than others, came to America to escape their past, but they carried with them a specific German culture and with it specific religious persuasions. Upon arrival at least they often acted as though they were determined to maintain German culture unchanged in America. What differentiated the so-called Germans from the French, the English, or even the Irish, was their apparent lack of cohesion. They were sharply divided by regional origin and culture; by such divergent dialects that English, in some cases, became their lingua franca; by church membership, and often by what can only be called rigid social or class differences. Because faith—and therefore the church—belongs to the personal realm, it is less exposed to normative outside influences. It is, therefore, less quickly challenged than other cultural traditions, meaning that a vital factor in the social control system is more protected than other cultural factors, such as the law or education.

In some ways, faith and religious beliefs associated with it may constitute one of the more enduring intangibles of individual and group behavior, comparable to such influences as may be caused by strong family ties or the love between partners. Personal religion, indeed, may be of even greater importance to the life of the individual than other intangible factors, because

---

2.   Adolf Harnack, *Protestantismus und Katholizismus in Deutschland* (Berlin: Georg Stilke, 1907), 5. (Translation.)

3.   Martin E. Marty, *Righteous Empire* (New York: Dial Press, 1970), 127.

it is concerned with the *telos*, the ultimate human uncertainty about the end of life. For mankind, faith may serve, in former times no differently than today, as a kind of assurance against an almost all-encompassing insecurity. If one assumes that emigrants are persons possessing more strength, self-assurance, and willpower than those who stay behind and accept the seemingly inevitable, it might also be argued that emigrants, most likely, have fewer questions about the correctness of their religious beliefs. Success in the process of migration from one society to another and in the construction of a new life will reinforce such persuasions. Faith and the organizational church are, therefore, of considerable importance in the immigrant's life, and changing them is likely to be one of the more significant aspects of the acculturation experienced by the second generation.

When I began to emphasize the essential role played by church and faith in society back in the 1970s, my views encountered an almost uniform opposition from German historians concerned with emigration from Germany to the United States.[4] At the time this seemed perplexing, and it took considerable resolve to continue my research concerned with the church as one of the significant institutions of society—certainly of multiethnic American society,[5] but also, even if less evident, of many other societies, including those of most European countries. Fortunately, I encountered American historians and social scientists willing to share their thoughts on vital questions of church and faith in mainstream American society, as well as in diverse ethnic minorities existing within the American cultural majority. At an early stage of my work, I had the added fortune of making the acquaintance of and learning from two American historians who may not have had a great number of common research interests, but who both contributed to my growing persuasion that non-quantifiable factors, among them faith or loyalty to a church, played a more significant part in the processes of society than we were led to believe by the then rather dominant quantifiers in American social history. Herbert Gutman did more than anyone to point out the intellectual fallacies of quantitative history in its purer form, and John Higham with patience led me to realize and consider

---

4.   There was no one among the small group of German historians teaching American history at German universities who was interested in American church history—Catholic, Protestant, or otherwise. Hartmut Lehmann's *Martin Luther in the American Imagination* (München: Wilhelm Fink Verlag, 1988) is one of the few German studies in recent years dealing with American religious questions or American church history.

5.   Reinhard R. Doerries, "Church and Faith on the Great Plains Frontier: Acculturation Problems of German-Americans," *Amerikastudien/American Studies* 24 (1979): 275–287; Doerries, *Iren und Deutsche*, especially chapter V, "Kirche und Glaube im neuen Land."

the undercurrents of American society prior to World War I. It did not require much perspicaciousness to recognize the church or religious organizations as a major force in the American social process.

While there is nothing to indicate that German scholars of American social history have changed their viewpoints of a quarter of a century ago—church and faith still seem to be of no particular interest to them[6]—modern church history has continued to be a very significant research area for American historians. Moreover, in the United States and elsewhere the visible increase of fundamentalist tendencies has been registered, at times with apparent misgivings. Fundamentalism, religious radicalism, and new churches or so-called "sects" have caused fears in traditional societies, and trends even to ostracize the new churches are not limited to societies lacking strong democratic political structures.[7] As in earlier periods, intolerance toward those on the fringes of religious society often appears more vociferous and violent in Europe than in America, even though American churches are no less rooted in faith than the churches of Europe. The New World with its New World Order merely appears to have been more receptive to outsiders and their churches and other religious organizations than much of European society has been and certainly than Germany with its history of bitter internal division caused by the intrinsically intolerant behavior of both Protestants (in Germany: evangelisch-lutherisch) and Catholics.[8] When studying the acculturation processes of Germans in American society, one of the more pressing questions then would appear to be how much and what kind of faith and religious behaviorism was transported to America by those who left German society, and how was what they brought with them Americanized.

At first glance it seems true that Germans or Prussians, no less than Americans, saw themselves as a chosen people. Yet, it would appear that chosenness was already present at the birth of America, while, by contrast, the German people oppressed by their kings and regional princelings were still

---

6.   Except for the work of a few German scholars on American history of the colonial and revolutionary periods, ongoing research largely ignores the churches and their history in America. See the annual bibliographies published by the German Society for American Studies.

7.   As an example of such reactions of modern Western societies, see the official steps recently taken against Scientologists in Germany.

8.   The ecumenical movement of recent decades and the considerable dependence of both churches on the government for financial support (church taxes) may have created the impression of a common position. In fact, however, the absence of other strong Protestant churches (except for the Reformed Church) has contributed to a continuing bipolarization that is in sharp contrast to the American multitude of churches and denominations.

struggling for proof of their chosenness, when in World War I they grasped for more power and instead lost what they had gained since 1870/1871. German immigrants then, it is argued here, not unlike other immigrants from Europe, often left a society harshly divided by religious fact, as well as by prejudice, and entered an American society that, however prejudiced, had never experienced the extent and the continuities of religious intolerance common to most of Western European national history. One may well consider religion, among other things, as a matter of the private sphere, as has been done in the past; but it is also true, in spite of all continued tendencies to privatize faith, that faith and the public organization of the faithful have exerted considerable influence on the development of American society.

The divisiveness of German Americans in religious matters has been so strong that it has prevented them from dominating any of the large churches in America. Catholics, Lutherans, and Freethinkers spent much of their strength feuding against each other, and the bitterness with which the groups pursued their differences in public was indeed extraordinary. Intolerance often reigned supreme.[9] There is, therefore, nothing on the German-American side that might be compared to the role Irish Americans played in the Roman Catholic Church. Even German Lutherans in America, battling each other over the Augsburg Confession and language maintenance, would not gather in one church and instead preferred to join other Europeans in splintered Lutheran synods.[10] They clearly accepted and benefited from the almost unlimited religious freedom in American society caused by the separation of church and state, as laid down in the First Amendment to the Constitution: "Congress shall make no law respecting an establishment of religion, or prohibiting the free exercise thereof."[11] They began to behave, in most instances, as other Americans of various faiths would: They learned to be free and independent of

9.   Doerries, *Iren und Deutsche*, 122–123. Carl Wittke, *Refugees of Revolution* (Philadelphia: University of Pennsylvania Press, 1952), 192–193, refers to the positions of the German churches in America on slavery to demonstrate the divergent views of German Americans.

10.   Russel B. Nye, *Society and Culture in America, 1830–1860* (New York: Harper & Row, 1974), 303; Lehmann, *Martin Luther*, 110–120.

11.   Separation of church and state did not imply that leaders of the churches and contemporary politicians would not have regular interaction to attend to institutional and political needs. See, for instance, David J. O'Brien, "American Catholic Historiography: A Post-Conciliar Evaluation," *Church History* 37 (March 1968): 82–83. See also Winfred E. Garrison, "Characteristics of American Organized Religion," *The Annuals of the American Academy of Political and Social Science* 256 (March 1948): 16: ". . . the First Amendment clearly meant: . . . no establishment of several or all churches by levying a tax to be divided among them . . . ," a practice still accepted in Germany without noticeable opposition.

government influences and, like Americans, they, who often had no experience in freedom and rebellion, came to oppose the hierarchies in the church and to operate as trustees of their often largely independent parishes. Lacking the structures of the Italian-American campanile society and not possessing the rich Irish-American memory of the endless struggle against Britain, the common Protestant enemy, German Americans, in most cases, adjusted to their surroundings and eventually became Americans. Exceptions, even such developments as the Missouri Synod with its almost nationalist language maintenance efforts,[12] or Cahenslyism, the German onslaught toward the end of the nineteenth century against Americanism within the then strongly Irish American and confident Roman Catholic Church,[13] merely demonstrate the comparatively serious lack of religious cohesion among the Germans. The point should not be overstressed, but, in contrast to the Irish-American takeover of the Roman Catholic Church from the French, both Wilhelm Löhe's efforts on behalf of German-American Lutherans and the Catholic Cahenslyite movement did not come from within American society, but rather received their main impetus from European forces outside of America, pursuing European cultural, as well as religious goals. Carl Schneider in his grand study of *The German Church on the American Frontier* put it straightforwardly: "The general feeling prevailed that the factors of race, folk, and nation were normative for the vital, spiritual development of the Germans in America."[14]

Indeed, when observing the Americanist Bishop John Ireland and his relationship with Theodore Roosevelt and the American nation,[15] the vision of one American church, possibly split into denominations as different as Catholics, Protestants, or Jews, becomes a veritable possibility. In notable contrast to Europe or Germany, *the* American church, however, if one can

12. See, for instance, Wilhelm Löhe, *Zuruf aus der Heimat an die deutsch-lutherische Kirche Nordamericas* (Stuttgart: Samuel Gottlieb Liesching, 1845). On Wilhelm Löhe's connection to Missouri Synod parishes, see Sidney E. Ahlstrom, A *Religious History of the American People* (New Haven: Yale University Press, 1972), 759.

13. Reinhard R. Doerries, "Peter Paul Cahensly und der St. Raphaels-Verein: Die Geschichte eines sozialen Gedankens," *Menschen Unterwegs* 2 (1981): 5–14.

14. Carl E. Schneider, *The German Church on the American Frontier* (St. Louis: Eden Publishing House, 1939), 471. Schneider finds this particularly remarkable because the earlier use of nationalism and folk by men such as Wilhelm Löhe predates the founding of the German Empire.

15. Theodore Roosevelt's comment about John Ireland in 1893: "Every true American, Catholic or Protestant, should be glad that there lives in the United States so stout a champion of Americanism as Archbishop Ireland. . . ." Cited in James Michael Reardon, *The Catholic Church in the Diocese of St. Paul* (St. Paul: North Central Publishing Company, 1952), 307.

speak of one societal institution in terms of a moral commitment, has been free of the state ever since the birth of the republic, and the community of the saints is but a memory from the period before there was an American nation.[16]

When taking account of the differing religious traditions among ethnic groups in America, one might feel inclined to appraise separately the influence of church and faith inside the ethnic group on the one hand, and the influence of the ethnic church and its activities on the larger American society on the other. Both aspects should be scrutinized when studying a specific ethnic group, and most promising would seem to be a comparative approach, drawing on the social processes experienced by other ethnic groups.

Most earlier German immigrants were religious, and it has been said that "their history is therefore largely the history of their churches."[17] Many of them were Lutheran and German Reformed, but the more peripheral German post-Reformation churches, in German society soon outcast as sects, were also represented in North America from the beginning. Moreover, American churches, such as the Methodists, Congregationalists, and Baptists, had made considerable inroads among German immigrants rather early in the nineteenth century, even though these churches were hardly known in Germany then. In several cases, early followers of such churches had migrated from Germany to America only to return to Germany for missionary work several years later. Some of the Germans who were won over by these missionaries later emigrated to America.[18] That Catholics were among the earliest German immigrants, and that they made up a considerable percentage of the Germans coming to America in the hundred years between the Napoleonic Wars and

---

16. There is no doubt, however, that some churches, certainly including the Roman Catholic Church, have tried to influence governmental work and the elections. O'Brien, "American Catholic Historiography," 82–83. The controversies over the Bennett Law in Wisconsin and the "Edwards Law" in Illinois, both in 1889, continue to be discussed among specialists.

17. Theodore Frelinghuysen Chambers, *The Early Germans of New Jersey* (Dover: Dover Printing Co., 1895), 41.

18. Thus, for instance, Methodism came to Thuringia. Renate Schwemer, *Die Auswanderung aus dem Großherzogtum Sachsen-Weimar-Eisenach vom Anfang des 19. Jahrhunderts bis zur Reichsgründung* (Ph.D. diss., University of Hamburg, 1944). Ludwig Rott, *Die englischen Beziehungen der Erweckungsbewegung und die Anfänge des wesleyanischen Methodismus in Deutschland* (Frankfurt: Studiengemeinschaft für Geschichte des Methodismus, 1968), 267–268. Better known are the Palatines who were brought to Ireland in the eighteenth century and there became faithful Methodists before later migrating to America. Walter A. Kittle, *Early Eighteenth Century Palatine Emigration* (Baltimore: Genealogical Publishing Co., 1965), 90–91. On early Congregationalist efforts among the Germans in the Midwest, see George J. Eisenach, *A History of the German Congregational Churches in the United States* (Yankton, SD: Pioneer Press, 1938) 1–17.

World War I had been largely ignored by historians, even in the United States. Only the influential publications of scholars such as Philip Gleason, Robert Cross, and Colman Barry finally demonstrated that Germans in America often were Catholics.[19]

One of the most significant influences of the church, inside the ethnic group as well as extending to numerous other sectors of the dominant American society, is the normative force. Depending on other ethnic traditions and cultural habits, the instruments employed to exert such normative force vary from one ethnic group to another. Also, it should be emphasized that it is not necessarily the size of the membership of a church that determines the extent of its influence. The spiritual authority behind such normative values is not easy to grasp, and it is even more difficult to measure the influences going out into society at large from such values. To what extent public behavior and policy-making are shaped by private faith must remain in most instances an unanswerable question. Few political figures open themselves so freely to the public as President Jimmy Carter, who made no secret of his being "born again" and whose political decisions therefore, justified or not, were judged differently than those of other national leaders. Nevertheless, there is no doubt that certain basic tenets common to most Christian and Jewish moral standards have religious roots and are kept alive less by institutional influence than by personal faith.

However personalized faith may be, we can be certain that institutions and associations of the church played a considerable part in the daily life of the immigrant, thus giving the church also a public quality. For the immigrant, Catholic as well as Lutheran, the institutionalized church was probably one of the most important vehicles in the difficult process of acculturation, the transcending from the familiar and clearly outlined European cultural surroundings to the world of seemingly unlimited choice and opportunity in America. In this respect, immigrants from German regions did not differ from the Scandinavians, the English, the Irish, or later arriving Italians and East Europeans. Protestant or Catholic, in large numbers they turned to the already existing churches of their faith and ritual, and where such did not yet exist, as was often the case, they erected their own, rather than joining one similar to their own. Though often without financial means, they made considerable personal sacrifices to establish parishes using their accustomed ritual and

---

19. See, for instance, Philip Gleason, *The Conservative Reformers* (Notre Dame: University of Notre Dame Press, 1968); Robert D. Cross, *The Emergence of Liberal Catholicism in America* (Cambridge: Harvard University Press, 1958); and Colman J. Barry, *The Catholic Church and German Americans* (Milwaukee: Bruce, 1953).

language. Once a group of people had created what might be called a parish, they would obtain a pastor or a priest, and, since in most cases he would have been trained by a particular denomination, he would use his connections and write for help, often from as far away as the country from which he and the immigrants had come.

Crying for help, these letters were written by the hundreds,[20] and they led to the formation of groups having for their main purpose what they saw as mission work among the immigrant churches but what, in fact, often was no more than what we would refer to as a fund drive. Some of these missions grew into important organizations. In most cases the collected funds were donated by the faithful attendants of worship services, quite average people. Motivations of those helping to organize such drives varied from pure missionary interests of many clergy, such as Friedrich Résé, to the almost political considerations of King Ludwig I of Bavaria, who disliked the fact that money collected in Bavarian parishes went to North America by way of the powerful French Oeuvre de la Propagation de la Foi. Because the Bavarian king wanted to have things his way, he permitted the founding of the Ludwig-Missionsverein.[21] Most comparable, other than the Oeuvre working out of Lyon, was the Austrian Leopoldinenstiftung founded in Vienna in 1829 to support Austrian Catholics in America.[22] The occasional comment that Lutherans in America received much less financial assistance of this nature than Catholics on the whole appears quite justified, but the relative lack of support, it should be pointed out, was caused by the way Lutherans were divided among themselves in the Old World and the New. Certainly, the unity of the Roman Catholic Church was of great benefit to Catholic immigrants.

The same kind of Catholic unity stemming from a worldwide Catholic Church was clearly evident in American society where the associationalism of the parishes could freely grow, ignored by the state and protected by a

---

20. In the case of German Catholics in the United States, the respective collections of letters have been saved in Munich, Vienna, and a number of monasteries in Germany. The letters from the priests in America to their dioceses are in many cases very informative documents about daily life and problems in German-American Catholic parishes. Because most letters are in German, they have not been used to any great extent by American historians, and German historians so far have shown almost no interest in this kind of documentation.

21. Concerning the background of this society see Willibald Mathäser, *Bonifaz Wimmer O.S.B. und König Ludwig I. von Bayern* (München: Priester-Missionsbund, 1937); Willibald Mathäser, *Der Ludwig-Missionsverein in der Zeit König Ludwigs I. von Bayern* (München: Salesianische Offizin, 1939).

22. The Leopoldinenstiftung, like the Ludwig-Missionsverein, was largely a result of the labor of the Vicar General from Cincinnati, Frederic Rese.

diocesan shield. To be sure, German Lutheran associations also grew in the unencumbered American environment, but they lacked the strength gained from a strong mother church and, it needs to be said, they were not forced to unite as Catholics were, or as Catholics may have thought they were, in view of vociferous and at times aggressive nativist anti-Catholic campaigns.[23] Philip Schaff, a leading German-American Reformed theologian, co-founder of the Evangelical Alliance, and a vociferous supporter of church unity, put it bluntly: "The Lutheran Church in America really is a unit in name only; in fact, it consists of a great number of synods that are quite independent of each other and some of which belong to a quite opposite dogmatic direction."[24]

When immigrant churches finally reached a certain financial security, they did not break off the old ties to forge ahead on their own. To the contrary, the former ties were often reinforced by American money, now flowing back, for instance, to help finance Lutheran seminaries in Germany training pastors for North America. The Evangelical-Lutheran Seminary Eben-Ezer in Kropp and a similar seminary in Breklum are examples of institutions working with funds coming back from the United States.[25] Most of the initiatives, Catholic or Lutheran, and later in America also German Jewish,[26] came from leading individuals, but the financial base was often created by the modest donations from a great number of very average parishioners on both sides of the Atlantic.

A further origin of the fast-growing associationalism was a much older tradition of self-help, thought to have originated in England and closely linked

---

23. Paul Kleppner, *The Cross of Culture* (New York: Free Press, 1970) who finds that Catholics under attack from the "German anticlerical Forty-Eighters" (77) were drawn to the Democrats.

24. Philip Schaff, "Die Deutsche Kirche in Amerika und der Deutsche Kirchentag," *Der Deutsche Kirchenfreund* 6 (February 1853): 67. (Translation.)

25. See Wilhelm Fr. Herrmann, "The Kropp Lutheran Seminary 'Eben-Ezer' Germany, and Its Relations to the United Lutheran Church in America" (Master's Thesis, Lutheran Theological Seminary, 1938). A. Späth, "Ein historischer Überblick über die früheren Verhandlungen des General-Konzils in Sachen Kropps," Erste Allgemeine Konferenz Deutscher Pastoren des General-Konzils der Ev. Luth. Kirche in Nord-Amerika in der Zions-Kirche, Rochester, NY, am 9. und 10. September 1908, Archives of the Metropolitan New York Synod of the Lutheran Church in America.

26. For instance, the Hebrew Emigrant Aid Society (HEAS) founded in 1881 in New York, followed by the Hebrew Immigrant Aid Society (HIAS) a few years later (organized by a *landsmanshaft*). Irving Howe, *World of Our Fathers* (New York: Simon and Schuster, 1976), 44–50.

to the idea of mutual assistance.[27] Regrettably, associationalism or, in German, *Vereinswesen* has received only scant attention in German historiography, and consequently we know very little about the German roots of the German-American *Vereinswesen*.[28] Workingmen's clubs and often forbidden political associations may have been among the precedents, but we lack satisfactory studies of German religious *Vereine*. German-American church associations were part of an enormous associational network permeating almost every sector of American society in the second half of the nineteenth century. Catholic associations received an added boost when the American church hierarchy suddenly declared membership in secret societies, that is, in most lodges, incompatible with membership in the Church and, therefore, partaking in the Holy Communion.[29] Because most associations, besides their leisure-time functions, also served economic needs not provided by society at large, such as burial insurance, accident insurance, orphanages, old people's homes, and the like, workers often considered membership in these associations a necessity, and the church was hard pressed to create an associational network of its own.[30] The leaders of these efforts were pastors, teachers, or other persons of civic influence in the parish.

Immigrant aid societies, such as the St. Raphael's Verein, the St. Raphael's Italian Benevolent Society, or the Irish Catholic Colonization Society, are good examples of this type of organization. In most cases they enjoyed church support and benefited from the good will of religious and civic leaders in the ethnic group. In some instances, they were encouraged and supported by

---

27. For these antecedents, see especially P. H. J. H. Gosden, *The Friendly Societies in England 1815–1875* (Manchester: University Press, University of Manchester, 1961); and P. H. J. H. Gosden, *Self-Help* (London: B. T. Batsford, 1973).

28. In Germany Thomas Nipperdey has been one of the very few historians seriously concerned with the role of the *Vereinswesen* in society. See, for instance, Thomas Nipperdey, "Verein als soziale Struktur in Deutschland im späten 18. und frühen 19. Jahrhundert," in *Geschichtswissenschaft und Vereinswesen im 19. Jahrhundert*, ed. Hartmut Boockmann, A. Esch, H. Heimpel, T. Nipperdey and H. Schmidt (Göttingen: Vandenhoeck & Ruprecht, 1972), 1–44.

29. Father John Riordan of the Leo House in New York made certain that Catholic immigrants from Germany understood the message: "Ich warne dich aber vor geheimen Gesellschaften, sogenannten Logen, welche meistens Unterstützungsvereine sind . . . weil aber viele derselben Freimaurerlogen sind, welche außer ihren Wohltätigkeitszwecken auch andere, kirchenfeindliche Zwecke verfolgen, die meisten gewöhnlichen Mitgliedern nicht bekannt sind, so darf ein katholischer Christ solchen Vereinen nicht beitreten." John Riordan, *Ein Erstes Wort in der neuen Welt, dem Katholischen Einwanderer Gewidmet* (New York: no publisher named, 1891), 20–21.

30. Doerries, *Iren und Deutsche*, 254.

emigration aid societies, such as the Società Italiana di San Raffaele, founded by the Bishop of Piacenza, Giovanni Battista Scalabrini,[31] or the Catholic Emigration Society of Ireland whose main purpose was to persuade Irish emigrants to travel to the American Midwest rather than stay in the cities along the Eastern seaboard.[32] The spirit of such associations was spelled out by the leading Americanist in the still Irish-dominated American Roman Catholic Church, John Ireland, and his friends among the hierarchy. In a pamphlet entitled *An Invitation to the Land* and designed for Irish immigrants in the port of New York, the message could not be clearer: ". . . he [the Irish immigrant] should possess that noble quality which western life so fully develops—SELF RELIANCE. Under God, it will be on himself he must depend for future success."[33]

Typically these societies, while associated with or being part of a parish or a diocese, not only attended to spiritual needs, but became involved, almost automatically, in much needed social work and regular service functions. Stephanus Keyl, the German Lutheran immigrant missionary in the port of New York, for instance, cooperated with the General Council and the Missouri Synod. In 1881 he received and dispatched to points farther west some 4,200 immigrants, gave financial advances to impoverished new arrivals, found jobs for 184 German immigrants, and, similar to the Irish priests, sent back money from the immigrants to relatives and friends left behind. Also typical for these associations was the close cooperation of Pastor Keyl with the city's most important German-American civic association, the Deutsche Gesellschaft der Stadt New York.[34]

Besides the ethnic associations with their often curious amalgamation of religious and socioeconomic purposes, the most significant ethnic activity was directed toward educating the next generation. Schools, however, were

---

31. Regarding Scalabrini and his work among the Italian Catholic immigrants, see Marco Caliaro and Mario Francesconi, *John Baptist Scalabrini: Apostle to the Immigrants* (New York: Center for Migration Studies, 1977).

32. The Catholic Emigration Society of Ireland was founded upon the initiative of Daniel O'Connell in 1841. James P. Shannon, *Catholic Colonization on the Western Frontier* (New Haven: Yale University Press, 1957), 16–18.

33. *An Invitation to the Land* (St. Paul: The Irish Colonization Bureau, 1877). Jewish aid societies in New York had the same goal when they admonished the Jewish immigrants to leave the squalor of the city and settle in rural America. Thomas Kessner, *The Golden Door* (New York: Oxford University Press, 1977), 20.

34. III. Verhandlungen der New Yorker Lokal-Conferenz vom Juni 1880 bis Juni 1886, 4. Oktober 1888, 38, Archives of the Atlantic District, Lutheran Church-Missouri Synod, Bronxville, NY.

for the immigrant not only an economic burden that required a considerable amount of cooperation across class lines, but they were also a prime vehicle for the passage of cultural traditions to the children. It is true that for the early immigrants, such as the Germans and the Irish, schools were needed to educate the young, not necessarily to perpetuate German Lutheran or Catholic or Irish Catholic culture. By allowing the priests to teach, the church often became the first institution capable of providing an education.

Later, in the American city, the ethnic school quickly took on other meanings, one of them, as Joshua A. Fishman and Vladimir C. Nahirny put it, being a counter force against "urban industrial American mass culture."[35] Since the merits of parochial schools continue to be a lively issue even in our time, it should be pointed out that church education organized by newcomers was in existence well before what we call public school systems came into being. Moreover, the forerunners of today's parochial schools were not limited to Catholic schools but were also organized by Lutherans, Quakers, Congregationalists, and other denominations.[36] In the United States demand for private church-run education has always been high, and the growth figures from Chicago, showing an increase from 14 schools with 5,770 students in 1865 to 134 schools with 84,429 students in 1910, are not exceptional.[37]

The Catholic Church in America needed some time until a Catholic school system became an official reality in 1884 at the Third Plenary Council in Baltimore. Then, however, the hierarchy left no doubt as to the seriousness of its intent: "No parish is complete till it has schools adequate to the needs of its children, and the pastor and people of such a parish should feel that they have not accomplished their entire duty until the want is supplied."[38] Evidently, the parishes followed the directive, and the Catholic school system, as a result, experienced a very impressive growth. Interestingly, while language maintenance played a major role in the bitter confrontation of Cahenslyism with Americanism, the church school as an institution or the appointment of,

---

35. Joshua A. Fishman and Vladimir C. Nahirny, "The Ethnic Group School and Mother Tongue Maintenance," in *Language Loyalty in the United States*, edited by Joshua A. Fishman, V. C. Nahirny, J. E. Hofman, and R. G. Hayden (The Hague: Mouton, 1966), 92–93.

36. Robert Middlekauf, "Before the Public School: Education in Colonial America," *Current History* 62 (June 1972): 279–281.

37. James W. Sanders, *The Education of an Urban Minority* (New York: Oxford University Press, 1977), 4.

38. *Pastoral Letter of the Archbishops and Bishops of the United States Assembled in the Third Plenary Council of Baltimore, to the Clergy and Laity of their Charge* (Baltimore: Baltimore Publishing Co., 1884), 17.

for instance, German- or Polish-speaking priests and nuns in such schools were not among the major issues. Perhaps Cardinal James Gibbons had it right when in 1907 he said about his Catholics: "With the English language as a constantly enlarging part of their course, they are gradually, almost unconsciously, brought into complete sympathy with American ideals, and readily adapt themselves to American manners and customs. This assimilation is constantly going on in our Catholic schools. . . ."[39] Not surprisingly, such foresight as expressed by the open and forward-looking Cardinal, was not shared by the more conservative leaders of the Missouri Synod. For them, the maintenance of German, closely linked to faith and culture, was an essential function of the church school system.[40] Possibly because their Lutheran parishes often were German only, and because no competitive factors were evident as in the Roman Catholic Church where Irish and German interests were set against each other, they insisted on German. The Missouri Synod, in fact, in several cases even rejected English speaking parishes.[41]

In the final analysis, though, prejudices expressed by both German Lutherans and Irish Catholics turned out to be very similar; both churches voiced loud accusations against the godless state school.[42] On a more positive side, it should be recalled that, of course, the ethnic schools, such as those of the German Freethinkers, who fought the influence of the churches, and the parochial schools served a much needed function for the children of the immigrants: They offered an education. Perhaps, though it is not possible to elaborate within the limits of this paper, it ought to be added that the immigrant by supporting a church school carried a tax burden heavier than that of his American neighbor who sent his children to the public school system.

---

39. Gibbons in *Catholic Standard and Times*, 21 December 1907, cited in James A. Burns, *The Growth and Development of the Catholic School System in the United States* (New York: Arno Press & and The New York Times, 1969 [first 1912]), 298–299.

40. Germanicus, "Ein Wort an die Deutschen," *Lutherisches Kirchenblatt* 3, 10 July 1886, 221. A. Schmidtkonz, "Was macht es uns zur Pflicht, in unseren Gemeinden christliche Wochenschulen zu errichten?" *Lutherisches Kirchenblatt* 3, 9 October 1886, 324.

41. Alan N. Graebner, "The Acculturation of an Immigrant Lutheran Church: The Lutheran Church-Missouri Synod, 1917–1929" (Ph.D. diss., Columbia University, 1965), 12.

42. Clemens A. Koppernagel, Chancellor of the Diocese of Harrisburg, Pennsylvania, to Leopoldinenstiftung, 17 July 1883, Archives of the Leopoldinenstiftung, Vienna. *Zweiter Synodal-Bericht des Wisconsin-Distrikts der deutschen evang.-luth. Synode von Missouri, Ohio, und anderen Staaten versammelt zu Sheboygan, Wis., vom 12.-18. Juni 1883* (St. Louis, 1883), 52.

While ethnic associationalism[43] and education may be the two most significant areas where the meaning of faith and the loyalty to a church can be registered, there are other areas of societal life, some of which in recent years have been rather more controversial than parochial education. The bitter struggle in America over the question of abortion, linked to the pro-life campaign strongly supported by the Roman Catholic Central Union of St. Louis (the former Deutsch Römisch-Katholischer Central-Verein) certainly would be one of the topics that might be considered for further comparative investigation of faith and church as they relate to specific ethnic groups. Also, the campaigns for language maintenance by Hispanic-American groups and the reactions of American society at large might be better understood if compared to earlier campaigns of a similar nature by, for instance, German and Polish Catholics.

Without wishing to offer the services of history to those concerned with religious questions connected to migration in our own time, there can be no doubt that a more informed view of the past may indeed assist the appraisal of the present. One might even be tempted to suggest that today's German society could benefit from understanding the American immigration experience.

---

43. Hermann Erbacher, *Die Innere Mission in Baden* (Karlsruhe: Verlag Evang. Presseverband, 1957), 5.

2

Community Versus Separation: A Northwest German Emigrant Settlement Region in Nineteenth-Century Ohio

Anne [Aengenvoort] Höndgen

S tudies on ethnic settlements and neighborhoods in the United States and on the processes of migration and acculturation among nineteenth-century European immigrants often use the term "cultural baggage" to refer to the specific sets of values, habits, and beliefs each national immigrant group is assumed to have taken with them to the new country. Nineteenth century German immigrants to the United States, for example, are often thought to have imported a cultural background sufficiently different from that of the French, Italian, or British to warrant the development of a nationally distinct and shared ethnic consciousness.

It has been less common for migration studies to pay equal attention to the *differences among* the members of a national immigrant group and the potential impact of these differences on processes of community formation and acculturation.[1] Research on nineteenth-century German immigrant groups in rural Ohio, however, suggests that community formation and acculturation among these immigrants were profoundly shaped by internal differences in creed and regional origin, and by the *group solidarities* and *group boundaries* that arose from these differences.[2] In Olivier Zunz's words, "Ethnicity may

---

1.   Acculturation is defined here as the process of coming to terms with the new (American) environment, which began immediately upon arrival and meant the gradual and partial adoption of cultural practices, values, and norms of the host society. (See Elliott R. Barkan, "Race, Religion and Nationality in American Society: A Model of Ethnicity—From Contact to Assimilation," *Journal of American Ethnic History* 14 (1995): 48.)

2.   Anne [Aengenvoort] Höndgen, *Migration—Siedlungsbildung—Akkulturation: Die Auswanderung Nordwestdeutscher nach Ohio, 1830–1914* (Stuttgart: F. Steiner, 1999). This essay largely builds on the third chapter titled "Migration and Community Formation: Selection and Group Formation Processes from Germany to Ohio," complemented by results from the other chapters dealing with the causes of the migration (II), the socioeconomic development of the settlement area (IV), and the acculturation processes the immigrants underwent in the nineteenth and early twentieth centuries (V). Especially regarding the chapters not receiving

be a quality which owes as much to the circumstances of settlement in a new country as it does to the culture imported from the old country."[3] The study of the migration and settlement processes that resulted in an unusually dense concentration of northwest German emigrants near the Ohio-Indiana border supports this insight empirically with detailed transatlantic evidence.

Today, the area under consideration comprises the three southernmost townships of Auglaize County in west central Ohio—German, Jackson, and Washington townships. Their non-Indian settlement history began in 1832 with the founding of the two hamlets of Stallotown (later Minster, Jackson Township) and Bremen (later New Bremen, German Township)[4] by two northwest German settlement societies. From 1838 onward, a section of land a few miles northwest of Stallotown and Bremen (later the village of New Knoxville in Washington Township) became dominated by immigrants from northern Westphalia. A large majority of the immigrant settlers came from a rather narrowly defined area in northwestern Germany within a forty-mile radius around the city of Osnabrück: from the rural plains and hills of the northernmost part of the Prussian province of Westphalia (Kreise [Counties] Tecklenburg and Warendorf), the western parts of the Kingdom of Hanover (District of Osnabrück, Amt [County] Diepholz), and the southernmost parts of the Duchy of Oldenburg (informally called the "Oldenburger Münsterland").

In 1850, eighty-five percent of all heads of household living in southern Auglaize County were German-born. In the same year, today's German and Jackson townships comprised the single most concentrated German rural settlement in Ohio.[5] After 140 years, in 1990, seventy to ninety percent of

---

in-depth treatment in this essay, the reader is referred to the above publication for the evidence underlying the conclusions presented here.

3.   See Olivier Zunz, "American History and the Changing Meaning of Assimilation: With Comments by John Bodnar and Stephan Thernstrom and Response by Zunz," *Journal of American Ethnic History* 4 (1985): 56.

4.   Auglaize County was created in 1848 from the western portion of Mercer County and the southern portion of Allen County. Thus, the first German immigrants to Minster and New Bremen actually settled in Mercer, while the first immigrants to New Knoxville settled in Allen County. In order to avoid confusion, however, the area will be referred to as Auglaize County throughout the text.

5.   With German immigrants making up more than twenty percent of the county's entire population in 1850, Auglaize County ranked first in Ohio in terms of the concentration of German settlement. It was followed by Mercer County (12.8 percent), Crawford County (12.6 percent), Putnam County (11.8 percent), and Seneca County (10.8 percent). Calculated from Hubert G. Wilhelm, *The Origin and Distribution of Settlement Groups, Ohio, 1850* [manuscript, Athens, OH, 1982], 30–31, table 6, 78–79, table 11.

Region of Origin	Number of Household Heads	In %
District (Landdrostei) of Osnabrück	69	21.6
"Oldenburger Münsterland"	106	33.1
Northwestern District (Region/Bezirk) of Münster	63	19.7
Remaining Westphalia	19	5.9
Remaining Kingdom of Hanover	40	12.5
Remaining Grandduchy of Oldenburg	7	2.2
Southwestern Germany[a]	7	2.2
Other German states	9	2.8
Total	*320*	*100.0*

[a] Emigrants from Baden and the Palatinate, the latter belonging to the Kingdom of Bavaria.

Sources: see appendix.

Table 2.1: Regional Origins of Identified German-Born Male Heads of Household in German and Washington Township, Auglaize County, 1850

Place of Birth	1850		1870		1900[a]	
	All[b]	*HH[c]*	*All*	*HH*	*All*	*HH*
	(2,920)	*(589)*	*(4,083)*	*(782)*	*(6,039)*	*(1,085)*
German States	50.8	85.1	29.0	70.1	-	20.9
Other Europe	0.8	1.9	1.4	2.3	-	1.0
Ohio	45.5	8.5	67.8	23.9	-	74.1
Other USA	2.8	3.6	1.6	2.7	-	4.0
Unknown	0.1	0.9	0.2	1.0	-	-
Total	*100.0*	*100.0*	*100.0*	*100.0*	-	*100.0*

[a] The 1900 Census was not made machine-readable in its entirety. Only the heads of households were recorded to facilitate comparisons with earlier censuses.

[b] All inhabitants.

[c] Only heads of households.

Sources: Manuscript Census Schedules for German, Jackson, and Washington Townships for 1850, 1870, and 1900.

Table 2.2: Places of Birth of the Southern Auglaize County Population, 1850–1900 (in %)

Minster, New Bremen, and New Knoxville inhabitants still reported German ancestry.[6] For the entire nineteenth century the numerical predominance of immigrants and their descendants from northwestern Germany in southern Auglaize County was challenged neither by Anglo-Americans nor by immigrants from other German states.[7]

At first glance, therefore, the three villages of Minster, New Bremen, and New Knoxville, located within fifteen miles of each other, should have had every reason to celebrate, like so many other "little Germanys," their common origin and settlement history in annual festivities such as German Days or a joint "Oktoberfest." However, from the very beginning of the settlement, the citizens of the three villages and the townships surrounding them opted for segregation and kept to themselves. Yet within each community a vivid sense of its ancestral northwest German heritage survived well into the twentieth century.

The contradiction between the undeniable ethnic homogeneity of the population of the three villages on the one hand and their voluntary seclusion on the other is striking. In retrospect, it seems attributable to three interdependent factors:

- The specific settlement history of each village/township;

- Certain forms of migrant selectivity, including processes of group and chain migration;

- Certain features of the immigrants' pre-migration life style and culture (mainly diverging religious beliefs and regional origins), which shaped community formation processes.

If we first look at the area's initial settlement period, the community-formation processes in southern Auglaize County had their formal origins in

---

6.   *The Evening Leader*, 6 February 1993, 1, 5.

7.   In 1870 "Prussians" alone accounted for over eighty-two percent of the German-born population in German, Jackson, and Washington Townships (Manuscript Census Schedules of these townships for 1870). The relevant publications on this area are: La Vern J. Rippley "The German Element of West Central Ohio," *German American Studies* 8 (1974): 89–105; Wolfgang Fleischhauer, "German Communities in Northwestern Ohio: Canal Fever and Prosperity," *The Report* (Society for the History of the Germans in Maryland) 34 (1970): 23–43; and Hubert Wilhelm, "A Lower Saxon Settlement Region in Western Ohio," *Pioneer America Society Transactions* 4 (1981): 1–10.

Country of Origin	Official Figures Entire State (Weisenberger)		Manuscript Population Schedules Exclusive of Larger Cities (Wilhelm)	
	absolute	*in %*	*absolute*	*in %*
"Germany"	111,257	51.0	70,236	48.1
Ireland	51,562	23.6	32,779	22.5
England	25,660	11.8	19,509	13.4
France	7,375	3.4	6,326	4.3
Wales	5,849	2.6	5,045	3.5
British North America	5,880	2.7	4,606	3.2
Scotland	5,232	2.4	4,003	2.7
Switzerland	–	–	3,000	2.0
Others	5,378	2.5	488	0.3
Totals	*218,193*	*100.0*	*145,992*	*100.0*

Sources: Weisenberger, *Passing*, 51, quoted the aggregate figures of the Seventh Census published by the Bureau of the Census in 1854. Hubert Wilhelm, "The Origin and Distribution of Settlement Groups, Ohio, 1850," (Unpublished Manuscript, Athens, Ohio, 1982), 27, used his own count of the 1850 census, disregarding the municipal districts of Cincinnati, Columbus, Dayton, and Toledo.

Table 2.3: Origins of Foreign-Born Population in Ohio, 1850

Cincinnati. From the 1830s until the Civil War, the city on the Ohio River was the "Gateway to the West," the most important transit point for migrants who arrived at the overseas ports of Baltimore, Philadelphia, and New York and were headed for the free soils of Ohio and the states farther west. For Germans, and for northwest Germans in particular, the Queen City quickly developed into one of the most popular destinations in the United States. In 1830 almost one fourth of its population was German-born.[8] By mid-century, the Germans also constituted the largest foreign element in Ohio as a whole.

Until the 1870s, about half of Ohio's immigrant population originated from one of the German states.[9] Around mid-century, the majority of these Germans lived in the western and northwestern portions of the state. It was only in those areas that the number of Germans exceeded fifty percent of all immigrants; in eight counties they even exceeded seventy-five percent. This relative over-representation of Germans among the other immigrant groups was caused by the fact that the sale of Ohio's western and northwestern Congress lands had commenced only in the mid-1820s, shortly before the first nineteenth-century "wave" of German emigration to the United States in the early 1830s. Also, the construction of the Miami and Erie Canal, which was to traverse the state from south to north, was begun in Cincinnati in 1825, and the counties along its prospective route suddenly became highly desirable for settlers in search of accessible, yet inexpensive land. As a result, a virtual corridor of German settlements began to emerge between Cincinnati in the southwestern, Piqua and Dayton in the west central, and Toledo in the northwestern portions of the state.[10]

8.　Francis P. Weisenburger, *The Passing of the Frontier: 1825–1850* (Columbus, OH: State Archaeological and Historical Society, 1968 [1941]), 42; Joseph Michael White, "Religion and Community: Cincinnati Germans, 1814–1870," (Ph.D. diss., University of Notre Dame, 1980), 28–29.

9.　Philip L. Brown, "People on the Move: The Foundation of Ohio's Ethnic Composition, 1870–1900," (Master's Thesis, Ohio State University, 1966), 24–25; *Population of the United States in 1860: Compiled from the Original Returns of the Eighth Census, under the Direction of the Secretary of the Interior by Joseph C. Kennedy, Superintendent of the Census* (Washington, DC: Government Printing Office, 1864), 398; *The Statistics of the Population of the United States: Embracing the Tables of Race, Nationality, Sex, Selected Ages, and Occupations: Compiled from the Original Returns of the Ninth Census under the Direction of the Secretary of the Interior by Francis A. Walter, Superintendent of the Census, Ninth Census*, vol. 1 (Washington, DC: Government Printing Office, 1872), 328, 336, 339.

10.　In the 1820s an extension of Ohio's waterway infrastructure was begun, mainly by connecting the Ohio River with the Great Lakes region and other Ohio rivers. The ensuing improvement in the movement of goods and people generated an entirely new settlement

Among the German immigrants pouring into Cincinnati's growing ethnic neighborhood "Over the Rhine" (the "Rhine" being the Miami and Erie Canal) were three families from the neighboring northwest German areas of Grafschaft Diepholz and Amt Damme: the Meslohs, Mohrmanns, and Stallos. These families, arriving in Cincinnati in 1830/1831, were the first among the future inhabitants of the northwest German Auglaize County settlements to cross the Atlantic Ocean.

They did not remain few for long. The pressing socio-economic conditions in northwestern Germany at the time drove a rapidly growing number of the rural inhabitants into harboring, and increasingly realizing, plans for emigration. These northwest German emigrants shared a very similar sociocultural and economic background. They came from one of the major German centers of rural textile production, the area between Münster in Westphalia and Cloppenburg in Oldenburg. Very broadly speaking, the exodus was a consequence of several socioeconomic developments:

- The decline of the traditional family-oriented cottage production of wool and linen, attributable to the increasing industrialization of the production process and competition from cheap British textiles flooding the German market;

- The decline of other non-agricultural sources of income (predominantly crafts and seasonal work in the Netherlands).

Relying on these additional sources of income, the rural population of the area had outgrown the agricultural potential of the soil in the eighteenth and early nineteenth centuries. With the decrease in income opportunities in the 1820s and early 1830s, an overpopulation crisis (relative to income opportunities from agriculture and other available resources) began to make

---

structure, with the canal cities and areas becoming much more densely populated than those not touched by waterways. See Carville Earle, "Regional Economic Development West of the Appalachians, 1815–1860," in *North America: The Historical Geography of a Changing Continent*, edited by Robert D. Mitchell and Paul A. Groves (Totowa, NJ: Rowman & Littlefield, 1982), 172–178; Ronald E. Shaw, "The Canal Era in the Old Northwest," in *Transportation and the Early Nation: Papers Presented at an Indiana American Revolution Bicentennial Symposium, April 24-26, 1981*, edited by the Indiana Historical Society (Indianapolis: Indiana Historical Society, 1982), 90–92, 100; Jack S. Blocker, "Market Integration, Urban Growth, and Economic Change in an Ohio County," *Ohio History* 90 (1981): 299; Thomas E. Ferguson, *Ohio Lands: A Short History*, (Columbus, OH: Ohio Auditor of State, 1987), 40. For the Miami and Erie Canal see *Miami and Erie Canal: Symbol of an Era* (Dayton, OH: n.d.).

itself felt, and the first individuals involved in the exodus were non-proprietary farmers, farmhands, and rural day-laborers and their families.[11]

Cincinnati was an alluring alternative to those suffering from severe socioeconomic pressures in Germany. It played an important transit role and had been featured in emigrant publications. Glowing letters sent home by early emigrants to family and friends soon attracted migrants from all over Germany, but particularly from the Westphalia-Hanover and Oldenburg-Hanover border areas. The impact in southern Oldenburg and western Hanover of enthusiastic emigrant letters was even mentioned in the contemporary German press. In May 1832 the *Oldenburgische Blätter* stated, "A letter written in January by the emigrant bookbinder Stallo from Cincinnati is probably greatly promoting emigration."[12]

The two events most essential for the further development of the future Auglaize County settlement both occurred during the summer of 1832. Within one month, about 130 of Cincinnati's northwestern German immigrant men formed two separate settlement societies—one Catholic and one Lutheran. For most new immigrants in a city, the first people to contact were friends and relatives, but the foremost institution to turn to was a church of their denominational affiliation, preferably one open to German members. In the early 1830s, German immigrants of the Protestant faith attended St. John's Lutheran Church, Cincinnati's first Protestant German parish (established

11. Over seventy-five percent of those Germans identified in the 1850 census for whom information on their former occupation was available (eighty-two men) had an agricultural background. Other sources (see note 5) also indicate the clear predominance of farmers and farm hands among northwest German emigrants.

12. *Oldenburgische Blätter*, No. 18, 1 May 1832, 142 ("Ein Brief, den der ausgewanderte Buchbinder Stallo aus Damme im Januar d. J. aus Cincin[n]ati geschrieben hat, mag viel zur Beförderung der Auswanderung beytragen . . . ."). The effect of Stallo's weekly letters also becomes obvious from contemporary comments. See Heinrich A. Rattermann, "Zwei Agitatoren der Auswanderung: Teil 2: Franz Joseph Stallo," *Der Deutsche Pionier* 7 (1875–1876): 11. The result was a marked concentration of emigrants from Stallo's hometown of Damme and neighboring villages in Cincinnati, see Armin Tenner, *Cincinnati, sonst und jetzt: Eine Geschichte Cincinnati's und seiner verdienstvollen Bürger deutscher Zunge: Mit biographischen Skizzen und Portrait Illustrationen* (Cincinnati, OH: Mecklenborg & Rosenthal, 1878), 320; and Antonius Holtmann, "Vom 'finstern Winkel Deutschlands' nach Amerika: Arbeit und Bestände der 'Forschungsstelle Niedersächsische Auswanderer in den USA' der Carl von Ossietzky-Universität Oldenburg," *Mitteilungsblatt der Oldenburgischen Landschaft* 76 (1992): 14. In 1832, however, the influential priest Friedrich Rese of Cincinnati (himself born in the Kingdom of Hanover) blamed Stallo's letters for luring many northwest German immigrants to Ohio without Stallo being able to keep his promises (2 December 1832 letter to Johann Horstmann, published in English in Louis A. Hoying, *Pilgrims All: History of St. Augustine Parish, Minster (1832–1982)* [Minster, OH: The Parish, 1982], 45–46.)

in 1814), while German Catholics shared St. Peter's Cathedral, Cincinnati's only Catholic church, with the city's many Irish immigrants. As studies on several immigrant groups have shown, parish communities like these not only provided spiritual guidance, but also served as an important focus of social life and information.[13] Naturally, then, the call for the establishment of a Catholic settlement society in April 1832 was not advertised in the press but was read from the pulpit of St. Peter.[14]

Settlement societies were more likely to originate from a congregation if, as in the case of the two Cincinnati parishes mentioned above, the members also shared a similar regional background. The Catholic settlement society of 1832 was made up almost exclusively of immigrants from southern Oldenburg and several Catholic parishes in the adjacent District of Osnabrück, while (as far as can be reconstructed) the members of the Lutheran society originated from Protestant communities in the Duchy of Osnabrück and the nearby County of Diepholz (both belonging to the Kingdom of Hanover).

The tendency for Catholics and Protestants to join separate settlement societies was related to the fact that these denominations had not coexisted harmoniously in their German regions of origin. The denominational history of southern Oldenburg and the Duchy of Osnabrück had been characterized by constant fissures, and by the early nineteenth century the area resembled a denominational checkerboard. In contrast to the rest of the Grandduchy of

---

13. The essential role and manifold functions of religious communities during the immigration and acculturation process have often been emphasized. A summary review can be found in Jay P. Dolan, "The Immigrants and Their Gods: A New Perspective in American Religious History," *Church History* 57 (1988): 68–70; and Timothy L. Smith, "Religion and Ethnicity in America," *American Historical Review* 83 (1978): 1158–1159 and 1168–1170. An introduction with particular reference to German immigrants is Reinhard R. Doerries, "Immigrant Culture and Religion: Church and Faith Among German Americans," in *Germans in America: Retrospect and Prospect: Tricentennial Lectures Delivered at the German Society of Pennsylvania in 1983*, edited by Randall M. Miller (Philadelphia, PA: The Society, 1984), 85; and Jay P. Dolan, ed., *The American Catholic Parish: A History from 1850 to the Present*, vol. 2 (New York: Paulist Press, 1987), 308–309.

14. Heinrich A. Rattermann, *Zwei Agitatoren*, 11. At least two other Catholic settlements populated by immigrants from southern Oldenburg (Oldenburg, Indiana; Teutopolis, Illinois) had their origins in Cincinnati parishes. Several Protestant settlements in Indiana were comprised of former members of the Cincinnati "Plattdeutsche Kirche" (Northern German Lutheran Church). See Franz Josef Tengenkamp, "Teutopolis—dütske Stadt in Illinois, USA," *Jahrbuch für das Oldenburger Münsterland* (1987): 142–143; David S. Dreyer, *A History of Immigration to the Batesville Vicinity: Commemorating the Sesquicentennials of Oldenburg, Huntersville and Penntown, and the 900th Anniversary of Venne, Germany* (Indianapolis: Bredensteiner Print Co., 1987), 7; Mary Gilbert Kelly, *Catholic Immigrant Colonization Projects in the United States, 1815–1860* (New York: U.S. Catholic Historical Society, 1939), 133–134.

Oldenburg, its southern part, the "Oldenburger Münsterland," was mainly Catholic, yet many villages had Protestant minorities. Conditions in the Duchy of Osnabrück were the reverse. In some parishes, Catholics and Protestants even had to share the same church, which led to considerable antagonism. Along the border between the two districts, many people experienced a diaspora situation, sometimes even a minority-within-a-minority situation, where denominational boundaries split farms and families.[15] In the annual church visitation reports of the 1820s, officials worried about the atmosphere of "distrustful jealousy" prevalent in the border parishes of southern Oldenburg and the Duchy of Osnabrück. The area from which most of the later inhabitants of the village of New Knoxville originated—the eastern part of Kreis (County) Tecklenburg, including the village of Ladbergen—was also a thoroughly (98 percent) Protestant Reformed island within a larger administrative entity of a different denomination, the almost entirely (ninety percent) Catholic District of Münster. There had been frequent, sometimes violent quarrels between Catholics and Protestants, who felt discriminated against, in other parts of Kreis Tecklenburg. And it is reported that the inhabitants of Ladbergen shunned contact with the villagers from Catholic Ostbevern living in the immediate vicinity.[16] Raised in this tense milieu, the emigrants of both denominations may well have begun to feel a strong sense of belonging together, and they were unlikely to drop their misgivings regarding the other denomination upon

15. Hannelore Oberpenning, "Verwaltungsgeschichte Dammes—ein historischer Überblick," in *Damme: Eine Stadt in ihrer Geschichte*, edited by Klaus J. Bade et al. (Sigmaringen: Thorbecke, 1993), 17–44; Christoph Reinders-Düselder, *Ländliche Bevölkerung vor der Industrialisierung: Geburt, Heirat, Tod in Steinfeld, Damme, Neuenkirchen, 1650–1850* (Cloppenburg: Museumsdorf Cloppenburg, Niedersächsisches Freilichtmuseum, 1995), 15, 48–52; Heinz-Joachim Schulze, "Vom Niederstift Münster zum Oldenburger Münsterland: Das Werden einer historischen Landschaft," *Oldenburger Jahrbuch* 80 (1980): 77–97; Gerhard Wintermann, "Aus 130 Jahren kirchengeschichtlicher Entwicklung in Südoldenburg (1803–1933)," *Jahrbuch der Gesellschaft für Niedersächsische Kirchengeschichte* 71(1973): 41–71; Karl Willoh, *Geschichte der katholischen Pfarreien im Herzogtum Oldenburg*, vol. 1 (Köln: Bachem, 1898), 121–134, 207–209.

16. Staatsarchiv Oldenburg Rep. 31–12–24, No. 21, Fol. 109–110, 204; Stephanie Reekers, *Westfalens Bevölkerung 1818–1955: Die Bevölkerungsentwicklung der Gemeinden und Kreise im Zahlenbild* (Münster: Aschendorff, 1956), 32–34; A. Diening, *Topographisch-statistische Übersicht des Regierungs-Bezirks Münster: Aus amtlichen Quellen zusammengestellt* (Münster: Regensburg, 1846), 1, 10–11; Albin Gladen, *Der Kreis Tecklenburg an der Schwelle des Zeitalters der Industrialisierung* (Münster: Aschendorff, 1970), 62–68; Friedrich Saatkamp, *Ladbergen: Aus Geschichte und Gegenwart eines 1000-jährigen westfälischen Dorfes* (Lengerich: Heimatverein Ladbergen, 1975), 34-35.

arrival in the United States: In Auglaize County, immigrants from Ladbergen and Ostbevern again lived close, yet apart–in New Knoxville and Minster, respectively.

Against this backdrop, the settlement decision made by the two northwest German settlement societies in 1832 seems paradoxical at first. Despite the difficult past and the vastness of the continent, the scouts of the Catholic and the Lutheran settlement societies, having explored various localities in Indiana, Illinois, and Ohio, were commissioned to buy immediately neighboring tracts of land. Within a few weeks the two societies bought sections of land that were only seven miles apart, yet separate. Why? We will, of course, never know for certain. However, the familiarity and security provided by an almost-identical dialect as well as a similar regional and socio-economic background seem in this one instance to have overruled the distrust Catholics and Protestants felt toward members of the other faith. To settle separately, yet directly adjacently seems a compromise between two deeply ingrained instincts: religious seclusion, on the one hand, and a longing for familiarity in a strange land, on the other. This dichotomy of segregation and community was to become the most characteristic and influential feature of the southern Auglaize County settlement area during the nineteenth and much of the twentieth centuries.

The two settlement societies not only expressly excluded members of other denominations. They also rejected the numerous immigrants from southern or southwest German states who lived in Cincinnati and attended the same churches. For the Protestant society this can be traced back to tensions that arose between south and northwest German Protestants after 1830. In the Lutheran congregation of St. John's, the southwest German parishioners repeatedly accused their pastor of unduly favoring the "Low German" (or northwest German) members. The quarrel surfaced in 1832 and resulted in the decision of over thirty northwest German parishioners and their families to leave the congregation. Seen in this light, the founding of the German Protestant settlement society is likely to have been the result of inter-regional conflict among German immigrants in Cincinnati.[17]

---

17. Emil Klauprecht, *Deutsche Chronik in der Geschichte des Ohio-Thales und seiner Hauptstadt Cincinnati in's Besondere: Umfassend eine ausführliche Darstellung der Abentheuer, Ansiedlungen und des allgemeinen Wirkens der Deutschen im Flußgebiete von der Entdeckung des Mississippi-Thales an bis auf unsere Tage* (Cincinnati: G. Hof & M. A. Jacobi, 1864), 172. In 1838 the situation eventually became unbearable and culminated in the split of St. John's congregation and the founding of the Northern German Lutheran Church ("Plattdeutsche Kirche"). See Wolfgang Grams, "Lebensläufe in der Fremde: Die Norddeutsche Lutherische ('Plattdeutsche') Gemeinde in Cincinnati (1838), eine Osnabrücker Gründung," (Unpublished Manuscript, Oldenburg, 1991); and Haefner, "Geschichte der Dritten Deutschen Protestantischen Gemeinde," *Der Deutsche Pionier* 17 (1886): 78–80, 164–170.

German regional origin, then, was the other major factor that determined group formation and the development of group boundaries in the early history of the German settlement in southern Auglaize County. Throughout the nineteenth century, immigrants from southern Germany remained a tiny minority among the large numbers of northwest German immigrants and their descendants.

Once the villages of Bremen (renamed New Bremen in 1835) and Stallotown (renamed Minster in 1836) had been founded in 1832, a slow and arduous settlement process began, one which suffered substantial setbacks due to cholera epidemics in 1833 and 1849/1850. In 1850, eighteen years after the arrival of the first pioneers, the settlement area comprising German, Jackson, and Washington townships had a population of barely three thousand. After the 1860s, the influx of new settlers, especially from northwestern Germany, dropped considerably, and as a result, the population had only doubled by the turn of the century (in 1900, slightly more than six thousand inhabitants lived in the area).[18] This was mainly due to the by now limited availability of arable land, the irrevocable decline of the canal era, the belated arrival of railways in west central Ohio, and the stagnating commercial base of southern Auglaize County. To most immigrants arriving after 1850, the area must have appeared increasingly less attractive compared to the vast tracts of inexpensive farmland available on the Great Plains.

The migration processes shaping the further settlement of southern Auglaize County served to strengthen group solidarities within and group boundaries between the two settlement societies. Migration chains, group migrations, and specific kinds of migrant selectivity reinforced the invisible borderline drawn between Catholic Minster and Lutheran New Bremen. As if to underscore this development, a third distinct immigrant group arrived in the area beginning in 1836. Northern Westphalians belonging to the Reformed denomination settled in New Knoxville and surrounding area—in the immediate vicinity of Minster and New Bremen—yet again deliberately keeping to themselves. New Knoxville, which, though not founded by Germans, was firmly in the hands

---

18. The population growth in German, Jackson, and Washington Townships in 1850–1900 was as follows: 1840, 1.958; 1850, 2.918; 1860, 4.259; 1870, 4.092; 1880, 5.811; 1890, 5.666; 1900, 6.039; 1910, 6.118 (*Ohio Statistics: Annual Report of the Secretary of State to the Governor of the State of Ohio, including the Statistical Report of the General Assembly, for the Year... [1868–1940]* [Columbus, 1869–1941], here 1871: 273; 1891: 789, 795–796; 1911: 354, 365, 372–373; and *Sixth Census of the United States, 1840*, Population Schedule. Manuscript Returns for Auglaize County, Washington DC, National Archives Microfilm Publications.)

of immigrants from the village of Ladbergen in northern Westphalia, became the center of an extraordinarily large Evangelical-Reformed congregation in southern Washington Township.

A letter by Hermhinrich Bröring, an emigrant from Vechta in southern Oldenburg, testifies to the feeling of familiarity that chain and group migrations could evoke in a strange land. In March 1845 he wrote to his family in Germany:

> We attend Minster church at a distance of one hour and a quarter. We usually meet Frans Ervers and Jan Brackmann there every Sunday. Hermhinrich Kläne von Stuckenborg is our next-door neighbor—we have so many familiar neighbors! We further let you know that Hermhinrich Gudenkauf and the Heuing brothers of Krimpenfort live half an hour away from us, and that the people from Hagen and Vechta living in our area are all quite well and happy.[19]

Quite clearly, the Bröring family was surrounded by Catholic friends from their home district of Vechta.

In a further refinement of the settlement pattern *within* the three Catholic and Protestant communities, immigrants from neighboring German villages very often settled immediately next door to one another. A household-by-household analysis of the 1850 census reveals striking clusters of migrants from the same counties and even villages in all townships. In New Bremen, for example, six immigrant families from the Osnabrück parish of Belm lived almost door to door, as did the seven families in German Township north of New Bremen whose heads all originated from Amt Diepholz in Hanover. The most notable "transplant" group was found in New Knoxville, where twenty-eight out of forty German families and individuals whose origin could be traced back to Germany were born in the tiny village of Ladbergen. Only one of the forty household heads identified in New Knoxville originated from an area other than northern Westphalia or the District of Osnabrück. This

---

19. Hermhinrich Bröring, letter of 5 March 1845 (letter collection of Rita Hoying, Minster). The German original reads: "Wier gehen nach Münster zu der Kirche wo wier eine Stund und ein viertelstunde von entvernt sind. Wo wier gewöhlig jeden Sontage Frans Ervers und Jan Brackmann zu sehen bekommen. Hermhinrich Kläne von Stuckenborg ist unser erste Nachbar wier haben all so viele Nachbaren. Weiters tuhen wier euch zu wissen das Hermhinrich Gudenkauf und die Gebrüder Heuing von Krimpenfort eine halbestunde von uns wohnen und alle die von Hagen und Vechta in unser Gegend wohnen sind alle noch recht Gesund und munter."

migration of small groups of neighbors and kin, quite common in destinations of heavy chain and group migration,[20] again provided the immigrants with a sense of security and familiarity in an alien environment.

In tracing the specific make-up of the southern Auglaize County population, it also proves instructive to consider those immigrant groups for whom Auglaize County did *not* become a permanent home. Those people who, despite an economic and regional background similar to that of the actual Auglaize County settlers, did not choose to make Auglaize County their final destination; those who took a look, but did not stay; and those who remained but did not draw any follow-up migration. All these are variant forms of migrant selectivity, and they, too, help to explain the remarkably "closed" nature of Minster, New Knoxville, and—to a much lesser degree—New Bremen.

The Ladbergen–New Knoxville migration chain is notable because it only drew a certain circle of families from Ladbergen to Ohio. Migration chains from Ladbergen to other destinations in the United States, for example to Holland, Indiana, and to the counties of Warren and St. Charles in Missouri, consisted of different family names, and there was virtually no intersection of family names among these three migration chains.[21] Thus, divergent migration traditions developed even on a sublocal or neighborhood level, and the development of "mini-chains" of this kind greatly promoted the homogeneity and group solidarity among the citizens of each of the American destinations.

Among those who came to Auglaize County but did not stay were, for example, leaders of immigrant groups from southern Oldenburg and the District of Osnabrück who visited Stallotown/Minster in the 1830s where their Catholic countrymen now lived. They came with the explicit objective of exploring settlement opportunities, yet they were immediately turned off, appalled by what they considered their former neighbors' poor settlement

---

20. Uwe Reich, *Aus Cottbus und Arnswalde in die Neue Welt: Amerika-Auswanderung aus Ostelbien im 19. Jahrhundert* (Osnabrück: Rasch, 1997); and Robert W. Frizzel, "Migration Chains to Illinois: The Evidence from German-American Church Records," *Journal of American Ethnic History* 7 (1987): 59–73, give examples of similar migration processes for other German immigrant groups.

21. See the list of emigrants from Kreis Tecklenburg and Ladbergen in Missouri in Walter D. Kamphoefner, *Westfalen in der Neuen Welt: Eine Sozialgeschichte der Auswanderung im 19. Jahrhundert* (Münster: Coppenrath, 1982), 186–190, tables B.2, B.3. For Ladbergeners in Holland, Indiana, see Friedrich Saatkamp, *Ladbergen: Aus Geschichte und Gegenwart eines 1000-jährigen westfälischen Dorfes*, 239.

decision (prior to extensive drainage the soil was still so swampy that even in the village streets pedestrians waded "up to their knees" in mud).[22] This may explain why no significant migration chain to the Minster area developed after the first large groups of migrants from Oldenburg and the Duchy of Osnabrück had settled there. It seems that for those few northwest German immigrants who in later years *did* come and stay, the opportunity to settle close to family and friends outweighed the topographical disadvantages, that is, the labor-intensive soil of the area and the limited amount of land still for sale. They might, therefore, be termed "conservative" migrants, because they, just like the pioneer immigrants in the area, chose security over more immediately profitable soils in other places.

Finally, there is the case of two small immigrant groups, each of identical regional origin in Germany, which were among the first to settle in southern Auglaize County but did not trigger any chain migration. In 1833 four Palatine families from the village of Lauterecken and four families from Amt (County) Eierdorf in Franconia bought land in New Bremen and Stallotown/Minster, respectively. The fact that these groups did not set off any further migration from their home areas was very probably a result of their being southern Germans—a tiny linguistic and cultural minority among the comparatively large and growing numbers of northwest German immigrants in Auglaize County. Interestingly, both the Palatine and the Franconian immigrant groups, though crossing the Atlantic on ships crowded with people from their home regions, left their familiar environments to settle among northwest Germans whose language they hardly understood. There is no immediately satisfying explanation for this decision, but it seems possible that when the vessels of both groups arrived at Baltimore harbor within less than a week in June 1833, they accidentally met and decided to travel and settle together.[23]

These reflections on migrant selectivity and migration processes indicate that there were many different ways in which regional origin and religion influenced the specific settlement pattern of southern Auglaize County as it appeared in 1850. It has also become clear, however, that despite the remarkable effectiveness of group and chain migration in "channeling"

---

22. Letter by Heinrich Joseph Böhmer, a former teacher from southern Oldenburg, published in *Vechtaer Sonntags-Blatt*, Vol. 2, No. 21, 23 May 1835, 82. The newspaper printed several of Böhmer's letters in full.

23. [Lang, Wilhelm], "Karl Boesel," *Der Deutsche Pionier* 17 (1886): 211–212; Franz Hergenröther's memories can be found in "Ansiedlung von Minster, Auglaize County," *Der Deutsche Pionier* 1 (1869/1870), 148; *Passenger Lists of Vessels Arriving at Baltimore 1920–1891*, roll 1, NA.

emigration from a specific point of departure to a specific destination, this did not happen automatically. The attraction of the fact that somewhere in the United States friends and family had already built homes seems quite often to have been overruled by individual preferences and spontaneous reversals of settlement decisions. This may have been especially frequent among emigrants originating from localities that had developed more than one major migration chain—in this case, emigrants from Ladbergen and southern Oldenburg, the latter not only settling in Auglaize County, Ohio, but also, for example, heading in large numbers to Oldenburg, Indiana, and Teutopolis, Illinois, in the 1830s and 1840s.[24]

At a more abstract level, the transatlantic empirical evidence gathered in this case study—based on individual record linkage placed in the context of contemporary letters and regional/local histories—has provided support for Dorothy Johansen's hypotheses on "migrant selectivity" and "self-selectivity." As early as 1967 Johansen claimed that migrants preferring one migration alternative over others shared a certain value system and certain expectations with regard to their environment and future lifestyle. By communicating their satisfaction or dissatisfaction to family and friends at home they, deliberately or not, quite effectively selected the migrants who would follow.[25] The observation that Kathleen Conzen made regarding German-Catholic immigrants in rural Minnesota and Wisconsin holds equally true for our three "German" townships in southern Auglaize County: Most immigrants there shared a "preexisting commitment to a certain lifestyle."[26] Their strong religious affiliations, similar regional and local origins, and similar socioeconomic backgrounds were the essential ingredients in this lifestyle.[27]

---

24. Franz Josef Tegenkamp, "Teutopolis"; David S. Dreyer, *History of Immigration*; Mary Gilbert Kelly, *Catholic Immigrant Colonization Projects*, 133–134. Kamphoefner also discovered some Damme people in Missouri. See *Westfalen in der Neuen Welt*, 106–110.

25. Dorothy Johansen, "A Working Hypothesis for the Study of Migrations," *Pacific Historical Review* 26 (1967): 11–12. Self-selectivity of migrants is again becoming more widely discussed. A session at the 1996 Social Science History Association annual convention in New Orleans was devoted to the subject of "Self-Selectivity of Migration and Chain Migration."

26. Kathleen N. Conzen, *Making Their Own America: Assimilation Theory and the German Peasant Pioneer: With Comments by Mack Walker and Jörg Nagler* (New York: Berg, 1990), 15–16, 33.

27. That this is a phenomenon far from exclusive to German immigrants becomes obvious when looking at research done on nineteenth-century Scandinavian and Dutch immigration to the United States. Looking at Norwegian Lutheran immigrants, Ann Marie Legreid and David Ward wrote: "Church activities promoted the development of a strong sense of solidarity that carried over into purely secular activities." Legreid and Ward, "Religious Schism and the Development of Rural Immigrant Communities: Norwegian Lutherans in Western Wisconsin,

Religion, it seems, not only played a crucial role during the initial settlement period of an immigrant village but also profoundly shaped the way the community later regarded itself, especially in terms of its relations with outsiders. Not surprisingly, over the course of the nineteenth century the German settlement area in Auglaize County developed many of the features characteristic of rural ethnic settlements with strong denominational ties that dotted and still dot the landscape of German settlement areas in Ohio, Indiana, Illinois, Wisconsin, and other Midwestern states.[28] An article entitled "God's Country" in *Ohio Magazine* (1992) identified allegedly characteristic traits of several Catholic settlements in southern Mercer and Auglaize Counties: the area's many "amazing churches . . . with a towering steeple," its "built-in conservatism," the "neatness, order and efficiency," but also its "closed society" deeming itself "special in God's eye."[29] The important term in this quote is "closed": Well into the twentieth century, the voluntary seclusion of the Catholics of Minster/Jackson Township and the Reformed Protestants of New Knoxville/southern Washington Township remained surprisingly pronounced. As late as in 1950 an observer noted that as a result of the seclusiveness of the village, newcomers to New Knoxville had to learn quickly:

1880–1905," *Upper Midwest History* 2 (1982): 13. A case study examining the prominent role of the Catholic church among Dutch immigrants to rural America was provided by Yda Schreuder, *Dutch Catholic Immigrant Settlement in Wisconsin, 1850–1905* (New York: Garland, 1989). For a study on Dutch emigrants of the Reformed creed in the northwestern United States, see Rob Kroes, "Amsterdam, Montana: In America, Not of It? A Fractured History of Ethnic Continuity," in *Emigration and Settlement Patterns of German Communities in North America*, edited by Jörg Nagler, Eberhard Reichmann, and LaVern J. Rippley (Nashville, IN: Max Kade German-American Center, Indiana University-Purdue University at Indianapolis, distributed by NCSA Literature, 1995), 129–144.

28. See the studies of Walter A. Schroeder, "Rural Settlement Patterns of the German-Missourian Cultural Landscape," in *The German-American Experience in Missouri. Essays in Commemoration of the Tricentennial of German Immigration to America, 1683-1983*, edited by Howard W. Marshall and James W. Goodrich (Publications of the Missouri Cultural Heritage Center, No. 2, Columbia, MO 1986), 40; Robert C. Ostergren, "European Settlement and Ethnicity Patterns on the Agricultural Frontiers of South Dakota," *South Dakota History* 13 (1983): 69–79; Russell L. Gerlach, *Immigrants in the Ozarks: A Study in Ethnic Geography* (Columbia: University of Missouri Press, 1976); Kathleen N. Conzen, "Deutsche Einwanderer," 362–375; Kathleen N. Conzen, *Making Their Own America*, 2–3, which provides additional secondary literature on local settlements. For Indiana see David S. Dreyer, *History of Immigration*; for Illinois see Franz Josef Tegenkamp, "Teutopolis."

29. John Baskin, "God's Country," *Ohio* 15 (1992), 116, 121, 137. To this list could be added a prevalence of German names in the phone book, multigeneration marriage links, and traces of the German language still existing today.

. . . neighbors expect them to join a church, to pay their debts, to work hard and to take good care of their own. If they meet community standards, they are accepted into this fellowship. If they fail, they probably come to resent what must seem a clannish resistance to the outlander.[30]

In neighboring New Bremen with its declining predominance of Lutheran Protestants, the pronounced degree of piety in New Knoxville was apparently regarded with wonder. A New Bremenite once commented on the people from New Knoxville: "They know angels down there."[31] It seems that the somewhat separatist attitudes reigning in Minster and New Knoxville toward people from out of town in general, and toward the other "German" villages in the neighborhood in particular, was mitigated neither by the immigrants' common northwest German origin nor by a common language (Low German).[32]

The segregation observed in nineteenth- and twentieth-century Minster and New Knoxville was not merely a product of the denominational homogeneity of these villages that had resulted from the migration process. Their specific cultural heritage, in this case the exclusionist (and often zealous) religious beliefs that the first settlers of these villages had brought with them to the New World, intensified the separatist attitudes of the immigrants. During the first massive northwest German emigration phase in the 1830s to 1850s, Germany experienced a time of intense theological and doctrinal quarrels within the Protestant and, to a lesser extent, the Catholic church. Among Protestants, a growing neo-pietist awakening movement competed with theological rationalism and alleged "liberalism" that had developed as a result of the Enlightenment.[33] In the Reformed village of Ladbergen, the congregation was profoundly influenced by the neo-Calvinist teachings of the well-known Krummacher family of theologians and ministers, whose three most prominent members preached with moral rigor in northwestern Germany,

---

30. "Great Churches of America: II. Evangelical and Reformed, New Knoxville, Ohio," *Christian Century*, 22 February 1950, 235–236.

31. The quote by Friedland Purpus from 1960 is taken from a collection of tapes containing interviews that Wolfgang Fleischhauer of The Ohio State University conducted between 1959 and 1962 with German/Low German-speaking inhabitants of southern Auglaize County. The tapes are kept at the Ohio Historical Society in Columbus (here: tape 11).

32. A complex analysis of the relationship of ethnicity and religion can be found in Harold J. Abramson, "Religion," in *Harvard Encyclopedia of American Ethnic Groups*, ed. Stephan Thernstrom et al. (Cambridge, MA: Belknap Press of Harvard University, 1980), 869–875.

33. Hans-Ulrich Wehler, *Von der Reformära bis zur industriellen und politischen 'Deutschen Doppelrevolution' 1815-1845/49*, 2nd ed. (München: Beck, 1989), 459–467.

including Ladbergen, during the first half of the nineteenth century.[34] After the first group of Ladbergeners arrived in Washington Township in 1833, the first pastor they could secure for their small congregation was also "touched by rationalism." He tried to insert a paragraph about the "freedom of choice in the quest for religious truth" into the congregation's new constitution. This "frivolous" idea led to a dangerous rupture within the community, and, according to one church history, it was only the conservative faith of those being taught by Krummacher that saved the congregation from falling apart.[35] Among the northwest German Catholic emigrants, a discontent with "modern" religious thought is less clearly visible than in the Protestant congregations. Still, the first temporary priest of Minster, Ohio, a teacher and chaplain from the District of Osnabrück, had left his profession and Germany out of dissatisfaction with rationalist tendencies within the church and his school.[36] The influence of German theological thinking on the large Catholic emigrant contingent from southern Oldenburg became strong only in America, when, in 1845, the southern parts of Auglaize and Mercer Counties were put under the religious auspices of the zealous order of the Society of the Most Precious Blood (CPPS). The Provincial of the American Province of the order, a Swiss monk by the name of Franz Brunner, had his headquarters near Minster. Much like the Protestant Krummacher clerics, Brunner fought against the "evils of liberalism" and the "excessive worldy sin" of his times.[37] Complete quiet

34. Data on the Krummacher family in *Meyers Konversationslexikon*, 5th ed., Vol. 10 (Leipzig/Wien: 1897), 780. For Ladbergen see Saatkamp, *Ladbergen*, 78–79, 83.

35. Quotations translated from the manuscript by Pastor Moritz Noll, "Geschichte der ersten deutsch evangelischen reformirten Gemeinde zu New Knoxville, Auglaize County, Ohio," New Knoxville 1893.

36. When Father Johann Wilhelm Horstmann emigrated in 1833, he took with him a group of eight to ten Catholic families. They founded Glandorf, another entirely German settlement in Putnam County, northwestern Ohio. See Karl Kiel, "Gründe und Folgen der Auswanderungen aus dem Osnabrücker Regierungsbezirk, insbesondere nach den Vereinigten Staaten, im Lichte der hannoverschen Auswanderungspolitik betrachtet," *Mitteilungen des Vereins für Geschichte und Landeskunde von Osnabrück* 61 (1941): 121, 123; Michael Leach, *Called to the Vineyard: A Definitive Study of the Religious Community in Glandorf, Putnam County, Ohio (1834–1900), and its Societal Impact as Symbolized by St. John the Baptist Roman Catholic Church* (Glandorf, OH: 1982), 7–11. The emigrants in Horstmann's party, just like the immigrants to Auglaize County, should not be thought of in the first place as being religiously motivated. Like the vast majority of northwest German emigrants, they were primarily looking for socioeconomic improvement and took this opportunity to travel as a group under the leadership of a trustworthy priest.

37. Hoying, *Pilgrims All*, 81–82. A thorough history of the Precious Blood Order in the United States up to 1860 with special reference to Franz Brunner is provided by Paul J. Knapke,

on Sundays had to be obeyed instead of the customary family visits, walks, festivities, and other Catholic Sunday entertainments. Brunner's ideal was a community where "gossip and chatter are never heard, nor does one see an idle man."[38] This was the strict code of values that had a profound impact on the Catholic and Evangelical congregations of nineteenth century Minster and New Knoxville.

It does not come as a surprise, therefore, that both villages, small as they were, became important national and international mission centers for their respective creeds (the Society of the Precious Blood in Minster after 1845; "The Way International" in New Knoxville since the 1950s). Both produced an unusually large number of clerics, monks, and nuns. In the 1950s the Reformed church in tiny New Knoxville was elected one of the twelve "great churches" of America worthy of study, in part because of its extraordinary "output" of clerics and missionaries (42 in its 120 years of existence).[39] In a survey conducted in 1935, the New Knoxville Church was one of only four very large Reformed congregations in Ohio with a membership of over a thousand. Minster's St. Augustine parish in its turn had generated two bishops, thirty priests and twenty-six nuns by 1940.[40]

While Minster and New Knoxville remained fairly homogenous in their predominant denomination as well as in their citizens' German home regions during the entire nineteenth century, New Bremen soon began to exhibit greater diversity and economic, social, and denominational openness.[41] While Minster and New Knoxville only had one or at times two churches, the former unity of New Bremen's church (and consequently its community) was shaken by several ruptures within the Lutheran congregation in the second half of the nineteenth century, and churches of diverging Protestant affiliation were established. These ruptures were the result of theological arguments as well

History of the American Province of the Society of the Precious Blood, 2 vols. (Carthagena, OH: Messenger Press, 1958).

38. Knapke, _History of the American Province_, 40, 127–128 (quotations from letters by Franz Brunner).

39. "Great Churches of America."

40. A list of Minster parishioners who entered religious life can be found in Hoying, _Pilgrims All_.

41. The following paragraphs sketch a few results from the acculturation chapter of my thesis entitled "Cultural Change and Cultural Stability."

as arguments about which larger church organizations (Lutheran, Reformed, Evangelical) the parishes should join.[42] Strife within congregations was certainly not an uncommon part of nineteenth-century community life. Studies have shown that initially repressed dogmatic arguments quite often prevailed over the need for harmony in a strange land.[43] In the case of New Bremen, the fading of its character as a "one-church village" was reinforced by the fact that the earlier formal division between northwestern and southern German immigrants disappeared in New Bremen when, in 1878, several demographically heterogenous hamlets on the outskirts of the town were incorporated.

In addition, an analysis of social and club life in Minster, New Knoxville, and New Bremen reveals that social activities in the former two villages almost exclusively revolved around associations in some way connected to the largest congregation in town. New Bremen, on the other hand, was the home of several secular clubs and lodges, while the very existence of lodges provided their deeply religious neighbors in Minster and New Knoxville with a cause for taking offense.[44] With no one church to unify the town, New Bremen's inhabitants proved to be more secular and, as it turned out, more oriented toward the American host society in their standards of behavior and living, i.e., in their acculturation, than the people of Minster and New Knoxville. New Bremenites were the first to publish an English-only newspaper and the first to adopt popular American styles in vernacular architecture. Perhaps as a consequence of this

---

42. *150th Anniversary St. Paul United Church of Christ, New Bremen, Ohio, 1833–1893* (New Bremen, 1983), 7–13; *New Bremen Centennial, 1833–1933, July 1–4* (New Bremen, OH: New Bremen Historical Society, 1933).

43. Gerhard Wiesinger, *Die deutsche Einwandererkolonie von Holyoke, Massachusetts, 1865–1920* (Stuttgart: F. Steiner, 1994), 193–194; John Gjerde, *The Minds of the West: Ethnocultural Evolution in the Rural Middle West, 1830–1917* (Chapel Hill: University of North Carolina Press, 1997), 19, 107; Robert C. Ostergren, *A Community Transplanted: The Trans-Atlantic Experience of a Swedish Immigrant Settlement in the Upper Middle West, 1835–1915* (Madison: University of Wisconsin Press, 1988), 211–217, 233. Kroes, "Amsterdam, Montana," 141–144, on the other hand, found that the theological arguments occurring among Dutch Reformed immigrants in a Montana settlement did not have a disunifying result. In effect, the complicated disputes even served to reinforce the settlers' attitude of being a select group of people sharing important values.

44. While lodges and fraternities fulfilled important tasks in integrating immigrants, the Catholic Church remained hostile toward freemasonry and lodges like the Knights of Pythias and the Odd Fellows, two of the ones present in New Bremen after 1870. See Mary Ann Clawson, *Constructing Brotherhood: Class, Gender, and Fraternalism* (Princeton: Princeton University Press, 1989), 126. The more orthodox Lutheran synods also did not allow their congregants to seek lodge membership.

| Admin. Entity | Census 1850 | | Census 1870 | | | |
| | Real Estate | | Real Estate | | Mobile Property | |
	Av. [a]	StD [b]	Av.	StD	Av.	StD
New Bremen	1,170	2,072	2,100	3,589	2,026	4,004
Minster	894	1,589	1,691	2,515	1,544	3,733
German Twp.	678	457	2,656	2,139	450	933
Jackson Twp.			3,707	2,326	327	115
Washington Twp. [c]	654	472	3,912	3,263	403	882
All	*769*	*1,053*	*2,792*	*2,983*	*753*	*2,124*

[a] Average (mean).

[b] Standard Deviation.

[c] Including the hamlet of New Knoxville.

Sources: Manuscript Census Schedules for German, Jackson and Washington Townships, 1850 and 1870.

Table 2.4: Average Property Value in Auglaize County Administrational Entities

greater openness, New Bremen became the most economically successful of the three German villages throughout the nineteenth and early twentieth centuries, being home to the largest department store and, for decades, the only bank in the area.[45] An analysis of the 1850 manuscript census shows that New Bremenites were wealthier in terms of real estate than the inhabitants of all other administrational entities in southern Auglaize County. In 1870, their movable property was almost twenty-five percent more valuable on average than that of their neighbors, although in terms of real estate the rural townships had caught up with New Bremen (see table 2.4).

It seems that the economic growth and comparative denominational openness that began to characterize New Bremen in the 1860s accelerated the process of acculturation in some areas of life. New Knoxville and Minster, on the other hand, exhibited a remarkable degree of cultural stability with regard to creed, language, and seclusive attitudes well into the twentieth century. It should be repeated, however, that in all three villages the pace of acculturation was much slower than that observed for urban immigrant groups or for immigrants living outside ethnically homogeneous settlement clusters.

In many respects, the settlement and acculturation processes exhibited by the townships and villages in southern Auglaize County may correspond to findings for other rural ethnic enclaves and are thus part of a pattern that is independent of specific (social, economical, regional, or religious) conditions in the sending and receiving cultures.[46] However, a closer look at the migration, settlement, and acculturation processes that shaped the history of each village reveals digressions from this pattern. Taking into account that the northwest German immigrants settling in Auglaize County shared a very similar socioeconomic, regional and linguistic origin, these digressions are remarkable because they point to the importance of *Heimatfaktoren* (background factors)—characteristics shared by certain German immigrant sub-groups—that could exercise a potentially powerful influence on the outcome of the entire migration process (migration, group formation, community formation, acculturation). The surprising outcome in this case is that the shared national, regional, social, and linguistic backgrounds of northwest German immigrants did not suffice to create and sustain a shared "German" ethnicity that the German settlers were conscious of and desired. In

---

45. *Minster Post*, 24 September 1896; William J. McMurray, ed., *History of Auglaize County* (Indianapolis: Historical Publishing Co., 1923), 420, 422, 442, 478.

46. See the acculturation model developed for German immigrants in Conzen, "Deutsche Einwanderer."

terms of cause as well as effect, German ethnicity was only a secondary force compared to the strong impact of denominational and local ties back to the immigrants' home regions. These determined the patterns of group solidarities and group boundaries that were at the heart of all migration and acculturation processes in southern Auglaize County.[47]

---

47. Timothy Smith has characterized the predominance of religious over national affiliation as a "redefinition of ethnic boundaries in religious terms" (Smith, "Religion and Ethnicity," 1168).

Appendix

Note on sources for table 2.1: The manuscript census schedules of German and Washington Townships for 1850 served as the basis for the process of identification by individual record linkage. Sources for northwestern Germany were the emigrant lists in: Friedrich Müller, "Westfälische Auswanderer im 19. Jahrhundert: Auswanderer aus dem Regierungsbezirk Münster, 1803–1850," *Beiträge zur Westfälischen Familienforschung* 22–24 (1964–1966): 7–389; Friedrich Ernst Hunsche, *Auswanderungen aus dem Kreis Steinfurt: Mit Beiträgen im Anhang von Friedrich Schmedt* (Steinfurt: [Oberkreisdirektor], 1983); Johannes Ostendorf, "Zur Geschichte der Auswanderung aus dem alten Amt Damme (Oldenburg) nach Amerika in den Jahren 1830–1880," *Oldenburger Jahrbuch des Landesvereins für Geschichte und Heimatkunde* 46/47 (1942–1943): 165–297. Unpublished sources: For the Principality of Osnabrück the emigrant data bank at the Niedersächsisches Staatsarchiv Osnabrück. For southern Oldenburg the emigrant list compiled by local historian Father David Hoying, Minster, OH (several hundred entries). This latter source is far more informative for southern Oldenburg than the emigrant index card file at the Niedersächsisches Staatsarchiv Oldenburg. Important additional information was obtained from American church records and regional histories containing biographical information: Death Records St. Peter / St. Paul / Zion Church, New Bremen Public Library (card index file); Death Records First United Church of Christ, New Knoxville parish archive (The church records of St. Augustine Parish were analyzed by Father D. Hoying for his above-mentioned emigrant list); C. W. Williamson, *History of Western Ohio and Auglaize County, with Illustrations and Biographical Sketches of Pioneers and Prominent Public Men* (Columbus, OH: W. M. Linn & Sons, 1905); *Combined Atlases of Auglaize County, Ohio: 1880, 1898, 1917* (Evansville, IN 1975).

3

The Dialectics of Ethnic Identity: German Jews in Chicago, 1850–1870

Tobias Brinkmann

I was born as a Jew. Politically I am an American, a patriotic, enthusiastic, and loyal American citizen as anybody can be. Spiritually I am German. I have been influenced by Schiller, Goethe, Kant, and other spiritual German heroes. I drank from the sources of German literature, and I sat at the feet of German teachers, and with a certain sense of pride I can say: I am spiritually a German.[1]

The term "German-Jewish period" is regularly used by scholars of American-Jewish history to describe the years before the rise in Jewish immigration from Eastern Europe in 1881. And indeed, between 1820 and 1880 more than one hundred thousand Jews migrated from the German states and neighboring territories to the United States. Quotes such as the one above by Reform rabbi Bernhard Felsenthal apparently demonstrate the strong identification of these Jewish immigrants with Germany. However, a closer look discloses an identity that is much more complex.

A review of the literature reveals a number of strikingly different definitions of the term "German Jews." Naomi Cohen, author of a general study on the "German-Jewish period," uses the term without further defining or examining its origins and usefulness.[2] Hasia Diner, on the other hand, covering the period 1820–1880 in the five-volume-study *The Jewish People in America*, questions the usefulness of the terms "German Jews" and "German-Jewish period." She claims that many Jewish migrants who arrived before 1880 came from a number of territories outside of Germany such as Hungary or Poland. And even most Jews who had lived in German territories such as Bavaria or Baden, Diner argues, had had little contact with German culture prior to

1. Bernhard Felsenthal, "Jüdische Thesen," in *Festschrift zum Siebzigsten Geburtstage A. Berliner's: Gewidmet von Freunden und Schülern*, edited by A. Freimann and M. Hildesheimer (Frankfurt am Main: privately published, 1903), 72–92. The article had been published originally in the Jewish monthly *Die Deborah* [Cincinnati] in September 1901.

2. Naomi Cohen, *Encounter with Emancipation: The German Jews in the United States 1830–1914* (Philadelphia: Jewish Publication Society, 1984).

migrating literally "out of the Ghetto" to America.[3] Neither Diner nor Naomi Cohen, nor most students of this period, however, have looked extensively at German-language sources. Cohen and Diner do not pay much attention to the Jewish Reform movement in America, which, on the eve of Jewish mass migration from Eastern Europe in 1880, counted most Jewish congregations in America among its followers and had a strong affinity to Germany. Diner does not make a distinction between origin in a specific country and identification with a country. Therefore, she cannot explain why Jews from Eastern Europe identified themselves as "Germans," writing: ". . . many American Jews who themselves—or their parents—had hailed from the lands of the east described themselves as 'Germans,' an identity thought to be prestigious, and ignored their Polish or other roots."[4]

Most scholars of nineteenth-century German immigration to the United States have ignored Jews and Jewish congregations and associations, although most German daily newspapers such as the *Illinois Staats-Zeitung* or the *New York Staats-Zeitung* frequently covered social events involving Jewish immigrants in the second half of the nineteenth century. One exception is Stanley Nadel's account of German immigrants in nineteenth-century New York City. During his research Nadel discovered many Jewish immigrants ranging from workers to millionaires who were active in German associations, often in leading positions. For Nadel, Jewish immigrants were an integral part of "Little Germany" in New York before 1880.[5] In his survey on Jewish immigration from Germany to the United States between 1820 and 1914,

---

3.   Hasia Diner, *A Time for Gathering: The Second Migration 1820–1880* (Baltimore: Johns Hopkins University Press, 1992), 232–233. The term "out of the Ghetto" was coined by Jacob Katz. See Katz, *Out of the Ghetto: The Social Background of Jewish Emancipation, 1770–1870* (Cambridge: Harvard University Press, 1971).

4.   Diner, *Time for Gathering*, 49. On the evolution of the Reform movement in Judaism from its German origins to its ultimate success in the United States, see Michael Meyer, *Response to Modernity: A History of the Reform Movement in Judaism* (New York, Oxford: Oxford University Press, 1988) and Michael Meyer, "German-Jewish Identity in Nineteenth-Century America," in *Toward Modernity: The European Jewish Model*, edited by Jacob Katz (New Brunswick, NJ: Rutgers University Press, 1987), 247–267.

5.   Stanley Nadel, *Little Germany: Ethnicity, Religion and Class in New York City, 1845–80* (Urbana, Chicago: University of Illinois Press, 1990), 99–103. Nadel is one of the few scholars working on German migration to the United States who includes Jews in his focus. For this see Nadel, "Jewish Race and German Soul in Nineteenth-Century America," *American Jewish History* 77 (1987): 6.

Avraham Barkai also uses the term "German Jews." He even claims that, until 1880, "German Jews" in America constituted a branch of German Jewry.[6]

Who were the "German Jews"? Or, to put it differently, were "German Jews" German immigrants of the Jewish faith, or were they Jewish immigrants from Germany with few or no connections to other immigrants from Germany? These seemingly simple questions open the way to rather more complex ones about the actual meanings of "German" and "Jewish" for the immigrants themselves, for their respective social environments in nineteenth-century America, and for historians who attempt to describe the changing ethnic identities of these immigrants.

In this article I explore two related issues for the period from 1850 to 1870 based on a study of Jewish immigrants in Chicago:[7]

1) What did "Germanness" mean to Jewish immigrants who arrived before the substantial increase in Jewish immigration from Eastern Europe? How can the term "German Jews" be defined?

2) How did "Germanness" relate to "Jewishness" and "Americanness" for Jewish immigrant leaders at different times?

The Complexities of Defining "Germanness"

The designation "German" requires a particularly careful analysis, because the German nation-state was only founded in 1871. The decision in favor of a *Kleindeutschland* excluded millions of German-speakers while including a number of minorities such as Poles and Danes. Not all Jewish immigrants in Chicago before 1880 came from what was to become the German Empire in 1871. Most originated from Bavaria, Hesse, Baden, Westphalia, and Posen. Others, however, embarked on their journey to America from Poland, Hungary, Bohemia, Lithuania, and Alsace.[8]

---

6. Avraham Barkai, *Branching Out: German-Jewish Immigration to the United States 1820–1914* (New York: Holmes and Meier, 1994), 228. Barkai and Nadel have used German-language sources extensively.

7. The article is based on my dissertation completed in 2000 at the Technische Universität Berlin, now published under the title, *Von der Gemeinde zur "Community": Jüdische Einwanderer in Chicago, 1840–1900* (Osnabrück: Rasch, 2002).

8. Herman Eliassof and Emil G. Hirsch, "The Jews of Illinois: Their Religious and Civic Life, Their Charity and Industry, Their Patriotism and Loyalty to American Institutions, from Their Earliest Settlement in the State unto Present Time," *Reform Advocate* [Chicago], 4 May 1901, 283–301.

Except for their language, German-speaking immigrants in the United States had little in common:

1) Most German-speaking immigrants were either Lutherans or Catholics, others belonged to a number of Protestant groups (or joined such groups in the United States), and some were Jewish.

2) Many German-speaking immigrants strongly identified with their respective home regions. Stanley Nadel has shown that in nineteenth-century New York German immigrants from certain regions had a high tendency to settle in the same neighborhood and to marry among their own.[9] Why were these regional bonds so strong? This can partly be explained by the survival of many small and mid-sized territories within the Holy Roman Empire that were often separated by religious affiliation. Many regions such as Westphalia or Franconia were only merged into larger states with the demise of the Empire in the early nineteenth century.

3) Immigrants from Germany migrated to North America over extended time periods. Other large immigrant groups came within relatively short periods. Most Jewish immigrants from Eastern Europe, for example, came to the United States between 1890 and 1914.[10]

4) The social makeup of German immigrants was anything but homogenous. Nineteenth-century immigrants ranged from agricultural laborers and struggling artisans to independent farmers with capital and small merchants. In America the social discrepancies increased even more, which can be explained by the

---

9. Nadel, *Little Germany*, 37–42, 48–50.

10. On this see Klaus J. Bade, "Die deutsche überseeische Massenauswanderung im 19. und frühen 20. Jahrhundert: Bestimmungsfaktoren und Entwicklungsbedingungen," in *Auswanderer—Wanderarbeiter—Gastarbeiter: Bevölkerung, Arbeitsmarkt und Wanderung in Deutschland seit der Mitte des 19. Jahrhunderts*, vol. 1, edited by Klaus J. Bade (Ostfildern: Scripta Mercurae Verlag, 1984), 259–299. For an updated essay see Klaus J. Bade, "Conclusion: Migration Past and Present—The German Experience," in *People in Transit: German Migrations in Comparative Perspective, 1820–1920*, edited by Dirk Hoerder and Jörg Nagler (Cambridge: Cambridge University Press, 1995), 399–412. On Jewish migration from Eastern Europe see Gerald Sorin, *A Time for Building: The Third Migration, 1880–1920* (Baltimore: Johns Hopkins University Press, 1992).

different social and cultural backgrounds of immigrants and their different times of arrival and chosen areas of settlement.[11]

Most German immigrants, however, shared a common language, and an orientation towards German *Kultur*. The latter concept is, of course, rather vague and difficult to define. Before 1880 Jewish immigrant leaders in Chicago identified strongly with Germany on a cultural and spiritual level, as will be explained below. They had little reason to identify with Germany on a political or national level, since in most German states Jews remained second-class citizens. While France emancipated its Jews swiftly in 1790/1791, the process of Jewish emancipation in the German states was a "tortuous and thorny path." Bavaria applied particularly harsh measures to reduce its Jewish population by forcing its Jews to migrate. A Jewish emigrant, asked in 1845 in Mainz whether he might consider returning to his Bavarian home village, replied: "I will only come back when North America becomes Bavarian." Full civil and social equality for Jews in the German states was only achieved with German unification in 1871.[12]

In order to interpret German ethnicity in the United States, it is necessary to differentiate between the actual background of the specific immigrants at the time of their arrival and their identification as "Germans" in America— either by themselves, their ethnic leaders, or their neighbors. These interrelated processes have been aptly described as the construction of ethnicity. Many immigrants from Europe who arrived in America after 1815 identified

---

11. On landless peasants and laborers see Rainer Mühle, "Colonist Traditions and Nineteenth-Century Emigration from East Elbian Prussia," in *People in Transit*, 35–55. On independent farmers and small artisans who left with capital see Mack Walker, *Germany and the Emigration, 1816–1885* (Cambridge: Harvard University Press, 1964).

12. Several German states emancipated their Jewish citizens before 1871. Baden was the first state in the German Confederation to do so in 1862, Prussia followed in 1869. On the emancipation of Jews in Europe see the essays in Pierre Birnbaum and Ira Katznelson, eds., *Paths of Emancipation: Jews, States, and Citizenship* (Princeton: Princeton University Press, 1995). On Germany see Reinhard Rürup, "The Tortuous and Thorny Path to Legal Equality: 'Jew Laws' and Emancipatory Legislation in Germany from the Late Eighteenth Century," *Leo Baeck Institute Yearbook* 31 (1986): 5–10. Quote translated from, *Der Orient [Leipzig]*, 28 May 1845, 22. The original German reads: "Ich werde nicht eher zurückkehren, als bis Nordamerika baierisch wird!" On the Bavarian policy toward Jews see Manfred Treml, "Von der 'Judenemanzipation' zur 'Bürgerlichen Verbesserung': Zur Vorgeschichte und Frühphase der Judenemanzipation in Bayern," in *Geschichte und Kultur der Juden in Bayern—Aufsätze*, edited by Manfred Treml and Josef Kirmaier (München: Haus der Bayerischen Geschichte, 1988), 247–265.

themselves as members of an ethnic group. At the same time, immigrants were increasingly defined by Americans in ethnic terms.[13]

In large American cities, German immigrants and their descendants formed not one homogenous and institutionally organized community, but rather loosely affiliated, constantly changing networks of numerous *Vereine*, congregations, and lodges. In the second half of the nineteenth century, working-class Germans and socially established German Jews were only two of several groups in Chicago whose lives remained socially and spatially worlds apart. But on certain occasions members of these groups interacted as Germans, for instance on the occasion of Lincoln's burial, or during the Fourth of July Parade in 1862 when the Germans and the Irish marched in separate cohorts displaying their ethnicity to the urban public.[14]

The Transformation of Jewish Communities in America

Two aspects are significant to understand the involvement of Jewish immigrants with German community life in mid-nineteenth-century American cities: The makeup of Jewish communities and—in contrast to Europe—the unusual degree of acceptance Jewish immigrants enjoyed in the United States.

The German immigrant community in Chicago was rather loosely organized, and the same can be said about the much smaller Jewish community. Even before the massive increase of Jewish migration to the United States after 1881, the Jewish community in Chicago cannot really be described as a tight *Gemeinschaft* along the lines of the traditional Jewish *Gemeinde* in Germany. When the first Jews from rural areas of Franconia and the Palatinate reached Chicago in the early 1840s, older Jewish communities on the East Coast and in Midwestern cities like Cincinnati were dividing along religious, social, and regional lines due to the same in-migration from South Germany and Posen. Jonathan Sarna has described this process as a transformation from the "synagogue-community" to a "community of synagogues."[15]

---

13. Kathleen Conzen et. al., "The Invention of Ethnicity: A Perspective from the U.S.A.," *Journal of American Ethnic History* 11 (1992): 8–9. See also David A. Gerber, *The Making of an American Pluralism: Buffalo, New York, 1825–60* (Urbana, Chicago: University of Illinois Press, 1989).

14. On plans for Lincoln's burial see *Illinois Staats-Zeitung* [Chicago], 30 April 1865. On the Fourth of July Parade, see *ISZ*, 4 July 1862. The two leaders of the German cohort were both prominent Jews; a Jewish lodge marched along with German worker's associations.

15. Jonathan Sarna, "The Evolution of the American Synagogue," in *The Americanization of the Jews*, edited by Robert M. Selzer and Norman J. Cohen (New York: New York University Press, 1995), 218–219.

But Jews in Chicago and elsewhere in the United States were not only splitting along religious lines. Early on, independent philanthropic and social associations were established, changing the composition of the traditional European-oriented Jewish community in America significantly. No longer were all Jews members of a religious congregation. Some now belonged to secular clubs, societies, and Jewish lodges; some were affiliated with a congregation and a secular association; while still others did not belong to a Jewish congregation or association but would occasionally attend a service or donate money to a Jewish charitable organization. The diversification of the older tightly knit Jewish *Gemeinschaften* into looser networks of various secular and religious associations and congregations that were splitting along religious or regional lines demonstrates the arrival of Jewish communities in America. The separation of church and state in the United States presented new opportunities for Jewish immigrants. Even after Jews in Germany were fully emancipated, they were forced by state governments to organize into one congregation in a given city or village, the so called "Einheitsgemeinde" (unified congregation). In America, by contrast, members of Jewish congregations could split whenever they felt it was necessary.[16]

Jewish leaders responded to the transformation of Jewish communities. Several organizations were established in the late 1850s with the purpose of unifying the Jews of Chicago. The first B'nai B'rith lodge in Chicago was founded in 1857 in order to narrow the widening gap between Jews from Bavaria and Posen. It may also have been established to attract Jews who had severed their ties to Jewish congregations in Chicago.[17] Two years later Jews in Chicago founded the United Hebrew Relief Association (UHRA) whose primary task was to centralize efforts to relieve Jewish poverty.[18] On a higher level, however, this association served as the focal point of the Jewish community network by offering corporate memberships to Jewish associations,

---

16. On the structure of Jewish *Gemeinden* in Germany and England after emancipation was granted, see Rainer Liedtke, *Jewish Welfare in Hamburg and Manchester, c. 1850–1914* (Oxford: Oxford University Press, 1998).

17. On the general history of the Independent Order B'nai B'rith see Deborah Dash Moore, *B'nai B'rith and the Challenge of Ethnic Leadership* (Albany: State University Press of New York, 1981). *Report of the Eighth Annual General Convention of the Independent Order Bnai Brith* (Cincinnati: Independent Order Bnai Brith, 1859), 33. In 1851 the revised constitution of the B'nai B'rith stressed the guiding principle of the order: "Gegründet zur Einigung der Juden in den Vereinigten Staaten von Nordamerika" (founded to unify the Jews in the United States of North America). Compare *Constitution des Unabhängigen Ordens Bnai Brith, Constitution of the Independent Order Bnai Brith* (New York: Independent Order Bnai Brith, 1851), n. p.

18. *First Annual Report to the Directors of the UHRA of Chicago* (Chicago, 1860).

congregations, and philanthropic societies in Chicago. The representatives of all member societies of the UHRA met annually to elect the board and to vote on the organization's budget. The establishment of the UHRA in 1859 marks the beginning of a Jewish-American community in Chicago with ties to most other Jewish congregations and associations. Until 1881—when Jewish immigration from Eastern Europe increased—the UHRA served as a "common platform" for Jews in Chicago. Rabbi Liebmann Adler praised the UHRA in 1874 for its work:

> Scarce two decades have elapsed since all the Israelites of this city were living as in the bonds of one family circle. Each knew the other. All worshipped harmoniously in one temple and shared others' woes and joys. How great is the change! Thousands scattered over a space of thirty miles, in hundreds of streets, divided by pecuniary, intellectual and social distinctions and even religious differences. Separation, division, dissolution, estrangement, repeated and continual, are the words which characterize the history of our brothers in faith until now. Dissolved in the mass of our population, we are losing the consciousness of homogeneity and the strength gained for each by concerted action. Praise upon you: The U.H.R.A.! You provided Chicago's Israelites with a common platform. Here come our Israelites through their representatives together.[19]

The first Jewish immigrants from Germany in Chicago were the first Jews ever to come to the city, and these Jews from the Palatinate and Franconia were also among the early settlers in the city. On the East Coast, Jewish immigrants were often despised by the Gentile establishment and remained outsiders for years to come. In New England only one Jewish community was established in the eighteenth century—in Newport, Rhode Island.[20] Boston was particularly hostile to Jews, and hardly any Jews came to the city before 1840. Jews in Boston were isolated outsiders for most of the nineteenth century, and the community remained very small until the 1880s.[21] In Midwestern communities

---

19. *15th Annual Report to the Delegates of the UHRA*. Adler's speech was printed in the (original) German and in the English translation reproduced verbatim here.

20. Stephen Mostov, "A Sociological Portrait of German Jewish Immigrants in Boston: 1845–1861," *AJS Review* 3 (1978): 127–128. Jews had already come to Newport by the late seventeenth century, but a congregation was organized only in the eighteenth century.

21. Mostov, "Sociological Portrait of German Jewish Immigrants," 127. Compare also Jonathan Sarna, "The Jews of Boston in Historical Perspective," in *The Jews of Boston*, edited by Jonathan Sarna and Ellen Smith (Boston: Northeastern University Press, 1995), 4.

Jews were more accepted members of urban society, at least on an official level. In an advertisement in a German-Jewish paper, published in Frankfurt am Main, the main Jewish congregation in Chicago claimed in 1857: "They [the Jews] have gained a position in this city that makes every true and spirited Israelite proud to carry the name 'Israelite.'"[22] In the 1850s the first Jews in Chicago were elected into political office, and immediately after the disastrous fire of 1871, the *Chicago Tribune* demanded that one of the leading Jews and Germans in Chicago, banker Henry Greenebaum, should become mayor to guide the city back to prosperity. Greenebaum declined, but the event illustrates the degree of acceptance Jews enjoyed in Chicago.[23] A few years earlier, in 1867, Chicago's leading businessmen had joined their Jewish colleagues in a boycott of a number of New York-based insurance companies that discriminated against Jews. This act of solidarity created a lot of publicity and, even more importantly, built trust between Jews and Gentiles.[24] In the late 1870s leading Jewish families were even accepted into the "high society" of Chicago.[25] Jewish community leaders were aware that this degree of acceptance was unusual, and they constantly worried about the social standing of Jews in Chicago and about the persistance of anti-Jewish prejudices. The need for acceptance was also an important driving force for religious reform, as is discussed below.

22.   *Der Israelitische Volkslehrer* 50 (1857): 286.

23.   Henry Greenebaum was a member of the city council from 1856 to 1858 and Edward Salomon from 1859 to 1861. Abraham Kohn became city clerk in 1861. For more information see Bernhard Felsenthal, "A Contribution to the History of the Israelites in Chicago," manuscript 1863, Col. Felsenthal, Bernhard. Box 130, CHS. On the proposal to elect Greenebaum as mayor, see *Chicago Tribune*, 21 October 1871.

24.   On the insurance boycott see *Chicago Tribune*, 12 April 1867. Under the surface strong prejudices existed against Jews in Chicago. An analysis of confidential business dossiers of a leading credit-rating agency in my dissertation proves, however, that anti-Jewish prejudices declined significantly between 1850 and 1880.

25.   In the *Chicago Society Directory* only seven women out of a sample of twenty-five leading Jewish families were listed in 1876. In 1880, when the ties to the German community were eroding, thirty-two names (mothers and daughters) are counted in a similar publication (*Bon-Ton Directory*), an indication of the entry of Jewish families into the "society" of Chicago. For details see Brinkmann, *Von der Gemeinde zur "Community,"* 296.

Jewish Immigrants and "Germanness" in Chicago

Until the 1870s most Jews in Chicago were German speakers.[26] They read the leading German paper, the *Illinois Staats-Zeitung*, which covered events in the Jewish community into the 1890s, an indication of a substantial Jewish readership. Even internal Jewish controversies were sometimes covered by the *Staats-Zeitung*, and several rabbis, especially Bernhard Felsenthal, wrote numerous articles for the paper on spiritual and cultural subjects, addressing Jews and non-Jews alike.[27] Being German speakers, Jews were often identified as Germans by outside observers, although they may not have considered themselves as such. Early in the 1850s an English visitor to Chicago observed that "most Jews here are Germans and speak that language."[28] The publication of two weekly English-language community papers after 1878 illustrates the fading of German as a spoken language. One of the two papers, the *Jewish Advance*, still had an extensive German section.[29] The following two case studies on social life and spiritual identification with Germany also illustrate that German was widely spoken in the 1850s and 1860s among Jewish immigrants in Chicago.

Jews and the Organization of a German Community in Chicago

Some Jews in Chicago were closely connected with the German community on a social level until 1900 and in a few cases even longer. Two biographical compilations of leading Germans in Chicago contain the names of famous Jews such as the Greenebaum brothers, Lazarus Silverman, and Henry Horner, to name just a few.[30] The involvement of most Jewish leaders in

---

26. Bernhard Felsenthal, *Kol Kore Bamidbar: Über jüdische Reform—Ein Wort an die Freunde derselben* (Chicago: Chas. Heß, 1859), 24. Felsenthal estimated that ninety percent of all American Jews either spoke and wrote only in German or preferred German.

27. Compare the bibliography in Bernhard Felsenthal, *Bernhard Felsenthal: Teacher in Israel* (Oxford, New York: Oxford University Press, 1924).

28. "Bericht eines englischen Conseils über den Stand der Juden in Chicago," in *Erzählungen meiner Erlebnisse*, edited by Salomon Ephraim Blogg (Hannover, Germany: Privately published, 1856), 43.

29. The papers were *The Chicago Occident* and the *Jewish Advance* [Chicago]. The *Advance* was discontinued after 1881. In 1869 Rabbi Israel Löw Chronik published and edited a shortlived German-Jewish monthly in Chicago, called *Zeichen der Zeit* (Signs of the Time).

30. See biographies of leading Jews in Emil Dietzsch, *Chicago's Deutsche Männer* (Chicago: Privately published, 1885), 36, 129, 193. See also *Chicago und sein Deutschthum* (Cleveland: German-American Biographical Publishing Company, 1901/1902).

the upper echelons of German community circles probably reflected the broad membership of Jews in German associations before the 1870s. Michael Meyer argues convincingly that German associations offered Jewish immigrants acceptance when they were still "outsiders" in greater America.[31]

Jews who were leaders of Jewish associations were equally active in German organizations. Rabbis and leading Jewish businessmen in particular were involved in German associations between 1850 and 1880: In 1853 Jews helped to establish the leading German philanthropic association, the "Deutsche Gesellschaft"—later known as the "German Aid Society"—which supported needy immigrants from Germany. Lawyer Julius Rosenthal acted as one of its early presidents and was a member of the board during the disastrous 1871 fire. Jacob Baiersdorf also served as president of the German Aid Society for some time.[32] During the Fourth of July parade in 1862 Henry Greenebaum and Edward Salomon led the German cohort.[33] In Emil Hirsch, who became the rabbi of the Sinai congregation in 1880, the Germans in Chicago found an intellectual of grand stature, one who was always ready to give speeches in English and German, one who could speak for the Germans of Chicago.[34] All these men also played leading roles within Jewish organizations in Chicago. These leaders could not have acted against the will of the members of Jewish congregations and associations. It was only after 1917 that the limits of involvement with the German cause were clearly drawn for Jewish community leaders. Emil Hirsch almost lost his position at Sinai in 1918, after he had repeatedly expressed his support for the German war effort.[35]

The large German community in Chicago was never cohesively organized, but Jews often led the efforts to bring all the Germans in Chicago together. The organization of the victory parade of 1871 was largely in the hands of Jewish community leaders. In fact, this was the only time that most Germans in Chicago were mobilized. The parade was organized in the office of Julius Rosenthal and

---

31. Meyer, "German-Jewish Identity," 252.

32. Article taken from *Der Westen* [Sunday edition of the *ISZ*], November 1909 [day not known], in Folder 129, German Aid Society, Historical Collections, Library of the University of Illinois at Chicago; Obituary of Julius Rosenthal, *Chicago Legal News*, 21 May 1905; Dietzsch, *Chicago's Deutsche Männer*, 36, 129, 193; *Cooke's City Directory: 1859–60* (Chicago: 1860).

33. *ISZ*, 4 July 1862.

34. On Hirsch see Hyman L. Meites, *History of the Jews of Chicago* (Chicago: Jewish Historical Society of Illinois, 1924), 141. On one of his most patriotic speeches praising the German war effort during the First World War see *Jahrbuch der Deutschen in Chicago für das Jahr 1916: Mit einer vollkommenen Geschichte des europäischen Krieges* (Chicago: Michael Singer, 1916), 31–33.

35. *Chicago Tribune*, 13 April 1918.

led by Henry Greenebaum; both were counted among the most respected Jews and Germans in Chicago.[36] Another issue that united the Germans in Chicago (and elsewhere) was the call for the imposition of strict controls on the use and sale of alcohol. Debates over prohibition were battlegrounds of class conflict and ethnic tension in nineteenth-century American cities. As early as 1867 Rabbi Chronik had invited leading Germans to his house to organize a drive against Sunday drinking laws.[37] In the early 1870s native-born businessmen again used the alcohol issue to strengthen their political position. After the fire of 1871, when attempts were made to introduce prohibition laws in Chicago, Henry Greenebaum helped the candidate of the anti-prohibition "People's Party" win the mayor's office by unifying the large majority of German and Irish voters. But success was shortlived. Once the threat of prohibition was removed, the political union of Germans broke down.[38]

Jews were prominently represented among the leading Germans of Chicago, but these leadership positions resulted more from social commitment to a large and dispersed community of groups than from real power over a tightly organized community. Why did Jewish leaders invest so much energy into organizing a German community? Between 1850 and 1880 the German community in Chicago was open and inclusive for Jews. German immigrant leaders did not discriminate against Jews. In fact, after the rise of modern anti-Semitism in Imperial Germany, the *Illinois Staats-Zeitung* and many other leading German papers in the United States took a firm line against anti-Semitism, criticizing even Bismarck in strong terms because he sought to use the anti-Semitic movement for his own ends.[39]

While there is plenty of evidence for the involvement of prominent Jews in the German community, there are, especially for the early period, almost

---

36. *ISZ*, 31 January and 3 March 1871; Eugen Seeger, *Chicago—Die Geschichte einer Wunderstadt* (Chicago: Privately Published, 1892), 131–132; *Deutsche Arbeiterkultur in Chicago von 1850 bis zum Ersten Weltkrieg: Eine Anthologie*, edited by Hartmut Keil (Ostfildern: Scripta Mercurae Verlag, 1984), 6.

37. *ISZ*, 9 December 1867. In Chronik's house a "Comite gegen Temperenz—und Sabbath—Zwangsgesetze" was organized. While many Germans socialized on Sundays, often in *Biergärten*, Jews who observed the Sabbath opposed Sunday laws because they were forced to keep their shops closed.

38. Karen Sawislak, *Smoldering City: Chicagoans and the Great Fire, 1871–1874* (Chicago: University of Chicago Press, 1995), 255–257.

39. On this see *ISZ*, 15 April 1881. A survey of the critical stance of German-American papers (*Cincinnati Gazette*, *New York Staats-Zeitung*) toward anti-Semitism in Germany can be found in *Der Zeitgeist [Milwaukee]*, 9 December 1880. For the general argument see Meyer, "German-Jewish Identity," 252.

no documents available that indicate widespread Jewish involvement in it.[40] After 1880 only individual Jews, notably Emil Hirsch and Henry Greenebaum, identified themselves with German associations in Chicago. Although as late as 1890 at least ten percent of the contributors to the German Aid Society were Jewish, they were passive donors and were not represented on the board as they had been earlier in the century.[41] The commitment to philanthropic organizations outside of the Jewish community was important for the Jewish leaders to counter anti-Jewish prejudices and to prove their willingness to open up to society. It is very likely that many Jews below the leadership level had social contacts with other German immigrants in the 1850s and 1860s, and even in the 1870s. But apart from the memories of individual immigrants, little material survives to corroborate the recollection of one of the old immigrants, Leopold Mayer, in 1899 that in the 1850s "the Germans, Jews and non-Jews, were one."[42]

It would be a mistake, however, to take the wide coverage of Jewish matters in the *Illinois Staats-Zeitung* and the fact that most Jews spoke German as evidence of a close relationship between Jews and non-Jews. In the 1860s Jews in Chicago organized their own social life, and numerous lodges of the Jewish fraternal Order B'nai B'rith were formed in the 1860s and 1870s. In 1869 the Standard Club, a prestigious club for Jewish businessmen, was organized, probably because Jews were excluded from non-German Gentile clubs. Jewish women also formed numerous organizations. In 1874 they organized the first Chicago chapter of the Unabhängiger Orden Treuer Schwestern (Independent Order of True Sisters).[43] After the 1870s German circles were increasingly replaced by those of the established urban society. Many leading Jewish families had become wealthy, a prerequisite to participating in the social life of the well-to-do in the city. These developments corresponded with residential mobility. Although most Jews had lived in the southern part of the Loop during

---

40.   There are hardly any sources such as membership directories available to document the history of German Americans in Chicago before 1880.

41.   *37. Jahresbericht der German Society of Chicago (Deutsche Gesellschaft von Chicago 1890/91* (Chicago, 1891). Greenebaum devoted much time to set up the German "Altenheim" on Chicago's West Side; on this see the numerous references to Greenebaum in Seeger, *Wunderstadt.*

42.   Quote in Eliassof, Hirsch, "The Jews of Illinois," 287.

43.   *Standard Club.* See also Meites, *Jews of Chicago,* 116–117. Second Annual Report of the District Grand Lodge No. 6. of the Independent Order B'nai B'rith (Chicago, 1870). File Johannah Lodge No. 9—Independent Order of True Sisters, Chicago Jewish Archives. Johannah Lodge abolished German as the official language only in the mid-1890s!

the 1850s, in the 1860s they began to move to the near and far South Side, the elite section of Chicago. Smaller groups lived on the West Side and the North Side. Although many Jews lived in close proximity to each other, they shared these neighborhoods with many native-born Gentile neighbors. At no time did large numbers of Jews seem to have lived in German middle-class neighborhoods.[44]

The German community in Chicago was a loose "ethnic" network, and prior to 1880 the Jewish community had a number of close connections with it, especially at the upper level. However, the small Jewish community was never a part of the large German community. In 1867 Jews organized a large parade to the construction site of the future Jewish hospital of Chicago. The parade included all the Jewish congregations, lodges, and associations, as well as Chicago's mayor. The *Illinois Staats-Zeitung* covered the event in detail and printed the speeches, and it is obvious that the hospital project was important for the Jewish community and its standing in the city of Chicago. Except for the language, however, "Germanness" was not an issue.[45]

The Jews of Chicago and the Civil War

Another good example of how Jews and Germans could simultaneously be closely involved yet clearly distict comes from the Civil War. When President Lincoln, who was acquainted with several Jews in Chicago,[46] called for troop reinforcements in the early summer of 1862, Jews in Chicago responded quickly by organizing a meeting on August 13, 1862. Within minutes six thousand dollars were collected to muster an all-Jewish company. The *Chicago Tribune* and the *Illinois Staats-Zeitung* praised "our patriotic Israelite fellow citizens" for their determined action.[47] One day later, even more Jews

---

44. These observations are based on samples I drew from UHRA membership lists from the 1860s to the 1890s. The data is included in Brinkmann, *Von der Gemeinde zur "Community."* On the Northwest Side of Chicago German-speaking Jewish workers seem to have lived in close proximity to non-Jewish German workers in the 1880s, for this see Hartmut Keil, "Immigrant Neighborhoods and American Society: German Immigrants on Chicago's Northwest Side in the Late Nineteenth Century," in *German Workers' Culture in the United States 1850–1920*, edited by Hartmut Keil (Washington, DC: Smithsonian Press, 1988), 43.

45. *ISZ*, 4 September 1867.

46. Meites, *Jews of Chicago*, 84–85. Abraham Kohn and Henry Greenebaum were both active in Illinois politics. They went to Springfield on several occasions and met with Lincoln.

47. *ISZ*, 15 August 1862.

attended a second mass-meeting. This was the first time that almost all the Jews in Chicago came together as Jews, and they formally decided to put aside their numerous differences, particularly with regard to religion, for the time being. Henry Greenebaum addressed the Jewish crowd in German and reminded them "that they owe the Union loyalty, because it gave them social and political freedom, a freedom they did not enjoy in Europe." His call was heeded: All Jews present agreed in their resolution, "that we, at this time, feel compelled—driven by our deep patriotic feelings, and by our adherence and love to the fatherland of our choice—to undertake as a community an effort for our fatherland that had adopted us." More donations were collected, and a company of almost one hundred Jewish volunteers was organized that evening, fully equipped by the Jews of Chicago. The size of the company is remarkable, since only around two thousand Jews lived in Chicago in 1862. The Jewish "Company C" became part of the "82nd Illinois" Regiment. This regiment was led by the famous Forty-Eighter Friedrich Hecker and was composed mostly of German immigrants.[48]

On August 20 another meeting took place to celebrate the formal entry of the Jewish company into Hecker's regiment. The Jewish women of Chicago donated the regiment's flag to Colonel Hecker, who attended the meeting along with Lorenz Brentano and other prominent Germans. The few but influential Forty-Eighters were the only other Germans in Chicago who owed their freedom to the United States besides the Jews. In his impressive speech Hecker drew a parallel between the struggle for Jewish emancipation in Germany and the fight for the emancipation of the black slaves in the South, saying: "I fought in my former home-country for the civil rights of Jews defending them against intolerance and race-hatred. You have repaid to me today. Just as emancipation was inscribed on our flags then, this flag will be the symbol of emancipation."[49] Jews and liberals had fought unsuccessfully for freedom, equality, and justice in Germany, but by emigrating to the United States and becoming Americans, they had emancipated themselves. Now it was their duty to fight together for the emancipation of the black slaves in the South.

The Jews of Chicago were praised for their quick response, and they were proud of themselves. Later in 1862 the directors of the UHRA declared in their annual report:

---

48. Ibid. On the number of Jews in Chicago see *Sinai*, September 1862, 232.

49. *Siani*, September 1862, 231. (Taken from the *ISZ* of 20 August 1862—the copy is probably lost.)

The very existence of that good Government, to which the Israelite especially is indebted for the enjoyment of political equality, and religious liberty, is threatened. . . . The Stars and Stripes, that emblem of justice and free institutions, have been trampled under foot by traitors at home, while the act, if not openly commended, is secretly cheered by Despots and Crowned heads of tyrannical Europe. . . . And nobly, yes thrice noble, and patriotically did the Israelites of Chicago respond in the emergency. With a burning love for country and freedom did they arise . . . and praise resounded throughout the land for their support of the war.[50]

The Jewish company and its soldiers did well in the war, although it suffered heavy casualties. Many soldiers were decorated and returned as officers. Edward Salomon became a brigadier general.[51] For Jews in Europe such careers were not even imaginable.

American patriotism proved to be a unifying force for the loose community of Jewish immigrants, transcending all religious, regional, and other differences. But the other important driving force for the decisive Jewish action was the rise of anti-Jewish prejudice during the Civil War.[52] Two events in particular indicate that Jews were not fully accepted in America: General Grant's infamous order No. 11 expelling all Jews from the "military department" under his command in Tennessee, and the army chaplain question. On both occasions, Rabbi Bernhard Felsenthal of Chicago wrote protest letters to politicians in Washington. Felsenthal was one of many Jews who called for Grant's order to be rescinded.[53] In the army chaplain question, Felsenthal's protest to Senator Wilson of Massachusetts may have been decisive. Wilson accordingly sponsored a bill to change the law on army chaplains from "ministers of some Christian denomination" to "ministers of some religious denomination."[54] These

50. *Third Annual Report of the UHRA*. The determined action indeed made big news "throughout the land" and beyond, see *Cincinnati Volksfreund*, 16 August 1862; *Allgemeine Zeitung des Judenthums* [Leipzig], 7 October 1862.

51. Meites, *Jews of Chicago*, 88–89.

52. Frederic C. Jaher, *A Scapegoat in the New Wilderness: The Origins and Rise of Anti-Semitism in America* (Cambridge: Harvard University Press, 1994), 196–200.

53. The order was lifted by President Lincoln. Felsenthal file (Letter to B. Felsenthal, "'Minister of Sinai Congregation' by the War Department," Washington, DC, 10 January 1863), Chicago Jewish Archives. See also: Joakim Isaacs, "Ulysses S. Grant and the Jews," *American Jewish Archives* 17 (1965): 3–15.

54. *Sinai*, August 1862, 200–201. Based on article in the *ISZ*.

two events were setbacks for American Jewry, but the outcome also offered some encouragement.

After the war, Rabbi Liebmann Adler published a number of patriotic speeches he had given in 1865 as sermons to his congregation. Adler's sermons were delivered in German, but they show that Jewish immigrants from the German states were patriotic Americans.[55] The religious sphere has been interpreted as a bastion of ethnicity by immigration historians.[56] The Jews of Chicago spoke German in their services and were inspired by the Jewish Reform movement in Germany and by Germany on a cultural level (see below), but in the synagogue they had always emphasized that they were free Americans and that they were proud of it. On the occasion of Lincoln's second inauguration, Adler declared: "Thank you, O God, for saving this free land. . . . Do you, you people, want to love a country and do what you can to keep it strong, when you are so powerful?"[57] Adler was not addressing the Jewish people in this paragraph, he was addressing the American people. The important theme of the suppression of Jews in Germany and Eastern Europe and the consequent need to defend the freedom of America was not an issue in these sermons. Adler spoke as an American to Americans, and he praised the democratic republic of the United States while condemning the monarchies of Europe.

Spiritual Identification with Germany

The spiritual and cultural involvement of Jewish immigrants in Chicago with Germany is best described by looking at the origins of Sinai congregation, Chicago's first Reform synagogue. Debates about the introduction of the German language sparked the Reform movement in Chicago.

Only a few years after the first Jewish congregation, Kehilat Anshe Maarab (Men of the West, KAM), had been established in 1847, the language issue began to cause tension. Several new members demanded that German be introduced as the language of the service, because nobody could understand

55. Liebmann Adler, *Fünf Reden: Gehalten in der Israelitischen Gemeinde Kehilas Anshe Maarab hierselbst an wichtigen nationalen Gedenktagen der Ver. Staaten* (Chicago: Illinois Staats-Zeitung, 1866), 20.

56. For an introduction see Edward Kantowicz, "The Ethnic Church," in *Ethnic Chicago: A Multicultural Portrait*, edited by Melvin G. Holli and Peter d'A. Jones (Grand Rapids, MI: William B. Eerdmans Publishing Co., 1995), 574–603.

57. Adler, *Fünf Reden*, 6.

Hebrew prayers.[58] In the mid-1850s German became the language of the service.[59] The conflicts over the introduction of German illustrated differing views on Judaism within the congregation. The founders of the congregation were rural Jews from Franconia and the Palatinate who clung to traditional forms of religious observance,[60] while those who pushed for the use of German were younger, better-educated men, some of whom had been educated at German universities. Leopold Mayer, one of these "youths," remembered almost fifty years later in 1899 that the services at KAM did not appeal to them, because "religion is for the living and not for the dead."[61] Two problems demanded immediate action: not only did the traditional service seem completely out of place and embarrassing to younger immigrants who had social contacts with Gentiles, but also many Jews simply stayed away from services and severed their ties with the community.[62]

After long debates a number of reforms were introduced: a choir was organized and—much to the distress of older members—an organ was acquired.[63] After a serious struggle the reform faction even managed to install an outspoken reformer as president.[64] The ensuing reforms boosted the reputation of the Jews in Chicago. In 1859 a visitor reported to Chicago's leading paper: "I understand that the new board of Administration has caused all th[e] change in the mode of service; . . . some time ago, a stranger, who visited their synago[g]ues, would hardly believe that he was among a civilized people . . . [but now the service is] so nice . . . that all prejudice against these, our fellow citizens, must give way."[65]

It seems, however, that the struggles within KAM were not only motivated by religious disagreements. The leader of the traditionalists, Abraham Kohn,

---

58. Bernhard Felsenthal and Herman Eliassof, *History of Kehillath Anshe Maarab: Issued under the Auspices of the Congregation on the Occasion of its Semi-Centennial Celebration, Nov. 4, 1897* (Chicago: Privately published, 1897), 23.

59. *The Occident* [Philadelphia], January 1855, 526.

60. Bernhard Felsenthal, "A Contribution to the History of the Israelites in Chicago," manuscript 1863, Col. Felsenthal, Bernhard. Box 130, CHS.

61. Quoted from Eliassof, Hirsch, "The Jews of Illinois," 287.

62. On the "indifference" of Jews in Chicago toward religious observance see *The Occident*, January 1857, 586.

63. *Die Deborah*, 8 August 1855; *Israelite* [Cincinnati], 8 July 1859.

64. Felsenthal, Eliassof, *History of Kehillath Anshe Maarab*, 31–34.

65. *Israelite*, 8 July 1859 (copied from *Chicago Daily Democrat*).

a Jew from Franconia, stated in a public letter that there was "no question of reform." The so-called "reformers" were all Jews from the Rhenish Palatinate who wanted to remove the president of the congregation, because he was "a native of Poland." Their motto was, according to Kohn: ". . . it must be a man from a [*sic* the] Pfalz."[66] Most of the young reformers—who came from the Palatinate—were not satisfied with the concessions they had won from the older members, but they did not have a clear agenda. At this point the struggle over reforms at KAM became part of a conflict between two men who offered two different directions for the young American Reform movement: Isaac Meyer Wise's move toward Americanization and David Einhorn's call for Germanization.[67]

In the early 1850s Wise, a young Cincinnati rabbi from Bohemia, set for himself the goal of organizing Judaism in America under one roof. He frequently visited many distant and small Jewish communities, and in 1854 he began to publish a weekly, the *American Israelite*, and one year later he started a German-language weekly for women, *Die Deborah*.[68] Wise saw himself as an Americanizer, and he called for the promotion of English as a spoken language. As the founding of *Die Deborah* indicates, however, he had to use German in order to convince Jewish readers to switch to English.[69] Wise was a reformer, but his interest in reform was more a matter of decorum. He was willing to make concessions as long as other Jewish leaders accepted his leadership role and supported his project of uniting American Jewry. Therefore, it is not surprising that Wise was well informed about the situation in Chicago. In July 1856 he visited the city for the first time.[70] He expressed support for reforms and criticized the "ultra-conservative" faction. Chicago Jewry seemed to be safely in his pocket. He claimed that many of the one thousand Jews in the city read his *American Israelite* and *Die Deborah*, and he emphasized that he had "no opponent here."[71]

In the same year Wise visited Chicago, David Einhorn came to America to begin his tenure at Har Sinai congregation in Baltimore. Einhorn was the first leading German-Jewish reformer to come to America. He

---

66. *Israelite*, 16 October 1857.

67. See especially Meyer, *Response to Modernity*, 235–250.

68. Meyer, *Response to Modernity*, 243.

69. *Die Deborah*, 24 August 1855. Nadel, "Jewish Race and German Soul," 9–10.

70. *Israelite*, 8 August 1856; 15 August 1856.

71. Ibid.

immediately challenged Wise's attempts to become the leader of American Jewry by publishing the *Sinai*, a German-language monthly, and attacking Wise regularly.[72] Einhorn was angered by Wise's approach to reform and his willingness to compromise on religious matters.[73] Wise called for an accommodation of the Jewish service to the "present age," but Einhorn demanded a thorough modernization of Jewish theology.[74]

In 1856 Einhorn received a letter from another recent immigrant, Bernhard Felsenthal in Madison, Indiana, who wished to contribute articles to the *Sinai*. Felsenthal was not an ordained rabbi, but he had university training and extensive knowledge of Jewish theology. Einhorn was enthusiastic to have found a correspondent for his paper who possessed a thorough *Bildung*.[75] Some time before March 1857 Einhorn had corresponded with several young reformers in Chicago who were acquaintances of Felsenthal's from the Palatinate.[76] Felsenthal and several of the reformers in Chicago were in fact part of a larger chain migration that moved Jews from villages along the border between the Palatinate and Hesse to Indiana and eventually to Chicago.[77] In 1857 Felsenthal himself moved to Chicago, where he initially worked as a clerk at the bank owned by Henry Greenebaum and Gerhard Foreman, two of the leading reformers at KAM.[78] In 1857 and 1858 the religious conflicts at the KAM congregation were discussed by Einhorn and Felsenthal in several letters, and in late 1858 and again in early 1859 Einhorn asked Felsenthal to become the leader of the reform faction at KAM.[79] Felsenthal then helped to organize the so-called "Jüdischer Reformverein" (Jewish Reform Association), where the reformers developed their program, and he published the manifesto of the early Reform movement in Chicago, "Kol Kore Bamidbar: Über jüdische Reform" (A Voice Calling from the Wilderness: On Jewish Reform) that grew

---

72. *Sinai*, February 1856, 4–10.

73. Meyer, *Response to Modernity*, 245.

74. *Israelite*, 30 September 1859. Wise had this to say about the "orthodox" faction in Chicago: "Our orthodox brethren must gradually be educated for the present age."

75. *Sinai*, February 1856, 412.

76. Letter Einhorn to Felsenthal, 10 March 1857 in Felsenthal Papers, AJHS.

77. This is covered in detail in Brinkmann, *Von der Gemeinde zur "Community."*

78. Emma Felsenthal, *Bernhard Felsenthal: Teacher in Israel* (Oxford, New York: Oxford University Press, 1924), 24–25. The Palatinate Jews also had a number of business connections with each other.

79. Letter Einhorn to Felsenthal, 30 November 1858; 20 January 1859, in Felsenthal Papers, AJHS.

out of a series of articles for Einhorn's *Sinai*.[80]

In the religious sphere Felsenthal was a Germanizer. Germany was important to him and to Einhorn as a cultural center, because the emergence of modern Judaism and the Reform movement in the first half of the nineteenth century had been closely linked with the spiritual revolution, the emergence of critical and rational *Wissenschaft* in Germany. Felsenthal emphasized in 1865: "We must not distance ourselves from German Judaism and its influences. As in medieval times the sun of Jewish *Wissenschaft* was shining on the Spanish sky, this sun is now shining on the German sky sending out its light to all Jews and Jewish communities, who live among the modern cultured peoples. Germany has replaced Sefard."[81] In 1859 he stressed: "The German people are still the first among the cultured peoples of the world, and we bow our heads in reverence before its spirit, its literature, its language. . . . We American-German Jews want to keep German in our Synagogues."[82]

For Felsenthal Reform Judaism in Germany had to serve as the model for Reform Judaism in America. The "Germanization" of Jewish theology was synonymous with the thorough modernization of Judaism. Felsenthal argued that reforms of the service leading to greater decorum such as the introduction of an organ were useless unless Judaism was redefined as a modern religion consistent with intellectual progress in the sciences and humanities. For him Judaism was a progressive religion centered around monotheism. Traditional religious practices that did not convey the essential religious truths were to be abandoned, and new elements had to be added, especially a sermon in the German language that would be understood by all congregants. It did not make sense, Felsenthal argued—and Einhorn praised him for it—to introduce copied versions of the Christian service by external reforms or by turning the Jewish service into a "Schaugepränge" (show) with choirs and music. Radical reform was a matter of spiritual *Bildung* rather than superficial accommodation to the "present age" along the lines proposed by Wise. Felsenthal did not oppose music as such in the service, but the congregants had to be affected in their inner spirit and "religious feelings" rationally rather than emotionally.[83]

80. *Sinai*, March and April 1859.

81. Bernhard Felsenthal, *Jüdisches Schulwesen in Amerika: Ein Vortrag gehalten am 13. Dezember 1865 in der 'Ramah-Loge' zu Chicago von Bernhard Felsenthal Prediger der Zionsgemeinde daselbst* (Chicago: Albert Heunisch, 1866), 37. Translation by author.

82. Felsenthal, "Kol Kore Bamidbar," 25.

83. Felsenthal, "Kol Kore Bamidbar," 19–20; David Einhorn, "Felsenthal's Kol Kore Bamidbar," in *Sinai*, May 1859, 115.

Another example for *Bildung* was the Sabbath. It was wrong to rush from the store to the service on Saturday for one hour, or not to attend the service at all, Felsenthal declared. But it was also wrong for Jews to obey the Talmudic rules without intellectually recognizing the important religious truths guiding them. Yes, one could smoke a cigar on Sabbath, or even better, attend a drama by Schiller or walk to the park in order to listen to a symphony by Beethoven. To educate oneself in this way was better than unthinking obedience to hollow laws without recognition of their inner spirit.[84]

It was very characteristic for "radical reformers" like Felsenthal to question the notion of authority as such, the authority of "holy" texts like the Talmud that had regulated religious observance and the daily lives of Jews for centuries, the authority of religious elites who had controlled religious affairs in the old ghetto, and the authority of the state that had interfered in the religious affairs of Jewish communities. In America there was no state interference in religious affairs, and Felsenthal often praised religious freedom in the United States.

Numerous quotes on the importance of spiritual Germany could be added, and Einhorn was even more outspoken on this matter. But the hymns Einhorn and Felsenthal sung to "Germany" can only be understood in their very American context. While Einhorn himself may have never felt at home in America, he was well aware that the reforms he was calling for had a chance to be realized only on American soil.[85] Felsenthal was very frank about this in "Kol Kore Bamidbar." In the United States (as opposed to Europe), Felsenthal argued convincingly that every individual Jew was "free" to evaluate Judaism and opt for reforms. The American Constitution guaranteed the separation of church and state; there were no old, established religious elites; and religious factions within a congregation could split from each other and form new congregations. He addressed the reformers in Chicago: "Do you want to expel them [the traditionalists]? Do you—and we speak to American Israelites—do you want to dictate to others how they have to pray to their God? Let us not fight, we are brothers, let us separate!"[86] The words, "We are brothers, let us separate!," read like a paradox, but the call for separation illustrates that the roots of the Germanization movement was American. Only in America could Jews split peacefully over religious matters, form their own congregations,

---

84. Felsenthal, "Kol Kore Bamidbar," 22–23.

85. Meyer, *Response to Modernity*, 248.

86. Felsenthal, "Kol Kore Bamidbar," 14.

yet remain united as Jews on a higher level, in secular and philanthropic associations like the B'nai B'rith and the UHRA. For Felsenthal America was a cultural desert, a land of spiritual superficiality. He praised Germany on a spiritual and cultural level, but politically, he emphasized, Germany was "elend" (miserable).[87]

In January 1860 Wise came to Chicago again, after visiting the city at least once in 1859.[88] Earlier Einhorn had warned Felsenthal that Wise would try to interfere in Chicago in order to take over the Reform faction.[89] Wise met with a reception that was not hostile, but he felt that the reformers around Felsenthal were busily preparing to establish their own "German" congregation. Wise again promoted modest external Americanization of the service: "Judaism changes not, but its forms, its outside has changed very often and must change again to suit our age and land, our taste, views, demands and wants." Wise could not admit that his position in Chicago was weakening and claimed not to have met any of these "radicals": "There is nothing in existence of it [radical Reform] except a pamphlet which starts with rationalism and ends in kitchen and stomach, with the extreme nonsense between. . . . This party will never succeed in Chicago." He described Felsenthal scornfully as "a pedantic and fantastic man . . .; [a] ship-wrecked egoist." Much to his dismay Wise had an encounter with Felsenthal at a meeting of the local B'nai B'rith lodge. Felsenthal took the opportunity to challenge Wise to a debate, but Wise left in disgust: "This gave my pedantic spectacled and ship-wrecked opponent an opportunity to criticise, scold, lament, decry, laugh, cry, and practising [*sic*] German grammar, of course when I was gone."[90] These descriptions were harmless compared to what Wise printed a few weeks later in his paper. Felsenthal was characterized in this way: "[a] long hook-nose upon which rest a pair of large silver spectacles, covering a couple of glass-like eyes . . . [like an] elephant . . . the famous . . . Chicago pamphleteer of radicalism."[91] Wise's scorn and sarcasm were only an indication of Felsenthal's success, otherwise Wise would have ignored the reformers, as he had done in September 1859 when "radical Reform" in Chicago was mentioned only once as a threat for

87. Felsenthal, "Kol Kore Bamidbar," 25.

88. *Israelite*, 13 January 1860; 30 September 1859.

89. Letter Einhorn to Felsenthal, 2 June 1859 in Felsenthal Papers, AJHS.

90. *Israelite*, 13 January 1860.

91. *Israelite*, 3 February 1860.

Jewish congregations there.[92] In 1860 a growing number of reformers joined the *Reformverein*. Einhorn was now openly and enthusiastically referring to Felsenthal as "unser Felsenthal."[93] In 1861 the new congregation, named Sinai after Einhorn's journal, was established when the reformers split from the KAM congregation.[94]

Some of the reform measures introduced at Sinai congregation show that Chicago reformers were inspired by the German model, but that they were American Jews when it came to reforms. From the beginning mixed seating of men and women was introduced at Sinai congregation.[95] Leading German reformers like Abraham Geiger were alienated by such reforms.[96] A Jewish traveler from Germany was also offended by the *Reformwuth* (reform madness) in Chicago in 1861.[97] German remained important as the spoken language in the service until the late 1870s, retaining its highly symbolic meaning until the turn of the century. Several Chicago congregations advertised for positions in the 1880s that required the ability to deliver sermons in German. In the mid 1880s American-born Joseph Stolz, one of the first graduates of the Reform-oriented rabbinical seminary Hebrew Union College in Cincinnati, exchanged a number of German letters with the Zion congregation in Chicago, whose board was looking for a suitable successor for Felsenthal, who had recently retired. Zion's board eventually invited Stolz to give a German sermon, and this sermon pleased the congregation so much that Stolz was hired.[98] The language requirement had little to do with day-to-day activities at the congregation, but it remained a symbol for the *Bildung* of the spiritual leader of the congregation and demonstrated religious progress.

---

92. *Israelite*, 30 September 1859.

93. *Sinai*, November 1859.

94. Bernhard Felsenthal, *The Beginnings of the Chicago Sinai Congregation: A Contribution to the Inner History of American Judaism* (Chicago: Privately published, 1898).

95. Felsenthal, *Beginnings of the Chicago Sinai Congregation*, 26.

96. Meyer, "German-Jewish Identity," 260–261.

97. Israel Joseph Benjamin, *Drei Jahre in Amerika 1859–1862* (Hannover, Germany: Privately published, 1862), 112.

98. See Joseph Stolz papers, in MS Coll. 242, American Jewish Archives.

Conclusion

The case of Jewish immigrants in Chicago illustrates that for Jewish immigrants in mid-nineteenth-century America the concept of Germanness must be analyzed on several different levels. Most Jews were German speakers until the mid-1870s. Jewish immigrants also had many contacts with other German immigrants during this period, and several leading Germans in Chicago, notably Henry Greenebaum, Edward Salomon, Julius Rosenthal, and Rabbi Emil Hirsch, were Jewish. But while most German associations included Jewish members and even officers, the organized Jewish community was distinct from the German community. During the Civil War Chicago's Jews put much emphasis on organizing a Jewish company. Jewish leaders realized that the war gave them the opportunity to show to other Americans that Jews were solid American citizens, and to prove to themselves that a new era of Jewish history had begun in the United States. During the war, the Jewish company fought in a German regiment, but Jewishness and American patriotism were much more important than Germanness for Jewish immigrants. As American Jews they felt obliged to defend the American constitution under which Jews enjoyed full civil equality, a status still denied to Jews in most European countries, notably in their former German home states.

The struggle of the reformers at KAM congregation shows how important the German Reform movement was for the emerging American movement. In fact, reforms represented a "Germanization" of the Jewish service. A closer look at Germanization reveals that it, however, cannot be separated from Americanization. Radical reforms such as mixed seating for men and women in the synagogue indicate that the German reformers consciously acted as American Jews. The Germanizer Felsenthal himself stressed that as "American Israelites" the reformers could and should split from their more traditional brethren, a move that was hardly imaginable, let alone legal, within the German *Einheitsgemeinde* at the time.

The term "German Jews" should, therefore, be used cautiously. The case studies indicate that "Germanness," "Jewishness," and "Americanness" were closely related. A historical analysis focusing on Jewish immigrants in mid-nineteenth-century America cannot ignore any one of these three categories.

4

Immigrant Religion and the Public Sphere: The German Catholic Milieu in America

Kathleen Neils Conzen

Roughly a quarter of the American population today acknowledges at least some German ancestry, and almost the same proportion of the American population is Roman Catholic in religious affiliation. A third or more of America's German immigrants were of Catholic origin, and perhaps a sixth of American Catholics today have German antecedents. What role did Catholicism play in shaping this significant segment of the German immigration, and what role did Germans play in shaping American Catholicism? These are central questions for a nation where religious belief has been and remains a vital force in public as well as private life. The formative influence of a diasporic Catholicism, I argue in this essay, is one of the least understood but most significant consequences of the transatlantic German migration, and I lay out five issues that pose particular challenges for its historical interpretation.[1] My case begins, appropriately perhaps, with a parable.

Klautches Mechel and the Haymarket Martyrs

American history knows Michael J. Schaack as one of its minor villains. He was the Chicago police captain who assiduously marshaled the evidence upon which the Haymarket anarchists were convicted in 1886, and who subsequently wrote a self-serving book cataloging the anarchist conspiracy

---

1. To avoid constant repetition of modifying language, I shall generally use "Catholic" to refer to persons raised within a Catholic cultural tradition even if not always formally practicing the faith or affiliated with Catholic congregations; and "German" to refer to German-speakers and their descendants in America, regardless of specific European national origin. German-speaking Catholics within different European states, including not only those that coalesced into the German Reich in 1871 but also Luxemburg, Switzerland, Austria, France, and Russia, shared much that was common in their Catholic tradition, and in America, despite initial differences of settlement patterns, tended to coalesce into a common Catholic culture. For similar reasons of stylistic economy, I occasionally use "Germany" figuratively to encompass all of German-speaking Europe when specific questions of state difference are not at issue.

and his own heroic role in its suppression.[2] He was at best overzealous, the historical record suggests, and quite likely corrupt. Haymarket remains today for American labor historians a powerful symbol of the ferocious repression faced by immigrant labor in its struggle for decent wages, working conditions, and the right to organize. In the historiography of German America, the six German-born Haymarket defendants endure as totemic emblems of a proud ethnic heritage of progressive activism. And Schaack, their tormentor, passes from the pages of history with his 1889 dismissal from the police force for venality, his antecedents unqueried, his subsequent fate unknown.[3]

Yet Michael J. Schaack was himself a prominent member of Chicago's German-American community. Born in 1843 in Septfontaines, Luxemburg, the son of a nail-maker, he emigrated to America with his family at age thirteen. After a brief time in Chicago, the family moved to the large Luxemburg farming settlement north of Port Washington, Wisconsin. But within two years, "Klautches Mechel," as he was known among nickname-prone Luxemburgers, was on his own, working in a brewery in Cairo, Illinois. Like many German Catholics he probably had little interest in the national passions that soon placed Cairo, at the strategic confluence of the Ohio and Mississippi rivers, in the cockpit of military action. In any event, he headed north in 1861 or 1862 to sit out the Civil War—and the draft riot that convulsed his Wisconsin hometown—by working as a sailor on the Great Lakes, before returning in 1866 to Chicago and a position with the Ludwig Detective Agency. His bravery in capturing a gang of thieves despite a hail of bullets and a knife wound gained him a spot on Chicago's police force in 1869. Fame, promotion, and the honorary title of "mayor" of the city's North Side German community accompanied his success in cleaning out local gangs, and in 1885 he was reassigned to the critical East Chicago Avenue station near the city's central docks, markets, and factories. Here his vigorous pursuit of the purported Haymarket bombers earned him the praise not only of the native-

2.   Michael J. Schaack, *Anarchy and Anarchists: A History of the Red Terror and the Social Revolution in America and Europe* (Chicago: F. J. Schulte & Co., 1889).

3.   For Schaack in Haymarket historiography, see Henry David, *The History of the Haymarket Affair: A Study in the American Social-Revolutionary and Labor Movements* (New York: Farrar & Rinehart, 1936), 222; Paul Avrich, *The Haymarket Tragedy* (Princeton: Princeton University Press, 1984), 209, 415–416; Bruce C. Nelson, *Beyond the Martyrs: A Social History of Chicago's Anarchists, 1870-1900* (New Brunswick: Rutgers University Press, 1988), 81, 196–197. For Haymarket's totemic role, see Bruce Levine, *The Spirit of 1848: German Immigrants, Labor Conflict, and the Coming of the Civil War* (Urbana: University of Illinois Press, 1992), 269–271; Hartmut Keil, ed., *German Workers' Culture in the United States 1850 to 1920* (Washington, DC: Smithsonian Institution Press, 1988).

born middle class, but also of major segments of the German community, which rallied to his defense when he was dismissed in 1889 for accepting bribes and trafficking in stolen goods. His dismissal, they argued, owed more to politics and socialist persecution than it did to any venality on Schaack's part, and with such backing, far from retiring in ignomy to a Wisconsin farm as subsequent historians would assert, he soon regained not only his pension, but reappointment and in 1891 promotion to the new position of Inspector of the North Side. He still held this rank at his death from diabetes at his Chicago home in May 1898. He left behind a wife whom he had married in 1871, three children, and over fifty thousand dollars worth of real estate investments.[4]

Michael Schaack cannot be dismissed simply as a lackey of Chicago's business community or even as the exemplar of an Americanizing ethnic middle class that he undoubtedly was. "He belongs to those Germans of modest middling circumstances who have earned something for themselves in honorable fashion," was how the *Illinois Staatszeitung* put it. And in his dedicated pursuit of those whom he saw as godless revolutionaries bent on violent destruction of the social order, he clearly spoke for its readers within the German business community who dubbed him their "Bürgermeister."[5] "No

4. Biographical background from Nicholas Gonner, *Die Luxemburger in der neuen Welt* (Dubuque: Luxemburger Gazette, 1889), 448–450; *Luxemburger Gazette* [hereinafter *LG*], 26 September 1886; 24 May, 31 May 1898; Chicago *Tribune*, 19 May 1898; Chicago *Times-Herald*, 19 May 1898. There is some disagreement between the accounts from the late 1880s, which clearly rely on information supplied by Schaack himself, and the 1898 *LG* accounts, which quote from obituaries in the *Illinois Staatszeitung*. The memorial notices have him two years younger at the time of his arrival in America and obscure his activities during the Civil War years. For efforts to dislodge him from the police force, see *LG*, 12 February, 2 April, 23 April, 23 July, 12 December 1889; 23 February, 11 May, 2 November 1897. For Schaack's estate, see *LG*, 7 June 1898. He indeed spent the summer of 1890 in his Wisconsin hometown of Port Washington but was reinstated and promoted to inspector in May 1891 (*LG*, 8 July 1890, 2 June 1891). For his patronymic nickname, see N. E. Becker, *Lexicon der eigenthümlichen Benennungen vieler Bewohner des Nördlichen Theils von Ozaukee Co., Wis. und Umgebung* (Chicago: Keystone Printing Co., 1908), 60. While the overwhelmingly Catholic Luxemburgers began developing their own American associations and press in the 1870s, they remained nested within the broader German-speaking community; Roger Krieps, *Luxemburger in Amerika* (Luxemburg: Bourg-Bourger, 1963), remains the only comprehensive interpretation of the Luxemburg ethnic experience.

5. Quoted in *LG*, 23 February 1897. For an interpretation of the role of the middle class within the ethnic community, see John Bodnar, *The Transplanted: A History of Immigrants in Urban America* (Bloomington: Indiana University Press, 1985). For Schaack's "Bürgermeister" title, see *LG*, 23 July 1889, 31 May 1898.

matter how much he has accustomed himself to American circumstance," the *Staatszeitung* insisted, "he has always remained a good German."[6]

But even more unmistakably his views reflected those of the German-speaking Catholic community within which he was raised. At the time of the Haymarket bombing, most Catholic German-American newspapers joined the *Luxemburger Gazette* in deploring the lot of workers faced with a "vampire-like" monopoly capitalism, "loosed from Christianity and all morality," that made a mockery of the notion of freedom. But they also condemned "communists, socialists, and anarchists" who led workers astray to seek "their Heaven on earth" while inciting them to violence and destroying the reputation of all immigrants in the process. "Since the fall of Adam, perfect contentment, unalloyed happiness, is possible neither for the individual nor for society," the *Gazette* reminded its Catholic readers. "Better times can come only when rich and poor—particularly the former—return to true, practical Christianity and the rule of life that Christ gave us: seek first for the kingdom of God and his righteousness, and everything else shall be given to you."[7]

Though apparently no longer himself a practicing Catholic, Michael Schaack allowed his devout wife to raise their children in the faith, and educated them at Catholic schools and the University of Notre Dame. He may indeed have belonged to various secret lodges forbidden to Catholics, but he was also a pillar of the Luxemburger Verein, the mutual benefit society that acted as the social focus for Chicago's deeply Catholic Luxemburgers, Eifelers, and Moselaners.[8] "As a genuine Luxemburger, our countryman has never forgotten his native dialect, and is ready with help and advice to any who turn to him," the *Luxemburger Gazette* noted, and over the years it followed his exploits with partisan pride.[9] It was probably no accident that less than two months after the Haymarket bombing, during the Luxemburger Verein's annual Kirmes

6. Quoted in *LG*, 23 February 1897.

7. *LG*, 11 May, 27 April, 17 August 1886. The *Gazette* was published by Nicholas Gonner in Dubuque, Iowa, but followed closely the news of Chicago's Luxemburger community—the nation's largest—and had a large readership there.

8. *LG*, 24 May, 31 May 1898. Schaack was variously reported as a thirty-second or thirty-third degree Mason, and incurred the enmity of many Chicago Catholics when he vigorously pursued a prominent Irish alderman on a murder charge. Consequently, as the *Tribune* noted (19 May 1898), "few people [i.e., non-Germans] in Chicago knew he was a Catholic and that he kept his faith in the church up to the last. It had been common to refer to him as a shining example of the A.P.A."

9. *LG*, 26 October 1886. For examples of reporting on his exploits, see *LG*, 12 February 1889, 4 February 1896, 23 February 1897.

celebration on Whit Monday, a long-standing informal election-campaign organization was reconstituted as a permanent Luxemburger Independent Club to work for the group's political ends, nor that Schaack was able to mold it into an effective power base for himself within the city's Democratic machine. Fellow Luxemburgers cheered his efforts to arrest and convict the Haymarket anarchists, and when reformers sympathetic to the convicted men agitated for his forcible retirement three years later, the Independent Club took full credit not only for his reinstatement, but for the outcome of a mayoral election that, they insisted, had turned on it.[10]

The Problem of German Catholicism in America

History, I suspect, owes Klautches Mechel little in the way of reputational rehabilitation; the old principle of smoke and fire undoubtedly applies. But he and his German Catholic confreres well merit more historiographical attention than they have yet received. As their attitude toward the Haymarket affair suggests, Catholics formed a distinctive subgroup within America's German-speaking community. German Catholic immigrants and their descendants supported an elaborate institutional structure that paralleled both the secular German-American ethnic array and non-German Catholic institutions. They developed a political culture distinctly at odds with that of other German Americans and a religious culture distinctive from that of other Catholics, and generally nurtured a set of conservative, communal values that became a significant influence within American public life. Both Joseph McCarthy and Eugene McCarthy, despite their Irish names, grew up within Midwestern German Catholic communities, for example, and their politics reflected contrasting sides of that cultural heritage.[11] German Catholics formed a recognizable voting bloc as early as the 1850s, and remained one as late as 1970, when political analyst Kevin Phillips highlighted their role in the

10. Gonner, *Luxemburger*, 212; *LG*, 26 June, 17 August 1886, 12 February, 2 April, 23 April 1889, 2 November 1897.

11. Michael O'Brien, *McCarthy and McCarthyism in Wisconsin* (Columbia, MO: University of Missouri Press, 1980); Eugene McCarthy, "Religion in Politics, Midwestern Variety," in *Once a Catholic: Prominent Catholics and Ex-Catholics Discuss the Influence of the Church on Their Lives and Work*, edited by Peter Occhiogrosso (Boston: Houghton Mifflin Company, 1987), 274–288.

emergence of a national Republican majority.[12] At the same time, not only
linguistic heritage but also demography, residential and educational patterns,
worldview, and liturgical preferences long distinguished many Catholics of
German descent from co-religionists of other ethnicities. They even, it has
been suggested, formed a partial exception to the stereotype that "Catholics
can't sing."[13]

The worldview that Schaack embodied was clearly as enduring and
influential a legacy of German immigration as was the labor activism of
his socialist opponents, or the institution-building of the liberal German-
American bourgeoisie. At a time when historians are probing anew the cultural
underpinnings of public discourse and behavior in a pluralist American society,
understanding the origins and influence of this German Catholic worldview
takes on particular relevance.[14] It would seem equally salient to any broader
project of modeling the contours and consequences of international migration
in the modern period.[15] Yet historians have more often reacted with the testy
dismissal reserved for exceptions that confirm no rule than with sustained
inquiry upon encountering Catholic Germans in America's historical record.
Their absence from standard accounts of Haymarket is symptomatic. Students
of the German-American working class tend to conflate it with those who
participated in the organized workers' subculture of the left, just as students
of German-American ethnicity in general have focused more on secular
than on religiously based manifestations of identity and adaptation.[16] For the

12. Kevin P. Phillips, *The Emerging Republican Majority* (Garden City, NY: Anchor Books,
1970); see also Samuel Lubell, *The Future of American Politics* (Garden City, NY: Doubleday
and Co., Inc., 1956).

13. Thomas Day, *Why Catholics Can't Sing: The Culture of Catholicism and the Triumph
of Bad Taste* (New York: Crossroad, 1991). Catholics of German descent long exhibited
significantly higher than average fertility, lower educational levels, and were more rural; see
Andrew M. Greeley, *Ethnicity in the United States: A Preliminary Reconnaissance* (New York:
Wiley, 1974).

14. Cf. Leo P. Ribuffo, "God and Contemporary Politics," *Journal of American History* 79
(1993): 1515–1531; Alan Brinkley, "The Problem of American Conservatism," *American
Historical Review* 99 (1994): 409–429.

15. Cf. Dirk Hoerder, "From Migrants to Ethnics: Acculturation in a Societal Framework," in
European Migrants: Global and Local Perspectives, edited by Dirk Hoerder and Leslie Page
Moch (Boston: Northeastern University Press, 1996), 211–262.

16. For German working-class radicalism see Bruce Levine, "Community Divided: German
Immigrants, Social Class, and Political Conflict in Antebellum Cincinnati," in *Ethnic Diversity
and Civic Identity: Patterns of Conflict and Cohesion in Cincinnati since 1820*, edited by Henry
D. Shapiro and Jonathan D. Sarna (Urbana: University of Illinois Press, 1992), 46–93; Levine,

bourgeois immigrants of the nineteenth century who effectively constructed German-America's public identity and first framed its historical interpretation, religious difference was an annoying distraction from the unity that Germans might otherwise possess, a fatal weakness in German efforts to assert ethnic influence on American life.[17] Subsequent historiography has largely followed their lead. With some notable exceptions, studies of German-American labor, politics, and culture and their role within American development continue to focus almost exclusively on the group's more liberal and radical elements.[18] Religious belief is dismissed as a factor in emigration, and interpreted as little more than a proxy for local cultures of origin in most studies of American community construction.[19] German Catholic bloc voting is quickly explained as an almost instinctive reaction to nativism, and few studies of immigrant

---

Spirit of 1848; German Workers' Culture; Steven J. Ross, *Workers on the Edge: Work, Leisure, and Politics in Industrializing Cincinnati, 1788–1890* (New York: Columbia University Press, 1985); Lawrence M. Lipin, *Producers, Proletarians, and Politicians: Workers and Party Politics in Evansville and New Albany, Indiana, 1850–1887* (Urbana: University of Illinois Press, 1994).

17. For this early historiography, see Kathleen Neils Conzen, "The Writing of German-American History," *Immigration History Newsletter* 12 (November 1980): 1–14.

18. Significant exceptions include Philip Gleason, *The Conservative Reformers: German-American Catholics and the Social Orders* (Notre Dame, IN: University of Notre Dame Press, 1968); Reinhard R. Doerries, *Iren und Deutsche in der Neuen Welt: Akkulturationsprozesse in der amerikanischen Gesellschaft im späten Neunzehnten Jahrhundert* (Stuttgart: F. Steiner, 1986); David A. Gerber, *The Making of an American Pluralism: Buffalo, New York, 1825–60* (Urbana: University of Illinois Press, 1989); Frederick C. Luebke, *Germans in the New World: Essays in the History of Immigration* (Urbana: University of Illinois Press, 1990); Jon Gjerde, *The Minds of the West: Ethnocultural Evolution in the Rural Middle West, 1830–1917* (Chapel Hill: University of North Carolina Press, 1997).

19. "Overinterpretation of religious motives should . . . be avoided"; Bade, "German Transatlantic Emigration in the Nineteenth and Twentieth Centuries," in *European Expansion and Migration: Essays on the Intercontinental Migration from Africa, Asia, and Europe*, edited by P. C. Emmer and M. Mörner (New York: Berg, 1992), 123. Cf. Dirk Hoerder, "Arbeitswanderung und Arbeiterbewusstsein im atlantischen Wirtschaftsraum: Forschungsansätze und -hypothesen," *Archiv für Sozialgeschichte* 28 (1988): 391–425; Wolfgang Helbich, *"Alle Menschen sind dort gleich. . . : " Die deutsche Amerika-Auswanderung im 19. und 20. Jahrhundert* (Düsseldorf: Pädagogischer Verlag Schwann, 1988); Walter D. Kamphoefner, "German Emigration Research, North, South, and East: Findings, Methods, and Open Questions," in *People in Transit: German Migrations in Comparative Perspective, 1820–1930*, edited by Dirk Hoerder and Jörg Nagler (Cambridge: Cambridge University Press, 1995), 19–34; Hans Fenske and Hermann Hiery, "Neue Literatur zur Geschichte der deutschen Auswanderung," *Historisches Jahrbuch* 116 (1996): 155–171.

opinion and action survey the extensive German Catholic press.[20] Nor, until recently, has Catholic historiography, long focused on the dominant and linguistically more accessible role of the Irish, exhibited any greater concern.[21] Despite increasing scholarly interest in the Catholic laity and in Catholicism as a cultural system, Germans still tend to appear in Catholic history narratives only at those points where their demands—for trustee control, for national parishes and sees—posed problems for the Catholic mainstream.[22] Too often, it would seem, we have assumed that all Catholics were Irish, and all Germans were freethinking or Protestant.

We even lack basic knowledge about the size and regional origins of America's German Catholic community. Neither German nor American authorities collected confessional information from the estimated 120,000 pre-1820 German arrivals and the roughly 5.5 million who followed in the subsequent

20. A valuable exception is John S. Kulas, *Der Wanderer of St. Paul: The First Decade, 1867–1877: A Mirror of the German-Catholic Immigrant Experience in Minnesota* (New York: Peter Lang, 1996); see also Walter D. Kamphoefner, "Liberal Catholicism and Its Limits: The Social and Political Outlook of the Louisville *Katholischer Glaubensbote*, 1866–86," *Yearbook of German American Studies* 31 (1996): 13–23.; Till van Rahden, "Beyond Ambivalence: Variations of Catholic Anti-Semitism in Turn-of-the-Century Baltimore," *American Jewish History* 82 (1994): 7–42.

21. Again, significant exceptions include Colman J. Barry, *The Catholic Church and German Americans* (Washington, DC: Catholic University of America Press, 1953), and Jay P. Dolan, *The Immigrant Church* (Baltimore: Johns Hopkins University Press, 1976).

22. Approaches toward a sociocultural history of American Catholics began with studies exploring the lay role within the Church, like Timothy J. Smith, "Lay Initiative in the Religious Life of American Immigrants, 1880–1950," in *Anonymous Americans: Explorations in Nineteenth-Century Social History*, edited by Tamara K. Hareven (Englewood Cliffs, NJ: Prentice-Hall, 1971) and Victor Greene, *For God and Country: The Rise of Polish and Lithuanian Ethnic Consciousness in America, 1860–1910* (Madison: University of Wisconsin Press, 1975), and are now maturing into sophisticated studies of Catholic culture like Paula M. Kane, *Separatism and Subculture: Boston Catholicism, 1900–1920* (Chapel Hill: University of North Carolina Press, 1994) and John T. McGreevy, *Parish Boundaries: The Catholic Encounter with Race in the Twentieth-Century Urban North* (Chicago: University of Chicago Press, 1996). David J. O'Brien, *Public Catholicism* (New York: Macmillan, 1988) is an important synthesis of the Catholic engagement with American public life. Jay P. Dolan, *American Catholic Experience: A History from Colonial Times to the Present* (Garden City, NY: Doubleday, 1985) is pathbreaking in its integration of social and institutional history. Dale B. Light, *Rome and the New Republic: Conflict and Community in Philadelphia Catholicism between the Revolution and the Civil War* (Notre Dame, IN: University of Notre Dame Press, 1996) is a good recent study that treats Germans within the context of conflicts with church authorities. See Patrick Carey, "Recent American Catholic Historiography: New Directions in Religious History," in *New Directions in American Religious History*, edited by Harry S. Stout and D. G. Hart (New York: Oxford University Press, 1997), 444–461.

century of mass immigration.[23] The widely cited estimate that roughly a third of the post-1820 German immigration was Catholic was created, in effect, by weighting the decadal totals of immigrants from the various German states by the proportions of Catholics within their respective populations.[24] But there is no particular reason to assume that the religious affiliations of emigrants mirrored those of any individual German state; Catholic populations were not evenly distributed geographically within states, and religious minorities were often disproportionately represented among emigrants from a given state.[25] Similar weighted estimates based on emigration and confession data for smaller German areal units at least suggest that Catholic proportions within

---

23. Georg Fertig, "Transatlantic Migration from the German-Speaking Parts of Central Europe, 1600–1800: Proportions, Structures, and Explanations," in *Europeans on the Move: Studies in European Migration, 1500–1800*, edited by Nicholas Canny (Oxford: Oxford University Press, 1994), 192–235; Hans-Jürgen Grabbe, "Besonderheiten der europäischen Einwanderung in die USA während der frühen nationalen Periode 1783–1820," *Amerikastudien/American Studies* 33 (1988): 271–290; Kathleen Neils Conzen, "Germans," in *Harvard Encyclopedia of American Ethnic Groups*, edited by Stephan Thernstrom (Cambridge, MA: Harvard University Press, 1980), 405–425. Even the best surveys of German-language parishes in the United States, such as those undertaken by German Catholic clergy at three intervals in the later nineteenth century, are inconsistent and incomplete in their statistical data, and obviously do not include persons of German origin or descent who belonged to non-German parishes; cf. E. A. Reiter, *Schematismus der kath. deutschen Geistlichkeit in den Ver. Staaten* (New York, Cincinnati, and Regensburg: Fr. Pustet, 1869); W. Bonenkamp et al., *Schematismus der deutschen und der deutsch-sprechenden Priester, sowie der deutschen Katholiken-Gemeinden in den Vereinigten Staaten Nord-Amerika's* (Freiburg im Breisgau: Herder'sche Verlagshandlung, 1882); Johannes Enzlberger, *Schematismus der katholischen Geistlichkeit deutscher Zunge in den Vereinigten Staaten Amerikas* (Milwaukee: Hoffmann Brothers Co., 1892).

24. Most such estimates are ultimately derived from Gerald Shaughnessy, *Has the Immigrant Kept the Faith? A Study of Immigration and Catholic Growth in the United States, 1790–1920* (New York: The Macmillan Co., 1925). His actual procedure was somewhat more complex but rested at base on German state-level Catholic proportions; for his methodology see 111–114; for decadal tables see 114, 123, 131, 140, 149, 159, 165, 169, 175, 180.

25. H. A. Krose, *Konfessionsstatistik Deutschlands, mit einem Rückblick auf die numerische Entwicklung der Konfessionen im 19. Jahrhundert* (Freiburg im Breisgau: Herdersche Verlagshandlung, 1904); Peter Claus Hartmann, "Bevölkerungszahlen und Konfessionsverhältnisse des Heiligen Römischen Reiches Deutscher Nation und der Reichskreise am Ende des 18. Jahrhunderts," *Zeitschrift für Historische Forschung* 22 (1995): 345–369; Antonius Liedhegener, "Marktgesellschaft und Milieu: Katholiken und katholische Regionen in der wirtschaftlichen Entwicklung des Deutschen Reichs 1895–1914," *Historisches Jahrbuch* 113 (1993): 283–353; Friedrich Blendinger, "Die Auswanderung nach Nordamerika aus dem Regierungsbezirk Oberbayern in den Jahren 1846–1852," *Zeitschrift für bayerische Landesgeschichte* 27 (1964): 452; Wolfgang von Hippel, *Auswanderung aus Südwestdeutschland: Studien zur württembergischen Auswanderung und Auswanderungspolitik im 18. und 19. Jahrhundert* (Stuttgart: Klett-Cotta, 1984).

the German emigration may have been closer to the two-fifths level during the mid-nineteenth century before dropping to a third or less by the 1870s, as the emigration impulse moved north and eastward from the more heavily Catholic German south and west.[26] Applying similar estimation procedures to the German-born tabulated in the 1870 U.S. Census, one of the peak years of German presence in America and a point when America's German Catholic subculture was reaching maturity, suggests a potential Catholic proportion among first-generation German Americans of thirty-seven percent, about a quarter of them from Baden and Württemberg in the southwest, a fifth from Bavaria, over two-fifths from Prussia (mainly Rhineland and Westphalia), and another ten percent or so from the more northerly states of Hesse, Hanover, and Oldenburg.[27] Clearly, Germans were surpassed only by the Irish and the Italians in the numbers of Catholics whom they contributed to the American population. By 1870 almost a sixth of all American Catholics belonged to

---

26. I calculated these estimates by applying regional Catholic proportions derived from Krose, *Konfessionsstatistik Deutschlands*, to the regional emigration estimates in Peter Marschalck, *Deutsche Überseewanderung im 19. Jahrhundert: Ein Beitrag zur soziologischen Theorie der Bevölkerung* (Stuttgart: Ernst Klett Verlag, 1973), tables 5 and 8, pages 38 and 45, and then calculating the Catholic proportion of that part of the total estimated emigration for which regional origins were specified. More detailed estimates for Prussia's thirty-seven administrative districts before 1871 and twelve provinces after 1871, generally confirm these trends; calculated from tables xl, page 118, and xxi, page 73 in Krose, *Konfessionsstatistik Deutschlands*, and table 8, pages 86–87, in Wilhelm Mönckmeier, *Die deutsche überseeische Auswanderung: Ein Beitrag zur deutschen Wanderungsgeschichte* (Jena: Gustav Fischer, 1912). Prussian statistics accounted for about thirty-six percent of the total estimated German emigration for the pre-1871 period and sixty-two percent of the more carefully tabulated total after 1871. A fuller discussion of these estimates and the problems associated with determining Catholic proportions within German immigration can be found in Kathleen Neils Conzen, "German Catholics in America," in *The Encyclopedia of American Catholic History*, edited by Michael Glazier and Thomas J. Shelley (Collegeville, MN: The Liturgical Press, 1997), 571–583.

27. *Ninth Census of the United States, Vol. I: The Statistics of the Population of the United States* (Washington, DC: 1872). These calculations assume that the estimated thirteen percent who failed to name a specific state of origin were distributed among the German states in the same manner as those who did give their origins; this may well not have been the case. Calculations for Prussia and Bavaria make use of estimates of Catholic proportions weighted according to district-level emigration figures. Ideally, of course, the American-born second and third generations should also be included in such estimates. The estimates also fail to allow for the influence of return migration. Likewise uncounted in these totals are most of the nation's fifty thousand German-speaking Catholic immigrants from Luxemburg; a significant portion of the German speakers from Alsace, Lorraine, and the Austrian Empire; and a minority of the Swiss.

German-speaking parishes; a century later, roughly the same proportion of American Catholics still acknowledged German descent.[28]

How then might a more focused historical inquiry account for the distinctive traces that these Catholics of German origin have left upon the American past? Implicit in current scholarship is an interpretation that would stress, on the one hand, the need of some immigrants—particularly, not yet secularized peasants—to import traditional religious practice as familiar comfort in a new and alien world, and on the other, the role of that new environment in forcing gradual adaptation and change. Thus, the story might go, imported German traditions of folk piety and parish polity, when confronted with the indifference of "American" (read "Irish") Catholics and nativist attack, encouraged the formation of a separate system of German national parishes. Within this system a distinctive brand of ethnic Catholicism developed, one politically defending itself against nativism and strong enough by the 1880s, particularly in the Midwest, to mount a partially successful challenge to liberalizing trends within American Catholicism, but one ultimately made obsolete by assimilation and episcopal centralization.[29]

Combining a generational trajectory and changes within American Catholicism itself, this interpretation captures important elements of the story. But it fails to take account of our growing understanding of the role of migrant selectivity, migration chains, and resultant settlement systems in structuring the immigrant adaptive experience.[30] Nor does it capture Peter D'Agostino's recent forceful demonstration that immigrant Catholicism can be understood only when the Church itself is seen as an "institutional emigrant" shaped in ongoing fashion by homeland developments and international institutional imperatives mediated through everything from religious orders

---

28. Shaughnessy, *Has the Immigrant Kept the Faith?*, tables xvii–xxvi; Alexander J. Schem, *Deutsch-amerikanisches Conversations-Lexicon*, vol. IX (New York: F. Gerhard, 1873), 437, citing Reiter, *Schematismus*, and *Sadlier's Almanac for 1873*; Harold J. Abramson, *Ethnic Diversity in Catholic America* (New York: Wiley, 1973), 13–14, relying on sample survey data.

29. Dolan, *American Catholic Experience*; O'Brien, *Public Catholicism*.

30. See, for example, Kamphoefner, "German Emigration Research"; Dirk Hoerder, "International Labor Markets and Community Building by Migrant Workers in the Atlantic Economies," in *A Century of European Migrations, 1830–1930*, edited by Rudolph J. Vecoli and Suzanne M. Sinke (Urbana: University of Illinois Press, 1991), 78–107. For an exemplary case study linking the migration process and subsequent cultural and religious change, see Jon Gjerde, *From Peasants to Farmers: The Migration from Balestrand, Norway, to the Upper Middle West* (Cambridge: Cambridge University Press, 1985).

and financial transactions to state and Vatican directives.[31] And above all, it overlooks the fertile insights of the vigorous recent historical scholarship on Catholicism in Germany. The homeland Catholicism that emerges from this new scholarship is hardly the static, uncontested "traditional religion" of immigration historiography stereotype. Rather, we see a revitalized community that responded creatively to the nineteenth-century challenges of cultural modernity and state centralization with an aggressively ultramontane piety nurtured within a newly enclosed socioreligious milieu, whose increasing twentieth-century permeability signaled alike the relative success of their defensive strategy and the growing pace of their national reintegration.[32]

The new historiography of German "milieu Catholicism" has itself neglected the vigorous currents of emigration flowing within Catholic Germany during this period. But when reexamined in the context of the transatlantic perspective it affords, I would suggest, German Catholicism in America emerges as a diaspora subculture long responsive to impulses flowing from the homeland. Thus, like its progenitor it was less the consolatory remnant of a fading peasant culture, than it was the aggressive, creative construct of a conservative modernity—a striking example of religion's continuing ability to structure migratory, adaptive, and political processes in a modernizing world.

---

31. Peter R. D'Agostino, "The Scalabrini Fathers, the Italian Emigrant Church, and Ethnic Nationalism in America," *Religion and American Culture* 7 (1997): 121–159.

32. Historians of modern German Catholicism continue to debate the contours of German society's confessionalization; the timing, extent, and social and cultural homogeneity of the Catholic "milieu"; and the factors underlying its formation and dissolution. For entry points into this scholarly growth industry, consult Margaret Lavinia Anderson, "Piety and Politics: Recent Work on German Catholicism," *Journal of Modern History* 63 (1991): 681–716; Michael Klöcker, "Katholizismus in der modernen Gesellschaft," *Archiv für Sozialgeschichte* 32 (1992): 490–509; Michael Klöcker, "Das katholische Milieu: Grundüberlegungen—in besonderer Hinsicht auf das Deutsche Kaiserreich von 1871," *Zeitschrift für Religions- und Geistesgeschichte* 44 (1992): 241–262; Eric Yonke, "The Catholic Subculture in Modern Germany: Recent Work in the Social History of Religion," *Catholic Historical Review* 80 (1994): 534–545; Joel F. Harrington and Helmut Walser Smith, "Confessionalization, Community, and State Building in Germany, 1555–1870," *Journal of Modern History* 69 (1997): 77–101; Jonathan Sperber, "*Kirchengeschichte* or the Social and Cultural History of Religion," *Neue Politische Literatur* 43 (1998): 13–35. For examples, see Thomas Nipperdey, *Religion im Umbruch: Deutschland 1870–1918* (München: Verlag C. H. Beck, 1988); Karl-Egon Lönne, *Politischer Katholizismus im 19. und 20. Jahrhundert* (Frankfurt am Main: Suhrkamp Verlag, 1986); Ernst Heinen, *Katholizismus und Gesellschaft: Das katholische Vereinswesen zwischen Revolution und Reaktion (1848/49–1853/54)* (Idstein: Schulz-Kirchner Verlag, 1993); Urs Altermatt, *Katholizismus und Moderne: Zur Sozial- und Mentalitätsgeschichte der Schweizer Katholiken im 19. und 20. Jahrhundert* (Zürich: Benziger Verlag, 1989); Jonathan Sperber, *Rhineland Radicals: The Democratic Movement and the Revolution of 1848–1849* (Princeton: Princeton University Press, 1991).

Clarifying the influences that shaped this subculture can help us understand its durability and its impact on those who lived within it and on broader American religious and political life. The remainder of this essay sketches the main contours of such an interpretation in preliminary fashion, as a challenge to further research; implicit within its framework is a triply comparative perspective assessing the American German Catholic experience within the context of the experience of Catholics in Germany, of other Germans in America, and of other American Catholics.[33]

The German Catholic Migration and Settlement System

By the end of the nineteenth century, there were more than 2,250 German-language parish-centered Catholic communities cutting a broad swath across the northern United States from the industrial cities of the east through the family farming heart of the Midwest and Great Plains, with outliers as far south as Alabama and Texas and out to the Pacific Northwest.[34] This far-flung settlement system was a fundamental factor in the vitality of America's German Catholic subculture. Its achievement, I propose, was a consequence of Catholicism's structuring role in the process of migration itself; of the Church's somewhat inadvertant role in stimulating the initial formation of significant migration chains, and its more purposeful one in linking those chains into a coherent American settlement system capable of sustaining a relatively autonomous ethnoreligious tradition.

The lack of reliable confessional data, the absence of real persecution of lay Catholics in nineteenth-century Germany, and the paucity of case studies of emigration from Catholic regions, have largely blinded historians to the religious dimension in German Catholic emigration.[35] The essentially

---

33. An unfootnoted narrative drawing upon this framework with more supporting detail can be consulted in Conzen, "German Catholics in America."

34. Enzlberger, *Schematismus.*

35. Cf. Walter Kamphoefner, *The Westfalians: From Germany to Missouri* (Princeton: Princeton University Press, 1987); Hoerder, "Arbeitswanderung"; Bade, "Transatlantic Emigration"; Hoerder and Nagler, eds., *People in Transit.* An exception in its Catholic focus is Anne [Aengenvoort] Höndgen, *Migration–Siedlungsbildung–Akkulturation: Die Auswanderung Nordwestdeutscher nach Ohio, 1830–1914* (Stuttgart: Franz Steiner Verlag, 1999). The Kulturkampf and other state efforts to influence the position of the Catholic church within Germany affected the availability of religious services, but did not otherwise place direct pressure on individual lay Catholics; Rudolf Lill, "Der Kulturkampf in Preussen und im Deutschen Reich (bis 1878)," in *Handbuch der Kirchengeschichte*, edited by Hubert Jedin, VI, 2 (Freiburg im Br.: Herder, 1973), 28–47; Ronald Ross, "Enforcing the Kulturkampf in the

economic character of the immediate motivations that led most Germans, Catholics included, to America has long been clear.[36] But direct persecution is not religion's only way of motivating and structuring emigration. Regardless of the formal stance of church authorities toward emigration, religion can influence susceptibility to emigration opportunities; it can create distinctive channels of communication and aid; it can nourish utopian longings. It can, in short, play a significant role among what Charles Tilly has termed the auspices of emigration, and this is indeed what scattered evidence suggests was the case in Catholic Germany.[37]

Catholicism's main role in the colonial period was negative, since British North America discouraged Catholic immigration while Austria and Russia courted southwestern German Catholics for Eastern European recolonization.[38] Occasional Catholics found their way to the middle colonies alongside Protestant relatives and friends, and ten German Jesuits arrived at different times between 1741 and the Revolution at the request of English colleagues to minister to them.[39] Only with the rise of mass emigration in the decades after 1815 did Catholic proportions significantly increase, in part as a natural consequence of the elaboration of older migration chains and the fortuitous formation of new ones. But now, Catholicism itself also became a structuring factor in at least three ways.

Bismarckian State and the Limits of Coercion in Imperial Germany," *Journal of Modern History* 56 (1984): 456–482.

36. Along with a host of newer studies, see Marschalck, *Deutsche Überseewanderung*; Mack Walker, *Germany and the Emigration, 1816–1885* (Cambridge, MA: Harvard University Press, 1964); Marcus Lee Hansen, *The Atlantic Migration, 1607–1860* (Cambridge, MA: Harvard University Press, 1940); Mönckmeier, *Die deutsche überseeische Auswanderung.*

37. Charles Tilly, *Migration to an American City* (Newark, DE.: University of Delaware, Agricultural Experiment Station and Division of Urban Affairs, 1965).

38. Cf. Hippel, *Auswanderung aus Südwestdeutschland*; Andreas Brinck, *Die deutsche Auswanderungswelle in die britischen Kolonien Nordamerikas um die Mitte des 18. Jahrhunderts* (Stuttgart: F. Steiner, 1993); Fertig, "Transatlantic Migration." For background on historic patterns of migration within Europe, see Canny, ed., *Europeans on the Move*; Leslie Page Moch, *Moving Europeans: Migration in Western Europe since 1650* (Bloomington: Indiana University Press, 1992). The main exception were the German-speaking Catholics recruited as agricultural colonists for French Louisiana between 1718 and 1721, where they farmed along the "German Coast" of the Mississippi above New Orleans and gradually assimilated into the French-speaking population; Helmut Blume, *Die Entwicklung der Kulturlandschaft des Mississippideltas in kolonialer Zeit; unter besonderer Berücksichtigung der deutschen Siedlung* (Kiel: Universität Kiel, Geographisches Institut, 1956).

39. Lambert Schrott, *Pioneer German Catholics in the American Colonies (1734–1784)* (New York: U. S. Catholic Historical Society, 1933), 43–88 passim.

First, the pervasive influence of confessional differences within German society found Catholics disproportionately represented among those with the strongest economic motives to emigrate. Great swathes of rural Catholic Bavaria, Baden, the Rhineland, and Westphalia remained, in the words of Clemens Bauer, "reservations of precapitalist and preindustrial economy." With higher birthrates and greater infant mortality than Protestant neighbors, Catholics were on average also more rural, less wealthy, and less well-educated, overrepresented in agriculture and handicrafts and underrepresented among the modernizing bourgeoisie. Scholars continue to debate the relative role of structural, cultural, and political factors in shaping these social "deficits," which by the late nineteenth-century provoked powerful Catholic demands for "parity" within German society.[40] But their influence on emigration is clear. In theory, Catholicism's anti-individualistic traditionalism might have precluded thoughts of self-improvement through emigration. In practice, it sustained high levels of settlement migration aimed at maintaining on abundant American land traditional ways no longer viable at home. During the decades when the lure of the ever-expanding American frontier was a prime stimulus to German emigration, Germany's Catholic peasants, artisans, and laborers were among those with the strongest economic motivations to respond.

They also had particular access to information about American opportunities, thanks to a second way in which Catholicism structured emigration: the channels of communication that the church, albeit inadvertently, supplied. Europe's post-1815 romantic reawakening of missionizing Catholicism meant that visiting clerics seeking financial aid and priests for American missions met a ready response from European Catholics concerned about Indian conversion

---

40. Harrington, Smith, "Confessionalization, Community, and State Building"; Ronald J. Ross, "Catholic Plight in the *Kaiserreich*: A Reappraisal," in *Another Germany: A Reconsideration of the Imperial Era*, edited by Jack R. Dukes and Joachim Remak (Boulder and London: Westview Press, 1988), 73–93; Peter Zschunke, *Konfession und Alltag in Oppenheim: Beiträge zur Geschichte von Bevölkerung und Gesellschaft einer Gemischtkonfessionellen Kleinstadt in der Frühen Neuzeit* (Wiesbaden, 1984); Hans Maier, "Zur Soziologie des deutschen Katholizismus 1803–1950," in *Politik und Konfession: Festschrift für Konrad Repgen zum 60. Geburtstag*, edited by Dieter Albrecht et al. (Berlin: 1983), 159–171; Liedhegener, "Marktgesellschaft und Milieu"; Werner Rösener, "Das Katholische Bildungsdefizit im Deutschen Kaiserreich—Ein Erbe der Säkularisation von 1803?" *Historisches Jahrbuch* 112 (1992): 104–127; Josef Mooser, "'Christlicher Beruf' und bürgerliche 'Gesellschaft': Zur Auseinandersetzung über Berufsethik und wirtschaftliche 'Inferiorität' im Katholizismus um 1900," in *Deutscher Katholizismus im Umbruch zur Moderne*, edited by Wilfried Loth (Stuttgart: W. Kohlhammer, 1991); Hans Rost, *Die Katholiken im Kultur- und Wirtschaftsleben der Gegenwart* (Köln: J. P. Bachem, 1908); quotation, Clemens Bauer, *Deutscher Katholizismus: Entwicklungslinie und Profile* (Frankfurt am Main: Josef Knecht, 1964), 33–34.

and the preservation of immigrant faith and nationality. Three European societies were established to support American missions: one in 1822 in Lyons, France (with significant German membership), a second in Vienna in 1827, and a third in Munich in 1838. They were important not only for the priests and funds ($8.7 million by 1914) that they sent to Catholic America, but also for the information about American opportunities and religious care that they diffused through Catholic Germany.[41] Thus, two Cincinnati priests, the Hanoverian Friedrich Résé and the Swiss-born John Martin Henni, each published pamphlets extolling the Midwest as the cradle of a German Catholic America during European visits in 1827 and 1836, respectively, and the lengthy 1845 published report of an Austrian cleric's American inspection trip for the Viennese society was an encyclopedic guide to the religious, economic, and political opportunities of every significant German Catholic settlement in the country.[42] Missionary letters printed in the annual reports of the societies were treasure troves of American information, news of American settlements dotted German-speaking Europe's growing Catholic press, and begging American clerics travelling from pulpit to pulpit diffused news of Catholic America in particularly immediate fashion.[43] European fascination with Native Americans turned every German-speaking Indian missionary into a potential immigrant recruiter, and many became formal colonizers, as did priests recruited directly to work among German immigrants.[44] By mid-century, the annual proceedings

---

41. Theodore Roemer, *The Leopoldine Foundation and the Church in the United States (1829–1839)* (New York: U.S. Catholic Historical Society, 1933); Theodore Roemer, *The Ludwig-Missionsverein and the Church in the United States (1838–1918)* (Washington, DC: Catholic University of America, 1933); Benjamin J. Blied, *Austrian Aid to American Catholics, 1830–1860* (Milwaukee: n.p., 1944).

42. Theodore Roemer, *Leopoldine Foundation;* Johann Martin Henni, *Ein Blick in's Thal des Ohio oder, Briefe über den Kampf und das Wiederaufleben der katholischen Kirche im fernen Westen der Vereinigten Staaten Nordamerika's* (München: 1836); Joseph Salzbacher, *Meine Reise nach Nord-Amerika im Jahre 1842* (Wien: Wimmer, Schmidt & Leo, 1845). The Résé and Henni visits respectively stimulated the founding of the Vienna and Munich societies.

43. There has been almost no direct research on these various kinds of linkages, but some insight into their complexity and functioning can be gained from studies of the decisions of religious orders like the Benedictines and Redemptorists to undertake American missions or in collections of letters of Catholic immigrants. See Jerome Oetgen, *An American Abbott: Boniface Wimmer, O.S.B., 1809–1887* (Washington, DC: Catholic University of America Press, 1997); Adolf E. Schroeder and Carla Schulz-Geisberg, *Hold Dear, As Always: Jette, A German Immigrant Life in Letters* (Columbia: University of Missouri Press, 1988).

44. William P. Furlan, *In Charity Unfeigned: The Life of Father Francis X. Pierz* (St. Cloud, MN: The Diocese of St. Cloud, 1952); Mary Aquinas Norton, *Catholic Missionary Activities in the Northwest, 1818–1864* (Washington, DC: The Catholic University of America, 1930). For

of the Katholischer Verein Deutschlands (Germany's national association of Catholic lay societies, founded in 1848) also included regular American reports, while its 1871 St. Raphaels Verein offered formal assistance to emigrating Catholics.[45] Thus, each German-speaking priest in America became a point of information and practical aid tied into an international network; each German parish priest a potential point of access. As German interest in emigration intensified in the 1830s, Catholic Germany was well on its way to developing what might be termed an emigration system of its own.[46]

That system was shaped also by a third factor that is more difficult to document, yet equally real: religious ideology. Despite the intensity of Catholic peasant emigration, possible links between religious belief and emigration have received surprisingly little attention within the burgeoning scholarship on Catholic Germany. We are unaccustomed to thinking of nineteenth-century Catholicism as a belief system motivating migration in search of refuge or utopia. Yet consider the embattled state of German Catholicism itself. Peasant piety was buffeted first by Enlightenment efforts to replace Baroque ritualism with a pastoral emphasis on teaching and morality, then by Napoleonic-era secularization that left sees without bishops and parishes without priests for years, and after 1815 by Catholic minority status and struggles with centralizing state authorities. Catholic renewal under such circumstances almost inevitably took the form of anti-modern, ultramontane loyalty to the papacy as an alternative source of authority, and led to recurring conflicts with

an innovative study of such connections, see Maureen A. Harp, "Indian Missions, Immigrant Migrations, and Regional Catholic Culture: Slovene Missionaries in the Upper Great Lakes, 1830–1892," (Ph.D. dissertation, University of Chicago, 1996). For instances of direct immigrant recruitment by early German priests, see Schrott, *Pioneer German Catholics*; V. J. Fecher, *A Study of the Movement for German National Parishes in Philadelphia and Baltimore (1787–1802)* (Rome: Apud Aedes Universitatis Gregorianae, 1955).

45. Doerries, *Iren und Deutsche*.

46. Recent studies of emigrant recruitment have paid virtually no attention to Catholic auspices. See Agnes Bretting and Hartmut Bickelmann, *Auswanderungsagenturen und Auswanderungsvereine im 19. und 20. Jahrhundert* (Stuttgart: F. Steiner, 1991); Stephan Görisch, "Die gedruckten 'Ratgeber' für Auswanderer: Zur Produktion und Typologie eines literarischen Genres," *Hessische Blätter für Volks- und Kulturforschung* 17 (1985): 51–70; Stefan von Senger und Etterlin, *Neu-Deutschland in Nordamerika: Massenauswanderung, nationale Gruppenansiedlungen und liberale Kolonialbewegung, 1815–1860* (Baden-Baden: Nomas, 1991); but see also Höndgen, *Migration*. Scattered information on the functioning of this Catholic system can be mined from missionary society reports, American parish and local histories, biographies of priests and histories of religious orders, reports in Catholic newspapers, etc. Systematic research would probably find its best sources in the archives of dioceses and religious congregations in both Germany and the United States, as well as in the Catholic press on both sides of the Atlantic.

governments over issues like the Church's role in marriage and education. One consequence, scholars agree, was an emotional devotionalism stimulated by revivalist missions and evident alike in the revitalization of old pilgrimage rites, a recurrent fascination with prophets and visions, and dramatic growth of membership in religious orders. Another was the gradual construction of a dense, defensive, and politicized Catholic milieu beginning in the late 1830s and culminating after 1871 in the formation of the Center Party and the subsequent successful resistance to Bismarck's Kulturkampf.[47]

Emigration could, of course, be a decisive way to sever outworn religious traditions, and indeed early immigrants from the Catholic areas of southwestern Germany enjoyed a reputation in America for the liberalism, secularism, and anticlericalism characteristic of that region. But emigration could also offer a promise of sanctuary for the pious, a refuge from the religious, economic, and political turmoil of a world gone awry. The great central valley of America, Henni prophesied in 1836, was destined to become the "arena of most effective working and flourishing of our holy religion."[48] Church authorities in Germany, less optimistic than their German-American counterparts, often sought to stem the tide of emigration, and the explicit chiliasm that led Ambros Oschwald

---

47. German Catholicism clearly harbored its own liberal, modernizing elements, particular within the urban middle classes, and scholarship suggests that the concept of a self-enclosed and complete "Catholic milieu" applies most fully only to the decades during and after the Kulturkampf, when anti-modern ideology was paired with adept institutional modernization. Recognition of such variation within German Catholicism, however, only underscores the potential within peasant communities for religious revitalization impulses encouraging the quest for shelter or salvation through separation and emigration. On these issues more generally see Heinz Hürten, *Kurze Geschichte des deutschen Katholizismus 1800–1960* (Mainz: Matthias-Grünewald Verlag, 1986); Erwin Gatz, "Zur Entwicklung der Pfarrei im Erzbistum Köln von der Säkularisation bis zum Zweiten Vatikanischen Konzil," *Historisches Jahrbuch* 105 (1985): 189–206; Jonathan Sperber, *Popular Catholicism in Nineteenth-Century Germany* (Princeton: Princeton University Press, 1984); Nipperdey, *Religion im Umbruch*; Klöcker, "Das katholische Milieu"; Maier, "Zur Soziologie"; Winfried Becker, "Der Kulturkampf als europäisches und als deutsches Phänomen," *Historisches Jahrbuch* 101 (1981): 422–446; Josef Mooser, "Katholische Volksreligion, Klerus und Bürgertum in der zweiten Hälfte des 19. Jahrhunderts. Thesen," in *Religion und Gesellschaft im 19. Jahrhundert*, edited by Wolfgang Schieder (Stuttgart: Klett-Cotta, 1993), 144–156; Rudolf Schlögl, "Katholische Kirche, Religiosität und gesellschaftlicher Wandel. Rheinisch-westfälische Städte 1750 bis 1830," in *Religion und Gesellschaft im 19. Jahrhundert*, 86–112; David Blackbourn, *Marpingen: Apparitions of the Virgin Mary in Nineteenth-Century Germany* (New York: Alfred A. Knopf, 1994); Thomas Mergel, *Zwischen Klasse und Confession: Katholisches Bürgertum im Rheinland 1794–1914* (Göttingen: Vendenhoeck & Rupprecht, 1994).

48. Henni, *Blick in's Thal des Ohio*, 5.

and 113 Badenese followers to found St. Nazianz, Wisconsin, in 1854 as a refuge from the ills of modern times was clearly exceptional.[49] Religion "caused" little German Catholic emigration in this immediate sense. It surely shaped, however, the way that opportunities were perceived and acted upon, it influenced the choice of those to whom immigrants turned for leadership and advice, and it directly affected patterns of settlement and community formation.[50]

Indeed, the best evidence for the structuring power of religion for German Catholic immigrants is the cohesive settlement system they created, shaped by the same mix of religiosity, church-derived information channels, and chain migration effects as the emigration itself. Strongest concentration occurred in Midwestern frontier areas where initial American settlement coincided with periods of heaviest Catholic immigration. Three-quarters of the roughly 2,250 German parishes in 1892 were located in the five Midwestern archdioceses of Cincinnati, St. Louis, Milwaukee, St. Paul, and Chicago, where roughly a third of all Catholic parishes were German.[51] The great majority were outside the cities normally associated with American Catholicism; fewer than ten percent

49. Hubert Treiber, "'Wie man wird, was man ist:' Lebensweg und Lebenswerk des badischen Landpfarrers Ambros Oschwald (1801–1873) im Erwartungshorizont chiliastischer Prophezeiungen," *Zeitschrift für die Geschichte des Oberrheins* 136 (1988): 293–348; Irmtraud Götz von Olenhusen, "Fundamentalistische Bewegungen im Umkreis der Revolution von 1848/ 49—Zur Vorgeschichte des badischen Kulturkampfes," in *Wunderbare Erscheinungen. Frauen und katholische Frömmigkeit im 19. und 20. Jahrhundert* (Paderborn: F. Schöningh, 1995), 131–170. Closer examination may uncover similar strains in other migrations. Consider the 1843 emigration to Ohio of Francis de Sales Brunner and his colleagues in the Congregation of the Precious Blood, participants in that same southwestern German "Catholic fundamentalism," and particularly the subsequent schismatic career of Joseph Albright; George F. Houck, *A History of Catholicity in Northern Ohio and in the Diocese of Cleveland*, vol. 1 (Cleveland: J. B. Savage, 1903), I: 13–21; Vincent A. Yzermans, *The Spirit in Central Minnesota: A Centennial Narrative of the Church of Saint Cloud, 1889–1989*, vol. 1 (St. Cloud, MN: The Diocese of St. Cloud, 1989), 23–25; Bob Riepe, *Journey of Hope* (Carthagena, OH: Messenger Press, 1985) (a fictionalized account to be used with care); Mark Schmid, *Sublimity: The Story of an Oregon Countryside, 1850–1950* (St. Benedict, OR: The Library Bookstore, 1951).

50. Cf. Joseph Scheben, *Untersuchungen zur Methode und Technik der deutschamerikanischen Wanderungsforschung* (Bonn: L. Röhrscheid, 1939); Mary Gilbert Kelly, *Catholic Immigrant Colonization Projects in the United States, 1815–1860* (New York: United States Catholic Historical Society, 1939), 49–57; Kamphoefner, *The Westfalians*, 73; Charles Herbermann, "A Catholic Colony in Ohio," *United States Catholic Historical Magazine* 4 (1891–1892): 125–134; Höndgen, *Migration*.

51. Calculated from Enzlberger, *Schematismus*; for more detail, see Conzen, "German Catholics in America," 574–575.

were in the sixteen large urban areas with six or more German parishes each.[52] This strong rural focus testifies to the self-selecting traditionalism of those who chose to settle under Catholic auspices. But the urban parishes were equally symbiotic parts of an integrated system knit together by continuing migration between city and country, and from one generation of settlements to the next, insuring constant diffusion and increasing syncretization of a distinctive German Catholic culture over time.

These parishes, when mapped, fall into about fifty geographical clusters ranging in size from three to thirty or forty contiguous rural and associated urban parishes each. Significant differences among these clusters in size, local dominance, and hence ability to sustain German Catholic cultural vitality can be accounted for, I would suggest, by a four-stage settlement process structured not only by changes in immigration flows and economic opportunities, but by the organizing role of the Church itself.[53] An initial formative phase, lasting until about 1830, was characterized by the low-volume migration of small groups of sometimes indifferent Catholics who encountered a weakly organized church with a chronic shortage of priests. Widely scattered among the broader German immigration, these immigrants were served, if at all, by itinerant priests who promoted occasional points of coalescence on each new frontier, sometimes around settlements of westering Irish or Maryland Catholics. The first concentrations coalesced around Jesuit missions at Conewago and Goshenhoppen in southeastern Pennsylvania in the 1740s and 1750s; not until after the Revolution did Germans from Philadelphia and Baltimore have the numbers, means, and self-confidence to form their own parishes, and it was 1833 before New Yorkers followed suit.[54]

---

52. Compiled from Enzlberger, *Schematismus*, and *Sadliers' Catholic Directory*; cf. Conzen, "German Catholics in America," 575.

53. The following discussion is based on a mapping and preliminary classification by size and date of foundation of all the parishes listed in Enzlberger, *Schematismus*, supplemented by research into the settlement history of the major clusters. The footnotes that follow are illustrative of these sources rather than exhaustive. See Conzen, "German Catholics in America," 575–576, for additional detail. For overview maps consult Heinz Kloss, *Atlas der im 19. und frühen 20. Jh. entstandenen deutschen Siedlungen in USA* (Marburg: Elwert, 1974).

54. Fecher, *Movement for German National Parishes*; Dolan, *Immigrant Church*; K. C. Watts, "Goshenhoppen," *Historical Records and Studies*, U.S. Catholic Historical Society, 21 (1932): 138–169; H. C. Watts, "Conewago: Our First Shrine to the Sacred Heart," *Historical Records and Studies*, U.S. Catholic Historical Society, 20 (1931): 28–63; John T. Reily, *Conewago: A Collection of Catholic Local History* (Martinsburg, WV: Herald Print, 1885); S. M. Sener, *The Catholic Church at Lancaster, Penn'a* (Philadelphia: 1894); "General-Vicar Joseph Ferneding," *Der Deutsche Pionier* 3 (1872): 353–362.

Such individualistic settlement was obviously costly in religious terms, and the solution that came to define what can be seen as a second, foundational phase of settlement, was pioneered by Dimitri Gallitzin, a Russian-Westphalian aristocrat who in 1795 became the first American-trained priest ordained in the United States. Four years later he settled among a group of Irish and German pioneers in Pennsylvania's Allegheny wilderness and began the self-conscious promotion of a Catholic colony that he named Loretto.[55] With the maturing of the Catholic informational network in Germany after 1830 and the intensification of emigration, such formal Catholic colonies—organized either in Germany or more often in the United States—became the favored settlement solution, and Catholic families arriving on their own found themselves quickly directed by clergy to the nearest colony.[56] The result was intensified clustering within church-centered communities at widely scattered rural sites, each at least initially quite homogenous in German regional origins, as well as the emergence of urban foci at inland entrepôts like Buffalo, Cincinnati, St. Louis, Chicago, and Milwaukee, and manufacturing centers like Pittsburgh and the Erie Canal towns. In these cities, and in the eastern ports of entry, German laity, priests, and their bishops worked out during this phase the basic institutional strategies to insure a German Catholic milieu for urban dwellers, including the recruitment of religious orders from Germany to guarantee the supply of priests and nuns.[57]

A third, expansionary phase emerged by the late 1840s, when the flood of German immigration overwhelmed the formal colonization process at the same time that older German Catholic colonies were actively seeking new land for their growing populations. Improved transportation and communication now insured rapid settlement of newly opened public lands, and frontier bishops could use America's new German Catholic press to lure settlers to

---

55. Peter Henry Lemcke, *Life and Work of Prince Demetrius Augustine Gallitzin* (London: Longmans, Green and Co., 1940); Siegfried Sudhof, *Von der Aufklärung zur Romantik: Die Geschichte des 'Kreises von Münster'* (Berlin: E. Schmidt, 1973).

56. Kelly, *Catholic Immigrant Colonization*, remains the best study of these colonies. For general patterns consult Emmet H. Rothan, *The German Catholic Immigrant in the United States (1830–1860)* (Washington, DC: 1946). For examples see *Of Pilgrimage, Prayer and Promise: A Story of St. Mary's, Westphalia, 1836–1986* (Westphalia, MI: Westphalia Historical Society, 1986); Höndgen, *Migration*.

57. Gerber, *Making of an American Pluralism*; Peter Leo Johnson, *Crosier on the Frontier: A Life of John Martin Henni, Archbishop of Milwaukee* (Madison: State Historical Society of Wisconsin, 1959); Kathleen Neils Conzen, *Immigrant Milwaukee, 1836–60: Accommodation and Community in a Frontier City* (Cambridge, MA: Harvard University Press, 1976); Rothan, *German Catholic Immigrant*; Dolan, *Immigrant Church*.

their dioceses and concentrate them for more efficient care.[58] Coincidentally, Bavarian and Swiss Benedictines—the former from the western Pennsylvania abbey they established in 1846, the latter from their 1853 abbey in southern Indiana—began their own westward expansion, encouraging settler coalescence around frontier priories in Minnesota, western Missouri, Kansas, and points west.[59] Instead of the scattered colonies of the second phase, third-phase expansion thus produced broad heterogenous belts of German Catholic settlement in Wisconsin, Iowa, Minnesota, Nebraska, and Dakota, while older colonies expanded outward at the expense of non-German Catholic neighbors, and new jumping-off cities like Dubuque, St. Paul, and Omaha acquired German Catholic communities of their own.

A final diffusion phase set in by the 1870s, when new communities were increasingly pioneered by the offspring of earlier settlers, speculation and efficient transportation made it more difficult for any one ethnic group to monopolize broad settlement areas, and the Church itself was sufficiently well organized that settlers could assume that religion would, in effect, follow the plow. One result was renewed scatter; another was the commercial organization of colonies, as developers competed to attract large, land-hungry, and skilled German Catholic farming families to land speculations everywhere from Florida to western Texas to Idaho's Palouse; a local alliance of German Catholic businessmen and church leaders from central Minnesota even negotiated with the Canadian government to establish a colony for their children—complete with Benedictine priory—in Saskatchewan in 1904.[60] But the real areas of growth now were in the German Catholic parishes of the cities, thanks not only to what was increasingly an immigration of young and single working people from Germany, but also to the urban migration of young people raised in the large German Catholic farm families of the Midwest.[61]

---

58. Johnson, *Crosier on the Frontier*; M. M. Hoffmann, *The Church Founders of the Northwest: Loras and Cretin and other Captains of Christ* (Milwaukee: Bruce Publishing Company, 1937).

59. Joel Rippinger, *The Benedictine Order in the United States: An Interpretive History* (Collegeville, MN: Liturgical Press, 1990); P. Willibald Mathäser, *Bonifaz Wimmer O.S.B. und König Ludwig I. von Bayern* (Bayern: Priester-Missionsbundes, 1937).

60. Jerome Weber, *Quest for a New Homeland: The Founding of St. Peter's Colony in Saskatchewan*, reprint of *Across the Boundary* by Bruno Doerfler (Muenster, SK: St. Peter's Colony, 1988); *Muenster, Texas: A Centennial History, 1889–1989* (Muenster, TX: Muenster Centennial Committee, 1989).

61. This is a process that remains as unstudied as the use of urban labor to amass capital for farm purchase that characterized earlier phases of the settlement process; for suggestive hints of

Thus German Catholicism, this argument suggests, was not merely part of the cultural baggage that immigrants brought with them; it was the vessel in which many made their voyage. Not all drew upon church auspices for their emigration or gravitated toward German Catholic settlements promising refuge and support for a familiar way of life. But those who chose to remain within the settlement system were self-selected by their adherence to its values and shaped a distinctive German Catholic milieu to safeguard and perpetuate them. Clearly, my case for the role of Catholic auspices in structuring emigration and settlement demands more detailed research on emigrant motivations, communication channels, migration chains, and colonization projects, and the implications of the four-stage settlement process for differential cultural vitality remain unexplored. But the responses of lay Catholics to the challenges facing them in nineteenth-century Germany cannot be understood without taking into account the choice of emigration that so many of them made. And the world they constructed in America will remain equally inexplicable until the processes that brought particular people to particular places for specific reasons are better understood.

Institutional Immigration

The vessel of German Catholicism, however, carried crew as well as passengers. An institutional immigration of priests and nuns, religious orders, lay people with close ties to the intellectual and material culture of Catholicism, and investment capital loomed disproportionately large within German as compared with other ethnic variants of American Catholicism. Its intensity and extended duration insured a constantly renewing leadership cadre that helps explain why America's German Catholicism was never just a simple construct of immigrant memory and American experience, but an integral extension of Germany's own Catholic subculture. This immigration has been more noted than analyzed within Catholic historiography, and most information comes from the histories of particular religious orders, which until recently have largely ignored questions about social background and recruitment, professional careers, worldviews, and social roles. But a few generalizations about the wellsprings and implications of this institutional immigration are possible.

---

the implications for urban religious culture, which is too often interpreted as a direct transplant from Europe, see Vincent A. Yzermans, *Spirit in Central Minnesota*, I: 446–457.

First, it is clear that the missionary impulse within European Catholicism—the lure of spiritual heroism in a romantic age—accounts in a broad sense for the willingness of so many religious to make the journey to America. But the pull of American spiritual need was complemented by the push of German circumstance. Warfare and secularization brought individual clerics to America as refugees; periodic state threats to religious orders encouraged congregations like the Swiss Benedictines in 1853 and German Jesuits in 1868 to establish explicit transatlantic refuges; the Prussian Kulturkampf sent large numbers of religious into actual American exile. On a more mundane and constant level, aspiring clerics unable to afford German seminaries could acquire training in America on far more reasonable terms, and newly ordained priests found improved chances for parish appointments and promotion. Others simply followed—or led—relatives and neighbors to America.[62]

The direct stimulus to nineteenth-century institutional immigration came, however, as it had during the colonial period, by invitation from Catholic America. American Catholicism long remained dependent on Europe for its priests. Prelates continued to recruit individual clergymen from Europe well into the twentieth century, but the post-1815 revitalization of religious orders soon offered a more cost-effective "outsourcing" option. By inducing religious orders to establish American foundations, bishops could delegate much of the responsibility for staffing, funding, and directing the religious care of German immigrants. Austrian Redemptorists, revivalistic preachers of Europe's Catholic awakening, were the first to accept the challenge, settling in the Cincinnati diocese in 1832 before moving to the large cities of the East. Other German, Swiss, and Austrian orders quickly followed, and soon their own mini-imperialisms within the United States gave further impetus to both urban and rural German Catholic expansion.[63] Despite several efforts to train

---

62. There is no American equivalent to Irmtraud Götz von Olenhusen's probing exploration of the professional world of the Badenese clergy in *Klerus und abweichendes Verhalten: Zur Sozialgeschichte katholischer Priester im 19. Jahrhundert: Die Erzdiözese Freiburg* (Göttingen: Vandenhoeck & Ruprecht, 1994). For an introductory look at emigrant priests from one German diocese, see *Auf nach Amerika! Beiträge zur Amerika-Auswanderung des 19. Jahrhunderts aus dem Paderborner Land und zur Wiederbelebung der historischen Beziehungen im 20. Jahrhundert*, edited by Ellen Rost, Otmar Allendorf, and Rolf-Dietrich Müller (Paderborn: Bonifatius, 1994). My insight on the professional motivations of emigrating clerical aspirants comes from abbotts' correspondence in the St. John's Abbey Archives, Collegeville, Minnesota.

63. Charles Shanabruch, *Chicago's Catholics: The Evolution of an American Identity* (Notre Dame, IN: University of Notre Dame Press, 1981); Otto Weiss, *Die Redemptoristen in Bayern (1790–1909): Ein Beitrag zur Geschichte des Ultramontanismus* (St. Ottilien: Eos Verlag, 1983); Thomas W. Mullaney, *Four-Score Years: A Contribution to the History of the Catholic*

priests in Europe specifically for America, American training proved a more effective—and cheaper—option, and in 1856 Henni, now bishop of Milwaukee, established a bilingual seminary that, along with the later Josephinum in Cleveland and the seminaries of the religious orders, supplied German-speaking priests to American dioceses well into the twentieth century.[64]

Numbers chart the relative success of these various strategies. Barely fifty German-speaking priests served the nation's estimated three hundred thousand German Catholics in 1843.[65] A little more than a quarter of a century later, a total of 1,169 German-speaking priests, only three percent of them (thirty-nine) known to be American-born, accounted for about thirty-five percent of all American clerics.[66] The heavy clerical immigration at the height of the Kulturkampf helped push the number of German-speaking priests to 2,067 by 1881, although the increase of the American-born proportion to eighteen percent also signified the beginnings of a transition to a home-grown German-American clergy. The largest single group among the immigrant priests (thirty percent) came from Westphalian and Hanoverian dioceses, many of them recent Kulturkampf refugees carrying the passions of embattled German Catholicity into pulpits across America; they were followed in order by priests from southwestern Germany (seventeen percent), the Prussian Rhineland (eleven percent), and Bavaria (eleven percent). Less than a quarter of the immigrant clerics, however, had been recruited as experienced priests; more than a third received most or all of their training in America, while the remainder arrived around the time of ordination. Two-thirds of the German-speaking priests were diocesan clergy. Benedictines were most numerous among those belonging to religious orders (twenty-eight percent), followed by Franciscans (twenty-

---

Germans in Rochester (Rochester, NY: 1916); Raymond Knab, "Father Joseph Prost, Pioneer Redemptorist in the United States," United States Catholic Historical Society, *Historical Records and Studies* 22 (1932): 32–84; Lawrence Mossing, *A Historical Study of the Sanguinists and the Early Catholicity of Northwestern Ohio from 1844 to 1870* (Canton, OH: Seiple Lithograph Co., [1952]); Norbert H. Miller, "Pioneer Capuchin Missionaries in the United States (1784–1816)," *Historical Records and Studies* 21 (1932): 170–234; Rippinger, *Benedictine Order*; Patrick J. McCloskey, *God Gives His Grace: A Short History of St. John the Baptist Province* (Cincinnati: The Province, 1994); Silas Barth, "The Franciscans in Southern Illinois," *Illinois Catholic Historical Review* 2 (1917–1920): 161–174, 328–338; *The Rise and Progress of the Province of St. Joseph of the Capuchin Order in the United States 1857–1907* (New York: Benziger Bros., 1907).

64. Weiss, *Redemptoristen in Bayern*; Rothan, *German Catholic Immigrant*; Johnson, *Crosier on the Frontier*; Houck, *History of Catholicity*.

65. Salzbacher, *Meine Reise nach Nord-Amerika*, 369.

66. Schem, *Conversations-Lexikon*, quoting Reiter's 1869 *Schematismus*.

three percent), Redemptorists (twenty percent), Jesuits (sixteen percent), and Capuchins (ten percent).[67]

German nuns and teaching brothers, their ranks similarly swelled by Germany's Catholic revival, were likewise courted by American bishops and pastors to staff parish schools and other institutions beginning in the 1840s. Perhaps a sixth of the flourishing American sisterhoods of the mid-twentieth century derived from German origins. Almost all were teaching and nursing orders; some of the largest and most widespread were recruited during the first wave of mass immigration before the Civil War, while later transplantations occurred during the Kulturkampf and again during the years of American urban growth before and after World War I.[68] Despite frequent tension over appropriate forms of governance and the adaptation of cloistered European rules to immigrant needs, these sisterhoods apparently attracted recruits from the German communities of America more quickly and in greater volume than did the priesthood. Many German parishes began producing exceptionally high numbers of vocations among the maturing second generation, and in these parishes women outpaced men in their choice of the religious life often two, three, or even four to one.[69] Such growth meant that these orders could expand along with the expansion of the German Catholic settlement system. Thus by 1892, the School Sisters of Notre Dame had founded nearly three hundred schools and orphanages in sixteen states, the District of Columbia,

67. These calculations are my own, derived from the listings in Bonenkamp et al., *Schematismus* (1882). The career tabulations are based upon only the 1,478 priests who contributed full information concerning their date and place of birth, their date of ordination, and their date of immigration. I used age fourteen as the cut-off point for "immigration as a child" and immigration within three years before and two years after ordination to identify those cases where immigration was part of the career process that led to priesthood.

68. Tabulation compiled from *Guide to the Catholic Sisterhoods in the United States*, edited by Thomas P. McCarthy (Washington, DC: Catholic University of America Press, 1964). Cf. Virginia Geiger and Patricia McLaughlin, eds., *Many Voices: Lectures Delivered at the Mother Caroline Friess Centenary Celebrations 1992* (Lanham, MD: 1993); Rippinger, *Benedictine Order*; Elinor Tong Dehey, *Religious Orders of Women in the United States* (Hammond, IN: W. B. Conkey, 1930).

69. James Hitchcock, "Secular Clergy in Nineteenth Century America: A Diocesan Profile," *Records of the American Catholic Historical Society* 88 (1977): 31–62; tabulations from assorted parish histories. It remains to be explored whether this gender differential simply reflects the oft-noted feminization of nineteenth-century piety or also involves greater demand for male labor in frontier families, the cost and time differential of training for the priesthood as compared with the convent, the lack of alternate opportunities for women as compared with men, or even the burden imposed on women by German Catholic family styles. On feminization see Colleen McDannell, "Catholic Domesticity, 1860–1960," in *American Catholic Women: A Historical Exploration*, edited by Karen Kennelly (New York: Macmillan, 1989), 48–80.

and Ontario, numbered over two thousand members, and in 1873 laid the basis in Baltimore for the first degree-granting Catholic institution of higher learning for women in America.[70]

An ancillary immigration of church-connected laity complemented the immigration of religious, thanks to the elaborate material culture of German Catholic worship and its European-derived emphasis on education and public involvement. Henni, for example, lured a German Catholic bookseller to Cincinnati in 1838, and when he became bishop of frontier Milwaukee his patronage drew not only a bookseller and a dealer in altar wines, but also noted teachers, musicians, church architects, and even, from 1847 to 1854, a school to train Milwaukeeans in the arts of church decoration.[71] By the mid-1830s, German-Catholic communities were attracting lay organists, teachers, and would-be journalists who, like their religious counterparts, felt both the push from anticlerical Germany and the pull of American opportunity. Bookstores and dealers in religious goods appeared early in cities with significant German Catholic populations, and by the 1850s, German publishers specializing in the Catholic trade were setting up American branches. The post-Civil War years saw a noticeable immigration of German architects trained in the neo-Gothic style that became the hallmark of America's German Catholic churches, along with artisans who established significant American firms producing religious goods.[72]

We need to know a good deal more about this institutional and para-institutional immigration before its full implications can be assessed. It certainly meant that America's German Catholicism was never purely a folk culture, a set of habits of the heart; it was also a consciously cultivated and evolving intellectual tradition. Institutional immigration guaranteed an educated leadership capable of dealing with Americans at a sophisticated cultural level, relieved immigrants from the full burden of supporting the complex religious establishment they demanded, and encouraged the rapid development of comprehensive education and health care systems. But it

---

70. *Many Voices*; Delores Liptak, *Immigrants and Their Church* (New York: Macmillan, 1989).

71. Johnson, *Crosier on the Frontier*; Harry J. Heming, *The Catholic Church in Wisconsin* (Milwaukee: Catholic Historical Publishing Company, 1896), 1135–1148.

72. Robert E. Cazden, *A Social History of the German Book Trade in America to the Civil War* (Columbia, SC: Camden House, 1984), 135–136, 227, 467–470; Heming, *Catholic Church in Wisconsin*, 1135–1148; Roy A. Hampton III, "German Gothic in the Midwest: The Parish Churches of Franz Georg Himpler and Adolphus Druiding," *U.S. Catholic Historian* 15 (1997): 51–74.

also helped insure that German-American Catholicism moved in tempo with homeland trends. Immigrant religious, maintaining close contact with German cultural wellsprings, readily interpreted American developments in familiar homeland terms and proposed tested homeland solutions to American problems. German motherhouse considerations influenced American clerical strategies, and imported texts and religious goods molded American piety. The tensions of such a transcultural leadership could be all too evident not only in dealings with America's English-speaking Catholic establishment, but also with parishioners (and nuns) who often had been in the United States a generation or two longer than their greenhorn priests.

Mentality and Pious Practice

Whatever the tensions in the relationship, however, the combination of lay commitment and institutional guidance appears to have produced a particularly coherent ethnoreligious culture of remarkable consistency throughout America's far-flung German Catholic settlement system. Wherever they clustered in self-selecting communities, German Catholics seem to have nurtured a characteristic set of religiously rooted mentalities, worldviews, and more consciously held beliefs and practices. Derived from both peasant traditions and transmontane revivalism, these values and habits shaped the decisions they made in their lives and the meanings they ascribed to them, and set them almost as much apart from English-speaking Catholics as from non-Catholic America.[73]

Basic to the worldview cultivated within German Catholic communities, I have argued elsewhere, was a deep sense of the permeation of the mundane with the divine, the orientation of earthly activity toward the afterlife, the impossibility of earthly perfection and the constancy of sin, the promise of forgiveness within the embrace of the Church. Endurance and duty were two prime virtues; ambition and display were sins against both God and the community. That community was a heritage of peasant need but also a religious demand. The individual did not face God alone, but worshipped in community, the prayers of many more readily heard than the prayers of one, prayer combined with physical action more efficacious than silent prayer alone. Family was not only a means of survival in a rural world, but also the

---

73. I am using "peasant" broadly here as shorthand for those raised within the values of the traditional agrarian and small-town communities of German-speaking Europe, regardless of the actual personal status of particular immigrants.

most basic community within which one approached God; the prayers and penances of the living the key to eternal happiness for those already dead; the woman's role not only to produce children to serve God and perpetuate the family, but to insure the prayers in which lay its salvation. Living in the world, the divine reached out to them through worldly things—rituals, sacramentals, song, elaborate churches—and innocent enjoyment could be found in the sociability and pleasures that the world offered.[74]

These were not quite the tenets taught by the priests and nuns, and not always those shared by other Catholics in America, but they were the folk assumptions inscribed in everyday action. It was a family and community-centered value system that made German Catholics effective pioneers and found ideal conditions for its perpetuation in the isolation of the countryside. The colony would support the needed church; the church would provide the education to retain children within the culture and the prayers to insure God's temporal and eternal favors; in perpetuating itself and maintaining a viable farm economy, the family sustained and extended the colony—a circle of faith protected by self-isolation from outside temptation. Indeed, rural colonies of sufficient size, Germans quickly realized, could draw on the force of government to reinforce their values, using their votes to control local schools, courts, taxation, and welfare.[75] In the cities, such a tight circle was never possible. Urban opportunity attracted Catholics of a more liberal, secularized

---

74. Kathleen Neils Conzen, *Making Their Own America: Assimilation Theory and the German Peasant Pioneer* (New York: Berg Publishers, 1990). Its generalizations about attitudes rest particularly on local newspapers, district court case files, and parish correspondence and reports in the St. John's Abbey Archives, Collegeville, MN. See also Höndgen, *Migration*, for a case study, and the compelling comparative synthesis in Gjerde, *Minds of the West*; helpful older studies include Ronald G. Klietsch, "The Religious Social System of the German-Catholics of the Sauk" (M.A. thesis, University of Minnesota, 1958); O. F. Hoffman, "Culture of the Centre-Mosel Germans in Manitowoc and Sheboygan Counties, Wisconsin," (Ph.D. diss., University of North Carolina, 1942); Alexis Hoffmann, "Natural History of a Rural Township" (1924 ms., St. John's Abbey Archives, Collegeville, MN). For a suggestive European comparison see Fintan Michael Phayer, *Religion und das gewöhnliche Volk in Bayern in der Zeit von 1750–1850* (München: Neue Schriftenreihe des Stadtarchivs München, 1970); Rainer Wirtz, "Religious Patterns of Interpretation and Mobilization in Vormärz Germany," in *Religion and Rural Revolt*, edited by János M. Bak and Gerhard Benecke (Manchester: Manchester University Press, 1984), 223–237.

75. Conzen, *Making Their Own America*; much suggestive information lies buried in parish histories like—to single out four from hundreds—Arthur A. Halbach, *Dyersville: Its History and Its People* (Milwaukee: St. Joseph Press, 1939); Albert Kleber, *Ferdinand, Indiana, 1840–1940: A Bit of Cultural History* (St. Meinrad, IN: n.p., 1940); Beatrice Wester Krier, *Tapestry of Luxembourgers* (Belgium, WI: by the author, 1987); Miller, *St. Michael's on the Hill: A 135th Year Commemoration* (Waite Park, MN: Park Press, 1993).

bent, and new sorts of economic and cultural potential encouraged attitudinal changes, even among the most conservative, that demand more study. But here too, the intense commitment to the German-speaking institutional parish testified to the vitality of the belief system.[76]

It was not simply a question of national pride, though, that was surely present as Germans adapted to an America they often regarded as culturally inferior. Nor was it just language difference, though this, too, was critical, despite the presumed universality of Latin worship. Henni's insistence that "language saves the faith" became a slogan among nineteenth-century German Catholics, reflecting not only the dependence of pastoral care on effective communication, but also the alternative available to disgruntled German Catholics in Protestant German-language services.[77] National differences in traditions of worship, piety, education, and parish governance made even bilingual parishes problematic. Germans had absorbed greater doses of Enlightenment support for parochial schools, worship in the vernacular, and lay control of parish property than their English-speaking fellow Catholics, as well as a far stronger attachment to the Baroque devotionalism of communal processions, pilgrimages, orchestral masses, and church ornamentation. It was no accident that conflicts over church music helped precipitate Philadelphia's German-Irish split in 1787.[78] And since German language and culture seemed inseparable from the grace-filled life they sought, German support for parochial schools to pass both on to their children became proverbial. An estimated two-thirds of Midwestern German parishes established schools within two years of their founding, compared with just over a quarter of their Irish counterparts.[79]

To realize in America the immigrant vision of a traditional community permeated by religion demanded a homogeneity of values that extended beyond the church to encompass every area of daily life, a homogeneity that the first generation, in particular, could never find in a mixed parish. Thus, German national parishes became de facto Church policy wherever German Catholics settled, and Germans clustered to insure the numbers needed to

76. See Conzen, *Immigrant Milwaukee*; Gerber, *Making of an American Pluralism*.

77. For the attribution of this slogan to Henni, see Barry, *Catholic Church and German Americans*, 10.

78. Fecher, *Movement for German National Parishes*, does not explicitly make this argument, but it is clear from the evidence he provides.

79. Stephen Joseph Shaw, "The Cities and the Plains, a Home for God's People: A History of the Catholic Parish in the Midwest," in *The American Catholic Parish: A History from 1850 to the Present*, edited by Jay P. Dolan, vol. 2 (New York: Paulist Press, 1987), 277–354.

maintain national parishes. In a characteristic rural pattern, these parishes clustered around the abbey or motherhouse serving the region, their steepled churches set within expansive precincts embracing rectory, school, convent, graveyard, picnic lawn, grotto, and parish hall, and flanked by the stores and saloons of the hamlets that developed around them. The Neo-Baroque piety of outdoor processions punctuated every major church feast, while the annual parish fund-raising fair became the functional equivalent of the old country *Kirmes*, votive chapels sprouted along country lanes, and miraculous occurrences occasioned familiar habits of multi-parish pilgrimage to local shrines. A broad array of devotional, service, and social associations, most with mutual benefit functions, sought to draw every category of parishioners regularly into community life, while periodic missions preached by itinerant revivalists stimulated special weeks of grace.[80]

With local government often little more than an extension of parish governance, German Catholic farmers realized early that they could hire Catholic teachers for the public schools and avoid supporting a separate parochial system. Though bishops were never comfortable with this approach, it was already common in Ohio in the 1830s, and Henni stressed its advantages to attract German Catholics to Wisconsin a decade later. Its prevalence throughout the rural Midwest is one reason why late nineteenth-century Germans were able to claim virtually universal compliance with the Church mandate for parochial schools. It resonated with Germany's system of public support for church schools and permitted many parishes to import the familiar figure of the *Kirchenvater*, the lay "church father" who combined the

---

80. Again, these generalizations are drawn from wide reading in parish and local histories, and from research in local sources for a book-in-progress on the German Catholic settlement area of Stearns County, Minnesota, where full documentation will be provided. Individual priests also early on established formal shrines as American analogs to noted German pilgrimage sites like Altötting or Kevelaar. Sanguinist Francis de Sales Brunner, for example, established the Maria Steig shrine to the Sorrowful Mother at Thompson, Ohio in 1850, within six years of arrival in the United States; Massing, *Sanguinists*, 177–182. For other examples see *Shrines: A Guide for the Catholic Pilgrim to Places of Special Veneration Located throughout the Diocese of Saint Cloud, Minnesota* (Diocese of St. Cloud: 1987); Gregory E. Faiers and Carolyn V. Prorok, "Pilgrimage to a 'National' American Shrine: 'Our Lady of Consolation' in Carey, Ohio," in *Pilgrimage in the United States*, edited by G. Rinschede and S. M. Bhardwag (Berlin: Dietrich Reimer Verlag, 1990), 137–148. Reports of miraculous apparitions in Germany similarly found American echoes; thus an issue of *Der Wanderer* (16 February 1878) that reported the latest news from Marpingen also included an article on "Eine merkwürdige Begebenheit," the miraculous appearance of a healing angel at a German parish in Mauch Chunk (today, Jim Thorpe), Pennsylvania. Such aspects of German-American popular piety have attracted little scholarly attention. For parish missions see Jay P. Dolan, *Catholic Revivalism: The American Experience, 1830–1900* (Notre Dame, IN: University of Notre Dame Press, 1978).

roles (and salaries) of public school teacher, organist, choir director, sacristan, and often—as the best educated layman in the parish—town clerk. In 1871 Henni opened the country's first Catholic normal school for lay teachers near Milwaukee, and men trained there or at colleges established by German orders played a central role in rural parishes well into the twentieth century.[81] This rural system came under increasing pressure after the 1884 church mandate that every parish have its own school. Teaching sisters, now available in sufficient numbers, were both cheaper and more subject to clerical authority than were lay teachers appointed by school boards. The system also began to draw legal challenges for blurring the boundaries between church and state. Parishioners, fearful of loss of control and female teachers alike, often resisted, sometimes successfully. Several rural German parishes in Minnesota's St. Cloud diocese, for example, were placed under interdict for their opposition but managed to retain variants of the older system far into the twentieth century.[82]

Urban German Catholics lacked the settlement concentration and political control that buttressed rural efforts to shape a fully Catholic way of life, relying on institutional completeness instead. Like their counterparts in the growing cities of the homeland, and for much the same defensive reasons, German Catholic parishes in American cities developed a well-deserved reputation for the cradle-to-grave organization of life. Beginning in the 1820s Henni, fresh from religiously divided, anticlerical Switzerland, pioneered in Cincinnati what became the basic instruments of urban German Catholicism. At the congregational level these included the elaborate church, choir, parochial school, and a broad spectrum of associations designed to "rescue wandering sheep and protect the remainder from the rapacious wolves of worldliness and modernity" while promoting personal piety. At the city level the instruments included the cemetery association, newspaper, orphan asylum, hospital, seminary and normal school, religious orders, and formal engagement with the

81. Nora Luetmer, "The History of Catholic Education in the Diocese of St. Cloud, 1855–1965" (Ph.D. diss., University of Minnesota, 1970); Johnson, *Crosier on the Frontier*; Vincent J. Higginson, *History of American Catholic Hymnals: Survey and Background* (Hymn Society of America, 1982); Bernadette Grabrian, "Milwaukee, Wisconsin: America's Nucleus of the St. Cecilia Society," *Sacred Music* 100 (1973): 3–12. Not all rural parishes relied on this system—some had parochial schools taught by nuns from the outset while others hired nuns as public school teachers. The rural Catholic school system needs more study; cf. Juliane Jacobi-Dittrich, *"Deutsche" Schulen in den Vereinigten Staaten von Amerika: Historisch-vergleichende Studie zum Unterrichtswesen im Mittleren Westen (Wisconsin 1840–1900)* (München: Minerva Publikation, 1988).

82. Yzermans, *Spirit in Central Minnesota*; parish correspondence files, St. John's Abbey Archives, Collegeville, MN.

public life of the city. We tend to interpret this institutional complex as a logical response to the immigrant's need for cultural continuity and the Church's desire to retain its adherents. But it was an important innovation whose European roots and wide American diffusion demand study.[83] The contrast with the more restricted range of Irish associations was telling. The Germans cultivated a stronger tradition of lay parish participation in part because they also ran a greater risk of seduction by the secular, frequently anticlerical *Vereinswesen* that flourished wherever nineteenth-century Germans settled.[84]

The coherent logic of a German Catholic belief system and praxis must not be overstressed, of course. An important challenge is to understand how relative cultural coherence was sustained across the settlement system, and to explore place-to-place variations owing to German background, American context, colonization phase, and the devotional emphases of particular religious orders. Both the role of women in German Catholic life, and the American counterpart of Germany's bourgeois Catholic culture, in which families like Michael Schaack's found their religious place, also merit greater

83. Johnson, *Crosier on the Frontier*; Peter Leo Johnson, *Stuffed Saddlebags: The Life of Martin Kundig, Priest, 1805–1879* (Milwaukee: Bruce Publishing Co., 1942); Altermatt, *Katholizismus und Moderne*. When looked at through the lens of German-American Catholicism, Henni emerges as one of the great institution-building and culture-shaping bishops of nineteenth-century America, but the German language world in which he moved meant that his activities have attracted little scholarly notice beyond an intelligent if limited biography. One might similarly argue that his role in shaping the conditions of American adaptation for a significant portion of the German immigration should have earned him a place on any list of nineteenth-century German-American leaders, but the secular focus of most ethnic scholarship has left his career in this context also unexamined. He was, for example, a significant disputant with nativist Yankees and German anticlericals alike, using the newspapers he founded in Cincinnati and Milwaukee to engage in ferocious doctrinal and political debates with his opponents. But he was also a canny civic promoter and a builder of bridges, particularly through music and art, with the broader non-Catholic middle-class community.

84. Conzen, *Immigrant Milwaukee*; Dolan, *Immigrant Church*; Joseph M. White, "Cincinnati's German Catholic Life: A Heritage of Lay Participation," *U.S. Catholic Historian* 12 (1994): 1–16; Shaw, "The Cities and the Plains." Also involved was fear of potential competition from Catholic Germany's two main nineteenth-century schismatic movements, the rationalistic Deutschkatholizismus of the 1840s and the Altkatholizismus that arose in protest against the doctrine of papal infallibility in the 1860s. The role of former Catholics in antebellum American freethinking congregations undoubtedly accounts for some of the Church's obsession with the threat that they posed. While the German Catholic press also mounted polemics against Old Catholics (e.g., *Der Wanderer*, 14 February 1874), they probably posed less of a direct threat in America, and America's modern Old Catholic church rests on non-German ethnic roots. This is an issue that merits more attention, and I am grateful to Andreas Dorn for calling it to my attention.

consideration.[85] The degree of enclosure achieved in these local communities and processes of cultural modulation over time remain open issues as do conflicts within (e.g., by gender or generation), acts of rebellion against, and paths of exit from the culture.

The Institutional Milieu

Beginning around mid-century and peaking in the 1880s, German Catholic America embarked on an ambitious effort to embed these parish-centered local communities within what can be viewed as a broader ethnoreligious milieu: a self-sufficient social world, an encompassing national array of confessionally defined ethnic associations, and a confessionally mediated engagement with the public issues of the day. The timeline of institutional elaboration can be quickly summarized. A necessary first step occurred with Henni's 1837 Cincinnati publication of the nation's first German Catholic newspaper, *Der Wahrheitsfreund*, in conscious imitation of Europe's emergent Catholic press. It quickly gained national circulation and imitators, bringing German Catholics throughout America in touch with one another and with events in Catholic Europe. Sixty-one German Catholic newspapers appeared over the course of the nineteenth century, along with a wide range of more specialist periodicals and a plethora of devotional publications, apologetics, histories, and lighter literature.[86]

Milieu formation gained further impetus in 1846 when the western Pennsylvania Benedictines laid the initial foundations for a German Catholic higher education system.[87] Then in 1855 came Der Deutsche Römisch-Katholische Central-Verein von Nord-Amerika, seven years after the first national convention of Catholic associations in Germany and coincident with national-level organization among secular German Americans. An umbrella federation of parish benevolent societies supporting their practical insurance programs, its annual meetings soon provided a platform for airing broader

---

85. See Jacob Borut and Obed Heilbronner, "Leaving the Walls or Anomalous Activity: The Catholic and Jewish Rural Bourgeoisie in Germany," *Comparative Studies in Society and History* 40 (1998): 475–502; Obed Heilbronner, "In Search of the (Rural) Catholic Bourgeoisie: The Bürgertum of South Germany," *Central European History* 29 (1996): 175–200.

86. Georg Timpe, "Hundert Jahre katholischer deutscher Presse," in *Katholisches Deutschtum in den Vereinigten Staaten von America*, edited by Georg Timpe (Freiburg im Breisgau: Herder, 1937), 4–33; Cazden, *German Book Trade in America*; Bonaventura P. Hammer, *Die katholische Kirche in den Vereinigten Staaten Nordamerikas* (New York: Chas. Wildermann, 1897).

87. Oetgen, *American Abbott*; Colman J. Barry, *Worship and Work: Saint John's Abbey and University, 1856–1956* (Collegeville, MN: Saint John's Abbey, 1956).

German Catholic concerns.[88] Local and state federations of benevolent and other societies followed, along with American branches of Catholic Germany's Kolping Society to aid young single workers in 1856, and the Cecilian Society to reform sacred music in 1873.[89] But only in the 1880s did America's German Catholics begin to approach European levels of national organization. First in 1883 came an American branch of the St. Raphael Society, then in 1887 a national association of German-American priests, which that same year called the first annual national assembly of lay Catholic societies, the Katholikentag, in direct imitation of the German model. The Katholikentag in turn prompted short-lived national associations for the German Catholic press, for young German Catholic men, for subgroups like the Luxemburgers, and for the support of poor German-American mission parishes.[90]

What accounts for these waves of organizational energy separate from the German-American mainstream, and what were their consequences? They can certainly be interpreted as defensive reactions to the American nativism and the anticlericalism of fellow German immigrants that particularly marked these periods. Encountering in America the same threats of modernity that they fled in Germany, like their European co-religionists America's German Catholics created an expanding associational circle to enclose and defend their communities.[91] But equally striking is the extent to which their national organization moved in time-lagged rhythm with currents flowing within Catholic Germany. The homeland's milieu Catholicism reached across the Atlantic to offer stimulus, perceptual filters, and vocabulary for a comprehensively

88. Gleason, *Conservative Reformers*.

89. Georg Timpe, ed., *Katholisches Deutschtum in den Vereinigten Staaten von America*, (Freiburg im Breisgau: Herder, 1937); Vincent A. Yzermans, *With Courage and Hope: The Catholic Aid Association, 1878–1978* (St Paul: Catholic Aid Association, 1978); Enzlberger, *Schematismus*; Higginson, *American Catholic Hymnals*; Karl Gustav Fellerer, ed., *Geschichte der katholischen Kirchenmusik*, vol. 2 (Kassel: Bärenreiter-Verlag, 1976), 348–352.

90. Gleason, *Conservative Reformers*; Berry, *Catholic Church and German Americans*; Enzlberger, *Schematismus*; Hammer, *Die katholische Kirche*; Richard J. Witry, ed., *Luxembourg Brotherhood of America 1887–1987* (Park Ridge, IL: n.p., 1987); Stephen Joseph Shaw, "Chicago's Germans and Italians, 1903–1939: The Catholic Parish as a Way-Station of Ethnicity and Americanization" (Ph.D. diss., University of Chicago 1981).

91. Heinen, *Katholizismus und Gesellschaft*; Levine, "Community Divided"; Gerber, *Making of an American Pluralism*; Conzen, *Immigrant Milwaukee*; Stanley Nadel, *Little Germany: Ethnicity, Religion, and Class in New York City, 1845–1880* (Urbana: University of Illinois Press, 1990). For an example of how German and Yankee anti-Catholicism could combine to create a locally adverse climate, see C. Walker Gollar, "Early Protestant-Catholic Relations in Southern Indiana and the 1842 Case of Roman Weinzaepfel," *Indiana Magazine of History* 95 (1999): 233–254.

organized German Catholic life in America. But organizational enclosure in the diaspora could never be as complete or successful as in Germany, I would suggest, in good part because, while its initial logic rested on defense against America's own forms of Kulturkampf, in the end the chief opponent of German efforts to preserve an ethnic Catholicism became the Catholic Church itself.

Certain tensions were long-standing consequences of the German minority position within an Irish-dominated and centralizing American church where uniformity was a rational administrative goal. Clashes with the American hierarchy over the German custom of administering parish property through a *Kirchenrat* (council of lay parishioners) dated back to the late eighteenth century. Such "trusteeism" was not an exclusively German problem, but since cultural differences made German parishes, from the bishops' perspective, more difficult to tame, it came to be seen as a characteristically German failing. The majority of German parishes probably enjoyed real trustee governance in practical affairs well into the twentieth century, but tensions persisted as long as the German parish system itself.[92] They were exacerbated by characteristic conflicts within German parishes themselves and by strains endemic to the national parish system. Early Catholic immigrants did not necessarily leave behind ingrained anticlerical and Febronian (state control) attitudes, nor did Germans from different areas of the homeland necessarily come together easily in shared parishes. Add unfamiliarity with voluntary financial support for churches, the early shortage and uncertain quality of priests, and the lay base of independent power in rural school boards, and the reputation of German parishes for quarrelsomeness becomes explicable. So, too, does the initial willingness of bishops to countenance German-speaking national parishes overlapping the English-speaking territorial parish system, and to consign their supervision to a vicar general or the superior of a religious order. But this in turn led to frequent German charges of neglect. Not until 1833 was the first German-American bishop appointed, when the Right Reverend Rése was named to the see of Detroit; by 1882, on the eve of the push toward national German Catholic organization, the United States had just

---

92. White, "Cincinnati's German Catholic Life"; Fecher, *Movement for German National Parishes*; Light, *Rome and the New Republic*; Patrick W. Carey, *People, Priests, and Prelates: Ecclesiastical Democracy and the Tensions of Trusteeism* (Notre Dame, IN: University of Notre Dame Press, 1987). For parish governance in Germany see Wilfried Evertz, *Seelsorge im Erzbistum Köln zwischen Aufklärung und Restauration 1825–1835* (Köln: Böhlau Verlag, 1993); Erwin Gatz, ed., *Die Bistümer und ihre Pfarreien*, (Freiburg: Herder, 1991).

one German archbishop, twelve bishops, and two apostolic vicars in nascent frontier dioceses.[93]

These statistics emerged from careful self-surveys conducted by America's German-speaking priests in 1869, 1882, and 1892, themselves symptoms of heightened ethnic tensions within American Catholicism that helped stimulate the Church's late nineteenth-century "Americanism" crisis. Those tensions are conventionally attributed to conservative German suspicion of the rapprochement with modern America advocated by liberal prelates anxious to rid the church of its "foreign" stigma, but exacerbated also by greater German tolerance for alcoholic beverages and suspicion of labor unions and secret societies.[94] Viewed from the German perspective, however, three other factors seem equally central: the rising self-confidence of German Catholic laity, a career crisis among German-speaking clergy, and the imperative of bishops, German and non-German alike, to eliminate the contradictions of the national parish system.

The organizational activity of the 1880s clearly owed much to heightened consciousness of identity raised by Germany's Kulturkampf. Newspapers and letters from Europe kept immigrants informed, recent arrivals occupied numerous pulpits and classrooms, and the last great German immigration wave of the early 1880s brought into American parishes a mentality shaped by Catholic resistance and victory.[95] It was sustained also by the growing prosperity of an increasingly second and third generation German Catholic community. But the maturing of the German immigration (and the disproportionate number of recent clerical immigrants whose English surely was imperfect) also guaranteed heightened career competition among

---

93. Barry, *Catholic Church and German Americans*; Fecher, *Movement for German National Parishes*; Robert Frederick Trisco, *The Holy See and the Nascent Church in the Middle Western United States, 1826–1850* (Rome: Gregorian University Press, 1962); Liptak, *Immigrants and their Church*; Bonenkamp et al., *Schematismus*.

94. The nationalist tensions that are my focus here were only part of a broader debate about the position of the Church in the modern world that culminated in papal condemnation of "Americanism" in 1899 and, historians have argued, American Catholic subcultural separation; cf. O'Brien, *Public Catholicism*; Barry, *Catholic Church and German Americans*; Trisco, *Holy See and the Nascent Church*; Gleason, *Conservative Reformers*; Gerald Fogarty, "The Catholic Hierarchy in the United States Between the Third Plenary Council and the Condemnation of Americanism," *U.S. Catholic Historian* 11 (1993): 19–35; Doerries, *Iren und Deutsche*; Dolan, *American Catholic Experience*. I have drawn on these sources for my reading of the Americanism controversy in the following paragraphs.

95. Cf. Rory T. Conley, "Arthur Preuss, German-Catholic Exile in America," *U.S. Catholic Historian* 12 (1994): 41–62.

German- and English-speaking priests. Who should take charge of the mixed-ethnicity parishes that social mobility was creating? And when national parishes for German immigrants existed within territorial parish boundaries, whose responsibility were the English-speaking children? Thus, Henni's 1878 nomination of a German coadjutor with right of succession for his Milwaukee diocese triggered protest from English-speaking priests who felt blocked from advancement, while similar protest erupted among German priests in St. Louis in 1884 over the subordinate status of national to territorial parishes. When the Third Plenary Council in Baltimore failed to resolve this issue, Peter Abbelen, a Milwaukee priest, delivered an 1886 Memorial to Rome from Midwestern German priests who sought, and received, affirmation of the co-equal status of national parishes and the right of parents to keep their children in national parishes. But what Germans saw as equal rights, others interpreted as special privileges. The ensuing newspaper and pamphlet war converted the arcana of canon law into an issue of national pride uniting German-American clergy and laity, and led directly to the Priester-Verein and the Katholikentag, which then became further evidence for German divisiveness and resistance to assimilation.

The overt stimulus for the first Katholikentag was the need to raise money for the St. Raphael Society's planned immigrant hostel in New York, and the next major stage in the mounting crisis came from that Society also. In 1891 its founder, Peter Paul Cahensly, a Rhineland merchant, carried to Rome a Memorial requesting Church support for national parishes, foreign-language ministries, and immigrant representation in the hierarchies of immigrant-receiving nations. Its impetus came from Italy, and it was signed by delegates from seven nations, but Rome quickly tabled the proposals once distorted cables to American newspapers converted "Cahenslyism" into a plot "to found a religious and political Prussia in the United States." Emboldened episcopal Americanizers followed with proposals to concede significant educational authority to the state, and a successful campaign to remove a conservative German theologian from the faculty of Washington's new Catholic University, provoking further German Catholic organization and greater demands for language safeguards within the Church than might otherwise have been the case.

German Americans, then, drew upon the organizational example of Germany's milieu Catholicism to defend themselves against assimilating pressure from the Church itself. Papal condemnation of "Americanism" in 1899 seemed to vindicate their position, but generational change and episcopal policy soon made their victory a pyrrhic one. Many of their new organizations proved short-lived, and the milieu they attempted to construct particularly porous, because culture wars were waging also within German Catholicism itself. Germans collided with the centralizing, standardizing campaigns of the American hierarchy, but German bishops were themselves part of that hierarchy. They had similar interest in bringing their dioceses under tighter control, accommodating religious practices to current Church understandings, and insuring a less public, more "respectable" brand of Catholicism. Thus, German as well as non-German bishops tussled with religious orders to regain diocesan control of prosperous parishes that they had gladly relinquished in leaner years. The German bishops who castigated Americanizers' public school proposals had dioceses filled with tax-supported rural "parish schools," and thus spoke to their own laity as much as to their Americanizing opponents when they demanded true parochial rather than mixed public/parish schools. Like their non-German counterparts they fostered newer forms of private devotionalism, curtailed elaborate processions, promoted pan-ethnic societies like the Knights of Columbus and the Catholic Youth Organization, and encouraged greater public involvement of women.[96] In effect, while defending the walls of a German Catholic milieu from outside attack, they helped sap it from within by weakening the logic of separation from other Catholics.

It is also important, however, to emphasize an even more powerful force undermining the German Catholic milieu even as it was being constructed. As Abbelen himself acknowledged, "gradual amalgamation . . . will come of itself, especially when and where immigration ceases." By the time episcopal *Gleichschaltung* peaked with campaigns to mandate English and mainstream German national parishes during the World War I era, generational transition and social mobility were rapidly altering the geographical base of the German Catholic settlement system itself. Children raised in the rural communities moved to urban parishes, while their urban counterparts moved from old national parishes to territorial parishes in better neighborhoods on the urban fringe, where intermarriage with other Catholics—particularly the Irish—

---

96. See Vincent A. Yzermans, *Frontier Bishop of Saint Cloud* (Waite Park, MN: Park Press, 1988); Joseph H. Lackner, "Bishop Ignatius F. Horstmann, Spokesperson for German-American Catholics?" *U.S. Catholic Historian* 3 (1994): 17–40; Benjamin J. Blied, *Three Archbishops* (Milwaukee: n.p., 1955); James H. Campbell, "New Parochialism: Change and Conflict in the Archdiocese of Cincinnati, 1878–1925," in *Ethnic Diversity and Civic Identity*, 94–130; Shanabruch, *Chicago's Catholics*; Steven M. Avella, "Sebastian G. Messmer and the Americanization of Milwaukee Catholicism," *U.S. Catholic Historian* 12 (1994): 87–107.

increased.[97] The urban second generation was often more comfortable using English than German, and as early as 1886 Milwaukee German Catholic schools were required to teach the catechism in both languages to insure that children understood their faith. Soon the city's parochial schools began teaching half-days in each language, and by the 1920s the language transition was virtually complete.[98] German survived longer in the countryside, but by the 1930s most rural parishes were also well into the language transition.[99] The German-language Catholic press declined rapidly after the turn of the century; only twenty-one of the persisting twenty-seven newspapers survived World War I, and only nine remained by 1937.[100]

Politics and the Public Sphere

The consequences of German Catholicism for American public culture proved more enduring than its institutional shell. German Catholics' distinctive historical voting pattern can be readily interpreted as a negative reaction to strains of nativism and evangelistic moralism within American political culture. But it is better seen, I would argue, as the product of an anti-statist localism grounded in the worldview of the German Catholic communities and shaped by perceptions of an American Kulturkampf aimed as directly at their values as were its European counterparts. Its logic governed both their historic allegiance to the Democratic Party and their Republican re-positioning during the renewed culture wars of the later twentieth century.

German Americans of all confessional stripes have often been accused, by their leaders at the time and by historians since, of political disinterest and ineptitude. What this meant in practice was that, unlike the Irish, they seldom voted as a single bloc and were underrepresented among officeholders. But also unlike the Irish, they were divided by religion, and the German Catholic milieu generated a distinctive political culture of its own, molded by self-interest, homeland example, and ideological conviction. Evangelical Protestantism's crusade to perfect America in its own image pervaded nineteenth-century American politics. Catholics shared the interest of other Germans in defending their voting rights, social habits, class interests, and

---

97. Abramson, *Ethnic Diversity.*

98. Shanabruch, *Chicago's Catholics*; Avella, "Sebastian G. Messmer"; Shaw, "Chicago's Germans and Italians."

99. Avella, "Sebastian G. Messmer"; Yzermans, *Spirit in Central Minnesota.*

100. *Katholisches Deutschthum.*

language. But other problems were uniquely their own, or shared with other Catholics: Protestant bibles in public schools, double taxation for parochial schools, court intervention in trustee controversies, nativist attacks on convents and churches, regulation of processions and religious garb.[101] They interpreted such attacks as an American Kulturkampf—which in many ways it was, waged like its European counterparts in a quest for cultural homogeneity to strengthen a centralizing state.[102] Thus, they found themselves replaying bitter homeland battles with fellow Germans often on the opposing side, and recourse to homeland methods was almost reflexive. The ending of Prussia's Kulturkampf was the lead story in the same issue of the *Luxemburger Gazette* that informed readers of the Haymarket bombing; even the wisdom of forming transatlantic versions of Germany's Catholic political and labor organizations was canvassed in America's German Catholic press.[103]

Above all, however, it was their vision of the social order that fundamentally structured the political engagement of those who lived within the German-American Catholic milieu. In a world where perfection was impossible, using government for social reform made little sense; national government's role was to preserve order. But activist local government, safely under the control of communal values, could insure distributive justice and well-being. Individualistic, profit-maximizing, and interventionist liberalism represented a modernity whose hostility to their values was dramatized not only by Europe's culture wars, but by the literal siege of the Vatican itself. "Catholics are persecuted because the restorative and invigorating spirit of their religion can never unite itself with the debilitating and all-polluting stink of rotten liberalism," wrote the editor of a Minnesota German Catholic journal in 1873.[104] Viewed from such a perspective, when German Catholics deviated from the more liberal politics of other Germans in nineteenth-century America, particularly in their general support for the Democratic Party, this was more than just racial prejudice or negative-reference rejection of anti-clericalism,

---

101. E.g., William A. Baughin, "The Development of Nativism in Cincinnati," *Bulletin*, The Cincinnati Historical Society 22 (Oct. 1964): 240–255.

102. Cf. Rudolf Lill and Francesco Traniello, eds., *Der Kulturkampf in Italien und in den deutschsprachigen Ländern* (Berlin: Duncker & Humblot, 1993); Ward M. McAfee, *Religion, Race, and Reconstruction: The Public School in the Politics of the 1870s* (Albany: State University of New York Press, 1998).

103. *LG*, 18 May 1886; *Der Wanderer*.

104. *Der Wanderer*, 22 March 1873.

nativism, and temperance.[105] It represented a self-conscious choice to use the localism and ethnic tolerance of the Democratic Party to defend their own "peculiar institution" from the pressures of a centralizing culture and state.

German Catholics learned early the practices of democratic self-governance in America. Many lacked experience with formal electoral politics in Germany, but most were familiar with the effective self-governance of peasant communities and formed part of the Catholic public that was mobilized in Germany from the 1830s onward.[106] Practical self-governance was part of the attraction of rural settlement in America, and soon Catholics like other Germans were managing township and even county governments in accord with their values.[107] There was less opportunity for such direct control in the cities, but the competitiveness of American politics insured that German Catholic voters were drawn into local party systems, and as Schaack's Chicago organization suggests, they played roles in machine politics that have yet to be adequately explored.[108] They could also rally effectively beyond the local community when necessary, finding allies wherever they could—other Catholics, other Germans as in 1889 Illinois and Wisconsin campaigns to

---

105. Joel H. Silbey, *The American Political Nation, 1838–1893* (Stanford, CA: Stanford University Press, 1991); Paul Kleppner, *The Cross of Culture: A Social Analysis of Midwestern Politics, 1850–1900* (New York: Free Press, 1970); Paul Kleppner, *The Third Electoral System, 1853–1892* (Chapel Hill: University of North Carolina Press, 1979); Richard J. Jensen, *The Winning of the Midwest: Social and Political Conflict, 1888–1896* (Chicago: University of Chicago Press, 1971). See also Robert P. Swierenga, "Ethnoreligious Political Behavior."

106. Sperber, *Rhineland Radicals*; Sperber, *Popular Catholicism*; Hürten, *Geschichte des deutschen Katholizismus*; Margaret Lavinia Anderson, "Voter, Junker, *Landrat*, Priest: The Old Authorities and the New Franchise in Imperial Germany," *American Historical Review* 98 (1993): 1448–1474; R. E. Sackett, "The Local Politics of the Prussian State: Nation-Building in Kempen of the Rhine Province, 1833–48," *Central European History* 21 (1988): 31–55; Utz Jeggle, "The Rules of the Village: On the Cultural History of the Peasant World in the Last 150 Years," in *The German Peasantry: Conflict and Community in Rural Society from the Eighteenth to the Twentieth Centuries*, edited by Richard J. Evans and W. R. Lee (New York: St. Martin's Press, 1986), 265–289; Heide Wunder, *Die bäuerliche Gemeinde in Deutschland* (Göttingen: Vandenhoeck & Ruprecht, 1986); Peter Blickle, ed., *Landgemeinde und Stadtgemeinde in Mitteleuropa: Ein struktureller Vergleich* (München: R. Oldenbourg Verlag, 1991).

107. For rural German Catholic self-governance see Kathleen Conzen, *German-Americans and Ethnic Political Culture: Stearns County, Minnesota, 1855–1915* (Berlin: John-F.-Kennedy-Institut für Nordamerikastudien, Working Paper 16/1989).

108. For the antebellum period the best urban case study is Gerber, *Making of an American Pluralism*; see also Conzen, *Immigrant Milwaukee*.

defend German-language instruction in the schools, even freethinking liberals during Cincinnati's 1869 Bible War.[109]

The values and needs of milieu Catholicism shaped public behavior even when Catholic issues were not directly at stake. Their concern was not only to act in accord with Catholic principles, but to protect the structure and independence of the community that embodied them. Thus, woman suffrage was opposed as a threat to women's place in the religious and social order. Support for agrarian reform always involved balancing the potential of a given program to enhance farm income—and the stability of the rural community—against the invasive state action that it might entail. The risk in labor union membership lay not only in unions' sometimes secret structure and socialist associations, but also in the coercive restrictions on individual and communal freedom they could demand. Thus, German Catholics tended to find what Richard Schneirov has described as the producers' republicanism of many native-born workers more congenial than the statist orientation of more radical immigrants, and probably helped buttress the practical shop-floor orientation of the American labor movement.[110] Lacking the numbers for the homeland solution of separate Catholic farmers' and workers' organizations, they followed the same policy principle as in the school wars, seeking nonsectarian bread-and-butter unions to match the nonsectarian public schools that their challenge to Protestant domination helped to create.

They applied the same principle in their broader roles as citizens. Lacking the power to shape a national state that would act according to their principles, they sought a state that would act as little as possible. Like other immigrants, they were early attracted to the Democratic Party for its anti-elitist rhetoric, but its tolerance for local difference helped cement their allegiance. It was not just that the presence of immigrants within the Democratic Party encouraged it to resist nativism and temperance legislation; German Catholics found their needs met by its stress on personal liberty grounded in communal self-

---

109. Roger Wyman, "Wisconsin Ethnic Groups and the Election of 1890," *Wisconsin Magazine of History* 51 (1968): 269–293; F. Michael Perko, *A Time to Favor Zion: The Ecology of Religion and School Development on the Urban Frontier, Cincinnati, 1830–1870* (Chicago: Educational Studies Press, 1988); McAfee, *Religion, Race, and Reconstruction.*

110. For this contrast (without attention to its religious dimension) see Richard Schneirov, "Political Cultures and the Role of the State in Labor's Republic: The View from Chicago, 1848–1877," *Labor History* 32 (1991): 376–400.There is little scholarship on German Catholics in the American labor movement. The turn of the century saw a proliferation of parish and city-wide Catholic workingmen's societies, as well as a revitalization of the Kolping movement; *Katholisches Deutschthum*, 156–161; Shaw, "Chicago's Germans and Italians."

governance and minimal central regulation or support.[111] A Milwaukee German Democratic paper summarized the party's appeal for German Catholics when it noted in 1860 that it represented "the principle of the right of communities . . . to regulate their internal affairs according to their own standards."[112] The dangers of centralization were underscored for German Catholics during the Civil War, when taxation threatened farms and businesses, and provost marshals in search of draft dodgers invaded their homes; only in Michael Schaack's Port Washington, Wisconsin, did large-scale rioting occur, but their reputation as unenthusiastic war supporters was well-deserved.[113] In 1868 a St. Paul German Catholic newspaper insisted that the central issues remained "too much government, arbitrary exercise of power, political corruption."[114] Not until the decades following World War II did they gradually move out of the Democratic fold. As American party positions changed, German Catholics' persistent anti-statism (and the isolationism related to it) helps explain the new attractiveness of the Republican Party, but so, too, does a heritage of public moral concern that by the later twentieth century found a more receptive home under the Republican wing. Their tradition never discountenanced governmental activism when they could control its terms. Thus, as Philip Gleason has shown, increasingly self-confident Central-Verein members, inspired in part by the example of Catholic Germany, mounted a Progressive-Era campaign to reform America in their own image of organic Christian corporatism, focusing on everything from settlement houses, labor unions, and agricultural cooperatives to birth control and abortion.[115]

---

111. On the Democratic Party see Jean H. Baker, *Affairs of Party: The Political Culture of Northern Democrats in the Mid-Nineteenth Century* (Ithaca: Cornell University Press, 1983); Joel H. Silbey, *A Respectable Minority: The Democratic Party in the Civil War Era, 1860–1868* (New York: Norton, 1977); Thomas E. Rodgers, "Liberty, Will, and Violence: The Political Ideology of the Democrats of West-Central Indiana during the Civil War," *Indiana Magazine of History* 92 (1996): 133–159; Peter B. Kovler, ed., *Democrats and the American Idea: A Bicentennial Appraisal* (Washington, DC, Center for National Policy Press, 1992); Paul Bourke and Donald DeBats, *Washington County: Politics and Community in Antebellum America* (Baltimore: The Johns Hopkins University Press, 1995).

112. *Tägliches Banner und Volksfreund* [Milwaukee], 27 June 1860.

113. Krier, *Tapestry of Luxembourgers*; Frank L. Klement, "Catholics as Copperheads during the Civil War," *Catholic Historical Review* 80 (1994): 36–57; Benjamin J. Blied, *Catholics and the Civil War* (Milwaukee: n.p., 1955); Kenneth H. Wheeler, "Local Autonomy and Civil War Draft Resistance: Holmes County, Ohio," *Civil War History* 45 (1999): 147–159.

114. *Der Wanderer*, 12 September, 3 October, 31 October 1868.

115. Gleason, *Conservative Reformers*; *Katholisches Deutschthum*.

The enclosed milieu of the German Catholic parishes dissipated, but much of its heritage lived on in the self-confident Catholic ghetto of the twentieth century.[116] Surveys as late as the 1960s found persons of German descent among Catholicism's staunchest supporters of parochial schools, church attendance, marriage and family doctrine, and anti-Communism.[117] The organic conception of society so deeply embedded in the German Catholic tradition helped Europe's Liturgical Movement put down some of its earliest American roots in the Benedictine abbeys and parishes of the German Catholic heartland, just as it lent support to New Deal and subsequent reform measures promising to enhance the security of family and community.[118] Among rural Germans it long supported high birth rates and an exceptional commitment to farming, giving much of today's Midwestern countryside a decidedly Catholic character and preserving, in the rural parishes, significant elements of the older German Catholic culture.[119] Its diasporic allegiances influenced voting on foreign-policy issues, its opposition to (and violation of) Prohibition was notorious, its support for right-to-life initiatives unwavering.[120] Its anti-statist, anti-liberal, familial traditionalism echoes today within the conservative Catholicism of the religious right, as unmistakably as its insistence on distributive justice finds a home in the Catholic left.[121]

Given the current state of scholarship, the interpretation that I have sketched here is necessarily a preliminary one. The influence of Catholicism on emigration and settlement, the diasporic interaction between Catholics in Germany and America, processes of cultural change and social mobility within the German-American Catholic world, relations with non-Catholic German Americans—all of these require much more research, particularly within the context of our growing understanding of Catholicism in German-

116. William Halsey, *The Survival of American Innocence* (Notre Dame, IN: University of Notre Dame Press, 1980).

117. Abramson, *Ethnic Diversity*; Andrew M. Greeley, *The American Catholic: A Social Portrait* (New York: Basic Book, 1977); Lubell, *Future of American Politics*.

118. Paul Marx, *Virgil Michel and the Liturgical Movement* (Collegeville, MN: Liturgical Press, 1957); Kenneth J. Heineman, *A Catholic New Deal: Religion and Reform in Depression Pittsburgh* (University Park, PA: The Pennsylvania State University Press, 1999).

119. Conzen, *Making Their Own America*.

120. Lubell, *Future of American Politics*; Phillips, *Emerging Republican Majority*.

121. Cf. Halsey, *Survival of American Innocence*; O'Brien, *Public Catholicism*; Mary Jo Weaver and R. Scott Appleby, *Being Right: Conservative Catholics in America* (Bloomington: Indiana University Press, 1995); Patrick Allitt, *Catholic Intellectuals and Conservative Politics in America, 1950–1985* (Ithaca: Cornell University Press, 1993).

speaking Europe. We have good data on how German Catholics voted, but few efforts to explain why, in terms of either public discourse or local community dynamics. We need to breach the wall of separation between church and other historiographies to understand interrelationships between developments within Catholicism and the public behavior of Catholics, and subject church members, leaders, and agendas to the same social and cultural analysis that has been applied to other American groups. We know far too little about German Catholic women, with their exceptional fecundity, their reputed hostility to woman suffrage, and their critical role in supporting the institutional array of the German Catholic milieu and thus also the charitable structure of urban America. Distinctive German Catholic experiences during the Civil War, World War I, and Prohibition remain a virtual terra incognita. How the German Catholic milieu—and its dissolution—influenced the American labor movement, agrarian reform, twentieth-century electoral shifts, and the cultural politics of the right: These too are central topics that need their historian.

But even without them, it is important to recognize the logic in the role played by German Catholics like Michael Schaack and his supporters within American public life. It was a logic rooted, I have suggested, not merely in ideology or obedience to Church authorities, but in the structure of their settlement system and in the deeply felt patterns of belief it embodied. Exploring that logic offers insight into the complex links of migration to subcultural formation within the modernizing transatlantic world. It underscores the importance of institutional as well as individual immigration, and emphasizes the diasporic character of America's immigrant subcultures, responsive to both homeland and receiving country currents. It clarifies the range of consequences of German immigration for American society, and illuminates a significant strain within the public behavior of members of America's single largest religious denomination. And in the process, I hope, it makes its case for the necessity of confronting rather than bracketing the role of religious belief in a truly comparative German-American history.

Part II:

Agricultural Patterns, Rural Society, and Ethnic Identity

5

Prescriptions and Perceptions of Labor and Family among Ethnic Group in the Nineteenth-Century American Middle West

Jon Gjerde

Critics for millennia have based observed differences on value judgments, and vice versa. Aristotle, for example, placed "the Hellenic race" midway between Europeans, who were "full of spirit, but wanting in intelligence and skill," and Asians, who were "intelligent and inventive, but wanting in spirit." Whereas Europeans retained comparative freedom but were incapable of ruling over others, and Asians were intelligent but always in a state of subjection and slavery, the Hellenic race was intermediate in character, encompassing both high-spiritedness and intelligence.[1] Characterizations such as these have if anything become more pointed in recent centuries as constructions of race have been linked to behavior and aptitude. Enlightenment thought, which categorized the lineal development of humanity into stages from hunting to commerce and classified its practitioners as "savages" and the "civilized," profoundly influenced the thinking of people with regard to varying cultural groups in the late eighteenth and early nineteenth centuries. By the late nineteenth century, the thought of Lamarck was used to justify arguments that cultural characteristics were inherited, and that racial differences could be accounted for in a sequence of sociocultural stages.[2] Science in the modern era became the handmaiden of racist thought.

Significantly, the structure of labor within the family and, more specifically, the work obligations among women, were often linked to these

---

1. Aristotle, *The Politics of Aristotle*, trans. Benjamin Jowett (Oxford: Clarendon Press, 1885), 96, 218, 248.

2. See, for example, Ronald T. Takaki, *Iron Cages: Race and Culture in 19th-Century America* (New York: Alfred A. Knopf, 1979); Reginald Horsman, *Race and Manifest Destiny: The Origins of American Racial Anglo-Saxonism* (Cambridge: Harvard University Press, 1981); and Daniel K. Richter, "'Believing That Many of the Red People Suffer Much for the Want of Food': Hunting, Agriculture, and a Quaker Construction of Indianness in the Early Republic," *Journal of the Early Republic* 19 (Winter 1999), 601–628.

notions of "progress," "enlightenment," and "intelligence." Writing about Native Americans, for example, Thomas Jefferson—profoundly influenced by Enlightenment categories—observed in 1781 that Indian women "are submitted to unjust drudgery" which was "the case with every barbarous people." He concluded that "it is civilization alone which replaces the women in the enjoyment of their equality."[3] A century and a half later, E. A. Ross, who for his part was swayed by Lamarckian thought, linked the benefits of work to higher fertility among the "lesser" European races. "William does not leave as many children as 'Tonio," he observed, "because he will not huddle his family into one room, eat macaroni off a bare board, work his wife barefoot in the field, and keep his children weeding onions instead of at school."[4]

Whereas such perceived differences and the value judgments attached to them have spanned centuries, it is noteworthy that they were surprisingly common in the rural Midwest, a region remarkably segmented by European ethnic groups, and a place where family labor was still common. Horace Miner, for example, who conducted anthropological fieldwork in Hardin County, Iowa, on the eve of World War II, perceived distinctly demarcated variations in household behavior among the different ethnocultural groups nestled in their rural neighborhoods. It was true, he wrote, that "the descendants of German immigrants [had] taken over the Yankee speech, dress, houses, manners of farming, and many of the values." Yet differences in relationships within the family had endured. After nearly a century of settlement in the county, the German neighborhoods remained "fully indoctrinated" to what Miner called a "dogmatic Lutheran and Evangelical tradition," which in turn spawned a corporate family organization that had become foreign to their Yankee neighbors.[5]

The foremost difference in Miner's eyes was a patriarchal tradition based on the German Americans' religiocultural systems of belief that was expressed in relationships between husband and wife and father and child. "The Germans," Miner observed, writing of them as a group with common practices, "believe

---

3.   *State of Virginia*, 60, cited in John Mack Faragher, *Sugar Creek: Life on the Illinois Prairie* (New Haven: Yale University Press, 1986), 114.

4.   Edward Alsworth Ross, *The Old World in the New: The Significance of Past and Present Immigration to the American People* (New York: Century Co., 1914), 303.

5.   Horace Miner, *Culture and Agriculture: An Anthropological Study of a Corn Belt County* (Ann Arbor: University of Michigan Press, 1949), 43. A fuller analysis of the varying family and community patterns among ethnocultural groups in the Middle West is Jon Gjerde, *The Minds of the West: Ethnocultural Evolution of the Rural Middle West, 1830–1917* (Chapel Hill: University of North Carolina Press, 1997), 159–221, 251–281, on which much of the following is based.

more in the subservience of the child and wife to the father, as the manager of the family farm." This behavior was considered "'bad' by the Yankees," Miner concluded, "as cultural differences usually are." The German father, in the Yankee critique, was no more than a "Tartar, working his family to the bone," whereas the American parent, in less corporate fashion, remunerated "his children and [gave] them independence of action." Yet independence, Yankee youth duly noted, could be costly. Subservience within the household, it seemed, was connected to accumulations of property "which are given the sons when they reach maturity." An arrangement within German households coupled the labor of children with land entitlements when they reached adulthood. Like grasshoppers observing ants, the Yankee youth "resent[ed] the German boy being given a farm."[6]

Miner's remarks are noteworthy as a twentieth-century example of a pervasive and protracted series of observations of competing, ethnoculturally defined family traditions that tied together patterns of household labor, affection and authority, and property.[7] A century earlier, Michel Chevalier perceived a similar pattern even if he focused less on parent-child relationships and more on the labor of women. "It is now a universal rule among the Anglo-Americans," he wrote, "that the woman is exempt from all heavy work, and she is never seen, for instance, taking part in the labours of the field, nor in carrying burdens." As a result, Anglo-American women have "also escaped that hideous ugliness and repulsive coarseness of complexion which toil and privation every where else bring upon them." Others, however, were not as fortunate. French-Canadian and Pennsylvania German women continued to toil in the fields "at least as much as the men" and as a result remained "wretched objects, who are feminine only with the physiologist." "It is the glory of the *English* race," Chevalier concluded, "that they have every where, as much as possible, interpreted the superiority of the man to the woman, as reserving to the former the charge of the ruder and harder forms of toil. A country in which

---

6. Ibid.

7. Oscar Lewis, for example, would write that in a rural Texan community "the Czech and German families are organized along patriarchal lines, with the wife in a subordinate position in the family and taking little or no part in affairs outside of the home. Czech women are not community leaders. . . ." Oscar Lewis, *On the Edge of the Black Waxy: A Cultural Survey of Bell County, Texas* (St. Louis: Washington University Studies, 1948), 100. And Miner's observations in this vein certainly were not the last. See Sonya Salamon, *Prairie Patrimony: Family, Farming, and Community in the Midwest* (Chapel Hill: University of North Carolina Press, 1992).

woman is treated according to this principle presents the aspect of a new and better world."[8]

Although women were objectified in both of his renderings, Chevalier nonetheless celebrated the advances of Anglo Americans in labor differentiation that he contended was part of a systematic shift in the distribution of power in the household—precisely the contrasts that Miner would comment on a century later. In "the earlier times," Chevalier argued, "everything was swallowed up in the father." As time passed, "the individuality—the rights, privileges, and duties—of the wife and children was the successive growth of ages." The United States was the locus of immense progress, an advance fueled by the religious and political systems under which the Yankee household existed. It was "under the influence of Protestantism and republicanism," Chevalier stressed, that "social progress had been effected by the medium of the spirit of individuality" since "protestantism, republicanism, and individuality are all one." Unlike the corporate German households that Miner would observe in 1940, "a farm," Chevalier argued during Jacksonian America, "is an inviolable republic in the state; each individual is a republic by himself in the family."[9] Indeed, the American farmer spared his wife "all the hard work and employments unsuitable to the sex," according to Chevalier, in large part because he was "initiated" to "the series of that succession of progressive movements which have characterized our civilization ever since it quitted its cradle in the East."[10] For Chevalier, the corporate family morality that undergirded the household mode of production was already breaking down among Americans in the Jacksonian era.

Although these characterizations were commonplace, they were contested by another narrative that disputed not so much the details of work as the moral principles that lay beneath them. Expressions of this viewpoint, constructed principally by immigrants, also have a long and varied history. Gottlieb Mittelberger, writing around the same time as Jefferson, observed that an Englishman "must not think of marrying a women if he is not able to support her without her having to work," because "woman must not be asked to do any

---

8. Michel Chevalier, *Society, Manners and Politics in the United States: Being a Series of Letters on North America* (Boston: Weeks, Jordan and Co., 1839), 342–343. My emphasis. That Chevalier understood labor differences as being at least in part related to ethnic differences is underscored in his observation that the variations could be traced to Europe. "In England," he wrote in a footnote, "a woman is never seen, as with us [in France], bearing a hamper of dung on her back, or labouring at the forge." Chevalier, *Society, Manners and Politics*, 342 n.

9. Chevalier, *Society, Manners and Politics*, 368–369.

10. Chevalier, *Society, Manners and Politics*, 430, 428.

work except such as they will do of their own free will."[11] A century and one half later, a Mexican corrido composed just a decade after Ross wrote observed that "today's young women / Do not think about housework / Who remembers the metate / Washing dishes and ironing / That would be unthinkable / All they want is to have fun. / That is why Our Lord / Has seen fit to punish us; / It's all the women's fault, / Because they've shortened their dresses."[12] Immigrants seemingly continued to hew to a tradition that rued the ill-effects of "progress" as commerce created a society dangerously reliant on luxury and sloth.

In focusing on the Midwest—the site of the observations of Chevalier and Miner—this article considers the conversation between ethnic groups, regarding their patterns of labor and life and the meaning they drew from it. I argue that the conversation reveals much about underlying conceptualizations of the family, its function, and its structure. It illustrates how American-born individuals used the trope of the European family to depict what Chevalier called the "advance" of individuality and distributions of power in a society that was part of a "series of that succession of progressive movements which have characterized our civilization." By utilizing the variations in labor roles, proponents of this ideology could deprecate "lesser" ethnic groups that lagged behind in the march of civilization. In contrast, Europeans used the labor patterns of Americans to warn against the dangers of life in the United States, to show the need for remaining true to invented patterns of labor among countrypeople, and ultimately to defend their group against diffusion from the outside.

Varying Patterns of Labor in the Rural Midwest

Observers had for decades remarked on the varieties of labor patterns in rural regions of British North America and the later United States. A major distinction between Canadian, German, and English women, as suggested by Chevalier, was whether or not women labored in the fields. Importantly, the custom of female field labor among immigrants endured. A German-

---

11.   Gottlieb Mittelberger, *Gottlieb Mittelbergers Reise nach Pennsylvanien im Jahr 1750, trans. Carl Theo. Eben, Gottlieb Mittelberger's Journey to Pennsylvania in the year 1750 and Return to Germany in the Year 1754: Containing Not Only a Description of the Country According to Its Present Condition, but Also a Detailed Account of the Sad and Unfortunate Circumstances of Most of the Germans That Have Emigrated, or Are Emigrating to That Country* (Philadelphia: J. J. McVey, 1898), 74.

12.   Maria Herrera-Sobek, *Northward Bound: The Mexican Immigrant Experience in Ballad and Song* (Bloomington: Indiana University Press, 1993), 283.

American community, according to a resident there in 1892, could "hardly be considered progressive in adopting new methods or appliances in farming. Father[,] mother[,] sister & brother all turn out & put in their entire time to the cultivation of their farms, in most all cases in the good old fashioned way."[13] Wives in some European enclaves toiled regularly in the field well into the twentieth century. Oscar Lewis, for example, noted the "important differences" in divisions of labor and the position of women in the European American settlements and "old-line Americans" in rural Texas. Whereas Czech and German women and children customarily worked in the fields, it was considered "degrading" for white American women to do this work.[14] And it was the conservative presence of women in the harvest fields, explained a female consultant, that reduced the incidence of "corn-pickers hands"—hands injured from corn-picking machinery—in a post-World War II Bohemian community.[15]

Other observers noted how European households explicitly utilized female workers to reduce labor costs and thereby to increase the income of the farm operation. Young wives typically worked with their husbands in the field. In one case, according to Herbert Quick, a female domestic was hired to take care of the young children while the wife "kept on doing a man's work." The calculations of cost and benefit were explicit. If the mother had taken on exclusively domestic duties, "they'd have had to hire a man, and hired girls were cheaper than hired men." As the family aged and the "children were big enough, they took their mother's place in the field and she took the hired girl's

---

13. August Kickbusch, 1892, Wausau, Marathon County, Wisconsin. Kate Everest fieldnotes. Kate Everest papers. WHS Arch. Other sources argued that use of implements increased even if labor responsibilities did not. The Milwaukee *Seebote* in 1876 noted that German workers in the field—"the farmer . . . with wife and child"—used the new labor-saving implements. Milwaukee *Seebote*, cited in *Dubuque National Demokrat*, 20 July 1876, 3.

14. Oscar Lewis did note that there was a difference between theory and practice since American women did work in the field on occasion although they did not like to admit to it. Lewis, *Black Waxy*, 24–25.

15. Edward Kibbe and Thomas McGorkle, "Culture and Medical Behavior in a Bohemian Speech Community in Iowa," (Unpublished paper, University of Iowa, 1957), 1–28. Peter A. Munch papers, Norwegian American Historical Association archives. Kibbe and McGorkle noted as well that after delivering babies, women did not postpone going back to work, including to labor in the fields. Few sources with European female voices are available to comment on their labor obligations. Interviews of first-generation Mennonite women reveal that they had not been forced to work in the field, but had wanted to help the farm operation. See Emerick K. Francis, *In Search of Utopia: The Mennonites in Manitoba* (Glencoe, IL: Free Press, 1955), 77.

place in the house."[16] Such a life course for married women was fraught with arduous labor. A fictional German farmer, whose mother and sister had worked with the men, saw nothing wrong with his wife so employed. "He expected it of his 'woman,'" wrote Ruth Suckow. And so the wife settled quickly into a life of work and rapidly "'lost her giggles,' as the family said."[17]

The Critique of Immigrant Patterns of Labor

If labor patterns differed across the ethnocultural boundaries, these very differences were utilized by observers as part of a larger narrative about ethnic difference. Critics of ethnic America tended to condemn the work regime of women and children that betokened arduous conditions for the weakest in the household. These critics were inclined to link such circumstances, moreover, with the apparent absence of affection between husband and wife. In sum, the narrative of immigrant labor was one that posited the inequalities inherent in a "backward" household apparently devoid of love and tenderness. By implication, it celebrated the American alternative as an environment that offered greater equality, compassion, and freedom for its members.

Herbert Quick, who grew up near German enclaves in his Iowa farm home, was attentive to the different proprieties of arduous fieldwork that women of different ethnocultural groups performed. The German housewife worked in the fields with her husband. "Nobody thought less of her for this field work," Quick observed, "that is, nobody in her circle of friends." Yet Quick connected labor differences to ethnic background and subtextually to "progress." "Among us Yankees," he continued, "the German habit of working women in the fields was the sure mark of the 'Old Countryman'. We didn't even allow our women to milk the cows." In yet another instance where "progress," race and ethnicity, and women's work were interconnected, Quick remembered "Old Ebenezer McAllister" who "used to say that among the Injuns the women did all the work, among the Hoosiers it was equally divided, and among the Yankees the men did it all."[18]

---

16. Herbert Quick, *The Fairview Idea: A Story of the New Rural Life* (Indianapolis: Bobbs-Merrill, 1919), 6. Another less conventional form of labor exchange was reported in 1878. An Anglo-American hunter missed a prairie chicken, but hit a "good natured German woman who was toiling in a harvest field." Refusing to accept apologies, "the practical farmer and his shot-bespattered wife" set him to work in the field "in place of the disabled female, who retired to her rural castle . . . to pick the shot out of her." *St. Paul Pioneer Press*, 23 August 1878, 6.

17. Ruth Suckow, *Country People* (New York: Alfred A. Knopf, 1924), 56–58.

18. Quick, *The Fairview Idea*, 6.

That Yankee men "did it all" was a reinforcement of a domesticity that simultaneously freed and trapped American women. Emily Hawley Gillespie, for her part as an American woman, despised the farm work that she felt was beneath her. After visiting her sister's home in 1883, Gillespie resented the farm work that her sister performed. "She looks more like a beggar than any thing else," Gillespie observed in her diary. "a perfect Slave to mans will & hard-work. indeed I am sorry. I do think woman ought to retain enough of their pride to keep themselves in a shape proper to their sex. no woman need to get so low as to do such filthy work." "I should despair," she concluded, "if my children, when I am gone, should remember me less than nobody in society."[19] Clearly, when adult women rejected fieldwork, added expenses to the farm operation were incurred. Especially during harvests, the employment of European women and children decreased the labor costs that had to be paid if, as Quick put it, one functioned "by the Yankee way."[20] On occasion, Americans objected to a sort of unfair competition made possible by what they considered immoral labor demands. Manitoban Anglo-Canadians went so far as to take their concerns to the Canadian House of Commons in 1878 and force the Deputy Minister of Agriculture to promise that their Mennonite neighbors would "conform to the superior moral standards of Canadian society."[21]

It might be argued that the labors of European immigrant women and children in the fields was a reflection of poverty, of the need to exploit all available labor within the household. That, at least, was the contention of a Midwestern foreign correspondent who observed in 1884 the toil of women who remained in Europe. In Bavaria and Switzerland, women who worked barefoot did half of the field work. Theirs was a life of "brutal work" where they had become "beasts of burden," the only liberty that they enjoyed was the "liberty to work." "How I should like to have these poor over-worked women see an American farmer's wife in her sweet home," the journalist concluded, "beautifully carpeted, surrounded with books and papers and eating meat and cake and pies three times a day!"[22]

---

19. Emily Hawley Gillespie diary, 15 August 1883, ISHD Arch. See also Judy Nolte Lensink, *A Secret to Be Burried: The Diary and Life of Emily Hawley Gillespie, 1858–1888* (Iowa City: University of Iowa Press, 1989), 270.

20. Herbert Quick, *One Man's Life: An Autobiography* (Indianapolis, Bobbs-Merrill, 1925), 196. Lewis noted that the failure to rely on the field labor of women and children caused Americans to hire more nonfamily labor. As a result, they took "a chance between high costs and high farm prices." Lewis, *Black Waxy*, 103.

21. Francis, *In Search of Utopia*, 77.

22. *Minneapolis Tribune*, cited in *Dubuque Daily Times*, 18 September 1884, 7.

Many American critics contended that wealth mattered little in what they often saw as an exploitation of female labor, which made the burdens imposed on European women in the United States all the more contemptible. Quick made a pointed comparison between the care of the cattle and the care of the wife in a German household. The husband "had built a concrete drinking tank for the cattle; all they had to do was to come and drink what they wanted." But "the woman who was his partner in life" was provided only "an iron pump handle and a gravel path" over which she carried buckets of water from the well to her kitchen. He had "money enough to build the finest farmhouse in the county," but he was too busy farming.[23] Unlike these Germans, the narrator observed, "When I married my wife I told her that if the time should come when we couldn't make a living without her working in the field we'd starve together. . . . I believe in division of labor on the farm, and I'm just mossback enough to think that women's work is round the house."[24]

The Creamery Man, in Hamlin Garland's short story of the same title, made similar observations. The "Dutchmen," which refers to German Americans, had fine houses and even bigger barns, but "their women were mostly homely and went around barefooted and barelegged, with ugly blue dresses hanging frayed and greasy round their land ribs and big joints." Their houses looked like a stable and "their women work so much in the field they don't have any time to fix up." "I don't believe in women workin' in the fields," the Creamery Man concluded. "My wife needn't set her foot outdoors 'less she's a mind to."[25]

Yet another example of male patronization, this criticism of patterns of immigrant women's farm work was fused with deprecations of an exploitation born out of the absence of love, if not of contempt, for the wife by the European male. Yankees were astounded by the lack of affection that seemed to characterize European patterns of courtship. In one case, an arranged marriage went awry when the wrong woman was sent from Germany to be

---

23. Quick, *The Fairview Idea*, 11–12.

24. Quick, *The Fairview Idea*, 7. The separate spheres of labor on the farm, some Americans admitted, were not without their problems. Quick's narrative continued: "My wife picked up that last sheet and read it. 'Much you know about it,' says she. 'Many a day when I've been nearly crazy with loneliness and monotony of housework it would have been a real kindness to me if I could have gone out and raked hay or driven the binder—out where the men were. That's what women want and need—to work with men.'"

25. Hamlin Garland, "The Creamery Man," in *Main-Travelled Roads, Being Six Stories of the Mississippi Valley* (Chicago: Stone and Kimball, 1894), 157–158. Quick, too, linked women's field labor to the condition of the home. A German woman, he wrote, "said she'd rather do that than the housework, and, considering the home, I really can't blame her." Quick, *The Fairview Idea*, 6.

married in her new Iowa home. That the prospective husband married the woman anyway challenged the "sentiment of love" that the Americans claimed to exist. The "acceptance of the substitute mate," Quick recalled, "and its failure to be regarded as anything but a good joke on [the husband] by his fellow-countrymen among us, had a tendency to set him and them off from us as a different order of beings."[26]

This purported lack of affection seemingly continued after marriage. One incident that was particularly unsettling encapsulates American condemnations of European patterns and warrants an extended quotation. When the family went into the field to labor, Quick remembered,

> Sometimes there would be a rattlesnake in a sheaf. One of our neighbors, a German settler fresh from the old country, took his wife into the harvest field to help with the binding. She took her baby along and parked it under a shock in the shade. One day the man came to the house of a neighbor just as they were sitting down to dinner. They invited him to join them and he accepted. After eating heartily, he confided to them that his wife was sick.

> "She vas vorkin' in te fielt," said he, "an' a snake stung her in de handt. Pretty soon she couldn't vork no more, ant so she vent to de house to git dinner; but ven I vent to dinner she didn't haf any got. I was hungry too."

That the wife died later that night only exacerbated the "shocked contempt" that the Americans felt. "A man who could stick to his work after his wife had been snakebit," concluded Quick, "send her to the house to get dinner after the virus in her veins had begun its deadly work, and then calmly sit down and eat a meal before mentioning it to a neighbor, stamped the entire class of immigrants in our rather narrow minds as being of a low order of intelligence."[27] Certainly, more work was done at a lower cost in these situations, but the absence of conjugal love created a household arrangement that, according to Quick's wife, "was a factory, not a family."[28] A "family" in Quick's world was one of separate spheres where husband and wife engaged in distinct but complementary undertakings.

---

26. Quick, *One Man's Life*, 118–119.

27. Quick, *One Man's Life*, 196–197.

28. Quick, *The Fairview Idea*, 7.

This narrative of labor practices was so pervasive that it also appeared in private diaries. Mary Woodward, a young American living in Dakota in the 1880s, deprecated in her diary the behavior of a German farm family that lived near her. A victimized son suffered many vicissitudes at the hands of his inflexible father. She wrote that he at last

> ran away from home, thinking he had gotten too big to be whipped— he was six feet tall. He went off, out of the vicinity for awhile, and then returned to work at Green's, three miles from home, where he has been all the fall, plowing. His family have not found him yet. He works in sight of home, and can see his sister plowing, and she can see him, but she doesn't dream who he is.

As a co-conspirator in the breakdown of what she considered a dour, brutal household, Woodward concluded: "I think that's fun."[29]

Characteristic of American comments on immigrant work patterns, Woodward's diary was also peppered with references to the labor of daughters. When writing of the German boy who ran away, Woodward also penned her observations about the labor of daughters on this well-to-do, yet parsimonious, household. "Elsie is plowing for her father, a stingy old German who makes women work out of doors," she wrote. "He thinks an hour long enough for them to prepare a meal, and affords them only the necessities of life, though he owns a half section [320 acres] of land with live stock and machinery."[30] In a notation some years later, Woodward remained disturbed about the work responsibilities imposed on immigrant daughters while she simultaneously admired their forbearance. "Such young, slender German girls," she wrote in 1888, "how they can work like men is beyond my comprehension. They drive four-horse teams standing up like any teamster."[31]

The memoir of Mary Schaal Johns, a German-American orphan who labored in a German household, later mused on differing prescriptions for work in the nineteenth-century Midwest. The conditions on the German farm were formidable. "In the summer," she wrote, "I went out and yoked the oxen. . . . Then while [her employer] plowed, I followed all day and whipped the oxen.

---

29. Mary Woodward diary, 25 October 1885, cited in Elizabeth Hampsten, *Read This Only to Yourself: The Private Writings of Midwestern Women, 1880–1910* (Bloomington: Indiana University Press, 1982), 229.

30. Ibid.

31. Mary Woodward diary, 16 February 1888.

I was too little to reach the off ox with my snake whip, so to strike him, I had to run around the plow. I was bare headed, bare-footed, and clad in only a little smock which I was sadly outgrowing."[32] After two years, a neighbor advised her to leave her employer. "'Mary, you leave [him],'" he recommended, "'You must get with some American family where you will learn English and American ways. . . . You can learn nothing following the plow!'"[33] When an opportune time came, she fled and ultimately entered the different world of "English and American ways." Flight to English and American ways—the very conflation of nation and language group is informative—was seen as an escape from a non-English-speaking environment insulated from the dominant and "progressive" mores of the host community. In its isolated state, the European family was portrayed as an environment that was characterized by inequality and occasional brutality. The connection of these circumstances to rural poverty was often negated when spokespersons argued that it was not so much privation as cruelty that characterized this patriarchal household.

The European Immigrant Response

Many European men and some European women saw the absence of grown women in the fields as a sign not of enlightenment, but of degeneracy. They argued that field labor—and productive labor in general—did not reflect a lack of compassion but rather portrayed labor as a means of maintaining discipline and structure within the home. Work performed by children, like the labors of wives, was prized within the household. A daughter skilled in dropping corn during planting, for example, was a source of family pride.[34] As a result, these commentators condemned the American home as a place of indolence and excess. A correspondent to *Die Iowa*, for example, who traveled throughout the Midwest, described his delight when he finally reached a German settlement

---

32. Mary Schaal Johns, "Home Mission Sermon and Schaal Family Reminiscence," unpublished manuscript, WHS Arch.

33. Johns, "Home Mission Sermon and Schaal Family Reminiscence," 5–6.

34. Quick, *The Fairview Idea*, 7. I have found few expressions by children in defense of child labor. One fictional account that does couples class with household labor systems. "The whole family had worked in the beet fields together" in the western prairies, wrote Ruth Suckow, "except the baby, and he almost did—the mother had to take him along because she was nursing him." When an "American" suitor of one of the daughters criticized the practice, she contended that her life "was American too!" When she had told him about "the way [her father] used to lick the kids to make them work" and he had become "indignant," she "had turned around and defended her father. 'He had to make us earn our bread.'" Ruth Suckow, *The Folks* (New York: Farrar and Rinehart, 1934), 546.

where he perceived proper arrangements between men and women. "To my joy," he wrote, "I found there the old good German custom of women and girls not avoiding work. . . . You see the healthy, sturdy girls everywhere, binding sheaves, sitting on the machine, or driving the corn plough. That's where the thousands of flitting about, gossiping, time-wasting dolls [*Puppen*], should go and get the example: from those German daughters."[35]

A central feature of the European critique of American family, then, was the accusation of indolence among women. To a Dutchman, "the women of the American people are terribly lazy."[36] A recently arrived Danish immigrant agreed three decades later arguing that "American wives are amazingly lazy. . . . It is quite appropriate to say that they sew not, they spin not, and they do not gather, but their menfolk feed them just the same."[37] A central image in the immigrant iconography of the American women became the rocking chair where, according to a Norwegian woman, "the wife sits . . . and reads or usually just drones."[38] As a result, a correspondent to *Die Iowa* observed that German men in Beatrice, Nebraska, preferred "to stay unwedded rather than enter marriage with an American girl." The paper a few years earlier had stated it even more succinctly. "In these times," contended the editor, "an 'American lady' is not a desirable wife."[39]

The common European perception that American women were lazy was paralleled by similar views with regard to the behavior of children and especially of daughters. "American girls," wrote *Die Iowa* in 1878 bluntly, "don't want to work and even condemn servant's work."[40] That children had

---

35. *Die Iowa*, 26 July 1877, 5.

36. "Sjoerd Aukes Sipma to my Relatives, to All the Farmers, and to the Director of Youth at Bornwerd," 26 September 1848, ISHD Arch.

37. Barbara Haukenberry, ed. and trans., "The Diary of a Danish Immigrant: Karl Pedersen in 1880," *Soundings: Collections of the* [UCSB] *University Library* 17 (1986): 19–31.

38. Helene Munch and Peter A. Munch, eds. *The Strange American Way: Letters of Caja Munch from Wiota, Wisconsin, 1855–1859, with "An American Adventure" by Johan Storm Munch,* (Carbondale: Southern Illinois University Press, 1970), 73. See Jon Gjerde, *From Peasants to Farmers: The Migration from Balestrand, Norway to the Upper Middle West* (New York: Cambridge University Press, 1985), 228–229, for other Scandinavian critiques of the lifestyle of American women.

39. *Die Iowa*, 7 November 1878, 8; 22 April 1880, 6.

40. *Die Iowa*, 15 August 1878, 5. *Die Iowa* contended further that "the maids here are almost all immigrant Europeans." Yet due to European work patterns, Americans even found young European women in short supply during harvest. A newspaper reported in 1869 that "the ladies of St. Paul complain considerably about the difficulty of securing and keeping hired girls" since the "hired girls (Norwegian and German) have gone out into the harvest fields to work." *St. Paul Daily Press,*

free time and parents neglected their responsibilities and abdicated their power resulted in incidents that weakened the family and, by implication, society. When boys were arrested for breaking and entering in 1882, for example, *Die Iowa* argued that it was parents who were at fault due to "their utter neglect."[41] Five years earlier, after a fifteen year old girl sickened herself with rat poison because her parents had forbidden her to dance, the paper could only conclude with sarcastic disdain that here was "another beautiful little scamp [*Früchtchen*]!"[42]

The abrogation of work enabled women and children the leisure to engage in activities outside the home, which reduced the influence of the "proper" spaces in the family and society. *Die Iowa*, for example, even took issue with American women's domestic labors in its report on a lecture series for women on efficient food preparation. "We think the important feature will be dealing with *pie and sweetmeat*," he wrote. "Then she will tell how to *get a dinner ready in fifteen minutes*."[43] The criticism of the free time that quick meal preparation occasioned was not based on increased work efficiency so much as on expanded leisure time that facilitated individual pursuits detached from family responsibilities. German Catholic editors repeatedly merged a condemnation of upper-class American women with an admonition for others not to abdicate their proper responsibilities. The "Ladies Literary Association," for example, was composed of "bluestockings" who "abused English, Latin, and, even Greek literature and art." Yet "can the ladies," the editor asked, "cook a competent soup or sew a button on their husbands' pants? We doubt it."[44] Elsewhere, the "local bluestockings" were condemned since they would do better "to write something on patching stockings, on making shirts, or on peeling potatoes" than on Schiller, Goethe, or Boccaccio.[45] Ultimately, mothers and daughters would come to resemble the woman who could "pray 'Our Father' in seven different languages" while her husband had

---

21 August 1869, 4. See also *St. Paul Daily Press*, 1 August 1868, 2. Willa Cather, *My Antonia* (Boston: Houghton Mifflin Company, 1918), clearly depicts the variations between European and American daughters.

41. *Die Iowa*, 11 May 1882, 8.

42. *Die Iowa*, 12 July 1877, 5.

43. *Die Iowa*, 8 February 1882, 5. The italicized text was written in English in the original.

44. *Die Iowa*, 15 January 1880, 8.

45. *Die Iowa*, 27 November 1884, 8. Yet another notice of the "Dubuque Bluestockings" asked: "How many of these women could cook a soup, do you think, or darn a sock?" *Die Iowa*, 25 October 1883, 8.

"to sew buttons on his own shirts."[46] Rather than learning to write creatively, "the young ladies," argued the editor, ought "to take a cooking ladle in hand instead of a quill, and to learn not how to ruin a *ready in five minutes* dinner, but rather how to make a good soup and prepare a juicy piece of meat so their husbands, if they ever catch one, would not have to rush to the liquor bottle and look like the black death."[47] Literary societies may seem a curious focal point for attack, but it is clear that they were viewed as the epitome of a public association enabled by leisure time that permitted the abrogation of conventional household responsibilities.

Leisure time, seized in part from the neglect of "proper" duties and in part from "vacations from the Lord," bred excess, another failing of American society.[48] The theater was marred by "brazen, immoral shows," while "the ways in which the figure of women [were] used in advertising designs [were] simply appeals to the lower passions and . . . a degradation of womanhood."[49] Fashion made people—especially women—"odd fools" when they dressed, for example, in precisely the same material as that worn by prison inmates.[50] When Americans embraced a new pastime of shooting at glass balls, it illustrated their character: "An American has absolutely no sense for moderation in things. Everything, even the most harmless pleasure, is exaggerated."[51]

The behavior of modern children, which epitomized leisure and excess as well, was just as disgraceful. "Young America" in 1876 was condemned by the *Dubuque National Demokrat* as composed of "corner loafers" who drifted about "cursing and swearing."[52] Still other Americans raised their children with "crazy ideas" including masquerades. "Masked children!" shrieked *Die*

---

46. *Die Iowa*, 12 October 1876, 8.

47. *Die Iowa*, 10 February 1876, 8. The italicized text was written in English in the original.

48. Even American churches were associated with leisure. A Baptist tabernacle, for example, was converted into a court for iceskaters; an Episcopal church, which taught "the Gospel of Henry VIII of England," held no church services at all in July and August since they apparently "do not require the Lord in summer." "Certain people," *Die Iowa* concluded, simply "have a very lowly conception of God's House." *Die Iowa* 21 September 1882, 8; 20 July 1882, 8.

49. *Die Iowa*, 23 October 1879, 8; *Catholic Tribune*, 28 September 1899, 4. Although the *Catholic Tribune* noted that it "may not agree with the ideas that actuate Women's clubs," it did agree with a resolution of the Federated Woman's Clubs of Illinois to prohibit "the figure of woman for advertising purposes in either a suggestive or an immodest and immoral manner."

50. *Die Iowa*, 12 October 1882, 8.

51. *Die Iowa*, 8 August 1878, 8.

52. *Dubuque National Demokrat*, 24 February 1876, 3. Children alone were not responsible for this disgrace because it was up to parents to be "severe enough and alert enough to keep their children from these hothouses of bad morals and vice."

Iowa, "Can these parents not see that by doting, they nurture and cultivate the sort of passions that are capable of making their children unhappy in later life[?]"[53] The so-called "Broom Brigade" in Fredericksburg, Iowa, where young women did military exercises armed with brooms, was castigated not for its militarism, but because it would be "better if they mended stockings and patched trousers or petticoats."[54] "American girls" [*Backfische*], struggling with "sheer boredom," in one report, took to riding horses with their *beaus*, a most unladylike pastime.[55] German Catholic writers condemned the custom of Santa Claus, but they found amusing a report of a girl who received a "simple darning needle and a ball of yarn" in her stocking on Christmas morning, a gift that reminded her of responsibilities that she had forsaken.[56] The beliefs among Scandinavians certainly were not praised by German Catholics, but at least "everybody worked in a Scandinavian family" and "even the well-to-do farm people sent their daughters to the cities to perform domestic service."[57]

If leisure enabled activities in an enlarging public sphere, opportunities to earn wages in the modernizing, industrializing economy was another prong in the assault on the family. Unlike those Scandinavians' daughters, young women increasingly were employed in occupations outside domestic labor. What was worse, they often preferred it.[58] As *Milwaukee Seebote* noted, "It is a sad comment on the times that housemaids are in short supply while retailers and manufacturers always get more young women than they need."[59] "It was another sign of the times and women's emancipation," *Die Iowa* agreed sarcastically, that young women would "rather cripple themselves sewing

53. *Die Iowa*, 19 May 1881, 5.

54. *Die Iowa*, 17 January 1884, 5.

55. *Die Iowa*, 24 August 1876, 8. The italicized text was written in English in the original.

56. *Hampton* [Iowa] *Freie Presse*, cited in *Die Iowa*, 17 January 1884, 5. *Die Iowa* argued that the tradition of Santa Claus illustrated how "Catholic feasts" were "mishandled and degraded." "Americans," it argued, "have lost the meaning" of Christmas since "gift giving St. Nicholas" had replaced Christ (18 December 1884, 8).

57. "Scandinavier in Amerika," *Luxemburger Gazette*, 29 June 1886, 4. Whereas women were castigated for their tendencies toward leisure, men were commended when they continued their labors. *Die Iowa* reported that a performance of Barnum's circus was attended mainly by American and Irish farmers. "There were few Germans visible," it noted, since "they do not abandon the harvest for the sake of a circus" (22 July 1880, 8).

58. On women in factories and the moral connections to it in mid-nineteenth century New York City, see Christine Stansell, *City of Women: Sex and Class in New York, 1789–1860* (New York: Alfred A. Knopf, 1982), 125–129.

59. *Milwaukee Seebote*, cited in *Die Iowa*, 16 August 1883, 8.

for starvation wages in a factory than work at good pay in a decent home."[60] Why? Labor in manufacturing or as a clerk permitted women to "go about in the latest getup, their hair artfully arranged upon their foreheads, as though God had begrudged them the bare [*freie*] brow that distinguishes us from the beasts."[61] Women reportedly relinquished positions as domestic servants in favor of less remunerative work as clerks because they had "more free time for circulating and prettying up." The overall pattern was disheartening for these observers. As a clerk, it was simpler "to get a *fellow* and to look down their noses on serving girls even though they—as slaves to the sewing machine or playthings of the buying public—stand far beneath them." Yet once they got that "fellow," clerks were less prepared to be wives and mothers: "[Servants] can run a house, [clerks] cannot. One knows children; the other does not. One helps to keep the man content and to raise a good family; the other not."[62]

Women of recent immigrant pasts were not as tainted by the world of commerce as their American counterparts. An exchange paper observed that Americans, when searching for domestics, ask "in the first place for a good 'green' German girl," which meant "a girl upon whom the odor of the ship yet clings, who wears her hair combed down, without 'bangs' or 'Langtry waves' or artificial hairpieces, a girl whose hands are red and with calluses and who can, of course, do everything that transpires in a house." Yet the transformation even of "green" immigrants was rapid: "Soon the 'green' one is no longer 'green'" since "she imitates her friend, sloughs off the old-fashioned get-up, stops parting her hair in the middle and letting her braids hang down the back."[63]

The spokespeople for this narrative expressed misgivings not only that an urbanizing and industrializing society created challenges for proper household relationships, but that it was a powerful force that accelerated deleterious innovations into the home. Greenhorns quickly became Gibson girls. Despite the perils of life in modern America, the solution was apparent: The construction of ethnicized walls to temper the diffusion of American ways into the community.

---

60. *Die Iowa*, 2 August 1883, 8.

61. *Die Iowa*, 16 August 1883, 8.

62. All this not to mention the "perils to which girls in the factory are exposed, to the vile language often used there; or to the calumnies against God and man, especially when the factory owner is of lax morals." *Die Iowa*, 3 May 1883, 8. The italicized text was written in English in the original.

63. German-language exchange paper, cited in *Die Iowa*, 24 January 1884, 5.

Conclusion

What was the larger meaning of these narratives about family labor?
Before proceeding we should take note of two factors. First, most of the
commentators we have discussed have male voices. Doubtless, the illustrations
used, indeed the entire narratives, would have varied if we were privy to a
wider array of observations by women.[64] Moreover, not all ethnic Europeans
or American-born men hewed to these constructions. A short story written
by Kristofer Janson in 1885, for example, projects the themes of patriarchal
inequality in a Norwegian household with an intensity equal to the American
observers cited above.[65] Conversely, American-born writers such as E. V.
Smalley celebrated the German family that, unlike American domestic life,
did not "place woman at the head of the household and make man her servant"
and whose children did not resemble "rampant, independent, self-sufficient
American youths."[66] Nonetheless, if these were not the only narratives
offered by immigrant and native-born people, they were nonetheless powerful
representations of the differing familial roles between ethnic European and
American families. And because the plots differed, each narrative had varied
uses for the spokespersons.

Second, as we discuss these narratives, we should at the outset be wary of
differentiating them as a division between views of "traditional" immigrant
and "modern" American constructions of the family. After all, each was
expressed in the late nineteenth century as the proper family form to respond
to a modernizing and ultimately industrializing and urbanizing world. If the
immigrant narrative relied on family forms that invoked a mythic past, it was
nonetheless a response to contemporary conditions. Each differentiated the
other as an improper response to the modern challenge.

I would like to suggest two uses for the varying stories about the proper
use of household labor. First, we should see the construction of work as
part of a larger narrative about proper household relationships. Immigrants,
particularly immigrants who confessed to religious faiths carried from

---

64. For a work that makes gender in the rural immigrant community central, see Carol Coburn,
*Life at Four Corners: Religion, Gender, and Education in a German-Lutheran Community,
1868–1945* (Lawrence: University Press of Kansas, 1992).

65. "Kvinden skal være Manden underdannig," in *Præriens Saga: Fortællinger fra Amerika*
(Chicago: Skandinaven's Bogtrykkeri, 1885), 5–60.

66. E. V. Smalley, "The German Element in the United States," *Lippincott's Magazine* 31
(1883): 355–363, cited in Wolfgang Helbich, *"Alle Menschen sind dort gleich . . .": Die deutsche
Amerika-Auswanderung im 19. und 20. Jahrhundert* (Düsseldorf: Schwann, 1988), 133–134.

Europe, often expressed disapprobation at the structure of the American family. Norwegian Lutheran Herman Preus, for example, argued in 1867 that Americans showed a "glaring lack of external discipline, obedience and order" that "inculcated in the children" the "principles of a false freedom and independence . . . that in time cannot but bear its tragic fruits in domestic relations with parents and masters and in civil relations with the authorities."[67] For their part, German Lutheran pastors in the early nineteenth century advised their flocks to scrutinize the *Eirishdeutsch*—a neologism describing Germans who had become Irish Germans, that is, Germans who had begun to speak English—who lacked farms as well kept, families as happy, or children as loyal as their own. When children ceased "going to church—to the church where they are taught to honor mother and father" and "to esteem honest toil," they are transformed. "They won't get up in the morning, but will loll in bed like ladies and gentlemen," the argument continued. "Neither will they be ordered about; with their new self esteem they will be an independent, mincing set." Enervated by materialism and a shiftlessness, "what a tearful thing when wayward children do not honor father and mother but squander the fruit of their toil."[68] These warnings about false freedoms, enervated children, and tragic domestic relations, which focused broadly on the family, were easily related to the necessity for comprehensive household labor on the farm. Work in this context was one building block for proper obedience and authority in the home. It was a means of tempering the luxury and enervation associated with the commercial, modern world.

In contrast, observers of the homes of the American-born perceived different arrangements by the mid-nineteenth century. Tocqueville, for example, from his French perspective, argued already in the 1830s that "paternal authority, if not abolished, has at least changed form," a development that was even "more striking" in the United States. There, "the father has long anticipated the moment when his authority must come to an end, and when the time does come near, he abdicates without fuss." "The son," on the other hand, "has known in advance exactly when he will be his own master

---

67. H. A. Preus, *Syv Foredrag over de kirkelige Forholde blandt de Norske i Amerika* (Christiana: Jac Dybwad, 1867), in *Vivacious Daughter: Seven Lectures on the Religious Situation Among Norwegians in America*, edited and translated by Todd W. Nichol (Northfield, MN: Norwegian-American Historical Association, 1990), 127–128, 64.

68. Summarized from *Evangelisches Magazin* in Heinrich H. Maurer, "Studies in the Sociology of Religion: II. Religion and American Sectionalism, The Pennsylvania German," *American Journal of Sociology* 30 (1924): 408–438. The spelling of "Eirishdeutsch" is from the original.

and wins his liberty without haste or effort . . . ."[69] Tocqueville noted how governmental structures informed family power. In aristocracies the father was not only the civil head of the family, but the carrier of its tradition and customs cemented with deference and "mingled with fear." The democratic family, to the contrary, hewed to a Lockian construction where "the father scarcely exercises more power than that which is granted to the affection and the experience of age." Every word "a son addresses to his father has a tang of freedom, familiarity, and affection all at once."[70] For Tocqueville, "democracy loosens social ties, but it tightens natural ones."[71] In sum, the responsibility of parents toward their children was lessened as was that of offspring toward their elders. Thus, when Albert Barnes at mid-century argued that "there is no class or order of men, except in the parental relation, who are entrusted by nature with any authority over any other,"[72] he admitted implicitly that that authority dissipated as children aged.

Second, if each narrative justified a particular family structure, each also provided the means to differentiate the failings of the other. The narrative of the American-born, by focusing on the inequalities that victimized individuals in the home, justified the right to intrude on the sequestered and isolated immigrant family. In a pluralistic society, where there often existed great concern about how private behavior influenced the public world, Americans of a variety of stripes could advocate entering the home in the hopes of improving the life chances for individuals, not to mention the direction of society writ large. If Quick could argue that German homes were not families but factories, if Ross could connect race suicide with child labor, if native-born Manitobans could take their concerns about family labor to the House of Commons, native-born North Americans from many perspectives could justify state intervention and intrusion into the home to enable individual rights. If these concerns were expressed with particular pointedness with regard to non-white Americans, they were also in place to deprecate the behavior of the European immigrant.

Conversely, the relentless diffusion of behavior into immigrant homes was a powerful justification for creating boundaries between the European and America. In no better milieu could ethnics illustrate the dangers of secularized American life than in the behavior of its young. If children were being led astray

---

69. Alexis de Tocqueville, *Democracy in America* (New York: Anchor Books, 1969), 585.

70. Tocqueville, *Democracy in America*, 587–588.

71. Tocqueville, *Democracy in America*, 589.

72. Albert Barnes, *The Casting Down of Thrones: A Discourse on the Present State of Europe* (Philadelphia: William Sloanaker, 1848), 3–24.

by American society, they were to be guarded from the innovations inescapably creeping into European-American homes both for their own sake and for that of their community. Fear of this diffusion, then, was a powerful justification for creating boundaries between ethnic groups and larger American society in order to prohibit the intrusions that endangered not only the community, but society itself. If the modern family seemed to be endangering not only the ethnic community but American society in general, ethnics could be patriots in an ethnically defined context to check the destruction that it wrought.

6

German-Origin Settlement and Agricultural Land Use in the Twentieth-Century Great Plains[1]

Myron Gutmann, Sara Pullum-Pinon, Susan Gonzalez Baker, and Ingrid Burke

Introduction

Historian James C. Malin, writing in the 1930s, observed that immigrants to the region he studied in Kansas frequently had a different relationship to farming and the land than did native Americans. Malin was especially concerned about mobility in the countryside and its relationship to farming. He stressed his perception of European immigrant farmers' devotion to their land: "Whenever the unstable native American came into competition with the immigrant stock of Germans, Swedes, and Bohemians, the American lost out. . . . The American did not possess the tenacious love of the soil for its own sake that was so conspicuous among these European stocks."[2]

In the sixty years and longer since Malin wrote, scholars have repeated and expanded his general conclusion. Immigrant farmers and their descendants farmed differently than did their neighbors of native parentage. German "yeoman" farmers are singled out, in particular, as practitioners of farming

1.   This research was supported by Grant No. R01 HD33554 from the National Institute of Child Health and Human Development. We are grateful to Martha Coleman and Brian Robinson for vital assistance in preparing the data, and to Geoffrey Cunfer and Michelle Butler for advice and assistance in preparing this chapter. For closely related work about a number of other ethnic groups, see Susan G. Baker, Myron P. Gutmann, and Sara Pullum, *Ethnicity and Land Use in a Changing Environment: The Great Plains in the Twentieth Century* (Austin: Population Research Center, 1999). Participants in the conference, "New Approaches to Migration Research: German-Americans in Comparative Perspective," at Texas A&M University, College Station, TX, April 22–24, 1997, sponsored by the German Historical Institute, gave generous comments on an earlier draft. Simone Wegge was especially helpful. We appreciate their assistance, but any remaining errors are our responsibility.

2.   James C. Malin, *History and Ecology: Studies of the Grassland*, edited by Robert P. Swierenga (Lincoln: University of Nebraska Press, 1984), 213.

strategies dedicated to the preservation of the land as part of a family "patrimony" in contrast to their neighbors whose farming practices reflected a more entrepreneurial orientation.[3] The generalization, based on ethnographic and community studies, still has value today. In a series of nearly 150 interviews with farm families in the Great Plains from 1997 to 1999, commitment to the land is a recurring theme among farmers and ranchers with German roots.[4] More than others in this group of interviews, German-descended farmers and their spouses hope that their children will take over from them. These farmers do not speak in terms of ethnic values, but their values appear in quotes like this more frequently than for others: "We'd like to have them farm, yes. It would be nice to turn [pass] the family farm down, because like this farm belonged to his uncle and he farmed with his dad and his brother, you know, it has kind of family value."[5]

In this chapter we test this generalization by looking at farming in the Great Plains of the United States at the beginning and the end of the twentieth century. We first ask whether the idea that German immigrants farmed distinctively at the beginning of the twentieth century holds up under close empirical scrutiny. We then assess whether German farming patterns that we find at the beginning of the century were still evident at century's end. Because there are no region-wide data about individuals, counties serve as our unit of analysis. This analysis builds on an approach we have used in a number of other studies.[6] An important innovation in this research is the explicit attempt to control for many of the possible environmental variations that can affect land

3.   Sonya Salamon, *Prairie Patrimony: Family, Farming, and Community in the Midwest* (Chapel Hill: University of North Carolina, 1992).

4.   This quote emerges from a set of approximately 150 farm family interviews conducted under the auspices of the research grant referenced in note one. We refer to this component of the larger project on population, environment, and agricultural land use as the Great Plains Farm Family Survey.

5.   Interview number WC21, Great Plains Farm Family Survey.

6.   For other studies making use of these data, see Myron P. Gutmann and Sara Pullum, "From a Local to a National Political Culture: Social Capital and Civic Organization in the U.S. Great Plains," *Journal of Interdisciplinary History* 29 (1999): 725–762; Myron P. Gutmann and Geoffrey A. Cunfer, *A New Look at the Causes of the Dust Bowl* (Lubbock: International Center for Arid and Semiarid Land Studies, Texas Tech University, 1999); Myron P. Gutmann, "Scaling and Demographic Issues in Global Change Research: The Great Plains, 1880–1990," *Climatic Change* 44 (2000): 377–392; Baker, Gutmann, Pullum, *Ethnicity and Land Use*; and Myron P. Gutmann, Geoffrey A. Cunfer, Ingrid C. Burke, and William J. Parton, "Government Agricultural Programs, Environment, and Land Use Decisions in the U.S. Great Plains, 1969–1992," (Unpublished paper presented at the Biennial Meeting of the American Society for Environmental History, Baltimore, March 1997).

use. In order to isolate an effect of ethnicity on farm practices across counties, we pay careful attention to soil, temperature, precipitation, and irrigation.

Ethnicity and Land Use: The Historiographical Tradition

A substantial historical literature links various immigrant communities with specific agricultural practices. That linkage has not only been found in the region that we call the Great Plains, but also for areas further to the east such as Illinois, Iowa, Wisconsin, and Minnesota. While those areas have different environments than the Great Plains, we have used the histories of ethnic farming in them to formulate our hypotheses. The agricultural tendencies associated with immigrant communities reflected both deliberate farming choices and more subtle organizing principles of community life. To the extent that ethnic communities were able to choose their land, they made varying attempts to shape it into a new home.

As Malin suggested, one indicator of community was a group's commitment to its location. Germans valued geographical stability and expected to pass their work and society on to the next generation. Their perception of agriculture revolved around a sense of permanence.[7] In contrast, American and English settlers followed an English pattern where land was a commodity and a tool for entrepreneurship.[8] These differences led to divergent population density and farm size. In comparison with their German counterparts, American communities were strung out, sharing few institutions.[9] German community members sought to reconstruct the peasant landscape they had left behind, and their communities were thus concentrated around a church and other community buildings.[10]

Another important choice for settlers was the type of agriculture that they pursued. Crop choices, in particular, were highly influenced by ethnicity. Germans grew more wheat than American settlers, and they were more likely

---

7.   Salamon, *Prairie Patrimony*, 16–17.

8.   Salamon, *Prairie Patrimony*, 17.

9.   John A. Hagwood, "The Attempt to Found a New Germany in Missouri," in *The Aliens: A History of Ethnic Minorities in America*, edited by Leonard Dinnerstein and Frederic Cople Jaher (New Jersey: Prentice-Hall, Inc., 1970), 137.

10.   Aidan D. McQuillan, *Prevailing over Time: Ethnic Adjustments on the Kansas Prairies, 1875–1925* (Lincoln and London: University of Nebraska Press, 1990), 5.

to grow any at all on a farm.[11] They grew less corn than American settlers. On the other hand, German immigrants, due to their smaller farms, concentrated on their former dietary staples: potatoes and small grains such as rye and barley.[12]

Immigrant ethnic groups also made livestock choices that were specific to their communities. Germans kept slightly fewer livestock than did Americans, according to Kamphoefner, but were more likely to have some animals on a farm. While Germans were more likely to keep cattle, they may not have been any more likely to keep dairy cows. Despite the stereotype that Germans were more likely than other groups to produce dairy items, Americans reported comparable figures of butter and cheese.[13] Germans were as likely as Americans to own swine, although in fewer numbers.[14]

The extent to which farmers devoted their land to any one enterprise varied greatly and reflected ethnic influence. For Germans crop diversity increased after the initial settlement period, as Old World preferences were reasserted. Until the strong intervention of market influences, Germans grew more crops per farm than any other group.[15] A number of factors affected land stewardship and mobility. Salomon argues that because American farmers were characterized by "entrepreneurship," they were highly mobile and did not work to maintain the fertility of their land.[16] The lack of attention that Americans paid to the longterm health of their land may not have affected crop yields for some time, however. It is possible that their neglect might have had an impact only after the Americans had moved on, selling the land to new immigrants from Europe. While Bogue describes settlers from the American South as "land butchers" who were perpetually mobile out of economic necessity, European immigrants, most notably Germans, had as their primary goal the

---

11. Bradley H. Baltensperger, "Agricultural Change among Nebraska Immigrants," in *Ethnicity on the Great Plains*, edited by Frederick C. Luebke (Lincoln: University of Nebraska Press, 1980), 174; Jon Gjerde, *From Peasants to Farmers: The Migration from Balestrand, Norway, to the Upper Middle West* (Cambridge: Cambridge University Press, 1985).

12. Walter Kamphoefner, *The Westfalians: From Germany to Missouri* (New Jersey: Princeton University Press, 1987), 129–130; Gjerde, *From Peasants to Farmers*, 181–185.

13. Terry G. Jordan, *German Seed in Texas Soil: Immigrant Farmers in Nineteenth Century Texas* (Austin: University of Texas Press, 1966), 91.

14. Kamphoefner, *Westfalians*, 128.

15. Baltensperger, "Agricultural Change," 179–181.

16. Salomon, *Prairie Patrimony*, 161–167.

establishment of a community. They were considerably less mobile.[17] Germans were unlikely to rent additional land in response to market forces and viewed the farm as a family enterprise to be passed from generation to generation.

This survey of wellknown descriptions of ethnic farming practices yields clear and testable propositions regarding the ways in which German-origin farmers used the land. We summarize them in the following list:

Crop Choice and Diversity:

- Germans were more likely to grow wheat than were the native born.

- Germans were more likely to grow crops that appealed to their traditional tastes in non-commercial quantities, especially small grains.

- Crop diversity increased for Germans during the late nineteenth century, then decreased as the market became a central priority, and traditional noncommercial crops fell out of favor.

Livestock and Livestock Products:

- Germans kept slightly fewer livestock per acre than did the native born.

- Germans were more likely to keep cattle and dairy cows than any other ethnic group.

- Germans were as likely to own swine as non-Germans, but in lesser numbers.

Farm Characteristics:

- Germans were likely to have mid-sized family farms organized around a farm-dependent village in which the church played a strong role in ethnic cohesion.

---

17.   Allan G. Bogue, *From Prairie to Corn Belt: Farming on the Illinois and Iowa Plains in the Nineteenth Century* (Chicago: University of Chicago Press, 1963), 5.

- Germans focused on passing land down to their children, keeping land in the family, and encouraging at least one child to stay on the farm.

One simple way to evaluate the spatial generalizability of these propositions is to examine data about agriculture for a number of counties, divided between those that were largely German and those that were not. The data we bring to bear are described more fully later in this chapter.[18] We select five counties in 1910 and 1990 that had the highest percentage German populations for that year.[19] We contrast each one with a nearby county that has similar environmental conditions but a much smaller proportion of Germans. The results, reported in table 6.1, show the percentage of cropland in rye and oats, the percentage of cropland in a single crop, cattle per thousand acres, and dairy cattle per thousand acres. Except for cattle in 1910 and dairy cattle in 1990, table 6.1 reveals no clear patterns differentiating counties with a large proportion of German-origin people from those with a small proportion. In the case of cattle in 1910 the more German counties had significantly more total cattle.[20] In 1910, for example, some German counties grew more rye and oats than nearby non-German counties, but others did not. The same was true in 1910 for other variables, and for 1990.

Our inability to confirm specific farming characteristics for Germans, based on individual county pairs, does not negate the generalizations drawn from the historical literature about the Great Plains and the Midwest. Rather, the findings require us to develop a more sophisticated strategy employing a larger sample of counties and more sophisticated methods.

---

18. The data and their sources are documented in Myron P. Gutmann, Sara Pullum, Geoffrey A. Cunfer, and Delia Hagen, *Great Plains Population and Environment Database: Sources and User's Guide. Version 1.0* (Austin: Population Research Center, 1999).

19. For 1910 and 1990, we chose the five counties in the Great Plains with the largest percentages of population who were German in each year. We define the German population in 1910 as those persons born in Germany or Austria, or those persons who had at least one parent born in Germany or Austria. For 1990, we define the German population as those persons who identified themselves as being of German or Austrian ancestry. The contrasting counties were no more than three adjacent counties away, and were, with the exception of Charles Mix County, South Dakota, in the lowest or second-lowest quartile of German presence for that year.

20. The difference is significant based on a standard test of differences between proportions. Hubert Blalock, *Social Statistics* (New York: McGraw Hill, 1979).

County	Germans, Percent of Population, 1910	Percent of Cropland in Rye	Percent of Cropland in Oats	Percent of Cropland in One Crop	Cattle per 1000 Acres	Dairy Cattle per 1000 Acres
Ellsworth, Kansas	27.64	0.05	0.82	61.28	77.36*	13.38
Reno, Kansas	3.60	0.27	3.85	44.86	64.85*	18.96
Pierce, Nebraska	33.46	0.40	27.68	50.22	111.41*	24.74
Clay, South Dakota	3.50	0.05	26.34	46.04	83.06*	20.75
Sherman, Nebraska	29.96	0.16	10.53	44.70	94.12*	24.77*
Custer, Nebraska	6.48	0.41	12.22	45.16	72.54*	12.71*
Stanton, Nebraska	38.85	0.53	26.03	46.50	123.80*	26.14
Union, South Dakota	6.37	0.00	16.88	47.69	103.14*	31.46
Richland, North Dakota	26.65	0.87	17.55	47.83	40.93*	15.73
Ransom, North Dakota	7.46	0.11	13.80	58.92	33.52*	12.04

* Starred variables have a statistically significant difference between German and non-German counties.

Table 6.1A: Specific County Pairs Based on Geographic Proximity and Contrasting German Presence, 1910

County	Germans, Percent of Population, 1990	Percent of Cropland in Rye	Percent of Cropland in Oats	Percent of Cropland in One Crop	Cattle per 1000 Acres	Dairy Cattle per 1000 Acres
Logan, North Dakota	87.82	0.10	4.88	48.62	95.81	5.90*
Sioux, North Dakota	18.11	0.05	2.21	62.15	36.27	1.05*
McIntosh, North Dakota	89.75	0.41	8.13	55.00	81.11	4.85*
Dewey, South Dakota	21.69	N/A	7.16	60.86	31.85	0.67*
Sheridan, North Dakota	79.43	0.23	4.36	54.84	46.74	2.70*
Benson, North Dakota	18.53	0.05	2.21	62.15	36.27	1.05*
Hutchinson, South Dakota	79.70	N/A	4.85	41.47	134.43	10.56*
Charles Mix, South Dakota	27.83	N/A	9.23	24.74	145.36	3.66*
McPherson, South Dakota	85.44	0.30	8.85	40.54	117.05	4.26*
Ziebach, South Dakota	17.12	N/A	4.05	45.50	30.23	0.03*

* Starred variables have a statistically significant difference between German and non-German counties.

Table 6.1B: Specific County Pairs Based on Geographic Proximity and Contrasting German Presence, 1990

Ethnicity and Land Use: A Research Strategy

We fit the hypotheses about how the people of the Great Plains farmed their land into a broader perspective that guides our overall project. In our conceptual framework (displayed in figure 6.1), four main elements affect land use: environmental effects, human population, economy and policy, and time period. Each of the four main elements has various subelements.

For this chapter, the most important determinants of land use are environmental effects and human population. We require much less detail about economy and policy, and the effects of time (other than climate change), because we are only dealing here with two time periods, separated by eighty years. The role of government intervention, market differences (such as prices), and the development of community and technology are all subsumed into the broad range of differences that exist between the farming environment in 1910 and 1990. When we remove the temporal differences reflected by changes in economy and policy, we are left with the spatial differences caused by the environment and various elements of the population.

At the heart of the changes that took place in the Great Plains between 1910 and 1990 were alterations in population, agriculture and economy, and the role of the government. There was also a small difference in climate between the two periods. The region's counties received, on average, about 10 millimeters of precipitation more each year in the period from 1895 to 1930 than they did in the period from 1960 to 1993. This is a two percent difference, and we believe that it did not have a noticeable impact on agriculture.

The region's social and economic evolution between 1910 and 1990 was much greater than the changes in climate. First, the population of the region nearly doubled in the period, even if that population growth has not been distributed evenly. Our Great Plains study area includes counties in ten states. The population in five of those states (North Dakota, South Dakota, Kansas, Oklahoma, and Nebraska), has in the aggregate changed very little since the beginning of the century, with slight shifts in emphasis between the states.[21] Three states that we identify as Mountain States (New Mexico, Montana, and Wyoming), more than doubled in size, but these states had small populations (about 400,000) in 1910, and continued to have small populations (about 940,000) in 1990. The substantial growth that took place in the population of the Great Plains was in the two remaining states, Texas and Colorado. The

---

21. Taking 1910 and 1990 as defining points obscures some of the history. The rural Great Plains states gained population until 1930, before falling back to the levels they attained in 1910.

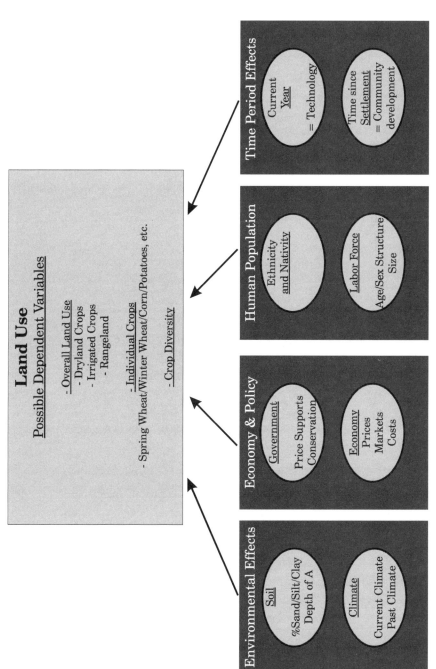

Figure 1: A Conceptional Basis for Understanding Ethnicity and Land Use

populations of the counties in Texas and Colorado that we include in the Great Plains more than tripled (from 1.2 million to more than 4.3 million). Most of this growth was in urban areas such as metropolitan Denver and a handful of Texas counties. The rural and agricultural population of the Great Plains changed relatively little in the twentieth century, except for some growth on the western fringe, an area that was not yet fully settled in 1910. On the other hand, the population of the urban and suburban Great Plains greatly increased.

The economy of the Great Plains also changed dramatically during the twentieth century. Agriculture became more specialized and solidified a market orientation that had already begun in 1910 as shown by the rise of a dominant wheat and ranching agriculture at that time. The thorough mechanization of farming was part of this process, one that resulted in the elimination of draft animals and a reduction in the widespread cultivation of corn, which was used by many farmers to feed their stock. Another aspect of agricultural mechanization was the diffusion of irrigation throughout the twentieth century, because a substantial part of the Great Plains lies over the Ogallala aquifer. These changes, together with the availability of artificial fertilizers, chemical herbicides, and pesticides, raised agricultural productivity. The rise in productivity is associated with a reduction in agricultural employment, which has fallen since the 1930s from more than half of the civilian labor force to less than one-tenth. To a certain extent, employment in services has grown and the service economy has partly replaced agricultural employment in the economies of the rural Great Plains.

The role of the government changed radically between 1910 and 1990, in the Great Plains as elsewhere. Government agricultural programs began in the 1930s, with the goal of reducing soil erosion and stabilizing farmer incomes. These programs have been successful in many ways, but they have had consequences that may have gone beyond the intention of their authors. Government programs have contributed in a major way to increases in farm productivity.[22] Moreover, these programs have tended to stabilize agriculture, rewarding farmers who plant the same crop mix year after year. They have also affected rural life in the Great Plains by bringing social programs and increased educational support to nonmetropolitan places. Much of the service sector employment that has compensated for declining agricultural employment has been in government, health, and educational services, all directly or indirectly provided with public funds.

---

22. Gutmann, Cunfer, Burke, Parton, "Agricultural Programs."

Sources of Data

Our analysis is based on county-level data about land use, soils, climate, population, and what we call ethnicity for 1910 and 1990, the latter based on the agricultural census of 1992. A brief summary of the sources that we have used is included below.[23] Availability of information, in part, governs our county-level analyses. Census data are reported for counties, and there are few sources at any smaller level of aggregation that meet our quality demands.[24] Counties also provide an effective level at which to visualize patterns evolving over time. Finally, our exploratory analyses in the broader Great Plains project reveal that county-level analyses yield meaningful results, as counties are sufficiently homogenous to constitute a sample with theoretical integrity, while also displaying sufficient variation to allow for statistical modeling.

Agricultural Land Use Data. The U.S. Censuses of Agriculture tabulate and report voluminous information about land use, agricultural productivity, and the economics of farming at the county level. Because there was not an agricultural census in 1990, we use data from 1992 in our agricultural analysis, matched to 1990 data about ethnic origins.

Soils Data. We employ data that report the average distribution of sand, silt, and clay in each county of the Great Plains. In addition, we report the average depth of topsoil in inches. We have a single source of soils data, which probably best represents conditions in the 1970s and 1980s. We are aware that soils have changed to some degree over the last century. However, no other large scale soil data are available.

Climate Data. In order to determine the role of climate in determining land use, we make use of the information distributed by the Historical Climatology Network (HCN). This represents monthly series of data for approximately 1,200 weather stations, dating back to the late nineteenth century in many cases. The monthly data available relate to precipitation, average maximum temperature, and average minimum temperature. Approximately 180 of these

---

23. For other examples of the use of these data, with specific references to sources, see the publications mentioned in notes one and three.

24. Gutmann, "Issues in Global Change Research."

stations lie within or near the area that we define as the Great Plains. Because these are station data, and because not every county contains a weather station, we have employed a procedure to interpolate and average the information for every month. We then assign an average value to each county. For our 1910 analysis, we have averaged precipitation and temperature for 1895 through 1930 for each county; for 1990, we have averaged those data for the years 1960 through 1993.

Population Data. Our most important population data measure the ethnic composition of the county population. The sources—and the meaning—of this information are quite different for 1910 and 1990. The data we use are drawn from the published county-level tabulations created by the Census Bureau for each of these years.

In 1910 the Census Bureau asked a question about the place of birth of each individual and the birthplace of each person's mother and father. The tabulated data report the number of persons born in a fairly detailed list of nations for each county in the study area. Moreover, they report the numbers of those native-born white persons whose parents were both born in an almost as detailed list of countries. These tabulations provide a measure of the ethnic origins of the population of a county in 1910, with some limitations. For instance, the ethnic origins of persons of third or later generation are not included, so that the descendants of very early immigrants to the United States (or pre-Revolutionary America) are not included. This feature of the data may diminish the presence of certain ethnic groups or eliminate them entirely. Germans are one of the groups that had begun to migrate early enough to have had their numbers diminished by 1910. Nonetheless, their locations and densities appear to be well represented in our 1910 data.

In 1990 the Census Bureau took an entirely different approach, and in addition to the question about nativity asked a question about ethnic origins. Question thirteen in the individual section of the long form questionnaire asked: "What is this person's ancestry or ethnic origin?" The Census questionnaire left a blank space, and the transcription process allowed two ancestries to be tabulated. We have made use of the first ancestry reported. A number of authors have considered the problems in ancestry reporting in 1990.[25] Despite the problems, the ancestry variables give us a good starting

---

25. Michael Hout and Joshua R. Goldstein, "How 4.5 Million Irish Immigrants Became 40 Million Irish Americans: Demographic and Subjective Aspects of the Ethnic Composition of

point for understanding the changing role of ethnicity in determining agricultural practice in the Great Plains in the twentieth century. We consider people born in Austria or Germany and the children of persons born there, to be German in 1910.[26]

Ethnicity in the Great Plains—Germans in 1910 and 1990

Research on ethnicity is often coupled in social science with the investigation of race. The Great Plains, however, reveals how distinct these two constructs can be. Over eighty-eight percent of the respondents to the 1990 Census in the Great Plains identified themselves as white. On the other hand ethnic variation in the Great Plains is quite robust with over thirty different ancestral countries being reported by Great Plains residents.

Not only is there more empirical variation in ethnicity than in race for the Great Plains, but, we contend, ethnicity offers a much more direct link to phenomena such as agricultural land use. Unlike race, a construct that natural and social scientists anchor, however tenuously, in real and perceived biological differences among people, ethnicity signifies membership in a group based largely on shared culture. Culture encompasses all the material objects people use to carry out social life, and all the nonmaterial aspects of human experience that make social life possible, including belief systems, value sets, and norms for conduct. To the extent that a group of people share these material and nonmaterial elements, they share a culture. Because this sharing is so much more likely to happen among people who live close to one another, cultural systems have a strong geographical base. Thus, identifiers like national origin have come to be considered as useful proxies for cultural identification in both folk definitions and scientific analyses. It is this shared culture, rooted in common national origin, that constitutes the core of ethnicity as a social construct. Our ethnic definitions for the population of the Great Plains presume that shared ethnic origin signifies, at some level, a shared culture. Ultimately, our objective

---

White Americans," *American Sociological Review* 59 (1994): 64–82; Ira Rosenwaike, "Ancestry in the United States Census, 1980–1990," *Social Science* 22 (1993): 383–390; Reynolds Farley, "The New Census Question about Ancestry: What did It Tell Us?" *Demography* 28 (1991): 411–429.

26. For a fuller discussion of ethnic groups in the Great Plains, see Baker, Gutmann, Pullum, *Ethnicity and Land Use*. In that analysis, we also included Russians among the "German" population, because many of the persons born in Russia but living in the Great Plains were of German ethnic origin.

will be to determine whether this shared ethnic experience manifests itself in the way that agricultural land might be used across time and space.

Our Great Plains study area includes over four hundred counties in ten states. Figure 6.2 illustrates the German presence in the Great Plains at the county level in 1910. The 1910 map reveals a stronger German-origin presence in the northern half of the Great Plains, with substantial spatial enclaves located in South Dakota and northern Nebraska. Propelling ourselves forward eighty years, we identify the German presence in the same areas in the 1990 Census. Obviously, a strict correspondence between the 1910 and 1990 ethnic variables is not possible. To characterize counties in 1990 solely on the basis of their first- and second-generation national origins would be to ignore the demographic reality of the region, namely, that international migration is no longer an engine for regional population growth. Therefore, our 1990 analyses rely on a variable capturing the primary ancestry claimed by the Census respondents of the Great Plains. Although the variables in 1990 (presented in figure 6.3) tap a different construct from that employed in the 1910 analyses, the comparisons are illuminating.

German ancestry dwarfed all other ethnic ancestral identifiers in the contemporary Great Plains, although it was still more heavily concentrated in the northern and central Great Plains than in the southern region. Despite this strong presence of populations of German ancestry considerable variation in the ethnic composition of individual counties continued to persist. Ultimately, the task for this research will be to evaluate whether the presence of a given ethnicity in a county explains, over and above environmental and general population factors, the land-use outcomes for that county.

Land Use and Environment in 1910 and 1990

The relationship between environmental conditions and land use constitutes the starting point for our analysis, because it is very difficult to determine whether ethnicity affects the choice of agricultural regime without holding the environment constant. Our own research and that of others show that a limited pool of environmental variables determine a substantial part of the variance in agricultural land use at the county level, at least in the later twentieth century.[27]

27. Ingrid C. Burke et al., "Interactions of Land Use and Ecosystem Function: A Case Study in the Central Great Plains," in *Integrated Regional Models: Interactions Between Humans and their Environment*, edited by Peter M. Groffman and Gene E. Likens (New York: Chapman Hall, 1994), 79–95; Ingrid C. Burke, William K. Lauenroth, and William J. Parton, "Regional and Temporal Variability in Aboveground Net Primary Productivity and Net N Mineralization

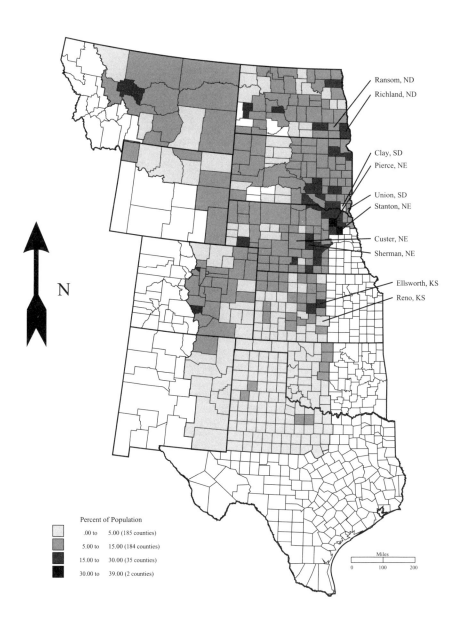

Figure 6.2: Germans as a Percentage of Total County Population, 1910

Gutmann et al.

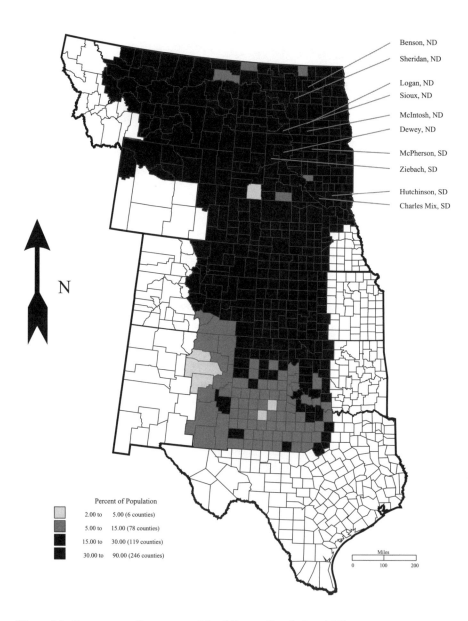

Benson, ND
Sheridan, ND

Logan, ND
Sioux, ND

McIntosh, ND
Dewey, ND

McPherson, SD
Ziebach, SD

Hutchinson, SD
Charles Mix, SD

N

Percent of Population

2.00 to	5.00 (6 counties)
5.00 to	15.00 (78 counties)
15.00 to	30.00 (119 counties)
30.00 to	90.00 (246 counties)

Miles

0   100   200

Figure 6.3: Germans as a Percentage of Total County Population, 1990

This research shows that almost all of the variations in agricultural land use in the Great Plains are explained by fluctuations in environmental variables, especially precipitation, temperature, soil texture, and slope. Not much room is left for human intervention, at least in these relatively recent data, in deciding between cropping and rangeland. All the variations controlled by the human population lie near the margin, in deciding whether to irrigate and which crop to plant. We confirm these relationships by undertaking a series of OLS regression analyses, with a single land use as the dependent variable in each. We list the variables and their definitions in table 6.2.

The first group of dependent variables comprises those that measure the extent of land use for crops.[28] We also include in this variable set the percentage of cropland devoted to the largest crop planted in the county, interpreted as the inverse of crop diversity. The second group of dependent variables includes those that measure the amount of livestock supported in the county, represented as the ratio of livestock inventory to farmland. These variables gauge the extent to which Germans preferred certain kinds of livestock. We summarize the portions of the regression results that are relevant here in table 6.3, panel A (about crops) and panel B (about livestock).[29] The models include a full set of independent variables, encompassing environmental characteristics and two important characteristics of farm life: average farm size and population density of each county.

The first conclusion to draw from table 6.3 is that although there are some exceptions, the r-squared values for most of the dependent variables are higher for 1910 than they are for 1990. This implies that environmental conditions

in Grasslands," *Ecology* 78 (1997): 1330–1340; Osvaldo E. Sala, William J. Parton, Linda A. Joyce, William K. Lauenroth, "Primary Production of the Central Grassland Region of the United States," *Ecology* 69 (1988): 40–45; W. K. Lauenroth, Ingrid C. Burke, Jose M. Paruelo, "Patterns of Production and Precipitation-use Efficiency of Winter Wheat and Native Grasslands in the Central Plains of the United States," *Ecosystems* 3(2000): 344-351; and Gutmann, Cunfer, Burke, Parton, "Agricultural Programs."

28.   In computing these dependent variables, we take into account the fact that while the 1990 census included a specific question about the total quantity of cropland on a farm, the 1910 census did not. We have computed a much more limited cropland variable for 1910 by taking the sum of land from which the following crops were harvested: wheat, corn, sorghum, oats, hay, rye, potatoes, barley, and cotton. This method presents two problems. First, we capture cropland harvested rather than planted. The Census offers no information on acreage planted in each crop. Second, we do not capture all of the cropland used, because a small fraction was harvested in less common crops.

29.   For a fuller discussion of the environmental determinants of historical land use in the Great Plains in the context of ethnicity, see Baker, Gutmann, Pullum, *Ethnicity and Land Use.*

County	Germans, Percent of Population, 1990	Percent of Cropland in Rye	Percent of Cropland in Oats	Percent of Cropland in One Crop	Cattle per 1000 Acres	Dairy Cattle per 1000 Acres
Logan, North Dakota	87.82	0.10	4.88	48.62	95.81	5.90*
Sioux, North Dakota	18.11	0.05	2.21	62.15	36.27	1.05*
McIntosh, North Dakota	89.75	0.41	8.13	55.00	81.11	4.85*
Dewey, South Dakota	21.69	N/A	7.16	60.86	31.85	0.67*
Sheridan, North Dakota	79.43	0.23	4.36	54.84	46.74	2.70*
Benson, North Dakota	18.53	0.05	2.21	62.15	36.27	1.05*
Hutchinson, South Dakota	79.70	N/A	4.85	41.47	134.43	10.56*
Charles Mix, South Dakota	27.83	N/A	9.23	24.74	145.36	3.66*
McPherson, South Dakota	85.44	0.30	8.85	40.54	117.05	4.26*
Ziebach, South Dakota	17.12	N/A	4.05	45.50	30.23	0.03*

* Starred variables have a statistically significant difference between German and non-German counties.

Table 6.1B: Specific County Pairs Based on Geographic Proximity and Contrasting German Presence, 1990

Panel B: Independent Variables Used and Their Sources

Variable	Source	Data Problems
Soil Characteristics:		
Percent of County Soil in Sand	U.S. Department of Agriculture: Statsgo Data Base	
Percent of County Soil in Clay	U.S. Department of Agriculture: Statsgo Data Base	
Mean Depth of County Topsoil (in inches)	U.S. Department of Agriculture: Statsgo Data Base	
Climate:		
Mean Precipitation in County (monthly in mm)	Computed from USHCN station data	
Mean Yearly Minimum Temperature in County (from monthly data in c)	Computed from USHCN station data	
Mean Yearly Maximum Temperature in County (from monthly data in c)	Computed from USHCN station data	
Variables Included Only in Ethnicity Models:		
Average Farm Size in County	U.S. Agricultural Census	
Average Population Density in County	U.S. Population Census	

Source: The Great Plains Population and Environment Database. The University of Texas Population Research Center, Great Plains Population and Environment Database: Version 1.0, Austin: Texas Population Research Center, University of Texas at Austin, 1998.

were more strongly correlated with land use in 1910 than in 1990. Without mechanization and lacking many late-twentieth-century farming innovations, farmers in 1910 tied their production more closely to environmental conditions than their successors did. The second conclusion we draw is that some crops have been more closely tied to environmental conditions than others. Potatoes, rye, and oats are less strongly linked to the environment than other crops. Wheat, on the other hand, is correlated to the environment in 1910 but not in 1990. We suspect this may be a function of the role of wheat fallow in dry areas, a practice that had not yet become widespread in 1910. Third, having a single largest crop is not strongly associated with environmental conditions. This leaves open the possibility that if monoculture is important in the Great Plains, it is associated with ethnicity, one of our research hypotheses.

When we turn to table 6.3, panel B, we see that environmental factors have a different relationship with farm size and livestock farming than they had with crop production. Farm size was much more closely correlated to our environmental variables in 1910 than in 1990, so that farm size in 1990 was largely a proxy for ranching rather than cropping. In areas where there was low precipitation, shallow topsoil, and sandy soil, ranching prevails. When we add population density to the model, we also see that in 1990 low population densities were significantly associated with large farms.

Each variety of livestock that we track in table 6.3, panel B, has a slightly different relationship with environmental considerations. When we look at total cattle, sheep, and swine, we see that their patterns changed over the course of the twentieth century. In 1910 there was little correlation between cattle or sheep and the environment. By 1990, on the other hand, there was a fairly strong relationship. In areas with greater precipitation and irrigation, it is possible to produce more hay, grass, and feed, and therefore to support more livestock per acre. There is also a negative relationship between minimum temperature and livestock, so that cattle do less well in very cold places than sheep and swine (which may winter inside). In 1990, however, swine were negatively associated with minimum temperature. We believe this reflects the strong correlation of hog farming with corn cropping, which also had a negative relationship with minimum temperature in 1990. In table 6.3, panel B, we hypothesize that farm size is associated with the propensity of farmers to ranch rather than farm for crops, and our results confirm this. Farm size is significantly associated with the percent of farmland that is cropland, with a negative sign.

	Percent Farmland in All Crops	Percent Cropland in:							
		Wheat	Corn	Hay	Potatoes	Rye	Oats	Barley	Largest Crop
1910:									
Soil Pct. Sand	-0.499*	-0.578*	-0.084	0.545*	0.041	0.013*	-0.001	-0.072*	0.319*
Soil Pct. Clay	-0.719*	-0.852*	-0.646*	0.736*	0.149*	0.001	0.200*	0.052	0.303*
Topsoil Depth	1.305*	2.366*	-1.116*	-2.511*	-0.044	0.002	-0.032	0.486*	-0.499
Precipitation	0.124*	-0.029*	0.122*	-0.469*	0.003	0.002*	0.009	0.015*	-0.034*
Max.Temperature	-2.686*	-3.590*	0.785	4.099*	0.439	0.192*	-0.970*	0.768*	-1.063
Min.Temperature	-1.100	2.014	0.674	-4.742*	-0.713	-0.300*	-0.257	-2.091*	1.695
Pct. Farmland Irrigated	N/A	N/A	N/A	N/A	N/A	N/A	N/A	N/A	N/A
Adjusted R-Squared	0.780	0.413	0.597	0.503	0.025	0.126	0.401	0.341	0.155
N	402	402	402	402	402	324	402	323	402

*Starred coefficients are significant at alpha=0.05 or less.

Table 6.3: OLS Regression Results:
Panel A: Environment and Cropping, Great Plains Counties, 1910 and 1990

| | Percent Farmland in All Crops | Percent Cropland in: | | | | | | | |
		Wheat	Corn	Hay	Potatoes	Rye	Oats	Barley	Largest Crop
1990:									
Soil Pct. Sand	-0.008*	-0.009*	-0.001	0.008*	-0.002	0.000	0.000	-0.001	0.001
Soil Pct. Clay	-0.008*	-0.008*	-0.002	0.006*	-0.002	0.000	0.000	0.000	-0.003*
Topsoil Depth	3.372*	1.940*	-0.861*	-3.463*	0.365	0.017	-0.126	0.001	-0.794*
Precipitation	-0.014	-0.091*	0.116*	0.088*	0.001	0.001	0.002	-0.036*	0.012
Max.Temperature	-6.068*	0.334	1.958*	4.607*	-0.334	-0.067	-0.700*	-2.079*	2.597*
Min.Temperature	5.569*	2.879	-5.315*	-7.797*	-1.287	0.061	0.526	-0.063	-1.792
Pct. Farmland Irrigated	0.833*	-0.849*	0.978*	-0.552*	0.641	-0.005	-0.060*	0.557*	-0.303*
Adjusted R-Squared	0.553	0.254	0.652	0.440	-0.003	0.031	0.244	0.510	0.123
N	404	396	306	420	17	112	256	177	420

*Starred coefficients are significant at alpha=0.05 or less.

Table 6.3: OLS Regression Results:
Panel B: Environment, Farm Size, and Livestock, 1910 and 1990 (cont.)

| | Percent Farmland in Crops | Percent Cropland in: | | | | | | | |
		Wheat	Corn	Hay	Potatoes	Rye	Oats	Barley	Largest Crop
1910:									
Population Density	1.873	0.895	0.349	-0.900	-0.247	-0.018	0.890	0.055	-1.191
Adjusted R-Squared	0.782	0.411	0.596	0.501	0.021	0.125	0.403	0.337	0.157
N	402	402	402	402	402	324	402	323	402
1990:									
Population Density	-2.569	11.236	-20.646*	17.804	-15.344	-4.675	-3.908	-1.469	27.754*
Adjusted R-Squared	0.663	0.251	0.656	0.477	-0.273	0.040	0.265	0.511	0.167
N	404	396	306	420	17	112	256	177	420

*Starred coefficients are significant at alpha=0.05 or less.

Table 6.4: Summary OLS Regression Results
Panel A: Population Density and Land Use Outcomes, Great Plains Counties, 1910 and 1990: Cropping Variables*
The coefficients presented in this table are the result of adding Population Density as an independent variable to the regression model shown in table 6.3, panel A. Only the coefficient for Population Density is reported. See text for further details.

	Average Farm Size	Livestock per 1000 acres of Farmland in:			
		Dairy Cattle	Total Cattle	Sheep	Hogs/Swine
1910:					
Population Density	-56.217	44.195*	59.289*	-8.924	5.309*
Adjusted R-Squared	0.099	0.966	0.556	0.249	0.526
N	402	402	402	402	402
1990:					
Population Density	-3763.746*	24.100*	-73.205	3.884	-0.186
Adjusted R-Squared	0.449	0.103	0.420	0.085	0.382
N	423	363	423	382	403

*Starred coefficients are significant at alpha=0.05 or less.

Panel B: Population Density and Land Use Outcomes, Great Plains Counties, 1910 and 1990: Livestock Variables*The coefficients presented in this table are the result of adding Population Density as an independent variable to the regression model shown in table 6.3, panel B. Only the coefficient for Population Density is reported. See text for further details.

The inclusion of population density in table 6.4 shows one of the ways that farming changed between the beginning and end of the twentieth century.[30] The overall level of cropland in counties was positively associated with population density (and significant) in 1910, but it was not statistically significant in 1990. The availability of a labor force led to an increase in cropland in 1910, but did not make much of a difference in 1990. Population density was also positively associated with cattle in 1910 (but not 1990) and negatively associated with farm size in both 1910 and 1990. The greater the population density, the smaller the average farm, but the more cattle per acre.

Ethnicity as a Predictor of Land Use Outcomes

Building from the environmental and general-population bases, our final set of analyses includes county indicators of German presence. For both 1910 and 1990, we use a variable that captures the percent of the population that is German. Table 6.5 presents simplified OLS regression results on a set of dependent land variables specifying aspects of cropping in the Great Plains, adding the indicator of German presence to the environmental and population characteristics presented above.

German Patterns in Cropping and Farm Size. Overall, ethnic information adds only a little explanatory power to the base models predicting how much farmland in a county is dedicated to cropping. Environmental and general-population variables alone account for nearly eighty percent of the 1910 variance in cropping, and over two-thirds of the variance in 1990. No additional variance is explained in 1910 by adding a measure of ethnicity, and the increase for 1990 is slight. Still, the analyses in both time periods suggest that, other things being equal, counties with a large German presence (immigrant in 1910/ancestry in 1990) were slightly more likely to crop their farmland than counties dominated by other ethnic populations.

While environmental opportunities and constraints appear to outweigh the effect of German influence, some differences in specific crops grown do emerge in table 6.5, panel A. In both the 1910 and 1990 analyses, including information about the population of Germans in a county significantly boosts the explanatory power of models seeking to estimate the percent of farmland

---

30. In order to emphasize the impact of the new variables added in the models reported in tables 6.4 and 6.5, we only report the regression coefficients for the additional variables, population density and percent German. For full regression results for these models, please contact the authors.

Percent Cropland in:

	Percent Farmland in Crops	Wheat	Corn	Hay	Potatoes	Rye	Oats	Barley	Largest Crop
1910:									
Percent German	29.095*	-49.567*	18.005	29.599	-5.655	1.767*	29.792*	-12.699*	-25.666
Adjusted R-Squared	0.785	0.423	0.596	0.504	0.022	0.135	0.433	0.351	0.162
N	402	402	402	402	402	324	402	323	402
1990:									
Percent German	6.917	2.791	7.269	-1.775	3.553	0.373	7.157*	-2.620	-15.132*
Adjusted R-Squared	0.663	0.249	0.656	0.476	-0.460	0.040	0.373	0.510	0.175
N	404	396	306	420	17	112	256	177	420

*Starred coefficients are significant at alpha=0.05 or less.

Table 6.5: OLS Regression Results
Panel A: Ethnic Composition and Land Use Outcomes, Great Plains Counties, 1910 and 1990: Cropping Variables*
The coefficients presented in this table are the result of adding both Population Density and Percent German as independent variables to the regression model shown in table 6.3, panel A. Only the coefficient for Percent German is reported. See text for further details.

	Average Farm Size	Livestock per 1000 acres of Farmland in:			
		Dairy Cattle	Total Cattle	Sheep	Hogs/Swine
1910:					
Percent German	1,392.143	28.987*	172.045*	-25.048	228.772*
Adjusted R-Squared	0.097	0.968	0.581	0.247	0.583
N	402	402	402	402	402
1990:					
Percent German	-1723.530*	5.201	85.847*	-3.592	70.080*
Adjusted R-Squared	0.436	0.108	0.432	0.083	0.395
N	423	363	423	382	403

*Starred coefficients are significant at alpha=0.05 or less.

Panel B: Ethnic Composition and Land Use Outcomes, Great Plains Counties, 1910 and 1990: Livestock Variables*

The coefficients presented in this table are the result of adding both Population Density and Percent German as independent variables to the regression model shown in table 6.3, panel B. Only the coefficient for Percent German is reported. See text for further details.

dedicated to specific crops. Some of the patterns confirm the historical/archival analyses based on local case studies of ethnicity and agricultural production; some call those observations into question.

While many immigrant farmers in the early period grew wheat for its commercial payoff, Germans who did so may have chosen it and other small grains based on traditional Old World farming practices.[31] Other historians state that in the early settlement period, Germans were more likely than other ethnic groups to grow small grains other than wheat, such as barley and rye.[32] In our analyses, we find that German presence is positively associated with rye in 1910 but not in 1990. We also discover that in 1910 Germans were less likely than other ethnic groups to grow barley, perhaps a sign that Old World preferences had begun to fade.

The crop equations present a complex set of ethnic effects on agricultural outcomes. Taken together, they suggest that German effects on crop choice were more prevalent in 1910 than in 1990, and may reflect a greater tendency for those counties with a strong immigrant presence to produce a wider variety of agricultural products for its own consumption. For example, in 1910 the production of rye and oats (both relatively non-market-oriented crops) was greatest in those counties with strong German presence. Even in 1990, the percent of cropland dedicated to the single largest crop (regardless of what it might be) was lowest in counties with a large German population. Diversity in production is associated with the German immigrant experience in 1910 and in the German enclaves of the Great Plains in 1990.

We present results about German influence on farm size and livestock raising in table 6.5, panel B. In terms of farm size, no significant ethnic effects appear for 1910, and overall explained variance in the equation is quite low. Whatever was driving variation in farm size in 1910 was not linked to the ethnic variation in the Great Plains population. However, by 1990, nearly half the variation in farm size across the Great Plains was explained by environmental, general population, and ethnic characteristics. Germans were likely to have smaller farms than other ethnic groups, supporting our notion that the ideal of the German family farm persists today.

31. Thomas R. Wessel, *Agriculture in the Great Plains, 1876–1936* (Washington, DC: The Agricultural History Society, 1977), 42–44.

32. Terry G. Jordan, *German Seed in Texas Soil: Immigrant Farmers in Nineteenth Century Texas* (Austin: University of Texas Press, 1966).

German Patterns in Livestock Production. Just as the historical literature would suggest, livestock production demonstrates some clear ethnic patterns, particularly in 1910. Germans were more likely than others to raise cattle generally, dairy cattle specifically, and swine on their farmland. Although the ethnic effects for the 1910 data are slightly stronger than in 1990, the pattern persists into the recent period.

Several general themes emerge from our attempt to incorporate a measure of German influence into models of agricultural land use. First, although German patterns of land use may have diminished as the population has distanced itself from the first generation, the presence of ethnic variation in the Great Plains still contributes to the variation observed in agricultural outcomes. Second, ethnic variation may matter more for some agricultural decisions than for others. Very little seems to be gained by adding ethnicity to models of overall crop production or to the production of some specific crops (such as corn or hay in both time periods). In contrast, ethnicity does seem to matter in the determinants of the production of wheat, rye, and oats. It also matters considerably in the models estimating how many and what kinds of livestock are incorporated into Great Plains farming. This observation suggests that we examine more closely the ways in which market factors (the risk/reward ratios of various crops and livestock types, for example) fit into the general farming strategies of different ethnic groups of farmers. The fact that German differences persist into the 1990 data suggests that such an exercise would be worthwhile not only for the past, but also for the contemporary period.

Thus, counties with a substantial German-origin ethnic community continue to demonstrate land use decisions that differ from counties where that presence is modest, controlling for basic environmental differences in soil quality and climate across the Great Plains region.

Conclusion

This research explores the historical generalization about agricultural production suggesting that ethnicity matters in understanding agricultural outcomes. Given the paucity of empirical data on the ethnic characteristics of farmers over time and across space, we have chosen to characterize farm counties in a key agricultural production region of the United States according to their ethnic composition near the beginning and end of the twentieth century, with particular attention to the influence of German-origin populations. Furthermore, we have tried to set aside the effects of environmental opportunities and constraints by building our ethnicity models on a solid foundation of environmental controls. The results reveal patterns conforming to some of the historical literature while calling other generalizations into question.

First, our results indicate that German ethnic settlement mattered for agricultural production both at the onset and end of the twentieth century in the American Great Plains. The consistent emergence of ethnic effects in our county-level data implies that population variables play a role in shaping the environment, at least as it appears with human management. The direction in which many of the ethnic effects cut in these analyses did not always correspond to the expectations raised by historical case studies focused on Germans in other parts of the United States. Our results confirm the historical generalization that German-dominant farming communities were more likely to plant wheat and some small grains in the early period of settlement. In contrast to our expectation that crop diversity would diminish over time in the wake of market and policy forces, our results suggest that crop diversity continues to be associated with the presence of a larger German-origin community in the contemporary period.

The results confirm expectations that counties with large German-origin populations would own more cattle, dairy cows, and swine per acre than counties with other ethnic profiles. These results do not confirm a statistical relationship between average farm size in 1910 and German-origin concentration, however. The 1990 data, on the other hand, do reveal a negative relationship between average farm size and the concentration of German-ancestry population in the county. The lack of a statistically significant negative relationship between German-origin settlement and average farm size in the early settlement period, combined with the historical literature focused on German settlement in particular localities suggesting that such a relationship did indeed exist, calls for further refinement of both the qualitative and quantitative approaches if the findings are to be reconciled.

Research challenges remain even after presenting these important findings. We cannot say, for example, how many of the results are driven by something in the shared culture of the inhabitants of these counties, rather than something in the environmental context. Still, the fact that ethnic effects persist over time and across space, after controlling for important differences in the opportunity structure presented by soil and climate, suggests that information about farming has been shared by people of common background living in a common territory.

Part III:

Politics and Ethnic Identity

7

German and Irish Political Engagement: The Politics of Cultural Diversity in an Industrial Age

Donald A. DeBats

The emerging interest in "social capital" as an explanatory factor in the development of democratic societies has a considerable capacity to shape new understandings of political life, both past and present. For historians, the idea of social capital renews and extends a longstanding appreciation of associational networks as central forces in sustaining American political engagement.[1] For political scientists, the interest in community structures and values that encourage (or fail to encourage) democratic politics recalls a time not so long ago when social networks rather than individualistic partisan identifications—or calculations of rational interest—were central matters in political studies.[2] A focus on social capital promises a more

---

1. For an excellent discussion of the application of this concept to a variety of societies, see the special double issue "Patterns of Social Capital," especially Robert I. Rotberg, "Social Capital and Political Culture in Africa, America, Australasia, and Europe," *Journal of Interdisciplinary History* 29 (Winter 1999): 339–356. On the concept applied to the United States, see Robert Putnam, "Bowling Alone: America's Declining Social Capital," *Journal of Democracy* 6 (January 1995): 65–78. For doubts about the historical applicability of the notion of social capital, see Jack P. Greene, "Social and Cultural Capital in Colonial British America: A Case Study," *Journal of Interdisciplinary History* 29 (Winter 1999): 491–509. For positive statements see Gerald Gamm and Robert D. Putnam, "The Growth of Voluntary Associations in America, 1840–1940," *Journal of Interdisciplinary History* 29 (Spring 1999): 511–557 and, with reservations, Mary P. Ryan, "Civil Society as Democratic Practice: North American Cities during the Nineteenth Century," *Journal of Interdisciplinary History* 29 (Spring 1999): 559–584. See also Theda Skocpol, "The Tocqueville Problem: Civic Engagement in American Democracy," *Social Science History* 21 (Winter 1997): 455–479; Theda Skocpol, *Diminished Democracy: From Membership to Management in American Life* (Norman: University of Oklahoma Press, 2003).

2. For a survey of that earlier work see Heinz Eulau, "The Columbia Studies of Personal Influence," *Social Science History* 4 (Spring 1980): 207–229. For a survey of more modern studies see K. S. Cook and J. M. Whitmeyer, "Two Approaches to Social Structure: Exchange Theory and Network Analysis," *Annual Review of Sociology* 18 (1992): 109–127. See also Bernard R. Berelson, Paul F. Lazarsfeld, and William N. McPhee, *Voting: A Study of Opinion Formation in a Presidential Campaign* (Chicago: University of Chicago Press, 1954) and Marvin E. Olsen, *Participatory Pluralism: Political Participation and Influence in the United States and*

analytical approach to the study of past and present political engagement as well as an opportunity to re-examine notions of American exceptionalism.[3]

For historians interested in issues of ethnicity and the place of immigrant groups in the political life of their adopted lands, social capital theory offers new ways of linking cultural organization and political participation, and more broadly of rejoining social and political histories. Historians have long noted the quickness of immigrant groups, "accustomed to a more tightly knit communal life," to form associations in their new homeland to "bind together their local ethnic communities."[4] That rich associational life so often seen as a hallmark of ethnic-group adaptation is in fact "a cornerstone" of the theory of social capital, which sees such activity as, "contributing . . . to the forging of horizontal networks of reciprocal trust . . . [w]ithout [which] it is difficult to sustain civic engagement and strong support for the democratic process."[5] In the simplest terms, the theory encourages us to ask whether we can better understand an ethnic group's engagement in the democratic process by uncovering the nature and extent of the social organizations established by that group. A new and more direct link is thus established between social and cultural activity on the one hand and political life on the other.

Just as reduced civic participation—more and more "bowling alone"—is seen as a worrying indicator of the decline of the democratic ethos in contemporary American society, so the earlier proliferation of such

---

Sweden (Chicago: Nelson-Hall, 1982). It is useful to recall, too, that the initial interest in the democratic contribution of groups to modern politics reflected a fear of mass powerlessness and atomization in modern industrial societies. The works of Harold Laski loom large here. For a survey of this literature see Francis W. Coker, "Pluralism," *Encyclopedia of the Social Sciences* 12, edited by Edwin R. A. Seligman (New York: The Macmillan Company, 1933), 170–173. For a critique of the vast rational choice literature as applied to politics, see Donald Green and Ian Shapiro, *Pathologies of Rational Choice Theory: A Critique of Applications in Political Science* (New Haven: Yale University Press, 1994).

3. For a critical look at the notion of the nineteenth century as a period defined by exceptional levels of political engagement, see Glenn C. Altschuler and Stuart M. Blumin, "'Where is the Real America?': Politics and Popular Consciousness in the Antebellum Era," *American Quarterly* 49 (June 1997): 225–267; Glenn C. Altschuler and Stuart M. Blumin, "Limits of Political Engagement in Antebellum America: A New Look at the Golden Age of Participatory Democracy," *Journal of American History* 84 (December 1997): 855–885; Glenn C. Altschuler and Stuart M. Blumin, *Rude Republic: Americans and Their Politics in the Nineteenth Century* (Princeton: Princeton University Press, 2000); Ryan, "Civil Society as Democratic Practice." For a sharp reply to the Altschuler and Blumin thesis see Harry L. Watson, "Humbug? Bah! Altschuler and Blumin and the Riddle of the Antebellum Electorate," *Journal of American History* 84 (December 1997): 886–893, especially 886.

4. Rowland Berthoff, *An Unsettled People: Social Order and Disorder in American History* (New York: Harper and Row, 1971), 273, as quoted in Gamm and Putnam, "Growth of Voluntary Associations," 531.

5. Rotberg, "Social Capital and Political Culture," 348.

associations impressed observers since de Tocqueville and may well, this theory holds, have underpinned the high levels of political engagement that typified the nineteenth century. "Societies with high levels of social capital function with greater, rather than lesser, participation of citizens."[6] From this it follows that the patterning of associational activity—the institutional history of voluntary organizations—that looms large in explanations of general political engagement might also help explain the course of political life seen in specific ethnic groups.

And yet, when we turn to the Germans and the Irish, the two largest immigrant groups in nineteenth-century North America, there is an obvious paradox in our understanding of the connection between social organization and political engagement. The rich, well documented study of associational life of German migrants emphasizes "an especially dense network of associations," but this observation sits alongside another literature that emphasizes no less the distinctly restrained nature of German political participation. The Irish, on the other hand, with a seemingly less extensive pattern of voluntary associations, are hailed in the literature as exemplars of extraordinary levels of political participation.[7] When we consider German and Irish immigrants, density of associational activity does not appear related to political involvement in the way that social capital theory would suggest. This seeming contradiction defines the organizing themes of this study and provides a new imperative for investigating whether German and Irish political participation were in fact as different as the literature suggests.

Close study of the realities of ethnic group political participation may also justify a more critical view of the literature linking social capital and a democratic ethos. Mary Ryan, who sees sustained associational activity as "an essential condition for, and component of, democratic politics," reminds us that voluntary associations can be far from democratic and argues that these institutions in themselves contribute little to the creation of a civil society. Democratically effective associations, Ryan believes, were more narrowly defined and characterized by "social inclusion, genuine participation, and power to affect the public realm." In fostering a democratic ethos, the internal

---

6. Rotberg, "Social Capital and Political Culture," 339.

7. Gamm and Putnam, "Growth of Voluntary Associations," 522; see also Kathleen Neils Conzen, "Immigrants, Immigrant Neighborhoods, and Ethnic Identity: Historical Issues," *Journal of American History* 66 (December 1979): 603–615 and James M. Berquist, "German Communities in American Cities: An Interpretation of the Nineteenth Century Experience," *Journal of American Ethnic History* 4 (Fall 1984): 9–30.

characteristics of associations and the social range of their membership may be more important than their simple presence. Even then, Ryan believes, associations should be understood as a component, but only a component, in the creation of that mix of voluntary organizations, mass political parties, public meetings, conflict, contention, and social movements that helped create an engaged democracy.[8]

This study brings to these theoretical questions and the empirical reality of nineteenth-century German and Irish political engagement an important new data source—the poll books. Poll books that survive in each of the three cases examined here make it possible to explore in ways not previously available the political life of German and Irish immigrants; from the poll books we can learn *who* actually went to the polls, which candidates and parties voters supported, and the social characteristics of both voters and nonvoters.[9] Linking political performance to information on associational activity may also help refine our understanding of the role of such activity in sustaining political engagement.

Poll book data—the written record of traditional British *viva voce* election law still in place in several American states and Canadian provinces at the midpoint of the nineteenth century—promise to take us beyond the assumption that immigrant communities engaged in politics in ways reflective of elite stances—a kind of New World version of Roeber's European principalities in which *cuius regio, eius religio* (subjects following their ruler's confession) prevailed.[10] If historians too often assume ordinary opinion from elite opinion, the poll books, as the definitive record of the actual behavior for all voters in a given locality, provide the ideal source from which to determine exactly how the ordinary voter *did* act politically. They allow us to "rethink the place of 'the people'" in nineteenth-century politics and to follow Reeve Huston's insistence that historians should more systematically explore the connection between the rank and file and the broader political world. The poll books are a concise recording of "the popular voices" of past politics for they take us into

8. See Ryan, "Civil Society as Democratic Practice," especially 560, 569, and 580.

9. The poll books for these elections can be located in the following Archives: Newport (Poll Books, Municipal, 1868–1878, Division of Archives and Records, Frankfort, Kentucky); Alexandria (Poll Lists, Arlington County, 1852–1861, Virginia State Library, Richmond, Virginia); Dereham (Poll Books, Oxford County, 1867, 1871, Regional History Collection, Files 133–134, 143–147, University of Western Ontario, London, Ontario).

10.   Jon F. Sensbach, "From Reich to Realm: German Immigrants in a New Land," *Reviews in American History* 22 (June 1994): 212.

the world of the ordinary nineteenth century voter, and the immigrant voter, in ways hitherto impossible.[11]

Viva voce law required the voter, in the New World as in the Old, to stand before his neighbors (*viva voce* disappeared well before women's suffrage) and call out in a loud voice his choice for all offices to be filled in that election. Clerks recorded those oral votes in poll books as a written record of the election and for the purpose of allowing the final vote tally to be adjusted after the close of the polls should any individual voter's eligibility be successfully challenged.[12] It is important to recall that while oral voting did not prevail everywhere in North America, nowhere was the vote secret. The ticket system, which prevailed where *viva voce* did not, required voters to place a brightly colored ballot paper in the voting box, thus endorsing a party's candidates and, not incidentally, assisting the party poll watchers in recording the choices of individual voters. The resulting canvass books, like the poll books, remind us of the absence of secrecy in North American elections at all times prior to the adoption of the Australian secret ballot in the closing years of the nineteenth century.[13]

If poll books take us into individual political worlds of the past, surviving nineteenth-century social inventories allow the reconstruction of the social worlds of those same voters. Linked, these individual level records provide unsurpassed insight into the political past. Some of the problematic issues

---

11. Reeve Huston, "The Nineteenth-Century Political Nation: A Tale of Two Syntheses," *Reviews in American History* 23 (September 1995): 419.

12. For a history of *viva voce* see Paul F. Bourke and Donald A. DeBats, "Identifiable Voting in Nineteenth-Century America: Toward a Comparison of Britain and the United States Before the Secret Ballot," *Perspectives in American History* 11 (1977–1978): 259–288. See also Paul F. Bourke and Donald A. DeBats, "Charles Sumner, the London Ballot Society and the Senate Debate of March, 1867," *Perspectives in American History*, n.s. 1 (1984): 343–357. For a full listing of the poll book studies in the United States and elsewhere, see Paul F. Bourke, Donald A. DeBats, *Washington County: Politics and Community in Antebellum America* (Baltimore: Johns Hopkins University Press, 1995), 346-347.

13. Canada adopted the secret ballot in 1874, and Virginia did so as a condition of rejoining the Union after the Civil War, while Kentucky continued to use *viva voce* in local elections until 1891, thus constituting, along with Western Australia, perhaps the last general elections anywhere to use oral voting. See Lionel E. Fredman, *The Australian Ballot: The Story of an American Reform* (East Lansing: Michigan State University Press, 1968); and George W. McCrary, *A Treatise on the American Law of Election*, 4th ed. (Chicago: Callaghan and Company, 1897). For an example of the use of poll lists, see Ronald P. Formisano, *The Birth of Mass Political Parties: Michigan, 1827–1861* (Princeton: Princeton University Press, 1971); and Ronald P. Formisano, *The Transformation of Political Culture: Massachusetts Parties, 1790s–1840s* (New York: Oxford University Press, 1983).

that have bedeviled the study of past politics—inference from aggregate to individual data and the typicality of socially homogenous districts—fall away; political history and social history are joined at the same level—the world of the individual.[14]

This study examines the associational activity and political behavior of German and Irish settlers in three localities: Alexandria, Virginia; Newport, Kentucky; and Dereham Township in Ontario's rural Oxford County. All three locales were in the mid-nineteenth century examples of the small- to medium-size communities generally regarded as stimulating both associational activity and high levels of political engagement.[15] In all three cases, too, the elections under study came at points of crisis likely to have encouraged political participation. The social and cultural diversity represented by these three case studies is striking. One was rural (Dereham Township), one was mercantile (Alexandria), and one was industrial (Newport). One was Canadian (Dereham), one was southern (Alexandria), and one was on the fringe of a Midwestern industrial city (Newport). This diversity of time, place, and political setting may assist in determining whether ethnic culture and its organization played a consistent role in shaping ethnic group political engagement. In all three places good runs of poll books survive, as do extensive social records. The overall diversity represented in these three case studies should underline the significance of common findings.

The study moves from a review of the literature on German and Irish political engagement in North America to a detailed consideration of these three places and the institutional expressions of German and Irish ethnicity in each. The focus then shifts to the central measures of German and Irish political participation—what proportion of Germans and Irishmen actually voted? Were the Germans in fact reluctant visitors to the polls, as the literature suggests, and were the Irish such keen participants? Was the rate of participation linked in

---

14. For the most recent statement of the problems of inferring individual from aggregate data, see Gary King, *A Solution to the Ecological Inference Problem: Reconstructing Individual Behavior from Aggregate Data* (Princeton: Princeton University Press, 1997). See also Paul F. Bourke, Donald A. DeBats, and Thomas Phelan, "Comparing Individual-Level Returns with Aggregates: An Historical Appraisal of the King Solution," *Historical Methods* 34 (2001): 127–134; Paul F. Bourke and Donald A. DeBats, "Individuals and Aggregates: A Note on Historical Data and Assumptions," *Social Science History* 4 (1980): 229–250; J. Morgan Kousser, "Ecological Regression and the Analysis of Past Politics," *Journal of Interdisciplinary History* 4 (Autumn 1973): 237–262.

15. Gamm and Putnam, "Growth of Voluntary Associations in America," find that "it was in the smallest and slowest-growing of the cities—the cities that stood, literally, on the urban periphery—where associational development was most vigorous" (549).

any obvious way to the general level of German and Irish associational activity in these three places, or was political participation more a function of the individual economic standing of the potential voters? The rich congregational records of Alexandria allow some detailed consideration of the relationship between a particular type of individual associational membership and political participation. Finally, the paper turns to the partisan choices of the German and Irish voters and examines through the poll books the notion, so strong in the literature, of a fractured German vote compared to a unanimous Irish political voice. The poll books allow us to determine with certainty which parties and candidates German and Irish voters *did* support. The linkage of social and political information allows an exploration of the political consequences of cultural divides between and within the German and Irish populations. How stable were those affiliations and under what circumstances would ethnic voters reverse their political partisan allegiances? In exploring these questions this study considers three indicators of nineteenth-century German and Irish political engagement—participation, partisan choice, and extent to which that partisan choice was ethnically cohesive.

The German and Irish Political Worlds: Differing Universes?

In both Canada and the United States German and Irish immigrants constituted, by the middle of the nineteenth century, the most visible national groups in increasingly complex societies.[16] Their presence in large numbers raised important new questions about the impact of so many "foreign" voices on a nation's political life. On the American side of the border these two intensively studied groups are generally represented in the literature as exemplars of starkly different political impulses. Modern scholarship on German Americans emphasizes the absence of a common national identity, a limited democratic experience, and a great deal of internal cultural division. The prevailing interpretation is of a divided German vote and a selective German engagement in American political life.[17] The American Irish, by

---

16. According to the U.S. census of 1860 and the Canadian census of 1861, the Irish-born represented 9.0% of the population of Canada and 5.1% of the population of the United States; the German born amounted to 0.75% of the Canadian population and 4.0% of the American population.

17. See, for example, Reinhard R. Doerries, "Immigrants and the Church: German Americans in Comparative Perspective," in this volume. Kathleen Neils Conzen, "Germans," in *Harvard Encyclopedia of American Ethnic Groups*, edited by Stephan Thernstrom (Cambridge: Harvard University Press, 1980), 405–425, especially 421. Walter D. Kamphoefner emphasizes the state-

contrast, have been consistently presented as enthusiastic, even boisterous, political participants, enlisted, almost without exception, in the cause of the Democratic Party.[18] Neither perception, however, arises from direct comparison of German and Irish political engagement. Indeed, those few general comparisons of German and Irish political involvement that have been undertaken suggest as much commonality as difference in the political life of German and Irish immigrants.[19]

Not surprisingly, Canadian scholarship on these matters marches to a different drum. This is especially true with respect to the Canadian Irish, the largest portion of whom arrived in Canada prior to the Famine, rather than after, as was the American experience. The Canadian Irish were proportionally more numerous and more Protestant than their compatriots south of the border. Studies of the Canadian Irish have lamented the lack of attention paid to this largest of national immigrant groups and the submergence of their experience in a distinctly American historiography.[20] Studies of the Irish in nineteenth-

based variations in German voting patterns. See Walter D. Kamphoefner, "German-Americans and Civil War Politics: A Reconsideration of the Ethnocultural Thesis," *Civil War History* 37 (1991): 232–246, especially 234–235. Bruce C. Levine emphasizes not so much temporary diversity as the movement of Germans in Chicago from solidly Democratic to insurgent Republican. See Bruce C. Levine, "Free Soil, Free Labor, and *Freimänner*: German Chicago in the Civil War Era," in *German Workers in Industrial Chicago, 1850–1910: A Comparative Perspective*, edited by Hartmut Keil and John B. Jentz (DeKalb: Northern Illinois University Press, 1983), 163–182, especially 171.

18. See, for example, Dennis Clark, *The Irish in Philadelphia: Ten Generations of Urban Experience* (Philadelphia: Temple University Press, 1973), especially 106–125. For a review of the study of the American Irish see Seamus P. Metress, *The Irish-American Experience: A Guide to the Literature* (Washington: University Press of America, 1981). Classic studies include Oscar Handlin, *Boston's Immigrants: A Study in Acculturation* (Cambridge: Harvard University Press, 1941); Carl Wittke, *The Irish in America* (Baton Rouge: Russell and Russell, 1956); George Potter, *To the Golden Door: The Story of the Irish in Ireland and America* (Boston: Little Brown and Company, 1960); William V. Shannon, *The American Irish* (New York: MacMillan, 1963); John B. Duff, *The Irish in the United States* (Belmont: Wadsworth Publishing Company, 1971); and Lawrence J. McCaffrey, *The Irish Diaspora in America* (Bloomington: Indiana University Press, 1976).

19. See, for example, Walter D. Kamphoefner, "German and Irish Big City Mayors: Comparative Perspective on Ethnic Politics" in this volume. See also Walter D. Kamphoefner, "Liberal Catholicism and Its Limits: The Social and Political Outlook of the Louisville *Katholischer Glaubensbote*, 1866–86," *Yearbook of German-American Studies* 31 (1996): 13–23.

20. See Donald Akenson, *The Irish in Ontario: A Study in Rural History* (Kingston: McGill-Queen's University Press, 1984); Cecil J. Houston and William J. Smyth, *Irish Emigration and Canadian Settlement: Patterns, Links, and Letters* (Toronto: University of Toronto Press, 1990), especially 1–9; Livio Di Matteo, "The Wealth of the Irish in Nineteenth-Century Ontario," *Social Science History* 20 (Summer 1996): 209–234.

century Canadian politics emphasize not enthusiastic and consistently partisan participation but the conflicting cultural pulls on the voter from Erin.[21] Thus the Catholic Irish of Québec were courted politically on the diverging grounds of nationality—that is as British subjects who should ally with other British voters—and as religious adherents who should vote with the French Catholics. In Québec, it appears that the Irish of whatever religion united in the main on nationality, that is Britishness, but it was a vote more conditional and considered than is suggested in the literature on the Irish south of the border.[22] Even in Upper Canada, where Irish Catholics and Irish Protestants tended to vote in opposite directions, the polarity was not absolute.[23] In many respects the interpretations of the Irish in Canada sound strikingly like contemporary interpretations of the Germans in America: a large, marginally engaged and divided group.

Variegation and contextualization, however, are themselves relatively new interpretations of German political engagement in the United States, as Walter Kamphoefner has reminded us. Earlier studies of German culture and politics tended to emphasize unity rather than division among German Americans. The focus then was on the "fit" of German culture with American culture, a perspective that reinforced the conclusions of early students of German-American political behavior. These views tended to present German Americans as a politically unified group that was at mid-century loyal to, and central to, the party of Lincoln.[24]

This view was eventually challenged and, in the hands of historians interested in the cultural basis of political engagement, the focus shifted to the persisting cultural differences among Germans in America. New research

---

21. For accounts of the shifting flow of Irish emigrants to Canada and the United States and the special attractions of Canadian conditions to Protestant Irish, see Kerby A. Miller, *Emigrants and Exiles: Ireland and the Irish Exodus to North America* (New York: Oxford University Press, 1985).

22. David De Brou, "The Rose, the Shamrock and the Cabbage: The Battle for Irish Voters in Upper-Town Quebec, 1827–1836," *Social History* 24 (November 1991): 305–334, especially 324–326.

23. Gail Campbell, "'Smashers' and 'Rummies': Voters and the Rise of Parties in Charlotte County, New Brunswick, 1846–1857," *Historical Papers* (1986): 86–116. Campbell estimates (103) that about seven percent of Irish Catholics voted against "the power of an entrenched Anglican and Presbyterian establishment."

24. Kamphoefner, "German-Americans and Civil War Politics." The notion of the German voter as central to Lincoln's victory was popular from William Dodd's 1911 essay to Joseph Schafer's rebuttal thirty years later. See Joseph Schafer, "Who Elected Lincoln?" *American Historical Review* 47 (October 1941): 51–63.

emphasized the diversity of the Germans, divided in their new home by many factors, not least the cultural differences carried over from Europe. Lacking a unifying national identity, divided even in specific regions by conflicting cultural understandings of issues such as property and liberty, Germans in the New World would take time to develop a sense of themselves as a group united by a common culture. The new interpretation also emphasized an apolitical and perhaps deferential stance on the part of German-born immigrants. Those who did engage in American political life often reflected in their approach the division between the pietistic and liturgical religious outlooks that contended in America no less than in Europe.[25] German Americans thus became exemplars of the evangelical/ritualistic divide that these historians found running through so much of nineteenth century American politics, separating Baptists and Methodists from Lutherans and Catholics. The Germans, however, were not seen as enthusiastic participants in these cultural politics; even when engaged, German Americans, "the most diverse ethnic group in America," became famous, at least in modern literature, for their factious approach to these politics.[26]

In recent years this view has been further particularized by an insistence that what was important in the political life of the Germans in America was not just the highly variegated cultural baggage that the immigrants brought with them but also the political context in which those people and that baggage landed. Moderating German political engagement was the nature of the political choice the German voter confronted in his specific locale. More specifically, where the Republican Party was untainted by nativist and anti-immigrant tendencies (not to mention temperance), Germans might well become supporters of the GOP. Where Republicans were associated with nativism or temperance, Germans drifted toward the Democratic Party, as they did in Wisconsin in the 1870s.[27] Precisely how this "contextual effect" interacted with the "baggage effect" is less clear.

---

25. See Sensbach, "From Reich to Realm," 210–215; Kamphoefner, "German-Americans and Civil War Politics." For an incisive review of the wider debate over the role of cultural differences in American political life, see Ronald P. Formisano, "Invention of the Ethnocultural Interpretation," *American Historical Review* 99 (1994): 453–477.

26. Quotation from Frederick C. Luebke, ed., *Ethnic Voters and the Election of Lincoln* (Lincoln: University of Nebraska Press, 1971), xi.

27. Paul Kleppner, *The Third Electoral System, 1853–1892: Parties, Voters, and Political Cultures* (Chapel Hill: University of North Carolina Press, 1979), 138; Kamphoefner, "German-Americans and Civil War Politics," 238.

There is, as noted, little of this nuanced sensitivity evident in the treatment of the American Irish. To conjure up the Irish voter on the American side of the border at virtually any time after the formation of mass parties in the 1830s and 1840s is to see an active participant in American political life and an enthusiast for the Democratic Party. Paul Kleppner argued long ago that the Irish Catholics were "the most strongly and consistently Democratic of the newer immigrant groups."[28] They were "highly visible and assertive" in their support for the Democrats.[29] Key to this partisan stance, as Noel Ignatiev has recently explained, "was the Party's rejection of nativism."[30] Indeed, "[t]he need to gain the loyalty of the Irish explains why the Democratic Party, on the whole, rejected nativism."[31] While the relationship between the Democrats and Irish was not "automatic," it was in place from the 1840s onward, informed by and strengthened by antagonism toward abolitionist Republicans.[32]

Yet in this view the Irish voter appears less sensitive than the German voter to the nuances of the local Republican establishment, especially whether it was associated with nativism—or was sympathetic toward blacks. Republican "rejection of nativism" seemingly had less impact on Irish than on German voters. Likewise, there is little notion in this literature that the Irish carried a contested political baggage with them. Nor is it clear why antipathy toward blacks should attract the Irish, but not the Germans, to the Democratic Party.[33]

The German-Canadian case for designation as a "charter group" rests on an early presence in Canada and a longstanding claim as the largest non-British, non-French group in Canadian society.[34] If the Canadian emphasis on internal divisions among German immigrants is familiar, the parallel concentration on the decline of ethnic feeling and identity is less so. In part this reflects the centrality of English-French tensions in Canadian approaches to issues of ethnic politics, and in part it reflects the early preponderance of British culture in the non-French portions of the emerging Canadian nation.

---

28. Kleppner, *Third Electoral System*, 61.

29. Kleppner, *Third Electoral System*, 69.

30. Noel Ignatiev, *How the Irish Became White* (New York: Routledge, 1995), 76.

31. Ignatiev, *How the Irish Became White*, 69.

32. Ignatiev, *How the Irish Became White*, 75.

33. Kamphoefner argues that combating nativism was the first priority. See Kamphoefner "German-Americans and Civil War Politics," 238. For an example of anti-black sentiment in the German language press, see Kamphoefner, "Liberal Catholicism and Its Limits," 14–17.

34. See K. M. McLaughlin, *The Germans in Canada* (Ottawa: Canadian Historical Association, 1985).

This preoccupation with the historical roots of French-English estrangement has led many Canadian historians to decry an overemphasis on the assimilation and melding of all other cultures into an "Anglo" identity and the neglect of a past Canadian political life more plural and less bifurcated.[35] The poll books allow a closer investigation of that political world too.

Three Settings

The worlds spanned by these case studies were very different. Alexandria in the late 1850s was a long established mercantile city on the Virginia side of the Potomac River, directly across from Washington, DC. The city, once part of the District, was prospering as the entrepot for the Shenandoah Valley. Newport in the early 1870s was a rapidly expanding—and far from peaceable—industrial town just across the Ohio River from Cincinnati; it was the site of one of the Ohio River valley's larger iron and steel mills—the Swift Iron Works. Dereham Township, in the southwest corner of Oxford County, Ontario, was a prosperous farming and dairy area not far from the northern shores of Lake Erie and, with the arrival of the railroad, ever more connected to the markets of Toronto and beyond. The three case studies represent modern forms of economic activity—commercial, industrial, and agricultural. We approach them at a moment of considerable political uncertainty: Alexandria, Virginia, on the eve of the Civil War; Dereham Township, Ontario, in the provincial election of 1871, one of the first elections following Canadian Federation in 1867; and Newport, Kentucky, at the precise moment in 1874 when the city was paralyzed by a bitter iron workers' strike.

All three communities were, by the standards of their time, midsized places. Mercantile Alexandria in 1860 recorded a population of just over 13,000, of whom 1,400 were slaves and 1,500 were free blacks. Industrial Newport in 1870 had a white population of just under 16,000 and fewer than 150 recorded black residents. The population of Dereham, increasingly involved in commercial dairy farming, reached 6,300 in the first Canada-wide census of 1871.

Just as these three places were very different in economic terms, so they were in their cultural composition. German and Irish migrants were present in each in very different proportions and in different ways. Moreover, the social inventories of the time recorded different features of the Irish and German

---

35. See Howard Palmer, *Ethnicity and Politics in Canada Since Confederation* (Ottawa: Canadian Historical Association, 1991).

populations. While the U.S. census schedules of 1860 and 1870 asked simply for the place of birth of residents, the Canadian schedule of 1871 also asked each respondent to identify his or her "origin." The census takers would explain, if asked, that this meant the patrilineal connection prior to entry to the North American continent; they were asking in effect for each resident's Old World ethnic identity. The Canadian census takers also instructed each resident to answer a question on religious affiliation. Religious information, so fragmentary, indirect, and hard won south of the border, is thus universally available for Canadians.

In terms of place of birth of its residents, industrial Newport was, not surprisingly, the most "ethnic" of the three; seventeen percent of the population had been born in Germany and another seven percent in Ireland. But of course there was a much greater presence of Germans and Irish within the electorates of these three places. There were 1,247 German-born adult males in Newport in 1870, making up thirty-five percent of the adult male population of the city; the 476 Irishmen over the age of twenty-one made up another fourteen percent of the potential voting population. Alexandria was in total only two percent German and eight percent Irish, but 111 German-born men and 331 Irishmen made up four percent and fourteen percent respectively of the city's adult white male population. Dereham was overwhelmingly populated by people of Canadian birth with only five percent of Irish birth and less than one percent of German birth. But the 1871 Canadian census of Dereham also recorded 343 men of Irish origin—a full twenty-six percent of the adult male population—and 109 men (eight percent of the total adult male population) who claimed German origin.[36] This study rests on the political performance of these 1,467 German men and 1,150 Irish men of voting age in three interesting, diverse locales.

Institutional Expressions of German and Irish Culture

The Germans of Upper Canada had for the most part passed through the United States on their way to the enormous tracts of Canadian land being opened for settlement in the early years of the nineteenth century. The Germans settled less in compact and institutionalized communities than in widely scattered family groups.[37] The German settlement in Dereham

36. Almost without exception those adult males of Irish or German birth appear in the Canadian census as being of Irish or German origin.

37.　Waterloo County, where Germans made up seventy-three percent of the population in 1871 and came to dominate cultural and political life, was an exception to the Canadian pattern, as

Township was notably scattered, inhibiting institutional development. One German historian remarked on the large number of Germans in the northern reaches of Oxford County, but observed that despite their numbers, there were few Lutherans because "they had never organized a church of their own."[38] In religious terms the Dereham Germans reflected the faiths of their non-German neighbors; by and large they were Methodists (fifty-nine percent) and Baptists (twenty percent).[39]

The Irish of Dereham, both those born in Ireland and those tracing their cultural roots there, were, in the pattern of the nineteenth-century Canadian Irish, largely Protestant. Those of Irish birth in Dereham Township were about sixty-three percent Protestant, a figure close to the Canada-wide average of fifty-five percent; those of Irish origin were even more likely to be Protestants with seventy-five percent (compared to a Canada-wide average of sixty-two percent) listing Protestant religions.[40] Even more than the Germans, the Irish of Dereham reflected in their religious affiliations the faiths of the communities in which they dwelt.

For neither group were there significant institutional expressions of ethnic identity. There were no specifically German organizations evident in the Dereham Township census or township directory and the Irish were represented only by the ubiquitous Loyal Orange Order—Lodge 648 of Culloden. The first Catholic church in the area was built in Tillsonburg in 1875; prior to that, Fr.

were the Mennonites, composed largely of migrants from Pennsylvania, who reflected in their settlement patterns a "desire for concentration and seclusion from strangers." McLaughlin, *The Germans in Canada*, 8–9; Heinz Lehmann, *The German-Canadians, 1750–1937: Immigration, Settlement and Culture* (St. John: Jesperson Press, 1986), 16.

38. Lehmann, *The German-Canadians*, 86–87. On the general settlement of Oxford County see Brian Dawe, *Old Oxford is Wide Awake! Pioneer Settlers and Politicians in Oxford County, 1793–1853* (London, Ontario: John Deyell Company, 1980), 3–25.

39. There were very small Mennonite, Catholic, and Lutheran populations in Dereham township. The only concentration of ethnic Germans was around the market town of Mt. Elgin. There were no German Catholics in Dereham Township. Dereham was forty-six percent Methodist and fourteen percent Baptist. While many of the German Methodists in Dereham migrated from the United States, there is no evidence that they brought with them the pattern of German-language Methodism.

40. For the religious disposition of Canadians of Irish "origin," see A. Gordon Darroch and Michael D. Ornstein, "Ethnicity and Occupational Structure in Canada in 1871: The Vertical Mosaic in Historical Perspective," *Canadian Historical Review* 61 (September 1980): 312. See also Houston, Smyth, *Irish Emigration and Canadian Settlement*, 8. Those of Irish origin in Dereham were thirty-eight percent Methodist, seventeen percent Anglican, twelve percent Baptist, seven percent Presbyterian, and twenty-five percent Catholic; Dereham overall was forty-six percent Methodist, seventeen percent Anglican, fourteen percent Baptist, nine percent Presbyterian, and eight percent Catholic.

O'Donovan of Woodstock held a service once every three months in McLean's Hall.[41] Nevertheless, anti-Catholicism was in the political air. In 1871 the local *Tillsonburg Observer* castigated George Brown, an emerging Reform Party leader, as exhibiting "a Popish intolerance." The *Observer* also publicized, albeit somewhat uncertainly, a lecture tour of "Baron de Camin" who would deliver in Tillsonburg his "Oration on Popery." The *Observer* was confident that "curiosity will fill the hall or church to overflowing."[42]

Both Irish and Germans were more socially distinctive in Alexandria and thus more institutionally present. The small German population of Alexandria was significantly Jewish and dominated the local Beth El synagogue.[43] If there were German Lutherans, they were not organized as such and a Lutheran church did not form in Alexandria until after the Civil War. German men in Alexandria were also concentrated in a few highly visible occupations—baker, confectioner, and clothier—running eighteen of the city's fifty bakeries and dominating the clothing trade. The Musikverein Alexandria was organized in the 1850s and the Hebrew Benevolent Society in 1857; they, together with the Alexandria Verein, provided the basis for the vast expansion of German cultural activities during the Civil War. New developments included a weekly German language newspaper (the *Alexandria Beobachter)*, Die Eintracht (a club that staged German plays), an Alexandria Turnverein, and two new singing groups (the Alexandria Maennerchor and the Concordia Gesangverein).[44]

The most obvious cultural expressions of Irishness in Alexandria were St. Mary's Catholic church, the boys' school (St. John's Academy), and the social clubs that both institutions supported. The local Hibernian Society was also much in evidence. Anti-immigrant politics was in the air here too. On the eve of the 1859 election, the local newspaper, the *Alexandria Gazette*, ran a letter to the editor criticizing efforts to induce members of the Young Catholics' Friend Society to vote for Henry Shackelford, a splinter Democratic candidate

41. See "Catholic Church Diamond Jubilee" in *Ingersol Sentinel-Review*, 28 Nov. 1935; "Woodstock" entry, *Oxford County Scrapbooks*, Vol. 14, n.p., Weldon Library, Regional History Collection, University of Western Ontario.

42. *Tillsonburg Observer*, 30 March 1871, 23 February 1871.

43. Tobias Brinkmann emphasizes the social divisions within the "German Jews" of Chicago and the social distance between the Jewish groups and other German communities in that city. In Alexandria, however, Jewishness defined the majority of the German population. On the Chicago pattern see Tobias Brinkmann, "The Dialectics of Ethnic Identity: German Jews in Chicago, 1850–1870" in this volume.

44. See Klaus G. Wust, "German Influences in the Settlement of Alexandria, Virginia," *Alexandria Gazette*, 5 March 1954.

for Congress. In an interview printed in the *Gazette,* Richard L. Carne, a teacher at St. John's soon to become the school's principal, rejected the charge that Catholic men were being mobilized for political purposes:

> the members of this Society would vote, some for Gov. Smith, others for Mr. Shackelford, and others again for Maj. Thomas . . . . [T]he Catholics of Alexandria were far less unanimous in their opinions on the subject than the members of several other churches. He had asked many Catholics the question of whether they had ever been called upon to vote against Gov. Smith on religious grounds, and always received a negative reply.[45]

The sly reference to voting against William Smith, the nominee of the regular Democratic Party for Congress, on "religious grounds," went to the heart of the matter—the alleged past association of Smith with the Know Nothing Party and his opposition to immigrants generally. The *Alexandria Gazette*, an opposition paper, delighted in the Democratic squabble, gleefully printing letters from a writer claiming to be a local Democrat, who laid out the details of Smith's anti-immigrant stance. It was alleged that in 1855, Smith, "on the stump" and in private conversations, "advance[d] some of the strongest arguments . . . by any one in favor of Know-Nothing principles." Smith did more "by his speeches and his influence . . . to build up and strengthen the Know-Nothing [P]arty in this District, than any other man in it." Smith was said to believe that the Know-Nothings did not go far enough, and it was alleged that he was in favor of a total repeal of the naturalization laws.[46] Smith's anti-immigrant views, based upon his assertions that immigration disproportionally assisted the Northern states and added to their political power, led him to pledge that, if elected to Congress, he would use all his influence and power "to break the flood tide of emigration now bursting on our shores."[47]

This seems to have been the pretext for the effort clearly afoot to urge Irish Catholics to vote for Shackelford, the alternative Democratic candidate. Smith's supporters heatedly denied the Know-Nothing allegation and the candidate went out of his way to court the German voters of Alexandria, speaking at the Saengerbund Festival in nearby Arlington Springs just before

45. *Alexandria Gazette*, 10 May 1859.

46. *Alexandria Gazette*, 20 May 1859.

47. Ibid.

the election, and "complimenting the German population for the many virtues and good qualities they display."[48] Whether Smith also used that occasion to discuss his well known temperance activities, which he would continue as a member of the Confederate House of Representatives, is not clear.[49] There is no doubt, however, that Smith was a candidate of limited natural appeal to the Irish and German voters of Alexandria.

The German-born and Irish-born of Alexandria were the two largest foreign-born groups in the city. They enjoyed, compared to their compatriots in Dereham Township, a greater, if still modest, range of associations and institutions that helped sustain their cultural identities and, as the Young Catholics' Friend Society suggests, also served as a basis of political mobilization. Certainly the appeals to voters in terms of their ethnic identity were more blatant in Alexandria than in Dereham.

The Germans of Newport, not surprisingly, were the most institutionalized of any of the six groups under consideration here. Newport was essentially an industrial suburb of Cincinnati, the second most German city in the United States in 1870, and a city often referred to as the "Munich of North America."[50] The Newport Germans benefited from the proximity of German cultural life in Cincinnati. But Newport, too, boasted a solid historical base of local German settlement. By 1873 there were six large "German" churches in the city—two Catholic (St. Stephen's and Corpus Christi, both with German-born priests), two Lutheran (St. Paul's and St. John's), the German Methodist Episcopal Church, the First German Baptist Church, as well as smaller United Brethren and German Reformed parishes. There were two Lutheran German schools, two German Catholic schools (St. Stephen's depended on Notre Dame sisters while Ursuline nuns served Corpus Christi) and one German Reformed school. The German language was important in Newport. Helena Klinger and J. J. Hetsch taught German in the city's high schools, and German remained a language spoken in churches well into the twentieth century.[51] The two large German Catholic churches sponsored, as in Alexandria, associations for young men and women. The city's German benevolent institutions included

---

48. See *Alexandria Gazette*, 14 March, 4 April, 14 April, 18 June 1859.

49. See John W. Bell, *Memoirs of Governor William Smith of Virginia* ([New York]: n.p., 1891).

50. See Henry D. Shapiro and Jonathan D. Sarna, eds., *Ethnic Diversity and Civic Identity: Patterns of Conflict and Cohesion in Cincinnati since 1820* (Urbana: University of Illinois Press, 1992), especially Levine, "Community Divided" and Miller, "Cincinnati Germans."

51. Lowell H. Harrison and James C. Klotter, *A New History of Kentucky* (Lexington: University Press of Kentucky, 1997), 221.

the German Beneficial Society and the Harugari; there was also the Newport Turngemeinde and two German Building Associations.[52]

The Irish of Newport were less institutionally present. The center of cultural life for Irish Catholics was the Church of the Immaculate Conception and its Immaculata Academy. But there were surprisingly few Irish organizations beyond the church in Newport, despite the considerable Irish presence in the town.

Newport was not a peaceable place for either the Irish or the Germans. Like so many Ohio River valley towns, Newport had a long tradition of anti-immigrant sentiment. The Know-Nothing upheavals of 1855, which featured pitched nativist riots in Cincinnati, rolled across the river into Newport where local anti-German feelings led to mass assaults, injuries, and a good many arrests. Significantly, it was the local Republicans who were most associated with this prewar nativism.[53]

Then in the fall of 1873 the city reeled from the first waves of economic panic that heralded the unprecedented era of economic depression about to engulf the entire region. The ironworkers, especially the largely immigrant heater and roller teams at the heart of the production process, were the first to feel the efforts of mill owners to reduce wages. The newly organized Ohio Valley Iron Association, a grouping of owners who accorded a prominent place to Alexander Swift, led the fight against the fledgling Ohio Valley Heaters and Rollers trade union. As Herbert Gutman demonstrated forty years ago, a surprising amount of the ensuing regional conflict between labor and management played out in Newport around the efforts of Alexander Swift to break the strike at his Newport works. The problem for Swift and the other mill owners was that, whereas in other regions the wages for heaters and rollers and their four-man teams were a function of the price of the finished metal, in the Ohio Valley works these wages were fixed. Owners like Swift thus confronted rapidly falling prices for finished iron but fixed wages for the cost of producing that iron. Bankruptcy loomed quickly as the owners found themselves caught

---

52. For details of the Newport German groups and activities, see W. Bonenkamp, J. Jessing, and J. B. Müller, *Schematismus der deutschen und der deutsch-sprechenden Priester, sowie der deutschen Katholiken-Gemeinden in den Vereinigten Staaten Nord-Amerika's* (Freiburg im Breisgau: Herder'sche Verlagshandlung, 1882), 182; and Johannes Enzlberger, *Schematismus der katholischen Geistlichkeit deutscher Zunge in den Vereinigten Staaten Amerikas* (Milwaukee: Hoffmann Brothers Co., 1892), 92. See also Newport City Directories for 1869 and 1873 in *Williams' Cincinnati Directory for 1869* (Cincinnati: Williams' and Company, 1869); *Williams' Cincinnati Directory for 1873* (Cincinnati: Williams' and Company, 1873).

53. See Steven J. Ross, *Workers on the Edge: Work, Leisure, and Politics in Industrializing Cincinnati, 1788–1890* (New York: Columbia University Press, 1985), 182–188.

up in a cascading competitive disadvantage. In early December 1873, the owners announced a twenty percent wage cut and then, in the face of resistance, a further cut of ten percent.[54]

Gutman argued that in smaller industrial towns like Newport, mill owners confronted strong community opposition to their efforts to reduce wages for skilled workers and to split skilled from unskilled labor. Not only did the striking workers resist, but so did the townspeople who personally knew the men and the families involved in this accelerating labor unrest. Indeed, the townspeople and their political voices, raised particularly against the use of the local police power in aid of the mill owners, provided the critical constituency for the strikers' cause.[55]

Certainly this appears to have been the case in Newport. Arrogant and determined, Alexander Swift brought in strikebreakers in January 1874 in an effort to reopen his mill, and hired private armed police to protect them. But the striking workers and their wives hounded the "scabs," threatening them with beatings and dumping pails of slops over them. Swift became even more irate as his strikebreakers melted away. He assailed the city authorities, and the Newport police in particular, for "not fully protecting his new workers" and threatened to bring in yet more blacks and Germans as new strikebreakers.

On February 21 a confrontation developed between strikebreakers and strikers. Fistfights rolled along the city streets, and three strikers were arrested by city police, only to be immediately released by sympathetic local judges. Alexander Swift, enraged, demanded that the city authorities prohibit protesters from gathering on city streets, but the city government again rebuffed his demand. Swift now issued pistols to his remaining strikebreakers, and the following day, in the midst of the predictable confrontation, one of the strikebreakers fired into the mob, killing Frederick Boss, a young butcher's apprentice. The crowd descended on the strikebreakers and, local folklore has it, chased them all out of town.[56]

In an atmosphere of increasing tension, Swift sought to apply new pressures. He appealed to the Catholic priests of Newport to urge the many rollers and heaters in their parishes to return to work. He initiated civil writs for damages against individual strike leaders. Finally, he appealed to the governor of Kentucky for National Guard troops to be sent to the streets of

---

54. Herbert G. Gutman, "An Iron Workers' Strike in The Ohio Valley, 1873–1874," *The Ohio Historical Quarterly* 68 (October 1959): 353–370.

55. Ibid., and Ross, *Workers on the Edge*, especially 190–191.

56. Gutman, "An Iron Workers' Strike."

Newport, and sought the deployment of Federal troops from the large garrison stationed at the Newport Army Barracks. On February 28 the city government of Newport capitulated and Democratic mayor R. D. Hayman banned "all unusual and unnecessary assemblages" in the city.[57]

Forty-eight hours later, on the morning of Monday, March 2, the voters of Newport went to the polls to elect most of the city government, including the powerful position of city clerk. An additional incentive for German and Irish participation in the Newport election was provided by the presence of so many foreign-born candidates on the ballot; of the forty-nine candidates running for the many local offices, eight were Germans, including the pastor of St. Paul's Lutheran church, who was seeking a position as a school trustee, and five were Irishmen. In Newport as in Alexandria and in Dereham Township, political crisis was in the air, and there was every reason to anticipate high levels of turnout.

We have seen that there was considerable variation in the prevalence of cultural associations in these three places. While the extent of associational activity in a locale is difficult to determine with precision, it does seem that Irish and especially German cultural identities were most solidly reinforced in Newport and least well expressed in institutional terms in Dereham Township. Commercial Alexandria had more German and Irish cultural institutions than rural Dereham but fewer than industrial Newport. Generally speaking, the Germans were better represented in institutional terms than the Irish. The question is whether the differing institutional levels of associational activity in these three very different locales was related, as the social capital theory suggests, to German and Irish political participation.

Participation

Complicating the determination of past rates of political participation are questions of voter eligibility and the extent of census undercounting, problems present in all three case studies. Canada in 1871 still restricted suffrage to property holders, although this restriction was unevenly applied. The best estimate is that about one third of adult males were kept from the polls by

---

57. On March 5 Governor Leslie ordered troops under the command of Captain Hendricks to be placed under the authority of the mayor as "troops in aid of the civil authorities." See P. H. Leslie to R. D. Hayman, March 5, 1874, printed in *Cincinnati Daily Gazette*, 7 March 1874.

the property qualification.[58] Calculating Canadian participation rates in terms of the age-eligible population (rather than participation of those meeting the property qualification) assists comparability with American data, but it also calls attention to the limits on political engagement south of the border. The United States of course did not have a property qualification for the vote in the 1860s and 1870s, but blacks were largely barred from the polls, and citizenship requirements were important in a nation that unlike Canada, did not confer citizenship on all residents. For all of these reasons, comparing across these three places in terms of the percentage of adult white males who attended the polls becomes analytically quite interesting.

The U.S. census of 1870 recorded for the first time the citizenship status of all adults and the Newport census allows some estimate of the numbers of adult males precluded from voting in the 1874 election on citizenship grounds. As it turns out, eighty-nine percent of Newport's adult white males were citizens; among the Germans and Irish the citizenship figures were nearly the same—eighty-six percent of German men were citizens as were eighty-four percent of Irish men. Citizenship requirements did not preclude disproportionate numbers of immigrant men from voting, and they were not a factor that could distinguish between the political participation rates of the Germans and the Irish.

Of course, all calculations of turnout are affected by the reliability of the basic census enumeration. Error rates were real and universal. While undercounts varied, recent work makes it prudent to assume that between ten percent and twenty percent of the population was missed in the average nineteenth-century census enumeration. This means that the "real" level of participation in American elections was probably at least ten percent lower than would be suggested by using aggregate census data.[59] Turnout rates based

---

58. See Gail Campbell, "The Most Restrictive Franchise in British North America? A Case Study," *Canadian Historical Review* 71 (June 1990): 159–188.

59. See in particular the special issue of *Social Science History* on the extent of undercounting in nineteenth-century U.S. censuses: Donald H. Parkerson, "Comments on the Underenumeration of the U.S. Census, 1850–1880," *Social Science History* 15 (Winter 1991): 509–515; Peter R. Knights, "Potholes in the Road of Improvement? Estimating Census Underenumeration by Longitudinal Tracing: US Census, 1850–1880," *Social Science History* 15 (Winter 1991): 517–526; John W. Adams and Alice Bee Kasakoff, "Estimates of Census Underenumeration Based on Genealogies," *Social Science History* 15 (Winter 1991): 527–543; Donald A. DeBats, "Hide and Seek: The Historian and Nineteenth-Century Social Accounting," *Social Science History* 15 (Winter 1991): 545–563; Kenneth Winkle, "The US Census as a Source in Political History," *Social Science History* 15 (Winter 1991): 565–577; Richard H. Steckel, "The Quality of Census Data for Historical Inquiry: A Research Agenda," *Social Science History* 15 (Winter

on individual level data promises a more accurate measure of turnout, for we can identify voters who appeared at the polls but were not on the census, partially correcting the undercount. Of course the reliability of any census base decreases as the interval between the enumeration and the election under study increases.[60]

With these caveats, corrective devices—and the poll books—in hand, we can return to election day in each of these communities and observe, almost as if we were present, all those who gathered at the polling places and voted. And we can note too all those who were present but who did not vote. Our expectation is that the turnout figures should be high, for the stakes were substantial. The 1859 election was Alexandria's last poll for state officers prior to the Civil War. The governor of Virginia, the lieutenant governor, a member of Congress, and a member of the state House of Delegates were all elected on May 26 of that year. In Dereham in 1871, the issue was the connection between politics in the Province of Ontario and the emerging national party system in a Canada created only four years earlier. The poll for representatives in the Ontario legislature was one of the first contested elections in the province since Federation. The election in Newport on March 2, 1874, for municipal officers—city clerk, sheriff, a plethora of local officials as well as members of the upper and lower chambers of the city council—was no less critical. When Newport voters went to the polls, they had in their minds the events of just two days past. As we have seen, the issue was not just urban disorder and the death of an innocent bystander, but the unprecedented pressure by organized

1991): 579–599. See also the sharp exchange between Gerald Ginsburg and Walter Dean Burnham: Gerald Ginsburg, "Computing Antebellum Turnout: Methods and Models," *Journal of Interdisciplinary History* 16 (Spring 1986): 579–611 and Walter Dean Burnham, "Those High Nineteenth-Century American Voting Turnouts: Fact or Fiction," *Journal of Interdisciplinary History* 16 (Spring 1986): 613–644. See also Bourke, DeBats, *Washington County*, especially 194–196. For a cautionary note on the accuracy of the Canadian census of 1871, see Edward Phelps, "Counting Ontario's People, 1793–1981: An Essay on Demographic Sources," *The Mirror* 1 (September 1981): 77–94.

60. That gap was six weeks in the case of Dereham (census enumeration 2 April 1871, election 25 March 1871), fifteen months in the case of Alexandria (election on 26 May 1859 and census concluding in August 1869), and forty-three months in the case of Newport (census concluding in July 1870 and election held on 2 March 1874). The greater the gap between census and election, the lower was the finding rate of voters in the census. In the case of Dereham there were only thirteen voters (2.1% of the total number of voters) in the 1871 election who were not on the census of that year; in Alexandria there were 233 voters (15.5%) whom we could not locate in the census records. We located nearly fifty-eight percent of the Newport voters in the 1874 election in the 1870 census returns, but there were 966 voters whom we could not locate in the 1870 census and for whom basic information on place of birth is missing.

capital on local authorities to use their powers to assist the breaking of the ironworkers' strike.

Observers at the time certainly thought turnout would be high in all three cases. The editor of the *Alexandria Gazette* speculated that a very high turnout would be the result of the animated contest for Congressional Representative.[61] This was the judgment of the *Cincinnati Daily Gazette*, too, and it observed, after the poll, that the Newport vote on March 2 was "heavier by fully 200 [ten percent] than any previous vote."[62] The actual rates of participation in each of these case studies are indicated in table 7.1.

	Germans	Irish	All
Alexandria[a]	27	24	57
Newport[b]	35	41	48
Dereham[c]	40	46	44

a) Alexandria—Numerator: 1,508 who voted for member of Congress, Governor, Lieutenant Governor, Attorney General, or member of the House of Delegates in the May 1859 general election. Denominator: 2,412 white males twenty-two and over on the census of 1860, plus 233 voters who did not appear on the census. German and Irish calculations based on voters and nonvoters of that place of birth as listed in the census and who were age twenty-two and above.

b) Newport—Numerator: 2,265 who voted for any office in the municipal elections held in March 1874. Denominator: 4,064 males seventeen and over on the census of 1870, minus the 331 men in the US Army assigned to the military barracks on the outskirts of Newport, plus 966 voters who did not appear on the census. German and Irish calculations based on voters and nonvoters of that place of birth as listed in the census who were age seventeen and above.

c) Dereham—Numerator: 607 who voted in election for member of the Provincial Assembly in the April 1871 election. Denominator: 1,356 males twenty-one and over on the census of 1871, plus thirteen voters who did not appear on the census. German and Irish calculations based on voters and non-voters of that origin as listed in the census who were age twenty-one and above.

Table 7.1: Turnout—Percent of Age-Eligible White Males Who Voted Alexandria, Virginia, 1859; Newport, Kentucky, 1874; Dereham Township, Ontario, 1871

Table 7.1 provides four important insights into past political engagement in these communities. First, despite crisis atmospheres and expectations of high turnout, the actual rates of participation in all three places were surprisingly moderate. In Alexandria just fifty-seven percent of adult white males present in the city cast a ballot. In strife-torn Newport less than half the age-eligible

61. See *Alexandria Gazette*, 9 April 1859.

62. *Cincinnati Daily Gazette*, 4 March 1874.

men went to the polls.[63] The property qualification for voting clearly depressed turnout in Dereham where forty-four percent voted, but levels of Canadian participation, even with a property qualification in place, were not that much lower than turnout in the United States. Second, it is striking that in both American cases the Germans and the Irish participated in these elections less enthusiastically than did the general population. Far from being drawn to the polls, even as ethnic issues were agitated, *both* Germans and the Irish shied away from voting. In Alexandria rates of political participation for the Germans and Irish were only half the city average; the level of political engagement among immigrant groups was closer to the norm in Newport but was still below the participation rate of the native-born.[64] Interestingly, it was in Dereham, where we are looking at first and subsequent generation immigrants, that Germans and Irishmen participated in politics in a manner most like their fellow citizens. Perhaps the Germans and the Irish were less politically distinctive in this environment precisely because here the immigrant ties were, for the most part, further in the past.

Third, there is little evidence in table 7.1 to support the notion, so prevalent in immigration literature, that there was a categorical difference between the political participation of the Germans and the Irish. Although in Newport and Dereham the Germans, whom the literature describes as less than enthusiastic politically, lagged behind the Irish by about fifteen percent, they outpolled the Irish in Alexandria by about the same amount.[65] Where participation rates

---

63. A total of forty-one African-American men are listed as having voted in Newport elections. The coverage of African Americans in the Newport Census of 1870 was uncertain and can only be regarded as a minimum estimate of the number of African-American residents and voters. The data are not suitable as a base from which to calculate a precise black turnout rate. Nevertheless, it appears that turnout among African Americans was at least as great, and was perhaps substantially higher, than the city average.

64. By and large, it seems, it was not citizenship that kept the Germans and Irish from voting in Newport. In 1870 eighty-one percent of Irish-born adult males were citizens as were ninety percent of German adult males. Similar percentages of both groups voted. At most eighteen percent of German nonvoters and twenty-one percent of Irish nonvoters were not citizens.

65. In evaluating these figures it is important to recall (see footnote 59) the number of voters not located in the census for whom there is no information on place of birth. This is a trivial number in Dereham, but it is somewhat more significant in Alexandria and Newport. If we assume that the ethnic distribution of voters missing from the census returns was the same as for the population of the city as a whole, we can assume that there were 5 Germans and 19 Irishmen among the ethnically unidentified voters of Alexandria and 164 Germans and 68 Irishmen among the unlocated voters in Newport. The inclusion of these additional "German" and "Irish" voters would raise the turnout rates in Alexandria to thirty percent of adult German men and twenty-eight percent of adult Irishmen. In Newport the hypothetical rates would be

favored the Irish, it was not by a grand margin. In Newport and Dereham German turnout was eighty-five and eighty-seven percent, respectively, of the Irish rate. The stereotypes of the politically recalcitrant Germans and the exuberant Irishmen seem overblown. The ordinary German voters in these three places do not appear to have been particularly uninvolved in political life any more than the Irish appear to have been fervent worshippers at the polls.

Finally, table 7.1 suggests that there was no close connection between aggregate ethnic associational activity and political engagement. Of the groups considered here, the Germans of Newport enjoyed the highest level of institutional cultural support, yet the turnout of Newport Germans was modest and surprisingly similar to that of the Germans in other communities. The simple presence of ethnic cultural associations was, simply put, a very poor predictor of the voting propensity of the individual members of that group.

There are of course caveats to these findings, the most important of which arises from the absence of electoral registers in Dereham to determine with precision those who met the province's property qualification for suffrage.[66] Tracing the voters of Dereham through the four elections held between 1867 and 1874 reveals that some thirty-two percent of age-eligible men failed to vote in any of these contests, a figure that nicely conforms to the general Canadian estimate of about a third of males excluded from the polls by the property stipulation.[67] Recalculating Dereham's overall participation rates on

---

more substantially changed: forty-two percent of German men voting and forty-nine percent of Irish males. In both cities these modified figures would leave the gap between German and Irish participation unchanged but raise both groups closer to the overall turnout figure; in Newport the Irish with an estimated turnout of forty-nine percent would just top the overall city average of forty-eight percent. These figures can be considered the maximum likely participation rates for the Germans and Irish of these two communities.

66. The suffrage in rural areas depended on ownership of real property with an annual assessed value of $200 or rental payment for the use of real property of at least $20 a year; in cities and towns, an annual assessed real property valuation of $300 or an annual rent of $30 was required. See *A History of the Vote in Canada* (Ottawa: Government Services Canada, 1997), 45–47. For a local statement of the requirement see the *Tillsonburg Observer*, 9 March 1871. See also Campbell, "The Most Restrictive Franchise?" Over time almost all qualified voters in Canada as in the United States did vote, if only once. See on this point Bourke, DeBats, *Washington County*, 181–202, especially 196.

67. The data set includes the Canadian provincial and federal elections of 1867, 1871, January of 1874, and May of 1874. In 1871 there were 1,160 men who would have been twenty-one at the point of the 1867 election. Of this age-eligible population, all but 371 voted in at least one of those four elections. This suggests that at the maximum, thirty-two percent of the age eligible population was disenfranchised by the property qualification. This is in fact very close to the Canada-wide estimates of the impact of the property limitation on the suffrage. If we track the 789 age-eligible men in Dereham who did vote across the four elections for which we have data,

this basis suggests a turnout of sixty-six percent of those eligible, a figure that approximates Gail Campbell's calculation, using a slightly different procedure, of a seventy-three percent turnout of age- *and* property-qualified men in the township.[68] For our purposes, however, it is striking that the *age-eligible* turnout in Dereham, where a property qualification limited the suffrage, still approximates the Alexandria and Newport rates, where there were no formal economic constraints on the right to vote.

Social Standing and Voting

Everywhere, however, political participation had an economic foundation. In all three case studies considered here the average voter was generally somewhat better off economically than the average eligible male who decided not to vote, as table 7.2 demonstrates. Of course, in Dereham the property qualification for the suffrage meant that voters were inevitably better off than nonvoters. As the reported estates of voters and non-voters in Alexandria and Newport show, however, non-voters here too were in the aggregate less well off than voters. Whether excluded by law or inclination, everywhere the less well off were less visible at the polls.

Generally speaking, the association between economic position and political participation extended to the Irish and the Germans of these three places. While there were exceptions to the rule (the Irish in Newport), in most cases those Germans and Irish men who participated politically had a somewhat greater economic stake in their community than their fellow ethnics who did not vote.[69]

---

we find that 218 or twenty-eight percent voted once, 278 or thirty-five percent voted twice, 206 or twenty-six percent voted three times, and only 87 or eleven percent voted in all four elections. In Canada as in the United States most voters, it appears, were occasional visitors to the polls. For the pattern on the American side of the border see Bourke, DeBats, *Washington County*, 181–201, 236–241.

68. See Gail Campbell, "Voters and Nonvoters: The Problem of Turnout in the Nineteenth Century: Southwestern Ontario as a Case Study," *Social Science History* 11 (Summer 1987): 187–210, especially 193. On the difficulty of calculating the effect, if any, of even seemingly harsh property restrictions on suffrage, see also Campbell, "The Most Restrictive Franchise?" Property qualifications remained in some provinces until well into the twentieth century. Ontario, however, had established universal male suffrage by 1898. As Campbell shows, the very restrictive property requirements on the law books were not always enforced at the polling place.

69. Voting, like economic well-being and religious membership, was likely related to permanency of residence in a community. In Alexandria, for example, seventy percent of adult white males who paid personal or property taxes and were thus listed in the 1859 tax lists voted

	Germans		Irish		All	
	Voters	*Nonvoters*	*Voters*	*Nonvoters*	*Voters*	*Nonvoters*
Alexandria						
Personal Estate	$250	$150	$100	$50	$200	$100
Real Estate	$1000	$1000	$800	$700	$3000	$2000
Newport						
Personal Estate	$200	$200	$100	$100	$200	$200
Real Estate	$2000	$1250	$1500	$1500	$2000	$1500
Dereham						
Acres Occupied	50	0	78	0	59	0
Acres Owned	50	0	61	0	50	0

Table 7.2: Economic Profile of German and Irish Voters and Nonvoters, Median Wealth Measures Alexandria, Virginia; Newport, Kentucky; Dereham Township, Ontario

If these data confirm the economic success of the Irish in Ontario, they also remind us that the Germans were better off than the Irish in the two American cities under consideration here.[70] Yet, as table 7.1 demonstrated, this greater wealth did not result in higher levels of German voting; in both cities, the Germans voted marginally less than the Irish, despite the German advantage in terms of economic position.[71] In Dereham, the Irish were in a stronger economic position than the Germans and participated in politics more.

We can see this aspect of German under-participation more clearly if we turn from self reported economic assets to the much more widely recorded, and perhaps more reliable, occupation data available from the census returns and city directories in these three places.[72] Table 7.3 ranks the occupations of

while only fifteen percent of those on the census of 1860 but not on the tax list of 1859 voted. Age is a less reliable predictor of permanency although the same pattern is evident. The median age of voters in Alexandria was thirty-eight while the median age of non-voters was thirty-three. Among other groups the differences were less striking. The median ages of German voters and non-voters were thirty-two and thirty-one. Among the Irish the median ages of voters and non-voters were thirty-six and thirty-five respectively.

70. Median reported value of personal property and real estate for all German adult males in Alexandria was $200 and $1,000 respectively, while the median Irish wealth figures were $50 and $800; in Newport the median value of self reported German personal property and real estate were $200 and $1,500, while for the Irish the figures were $100 and $1,500.

71. Livio Di Matteo argues that if early Irish immigrants to Ontario were slightly disadvantaged economically, this difference had disappeared by the mid to late years of the century. See Di Matteo, "The Wealth of the Irish."

72. Occupational data is available for a wider range of the population in all three case studies and was more likely to be accurately reported than were self-estimates of personal and real estate assets.

ALEXANDRIA

Occupational Status[a)]	Germans		Irish		All	
	Distribution	Vote	Distribution	Vote	Distribution	Vote
High	6	42	1	75	10	69
Medium	71	29	22	40	61	58
Low	22	17	76	19	29	38

NEWPORT

Occupational Status	Germans		Irish		All	
	Distribution	Vote	Distribution	Vote	Distribution	Vote
High	4	36	2	50	5	50
Medium	63	37	40	44	63	45
Low	33	32	57	39	32	41

DEREHAM

Occupational Status	Germans		Irish		All	
	Distribution	Vote	Distribution	Vote	Distribution	Vote
High	3	0	4	0	5	37
Medium	81	49	80	59	74	57
Low	16	12	15	8	22	12

a)   High Status: Professional, Major Proprietor, Manager, Merchant, Wholesaler, Major Public Official; Mid to High Status: Agent, Minor Proprietor, Minor Public Official, Clerk, Master Craftsman, Skilled Craftsman, Proprietor, Skilled Workers, Primary Producer; Low to Mid Status: Apprentice, Semiskilled Worker, Unskilled Worker, Other Employee

Table 7.3: Occupational Status of German and Irish Adult Males and Voting, by Percent, Alexandria, Virginia; Newport, Kentucky; Dereham Township, Ontario

the men of Alexandria, Dereham, and Newport according to a status hierarchy, dividing occupations into high, medium, and low categories.[73] In Dereham Township participation of Irishmen and Germans was similar at each level of the status hierarchy. But in Newport and Alexandria the Irish, while clustered in lower status occupations, participated more at every level of the status hierarchy than the Germans.

In Newport some thirty-nine percent of unskilled and semiskilled Irish workers went to the polls; among the low-status German workers, however, thirty-two percent voted. Even more striking given the general connection between economic position and political participation was the divergence between the political behavior of the German and Irish economic elite. In both American cities considered here the Germans enjoyed much greater representation in the highest status occupations than the Irish. But in Newport, fifty percent of high-status Irishmen voted as against thirty-six percent of high-status Germans while in Alexandria seventy-five percent of the small Irish upper-status group voted as against forty-two percent of the German status elite.

The economic pattern repeats a theme observed in associational terms: while German and Irish voting participation was surprisingly similar, we might have expected the Germans, better off financially and better represented in associations than the Irish, to have voted at higher levels than they actually

---

73. A complex dictionary of occupational status and function has been developed for these studies. Copies of the rankings are available from the author. On the changing German occupational structure see Hartmut Keil, "Chicago's German Working Class in 1900," in *German Workers in Industrial Chicago*, 19–36. Nora Faires emphasizes "the Germans' generally high occupational status relative to the status of the Irish." See Nora Faires, "Occupational Patterns of German-Americans in Nineteenth Century Cities," in *German Workers in Industrial Chicago,* 37–51, quotation on p. 40. See also Alan N. Burstein, "Immigrants and Residential Mobility: The Irish and Germans in Philadelphia, 1850–1880," in *Philadelphia: Work, Space, Family, and Group Experience in the Nineteenth Century: Essays Toward an Interdisciplinary History of the City*, edited by Theodore Hershberg (Oxford: Oxford University Press, 1981), 174–203. On the occupational situation of the Irish see JoEllen Vinyard, *The Irish on the Urban Frontier: Nineteenth Century Detroit, 1850–1880* (New York: Arno Press, 1976). On German occupational structure see Bruce Laurie and Mark Schmitz, "Manufacture and Productivity: The Making of an Industrial Base, Philadelphia, 1850–1880," in *Philadelphia*, 43–92; and Bruce Laurie, Theodore Hershberg, and George Alter, "Immigrants and Industry: The Philadelphia Experience, 1850–1880," in *Philadelphia*, 92–119. See also Kathleen Neils Conzen, *Immigrant Milwaukee, 1836–1860: Accommodation and Community in a Frontier City* (Cambridge: Harvard University Press, 1976); Russell Kazal, "Becoming 'Old Stock': German-American Assimilation in Two Philadelphia Neighborhoods at the Century's Turn" (Paper presented at the GHI Symposium, "New Approaches to Migration Research: German-Americans in Comparative Perspectives," Texas A&M University, April 1997).

did. It is in this sense, of voting less given their relatively stronger financial and institutional position, that we can talk about a German deficit at the polls. Of course, viewed more broadly, participation of both the Germans and Irish must be seen in a context of relatively low general participation. The reach of nineteenth-century politics, at least as seen in these three case studies, appears surprisingly shallow, with the result that those most attracted to politics were also those best placed in their community.

Individual Associational Activity and Political Participation: Alexandria

The unique records available in Alexandria allow us to pursue more carefully the link between associational activity and political participation. We have seen that there was no direct correlation between aggregate associational activity, whether for a locale or for a group, and aggregate political participation. In Alexandria, however, the religious records of the city that survive allow us to explore the connection between individual participation in a particular type of voluntary association—formal religious membership—and individual political participation.

That this remarkable information is available for the city of Alexandria is a measure of the fact that the city weathered so successfully the twin scourges of so much of Southern history—the Civil War and urban renewal. The Union Army captured Alexandria the day after Virginia seceded, with the loss of a single life and no physical damage to the city, simply by marching across the aqueduct over the Potomac that carried canal traffic between Washington, DC, and Alexandria. A century later urban renewal claimed some victims in the city, but once again the list of casualties was short. The result is that all twelve of the churches that served the white population of Alexandria in 1859 survive in Alexandria today. The membership lists from these congregations allow the compilation of a complete religious census for the white population of the city. (See the appendix for further discussion about the use of these membership lists.)

Connecting these religious records to the census, tax list, and poll books for Alexandria produces some surprises. Organized religion was, on the evidence of these records, distinctly limited in its reach in Alexandria and, like political participation, more limited than is often suggested. Just over a quarter (twenty-seven percent) of the city's adult white males appeared on any of the formal church records. While we are missing the female membership lists for two of the Methodist churches, it is unlikely that more than a third of Alexandria's white adults, male *or* female, were members of organized religious congregations. Among the Germans and Irish, the patterns were similar: Twenty-seven percent of German males and twenty-two percent of Irish men were listed in the city's religious records.

The Germans of Alexandria were mostly Jewish; over half (fifty-nine percent) of the German men who belonged to a religious group were members of the small and factious Beth El congregation. The rest were Catholic (fourteen percent), Episcopalian, or Presbyterian (ten percent each). The Irish, on the other hand, were overwhelmingly affiliated with St. Mary's, which had among its adherents eighty percent of those Irish whose religious membership we know; there was no significant Irish presence in any other of Alexandria's churches.

The connection with politics was clear in that those men who were associated with a church or synagogue were much more likely to vote than those who were not members. Some seventy percent of adult white males belonging to a religious congregation voted in the 1859 election as opposed to only forty-five percent for those not members. The same pattern is even more strongly evident among the city's German and Irish populations. Among German men who were members of a religious group, forty-eight percent voted, while only seventeen percent of nonmembers did so. The Irish pattern was almost identical: Forty-seven percent of church members voted but only twenty percent of nonmembers.

Before we assume that associational membership at an individual level did have the political effect suggested by social capital theory, we need to consider the fact that there was a strong covariance between economic well-being and church membership just as there was between economic standing and political participation. In Alexandria those white males with a religious affiliation reported in the 1860 census an average personal estate of $300—exactly twice that of the unchurched. The pattern in real estate was similar—an average of $3,550 for those affiliated with a church or synagogue against $2,000 for those without a religious connection.

The affinity between economic well-being and voting ran through all the religious institutions of Alexandria at an aggregate as well as an individual level: The higher the status of the institution, as measured by the occupational status of its members, the greater was the level of political participation. Table 7.4 arrays the twelve congregations of antebellum Alexandria in terms of the occupational makeup of their congregations and the percentage of members who voted in the 1859 election. Christ Episcopal Church, long regarded as the elite church of Alexandria and the church that Robert E. Lee and his family attended, headed the occupational standing of the city's congregations with five times the proportion of high-status members as the city at large. Voting turnout was highest (eighty-six percent) among members of Grace Episcopal Church, with a congregation more concentrated in middle- to high-status occupations, but Christ Episcopal was not far behind with eighty-two percent turnout.

Among the Germans the same patterns prevailed. Germans who belonged to a religious organization in Alexandria reported a median combined wealth in 1860 of $3,250, while those who did not reported assets of only $950. But this association between wealth and religious affiliation was not nearly so clear among the generally poorer Irish. Those with church memberships reported a median combined real and personal estate of $875, but nonmembers reported an almost identical holding of $800. What this suggests is that Irish, and hence Catholic, church membership was substantially more universalistic and less economically specific than other religious groups in the city. As we will see, this had important political consequences.

One of the most interesting features of table 7.4 is the gap between the relatively low rate of political participation (forty-four percent) among the members of the high-status Beth El congregation, heavily German, and the high turnout (sixty-four percent) of members of St. Mary's with its Irish presence and relatively low status occupational profile. To be sure, high-status Germans voted more than low-status Germans, and Germans who were members of Beth El voted more than those who were not part of a religious organization. In both respects they mirrored the city-wide pattern. But once again we see that the German rate of participation lagged behind that of comparable groups when considered in terms of their social advantages—in this case occupational standing. Conversely, members of St. Mary's, with a much more modest status profile, voted well above the Beth El rate.

In one sense the Alexandria data suggest a simple convergence: Religious membership disproportionally caught up the well-to-do in the city; the more well-to-do a church or synagogue's membership, the higher the degree of political participation. But this formulation ignores hints contained in the very different German and Irish profiles that suggest a possible independent impact of religious membership on political engagement. We can see this connection more clearly if we consider men of the same status level and examine the extent of voting among those who were religious members, and those who were not members.

Alexandria, Virginia, 1859–1860

Congregation	Status[a] of Members			Turnout
	High Status	*Mid to High Status*	*Low to Mid Status*	
Christ Episcopal	54	34	12	82
Second Presbyterian	41	57	3	78
St. Paul's Episcopal	30	60	10	73
Grace Episcopal	29	64	7	86
First Presbyterian	23	66	11	76
Baptist	23	61	16	61
Beth El	22	72	6	44
Quaker	21	58	21	77
Methodist Episcopal	16	64	20	74
Methodist Trinity	15	66	19	71
Methodist Protestant	9	70	21	71
St.Mary's Catholic[b]	9	57	34	64
City	10	60	29	52

a) Same status categories as Table 7.3. Based on adult males reporting an occupation.

b) The occupational inclusiveness of St. Mary's is even more evident if we delete those associated with St. John's Academy and consider only those whose names appear on a church record. Only ten percent of men associated with St. Mary's in this more precise way were employed in high status positions, thirty-nine percent were in mid-status occupations, and fully fifty-one percent were in low status occupations. St. Mary's membership reflected a far greater representation of the lower occupational orders than any other church in Alexandria.

Table 7.4: Status Composition of Congregations and Voting, by Percent

At all levels of the status hierarchy, men who were church members participated in politics more than their compatriots who were not. Associational membership was accompanied by a higher level of political engagement regardless of status. Thus, sixty-four percent of professionals who were church members voted, but only forty percent of professionals who were not church members went to the polls. Even more interesting is the impact of religious membership on political participation at the other end of the occupational scale. Only a quarter (twenty-six percent) of unskilled workers who were not church members voted, but nearly half (forty-nine percent) of unskilled workers who did belong to a church voted. Among the unskilled, church members were nearly twice as likely to vote as nonmembers. Among the highest status groups, those with religious affiliations were sixty percent more likely to vote than nonmembers; at the bottom of the status hierarchy, congregation members were eighty-eight percent more likely to vote than nonmembers. Individual

DeBats

Alexandria, Virginia, 1859–1860

Wealth Quintile	Percent of Adult Males Who Voted	
	Member of Congregation	*Not Member of Congregation*
Highest	83	71
Lowest	64	40

Table 7.5: Political Participation by Wealth and Religious Membership

associational activity, seen here in membership of a religious community, appears to have had its greatest political impact on those of the lowest status rankings. And here may be the explanation for the higher than expected (given their limited wealth and low occupational status profile) participation of the Irish in political life in Alexandria, and perhaps more widely.

Table 7.5 below shows the same pattern when we rank the entire city by wealth and compare the participation rates of those who were members of religious congregations with those who were not. Again the most well off voted more than the least well off, and within the economic elite of the city those who were church members voted more than those who were not. Men in the lowest wealth group voted less but the "church effect" was much greater. Put simply it appears that the political effect of individual associational membership was real, and this effect was markedly greater at the bottom of the wealth and status hierarchies.

If there is little in these case studies to support the notion that the general level of group organization in a locale led to higher general levels of political participation, it does seem that at the individual level, and especially for individuals least well off, associational membership may have had a significant effect on the likelihood of political participation. In exactly this way it may well be that Irish political participation was assisted by a Catholic Church that reached deep into the lower social orders and, especially in Alexandria where there does seem to have been a clear political component to the church's activities, spurred political participation within a socioeconomic group otherwise not likely to vote. Associational membership, at least religious membership, did appear to matter politically, but at the individual rather than the aggregate level, and it mattered most to those least well off.

Partisan Choices of German and the Irish Voters

If participation in political life was a function of individual economic well-being, occupational status, and some types of associational membership, the evidence from Alexandria, Dereham, and Newport also suggests the importance of cultural factors in the choices individual voters made once at the polls. Those partisan choices were inevitably made in a confusing and fluid political context. Alexandria on the eve of the Civil War was essentially a Whig/Opposition town at a time when the Democratic Party was increasingly ascendant in Virginia and in the South. In postwar Newport, Republicans held to power by the slenderest of margins in the midst of threatened social disorder. The voters of Dereham made political choices at a time of chaotic factionalism as a national party system struggled to emerge in the newly created Canada, and as the Reform and Tory parties came to grips with notions of government and legitimate opposition.

	Germans	*Irish*	*All*
Alexandria[a]			
Democratic	76	83	41
Opposition	24	17	59
Newport[b]			
Democratic	33	81	48
Republican	67	19	52
Dereham[c]			
Reform	68	39	45
Conservative	32	61	55

a) Election for Governor
b) Election for City Clerk
c) Election for Member of the Provincial Legislature

Table 7.6: Partisan Choice of Voters, by Percent, Alexandria, Virginia, 1859; Newport, Kentucky, 1874; Dereham Township, Ontario, 1871

Nevertheless, when we reflect on all of the ballots cast by the ordinary voters in these three very different contexts, some clear cultural patterns, summarized in table 7.6, are evident.[74] The most surprising finding is that the Germans in all three locales closely approximated the Irish in terms of their commitment to a single party. Just as the Germans in these three places voted about as frequently as the Irish, they also exhibited about the same degree of political unity as the Irish. In all three cases the Germans, like the Irish, were more united in their political choices than the larger populations of which they were a part. In Dereham and Newport German and Irish voters opposed one

74. Because the 1859 Congressional election in Alexandria was a three-way contest, this table uses the Alexandria vote for governor. The candidates were William Goggin, Opposition, and John Letcher, Democrat.

another while in Alexandria both groups supported the Democratic Party by roughly equal margins. The internal unity of the German and Irish voters in these three closely balanced political units is striking; in each case, the German and Irish voters were between sixty-one and eighty-three percent committed to one of the contending parties.

Once again there is little evidence to support the notion, so common in the literature, that the German voters were particularly divided in their partisan loyalties while the Irish were particularly cohesive. In these three case studies the Germans were similar to the Irish in their partisan cohesiveness. In Dereham the voters of German origin were, despite the paucity of German cultural institutions, more united in their political stance than the Irish. In Alexandria the Irish were more united than the Germans, but by a relatively small margin (eighty-three percent versus seventy-six percent); only in Newport was there a significant gap between the unity of the Irish and Germans (eighty-one versus sixty-seven percent). If the Irish are the exemplars of nineteenth century political unanimity, the Germans in at least these locales should also be seen as contenders for that title. Germans in these places were group partisans, just like the Irish; they constituted a political vote committed to one side of politics even when, as in these case studies, the political environment in which they lived was quite competitive.

In Alexandria the Germans and Irish were among the strongest supporters of the city's Democratic ticket. Indeed, the only two religious groups in the city that supported the Democrats were those dominated by these two immigrant groups—the voters from St. Mary's, heavily Irish, who voted fifty-six percent Democratic and those from Beth El, heavily German, who cast every vote for the Democrats. In no other congregation in the city did the Democrats even approach majority support.[75] Among Protestant church members only twenty-six percent voted Democratic.

The unity of the Irish and German vote in Alexandria was particularly striking, given the effort of the *Alexandria Gazette* to demonstrate that Smith, the Democratic congressional candidate, was a closet Know-Nothing adverse to the interests of immigrant voters. The *Gazette*'s campaign bore little fruit. In the congressional contest both Irish- and German-born voters continued to

75. Grace Episcopal: seventeen percent Democratic; Quakers: seventeen percent Democratic; Second Presbyterian: eighteen percent Democratic; First Presbyterian: twenty percent Democratic; Christ Episcopal: twenty-two percent Democratic; Methodist Trinity: twenty-six Democratic; St. Paul's Episcopal: twenty-nine percent Democratic; Baptist: twenty-nine percent Democratic; Methodist Protestant: thirty-five percent Democratic; Methodist Episcopal: forty percent Democratic.

favor the Democratic Party, albeit by reduced majorities. Some German and Irish voters defected, but a majority of the Irish (seventy-one percent) and a plurality of the Germans (forty-eight percent) voted for Smith despite all of his anti-immigrant statements and inclinations. Likewise, forty-five percent of Alexandria's Catholics, including William F. Carne, and almost all of the Jews voted for Smith.[76] Only eight percent of the Irish voters and fifteen percent of Germans supported Shackelford, the splinter Democratic candidate. The Germans and Irish of Alexandria were partisans, and remained so, even in the face of reasonable evidence that their party was running an anti-immigrant candidate.

The solidity of immigrant voting in Alexandria suggests a party loyalty that the short-term exploitation of cultural issues could not easily displace. Ethnic voters who were members of Beth El or St. Mary's were well established in their occupations, and in Alexandria these were the voters least likely to desert the party ticket. Party loyalty, like so much else, went hand in hand with solidity of place in the community. Neither was easily disturbed.

The Dereham case study allows us to explore the variability of ethnic partisanship before loyalties were fully formed. The chaotic factionalism of Canadian politics in early post-federation elections worked against stable political loyalties. Loyalty even to a candidate was complicated by the ebb and flow of factional groupings that saw political figures move from one political coalition to another.[77] The result was very high levels of voter movement between elections. Dereham Township, for example, appears in aggregate terms to have shifted only slightly toward the Reform Party between the provincial elections of 1867 (sixty-two percent Conservative) and 1871 (fifty-five percent Conservative), yet at an individual level there was remarkable inconsistency, with fully forty-five percent of those voters who participated in both contests changing party allegiance.

The Germans and Irish of Dereham were caught up in this shift, with the men of German origin voting seventy percent Conservative in the first election but nearly seventy percent Reform in the second. Among the Irish, by contrast, the Conservative vote rose, from fifty-five percent to sixty-one percent, as Irish Catholics, heavily Reform (ninety-three percent) in 1867, shifted to the Conservatives (sixty-two percent). By 1871 as table 7.6 showed, Dereham's German and Irish populations had moved in almost diametrically opposite

---

76. See Edward L. Stephens, *St. Mary's: 200 Years for Christ* (n.p., n.d.), 40.

77. See George Emery, "Adam Oliver, Ingersoll and Thunder Bay District, 1850–1851," *Ontario History* 68 (1976): 25–43, especially 34.

political directions; the Germans were the township's most volatile ethnic group and the Irish Catholics the most volatile religious group.[78]

The turnaround of the German vote (Conservative to Reform) and the Irish Catholic vote (Reform to Conservative) seems mainly to reflect the neighborhood in which these groups resided, and the pressures brought to bear on those particular neighborhoods by political notables. In all of this there is evidence of the deferential politics that still existed in late nineteenth-century Canadian political life.[79] The Germans of Dereham Township were heavily concentrated in the northeast, around Mt. Elgin, the political neighborhood of Ebenezer Bodwell, a local notable and member of Canada's national parliament. Ten of the fourteen Germans who changed their vote between 1867 and 1871 lived within the Mt. Elgin district, and each of these ten changed his vote from Conservative to Reform. This was exactly the political course that the Bodwell clan marked out, and it appears that those in the neighborhood followed the Bodwell lead. In a parallel process, but with an opposite direction, the Irish Catholics of Dereham, concentrated in the northwest of the township, near Ingersoll, moved *en masse* to the Conservative cause. The same "influential men in Ingersoll" who urged Stephen Richards to contest the 1871 poll for the Conservative cause made their influence felt on the Irish Catholic men who lived in close proximity.[80] Thus, eleven of the twenty Irish Catholics in Dereham who changed their vote between 1867 and 1871 lived very near to Ingersoll, and ten of these voted for Richards and the Conservative cause despite voting for the Reform Party four years previously.

---

78. In Dereham most male Germans of voting age were Methodists (fifty-five percent) and Baptists (sixteen percent); just five percent were Lutheran. There were no German Catholics and no German Jews in Dereham. The Irish were more dispersed in religious terms—split between Methodist (thirty-five percent), Catholic (twenty-three percent), Anglican (nineteen percent) and Baptist (twelve percent). In 1871 there was little difference between the political preferences of Irish Catholics (sixty-two percent Conservative) and the Irish at large (sixty-one percent Conservative), but just four years earlier the Irish Catholics had voted overwhelmingly (ninety-three percent) for the Reform party.

79. Gail Campbell, "People, Parties, and the Vote: Electoral Behavior in Southwestern Ontario Townships, 1854–1902," (Ph.D. Thesis, Clark University, 1983), 190–191. See also Sidney J. R. Noel, *Patrons, Clients, Brokers: Ontario Society and Politics, 1791–1896* (Toronto: University of Toronto Press, 1990).

80. *Tillsonburg Observer*, 30 March 1871; See also E. D. Tillson to Hon. Sir Francis Hincks, Tillsonburg, 30 January 1871, Tillson Letterbook, Volume 2. The first volume of the Tillson letter book is located in the Tillsonburg Museum; the second is held by Ms. Kate Rogers of Ottawa. I wish to thank Ms. Rogers for her generosity in making the contents of this volume available.

If we cannot watch precisely the process by which the Germans and Irish Catholics were "turned around" in their respective sections of Dereham, we can see political influence brought to bear very clearly in the southeast of the township, in Tillsonburg, where Edwin D. Tillson was, as the village name suggests, the local notable. He owned the mill and iron foundry and was the town's largest employer. Until 1871 Tillson had been a supporter of Adam Oliver and the Reform cause, but in that year he began a correspondence with fellow party member Sir Francis Hincks, the former premier of Ontario. Hincks was on the verge of joining the Conservative cause, and he sought to bring Tillson with him. The focus of the ensuing correspondence was a local patronage position—the Tillsonburg postmastership.

Tillson explained to Hincks that he sought the position not for his own benefit but so that he could employ in that office relatives of his now deceased business partner. Tillson asked his friends to notify the Conservatives in Ottawa that he had "fully deseided [sic] to support the . . . [P]arty . . . at the next election." Very much aware of the "considerable property" he possessed, Tillson said, "you know I can use more influence in getting out votes than any man in this neighbourhood." Two days later he observed that "I think I can have a good deal of influence in working up an election."[81]

Tillson had his postmastership by early February 1871, and, over the next few weeks, additional appointments came his way. Hincks then wrote to Tillson to ask him to "lend a helping hand" to the Conservative cause at the 1871 election, now only weeks away. Tillson evidently acted, for just after the election he wrote to Hincks proudly conveying the results: the voters of Tillsonburg, he reported, "have done their duty" and supported Richards, the Conservative candidate. The proof was in the details: "Of the eighty-one votes in Tillsonburg, we gave sixty-five for Richard's [sic][,] nine for Oliver[,] two sick[,] and five would not vote."[82] The victory was not total; there was just a hint of refusal among the five who "would not" vote. But in general, Tillson was indeed correct that the local voters had "done their duty": Of the twenty-three men who changed their vote in the Tillsonburg district between 1868 and 1871, twenty (eighty-seven percent) changed to the Conservative cause, the course which Tillson now so ardently advanced.

This process of change in Dereham, while it rested on cultural groups, was not in itself about cultural politics; more important was a politics of deference

---

81. E. D. Tillson to E. Dotty, Tillsonburg, 28 January 1871; E. D. Tillson to A. Walsh, Tillsonburg, 30 January 1871, Tillson Letterbook, Volume 2.

82. Tillson to Hincks, 30 January 1871; 25 March 1871, Tillson Letterbook, Volume 2.

in which local notables, in a circumstance of extreme political fluidity, were able to influence the political decisions of individual voters, whatever their social characteristics, who lived within their reach. Neighborhoods tended to reflect concentrations of religious and ethnic groups; as neighborhoods shifted political allegiances, so too did the cultural groupings. With political stability would come the possibility of more stable alliances between ethnic and partisan groups of the type evident in Alexandria.

If Dereham Township is an example of cultural politics in the making and Alexandria of established and stable cultural politics, the story of the Newport election of 1874 suggests some of the "class consequences" of enduring ethnic partisan affiliations. In Newport as in nearby Cincinnati there were residents from virtually every one of the states of the newly federated Germany—a social diversity that has always given rise to speculation about division within the German vote. Fredericke Hauke, editor of the *Volksfreund*, one of Cincinnati's German papers, observed that "[t]he Plattdeutsche is against the High German, the Swabian against the Bavarian, [and] the Wurtenburger against the Prussian."[83] Republican Party organizers of course sought a united German vote and printed (see illustration 7.1) the party ticket in German. Some of Hauke's divides were indeed evident within the German voters of Newport and even, paradoxically, in the alterations (see illustration 7.1) made to the preserved copy of the 1872 ticket. Yet if there was partisan division among the German voters, it is important to recall from table 7.6 that the Germans of Newport supported the Republican Party by a majority of two to one.

There was even less variation across German cultural groups in terms of participation. Because the census takers of Newport were so assiduous in recording the specific place of birth for Germans, we can examine in minute detail the rate of participation of emigrants from each German region. A degree of diversity is obvious, with those from Saxony and Baden (and interestingly, Oldenburg) slightly more enthusiastic about voting than those from Darmstadt, Württemberg, and Hanover. Underlying this again was an economic reality: Generally speaking (except for immigrants from Oldenburg) those less well off in terms of property ownership participated less than other German immigrants, such as those from Saxony, who were better off. On the other hand, participation rates for all birthplaces were within ten percentage points of the average rate for Germans as a group. German real and personal estate holdings were in general consistent across internal cultural divides and so was participation. Among the Germans, as among the general population,

---

83. Quoted in Ross, *Workers on the Edge*, 173.

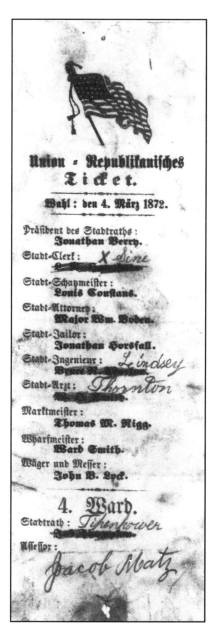

Source: Frankfort, KA. Newport, Kentucky, Poll Books (Municipal), Elections of March, 1872, Ward 4, Division of Archives and Records.

Illustration 7.1: 1872 German Language Republican Ticket

Newport, Kentucky, 1874

Place of Birth	Percent Republican
Hesse	92
Saxony	88
Württemberg	88
Bavaria	72
Hanover	67
Baden	63
Prussia	52
Oldenburg	0

Note: Partisanship only measured where there were ten or more voters from a named area. There were four voters each from Darmstadt, Nassau, and Mecklenburg. All voted for the Republican candidate as did the one voter from Hamburg and the two from Bremen.

Table 7.7: German Birthplace and Partisanship

those who possessed greater assets voted more assiduously than those who did not.[84]

As noted, when we turn to partisanship (table 7.7), there is evidence of greater diversity among the German voters of Newport. The strongest Republican support came from immigrants from Hesse, Saxony, and Württemberg. At the other extreme, voters from Oldenburg stand out: these Germans were, to a man, Democrats. Every other grouping cast a majority of its vote for the Republican Party. There was in this sense a certainty in Newport about the affiliation of the Germans: they were, with only the Oldenburg exception, Republican. The question of *how* Republican was a matter of cultural difference in Newport no less than in Alexandria or Dereham.

The confessional side of these partisan differences seems clear. Many of the Oldenburg emigrants to the Cincinnati area were drawn from the Catholic enclave at the southern tip of the Duchy, and it is likely that many of Newport's men from Oldenburg were members of one of the city's German Catholic churches. On the other side of the cultural divide, Newport residents born in Saxony were likely to be Protestants, and Saxon voters were almost as solidly Republican as Oldenburg emigrants were Democratic. We do not know individual religious affiliation in Newport, but it is likely that there

---

84. The only exception was the higher median estate holdings of the thirteen age-eligible voters from Darmstadt.

was a general association between Catholicism and the Democratic Party and Protestantism and the Republicans.[85]

In Newport most Germans were Republicans, and most Irish were Democrats; only German Catholics were likely sources of consistent support for the Democratic Party. These cultural divides between and within ethnic groups in Newport destroyed the possibility of partisan alliances built on economic issues. Even the intense labor dispute convulsing the city was not sufficient to create a working class vote.[86] There were 3,281 German males listed as unskilled workers in the 1870 census of Newport and 210 unskilled Irishmen. The unskilled Germans were less likely than Germans generally to vote for the Republican ticket, while the unskilled Irish were even more Democratic than Irish voters generally. Germans overall voted sixty-seven percent Republican; unskilled German workers voted fifty-two percent Republican. The Irish as a whole voted eighty-one percent Democratic while the unskilled Irish voted ninety-six percent for the Democrats. Put simply, the unskilled German workers and the unskilled Irish workers both voted fifteen points less Republican and more Democratic, respectively, than their ethnic fellows. But both groups of unskilled workers supported the party of their cultural group; the result was that the unskilled German and Irish workers were politically opposed.

Among the Germans only those unskilled workers from Prussia and Baden (and of course Oldenburg) gave the Democrats a majority.[87] The unskilled

---

85. While Bavaria was heavily Catholic, the heaviest emigration rates were from predominantly Protestant areas. Conversely, much of the emigration from Prussia flowed from its Catholic sections. For a discussion of Catholicism among many immigrants from Oldenburg to the Cincinnati area, see Anne [Aengenvoort] Höndgen, "Community Versus Separation: A Northwest German Emigrant Settlement Region in Nineteenth Century Ohio," in this volume.

86. The literature on the cultural division of the American labor force is vast. For early surveys of the literature linking labor history and social history, see David Brody, "The Old Labor History and the New: In Search of an American Working Class," *Labor History* 20 (Winter 1979): 111–126 and David Montgomery, "To Study the People: The American Working Class," *Labor History* 21 (Fall 1980): 485–512. See also Richard J. Oestreicher, "Industrialization, Class, and Competing Cultural Systems: Detroit Workers, 1875–1900," in *German Workers in Industrial Chicago*, 52–72 and Thomas J. Suhrbur, "Ethnicity in the Formation of the Chicago Carpenters Union: 1855–1890," in *German Workers in Industrial Chicago*, 86–103. Suhrbur focuses on the difficulty of uniting craft workers across ethnic lines; Oestreicher explores the circumstances that were associated with efforts to create working class solidarity across ethnic lines in Detroit in the strikes of 1891.

87. Unskilled workers from Prussia voted fourteen to thirteen for the Democratic candidate; the five unskilled workers from Baden split three to two in favor of the Democrats. On the other hand the unskilled German workers from Bavaria voted sixteen to eight in favor of the Republicans.

workers from Bavaria and Saxony remained solidly Republican as did the small group of ironworkers from those provinces. The Irish iron workers, of course, voted, like *their* compatriots, Democratic.

If the German and Irish voters of Dereham remind us of a time prior to the formation of stable links between cultural groups and political parties, Alexandria and Newport suggest the centrality and durability of those connections once formed. Cultural loyalties divided workers in Newport, even in the midst of a violent labor dispute that might have united them, just as cultural loyalties in Alexandria kept the Germans and especially the Irish loyal to the same political party despite an anti-immigrant candidate who was clearly antagonistic to both groups. In Dereham the connections between cultural groups and political groups were inchoate and subject to residual deferential politics. In Alexandria as in Newport political identities were more firmly rooted in cultural identities. Once formed these partisan connections proved highly durable, even, as in Alexandria and Newport, when powerful contemporary issues must have called those loyalties into question.

Conclusion

The individual political worlds of German and Irish voters as recorded in the poll books shed considerable new light on past political life. The poll books tell us that there were more similarities than differences in the political engagement of members of these largest of immigrant groups. The three case studies explored here provide little support for the notion that the Germans and the Irish represented dramatically different accommodations to nineteenth century mass politics in the New World. In all three cases the Germans and the Irish participated in politics at about the same level and exhibited in their voting behavior about the same degree of partisan unity. If the Irish voted slightly more than the Germans and were slightly more united around a party, the difference between the groups was a matter of degree, and a limited degree at that, rather than of kind.

A hierarchy of economic well-being separated voters and nonvoters, including the Germans and the Irish. The poor, the marginal, the least advantaged did not vote in large numbers in America and were prohibited from voting in Canada; self selection south of the border followed the same economic imperatives as did the property qualification to the north. Only in this sense did the Germans, generally better off than the Irish, fail to vote in the proportions expected.

There is little evidence in these case studies of a direct correlation between the simple number of associations in a locale or within an ethnic group—that famous social capital—and the engagement of ordinary citizens from that locale or group in political life. One cannot but suspect that institutional memberships were highly class specific and further benefited, in political terms, the political engagement of the economically privileged. Religious membership is a revealing measure of the extent of a connection between associational membership and individual political engagement. Overall the cumulative advantages of economic position are evident in the fact that those men who were members of religious congregations (a smaller coverage than much of the nineteenth-century literature suggests) were distinctly better off than men who were not members; likewise those who were members of religious organizations were substantially more inclined to participate in political life than those who were not. To paraphrase E. E. Schattschneider's famous quip about contemporary pluralist theory, the historical heavenly choruses of nineteenth-century voters and of religious adherents sang with clear middle class accents. For many, social capital simply paralleled economic capital. Associational membership, economic position, and political engagement all went hand in hand. In this broad sense it is difficult to see, as Mary Ryan observed, the democratic consequences of associational membership.

No less intriguing, however, are the hints in the Alexandria and Newport cases suggesting that, for individuals in lower social positions who were engaged in associational activity (here religious membership), the "political effect" of belonging to a group may have been highly potent. To be specific, the economic inclusiveness of the Catholic Church, encompassing in Alexandria and Newport no less than elsewhere "poor immigrant workers," may well have been an important factor in explaining the elevated rates of political participation demonstrated by the least economically advantaged among both the Irish and the Germans.[88]

If prosperous economic circumstances and community "belongingness" helped select those who came to the polls, cultural affinities certainly helped explain the political choices made once there. In rural Dereham cultural factors were readily evident in settlement patterns, and it appears that much of the change in partisan preference that marked this chaotic period arose from neighborhoods, of whatever ethnic composition or political persuasion, that could be "influenced" by local notables. Dereham provides a compelling North American example of a deferential political world more usually associated

---

88. Kamphoefner, "Liberal Catholicism and Its Limits," 13.

with the hierarchies of nineteenth century English politics.[89] In the Dereham
of the last third of the nineteenth century, we can see evidence of a residual
deference that manifested itself in mobilizing voters not in terms of their
social characteristics but according to whether they fell within the sway of
influential local notables. Perhaps to find such levels of deference in American
political life, one must return to a much earlier American experience, before
mass political parties established the relative stability of political identities so
apparent in mid-nineteenth century Newport and Alexandria. Perhaps too the
fluidity of cultural partisanship evident in Dereham would give way in time to
the stable associations seen south of the border.

In all three case studies, there was quite clearly a "German vote" that
closely approximated in size and unity the much more famous "Irish vote."
Though there were important cultural divides within the Irish and especially
the Germans, both groups demonstrated far more unity of allegiance to a
political party than did the broader communities within which they resided.
The German "bloc vote" was only marginally less powerful in these three
case studies than was the Irish. Likewise, German political participation was
only marginally less vigorous than the Irish. The internal divisions within
each group tended to reflect degrees of difference, not categorical divides, in
partisan attachment. The Irish Catholics and Irish Protestants of Dereham voted
for the same political party, differing only in the degree of their attachment.
The Germans of Newport, perhaps more sharply divided by different regional
cultures, nevertheless managed a surprising degree of overall partisan unity.
Above all, we can see in Newport how a politics built upon cultural diversity
vitiated the possibility of political alliances built on economic identities.

Nineteenth-century newspaper commentators and ethnic leaders often
wrote despairing general accounts of German political engagement in North
America, emphasizing what they saw as a lack of unity and enthusiasm. The
poll books of individual behavior suggest that compared even to the politically
praised Irish, this indictment was undeservedly harsh. In shedding new light on
the politics of cultural diversity that was so central to nineteenth-century North
America, the poll books reveal a political life of ordinary German immigrants
that was more similar to that of the Irish than traditional sources have generally
suggested. In the end, one is left puzzled by the willingness of commentators,

---

89. See, for example, Thomas J. Nossiter, *Influence, Opinion and Political Idioms in Reformed
England: Case Studies from the North-east 1832–1874* (Brighton: Harvester Press, 1975);
David Cresap Moore, *The Politics of Deference: A Study of the Mid-Nineteenth Century English
Political System* (New York: Barnes and Noble, 1976); Patrick Joyce, *Work, Society and Politics:
The Culture of the Factory in Later Victorian England* (Brighton: Harvester Press, 1980).

past and present, to accept the notion that German voters were categorically different from other immigrants in their approach to American politics. There is little evidence in these case studies of German "exceptionalism."

The poll books in the cases reported here permit a view of individual and group behavior free from the perspective of disillusioned leaders. These unique records make possible the rejoining of social history and political history at the level of the individual, a process that proves analytically useful on a wider front. Individual-level sources have a wonderful capacity to break down stereotypical views of past immigrant engagement with American politics and provide a corrective, as suggested here, to the conventional understanding of the German political record in North America.

It may be, too, that the limits and insights of social capital theory are best appreciated by focusing on individuals. The mere presence of associational groups in a city or within an ethnic population seems to have had little impact on the behavior of individuals within that city or group. For many, associational membership may have been simply another measure of economic success and hence lacking the political consequences suggested by the theory. On the other hand, associations that reached out to the less economically privileged and exhibited a political presence—exemplified most clearly here by Alexandria's St. Mary's Catholic Church—might well have made a very real contribution to democratic life, linking into the world of formal politics those at the bottom of the socioeconomic hierarchy. This suggests that our understanding of the democratic consequences of associational life might be directed particularly to those organizations whose memberships were defined not by cultural exclusivity but by connection to the currents in and the composition of the broader social order. In this, as in so many other respects, Irish and German immigrants appear to have shared a common American experience.

Appendix

There are three caveats associated with the religious census. First, there are two record gaps. It has not yet been possible to view membership records of St. Mary's Catholic Church, and this paper relies on names appearing in the marriage and burial records of St. Mary's or attendance at the church-run St. John's Academy. In addition some of the class records for the pre-Civil War Methodist Episcopal South have been lost; those used here are from the years immediately after the war. Second, it may be that membership lists maintained by churches for denominational groups, like Episcopalians, that emphasized infant baptism and universal adult membership are more inclusive than those for more evangelical churches in which membership required a confession of faith. Third, many individuals, and perhaps particularly men, may have been associated with a church without becoming a member. Alan Taylor, in his study of the Presbyterian church of Cooperstown, New York, found that some 241 men subscribed money to the building of the church, but only 44 of these became members. See Alan Taylor, *William Cooper's Town: Power and Persuasion on the Frontier of the Early American Republic* (New York: Knopf, 1995), 227. Ronald Formisano also notes the difference between the participation of men in nineteenth-century religious life and membership in congregations. Formisano found that no more than thirty percent of adult men in Bedford, Massachusetts, were church members in the early Jacksonian period but estimated that up to half, and perhaps more than half, of all potential voters were participants in the town's religious life. See Formisano, *Transformation of Political Culture*, 367–369. See also Paul E. Johnson, *A Shopkeeper's Millennium: Society and Revivals in Rochester, New York, 1815–1837* (New York: Hill and Wang, 1978), 152–161. On the other hand it is important not to over-emphasize the centrality of religion in past political life, given the figures on religious membership that do exist. Allan Bogue notes the tendency to give "scant consideration to the presence of large numbers of voters unaffiliated with any church." See Allan G. Bogue, "The New Political History in the 1970s," in *The Past Before Us*, edited by Michael Kammen (Ithaca: Cornell University Press, 1980), 250. Despite these limitations the religious records available for Alexandria are impressive in their comparative completeness. The specific records used for the religious census of Alexandria were:

EPISCOPAL CHURCHES:
St. Paul's Church—Vestry Records (Births, Marriages, Deaths, Confirmations, Communicants); Graveyard Inscriptions. Grace Church—Church Register (Communicants, Baptisms, Burials, Marriages, Confirmations). Christ Church—Vestry Book, 1854–1861.

BAPTIST CHURCHES:
First Baptist Church—Church Records, Volume 4, 1854–1871.

ROMAN CATHOLIC CHURCHES:
St. Mary's Church—Burial Records, 1798–1982; Marriage Records, 1855–1865; Records from St. Mary's Cemetery; Parishioners, 1855–1860; St. John's Academy School Register.

METHODIST CHURCHES:
Trinity Church—Register of Members. See Fern C. Stukenbrocker, *A Watermelon for God: A History of the Trinity United Methodist Church, Alexandria, Virginia, 1774–1974* (n.p., 1974). Methodist Episcopal South Church—Records of 1876 (members recorded without date of joining). See Kathryn Hedman, comp., *Washington Street United Methodist Church*; see also Leonidas Rosser's Diary in ibid., 292–348.
Methodist Protestant Church—Register of Membership; Quarterly Conference Records.

QUAKER:
Alexandria Society of Friends—Monthly Meeting Membership, 1823–1881. See Lorna A. Anderberg, *Comparison of Alexandria Quakers to the Population of White Alexandria* (n.p., 1987).

JEWISH:
Beth El Synagogue—see Max Rosenberg, ed., *Temple Beth El: A Centennial History of Beth El Hebrew Congregation Serving Northern Virginia since 1859* (n.p., n.d.); Ruth Sinberg Baker, *Adult Jewish Males Residing in Alexandria, Virginia during 1850s, 1860s* (n.p., 1980.); Isaac Leeser, *The Occident*; Hasia R. Diner, *A Time for Gathering: The Second Migration, 1820–1880* (Baltimore: Johns Hopkins Press, 1992), 106, 148–149.

PRESBYTERIAN:
First Presbyterian Church (Old Meeting House)—Church Register, Baptism Book. Second Presbyterian—Church Register, Baptism Book.

The names from all of these records were linked with the Alexandria census of 1860, the property (personal and real) tax lists for 1859, and of the poll books for the 1859 election.

8

German and Irish Big City Mayors: Comparative Perspective on Ethnic Politics

Walter D. Kamphoefner

According to conventional wisdom, German Americans were too diverse and disunited to constitute a powerful political bloc such as that posed by the Irish. The scholarly consensus is well summed up by Kathleen Neils Conzen in her article on Germans in the *Harvard Encyclopedia of American Ethnic Groups*: "Language difficulty, lack of familiarity with democratic practices, and the narrowly economic motivation of their immigration were some reasons for German political impotence. But more significant was the disunity that prevented overwhelming numbers from rallying behind a single party."[1]

There is no disputing parts of this characterization. Compared to the Irish, the confessional, regional, and occupational diversity of the Germans was just as apparent as their fluctuating political loyalties. It is not so certain, however, that slavish loyalty to one party brought large benefits in terms of policy output or even the makeup of the ticket. Precisely because of the independence of the Germans, political parties could ill afford to ignore their wishes. This was particularly true at the local level, where the leading issues were often in the highly emotionally charged areas of cultural politics, for example, education and alcohol. As urban historian John Alswang has observed, "The key to the machine's success has been its ability to provide services that government has been unable or unwilling to provide, and these services have been as

---

1. Kathleen Neils Conzen, "Germans," in *Harvard Encyclopedia of American Ethnic Groups*, edited by Stephan Thernstrom (Cambridge: Harvard University Press, 1980), 421. Similar characterizations can be found in Fred Luebke, *Immigrants and Politics* (Lincoln: University of Nebraska Press, 1969), 8–9; Fred Luebke, "The Germans," in *Ethnic Leadership in America*, edited by John Higham (Baltimore: Johns Hopkins U. Press, 1978), esp. 66–68; James Bergquist, "German Communities in American Cities: An Interpretation of the Nineteenth-Century Experience," *Journal of American Ethnic History* 4 (1984): 13–16; David Gerber, "Language Maintenance, Ethnic Group Formation, and Public Schools: Changing Patterns of German Concern, Buffalo, 1837–1874," *Journal of American Ethnic History* 4 (1984): 34–35.

importantly cultural as they have been economic."[2] Not only in questions of policy, but also in the area of personnel, Germans in local politics came off better than is generally realized. And with respect to the type of individual who presided over city government, the contrasts between Germans and Irish, and the propensity of the latter toward machine politics, can easily be exaggerated.

For the stereotypical Irish mayor one need look no farther than Edwin O'Connor's 1956 novel, *The Last Hurrah*, and the film of the same name, based on the life of James Michael Curley, who served as Boston's mayor for five terms spread across four decades. Son of an immigrant hod carrier who died young, Curley grew up with politics. Elected to the city council at age twenty-six, he next moved up to the Massachusetts House. Jailed for impersonating a friend on a civil service exam, he successfully ran for alderman from his cell. Before his first term as mayor he had been twice elected congressman; after his third term he became governor of Massachusetts, then after several setbacks returned to Congress. During his last stint in city hall he was jailed for five months on charges of congressional influence peddling but managed to hold onto the mayor's office.[3]

The profile of Germans in politics has been almost too low to evoke stereotypes, much less inspire novels or films. But if there is a stereotypical German mayor it would be someone like Rudolph Blankenburg, who served one term in Philadelphia's city hall during the Progressive era. The well-educated son of a German Reformed minister, Blankenburg immigrated at age twenty-two, married a Quaker woman, and became a Methodist. A successful businessman long active in reform circles, Blankenburg was nominated by a local third party and was also supported by the Democrats against the Republican machine, though in national politics he was a Republican. His administration was characterized by typical structural reforms: fighting corruption, promoting efficiency, and cracking down on vice. But he was thwarted by a Republican city council, deserted by his own allies when he refused to distribute patronage to them, and did not even seek reelection.[4]

2. John M. Alswang, *Bosses, Machines, and Urban Voters* (Baltimore: Johns Hopkins U. Press, 1977), 34.

3. Edwin O'Connor, *The Last Hurrah* (Boston: Little, Brown, 1956). The 1958 Columbia Pictures film starring Spencer Tracy was directed by John Ford. *Biographical Dictionary of American Mayors, 1820 to 1980*, edited by Melvin Holli and Peter d'A. Jones (Westport, CT: Greenwood, 1981), 86–87.

4. *Biographical Dictionary*, 32.

In fact, Blankenburg is not that far from the German norm, but many of the Irish mayors also resemble him as much as they do the colorful but atypical Curley.

Apropos of stereotypes, it should be noted that despite assertions that have found their way into some textbooks, the original "Boss," William M. Tweed, was not Irish, but an American born of Anglo-Protestant background.[5] While urban historian Melvin Holli considers New York mayor William F. Havemeyer, whose name reflects his German parentage, a "prototype of the twentieth-century structural reformers," two of the other four such exemplary mayors he cites were in fact Irishmen: James Phelan of turn-of-the-century San Francisco and John Purroy Mitchell, an "oddly puritanical Catholic" who occupied New York's city hall during World War I.[6] The first Irish Catholic to preside over Chicago was Edward F. Dunne, whom a recent biography characterizes as "the mayor who cleaned up Chicago." His German Republican successor, Fred "Fat Freddie" Busse, a Catholic saloonkeeper, better fits the machine stereotype often applied to the Irish. Moreover, his ethnicity figured strongly in his election, helping swing many otherwise Democratic German Catholics.[7]

To combat overgeneralization from colorful anecdotes, this paper presents a more systematic look at those members of the two leading nineteenth-century American ethnic groups who served as mayors in fourteen of the country's largest cities between 1820 and 1980. It draws upon the resources of the *Biographical Dictionary of American Mayors*, which covers the cities of Baltimore, Boston, Buffalo, Chicago, Cincinnati, Cleveland, Detroit, Milwaukee, New Orleans, New York, Philadelphia, Pittsburgh, St. Louis, and San Francisco (plus Los Angeles, which elected no Germans or Irish as mayor).[8] Along with a collective biography approach, this paper examines

---

5.   Tyler Anbinder, "'Boss' Tweed: Nativist," *Journal of the Early Republic* 15 (1995): 109–116.

6.   Melvin G. Holli, *Reform in Detroit: Hazen S. Pingree and Urban Politics* (New York: Oxford University Press, 1969), 163–168.

7.   John R. Schmidt, *"The Mayor Who Cleaned Up Chicago": A Political Biography of William E. Dever* (DeKalb, IL: Northern Illinois University Press, 1989), 19 and passim; Joel A. Tarr, *A Study in Boss Politics: William Lorimer of Chicago* (Urbana: University of Illinois Press, 1971), 177–178, 189.

8.   *Biographical Dictionary*, 418–431 and passim. Mayors were included only if they were elected at least once in their own right, omitting those who took office by appointment or succession and only served out their predecessor's term. I have for the most part accepted the editors' definitions of ethnicity and religion from their appendices. The Germans include at least three persons of mixed ancestry in the second generation, and five (including two with Irish-stock mothers) in the third. The Austrian Catholic Leopold Markbreit is included

the level of ethnic success in the fourteen cities in relationship to their ethnic population makeup. It joins a growing literature of urban studies, in particular the work of Jon Teaford, in downplaying the extent of machine influence in city halls between the Civil War and World War I.[9] Where machines did exist, they were more often ward-level and factionalized than citywide and extending to the top of the ballot.[10] As Teaford emphasizes, the mayor's office was largely a bastion of the business elite, especially its Anglo-Protestant members.[11]

In view of the reputation of the Irish as born politicians and their advantage of an English mother tongue, it comes as some surprise to learn that more first-generation Germans (twelve) than immigrant Irish Catholics (nine) were elected as mayors in the fourteen cities covered by the *Biographical Dictionary.* Irish Catholics have a slight edge in the second generation, making the totals practically identical for immigrants and their children: thirty-nine Germans and forty Irish Catholics (table 8.1). But in the third generation Germans again have a slight advantage, making the overall totals sixty to fifty-eight. Even

among first-generation Germans since he was clearly part of the ethnic language community, but George McClellan, Jr., born in Germany of American parents, is excluded. In cases where generation was ambiguous from the dictionary entry, I supplemented it with manuscript census information. However, I followed the *Biographical Dictionary* in its questionable decision to omit from the German category two third generation mayors: five-term Milwaukee mayor Henry Maier, a Lutheran whose mother, father, and stepfather were all of German stock, and John Poelker, a St. Louis Catholic whose parents both appear in the manuscript census as being of German parentage. Similarly, I omitted from the Irish Catholic category three persons listed in the *Biographical Dictionary* as being of unknown confession. Two of these men, George Maguire and George Kane, only held office for one year in St. Louis and Baltimore respectively and would have had minimal effects on the totals. Milwaukee Socialist Daniel Hoan, whose father was born in Canada of Irish parents, was elected seven times and served a total of twenty-four years, but he could hardly have been Catholic given his partisan affiliation, and he certainly did not represent an Irish ethnic constituency.

9.   Jon C. Teaford, *The Unheralded Triumph: City Government in America, 1870–1900* (Baltimore: Johns Hopkins U. Press, 1984). In a similar vein see also Terrence J. McDonald, *The Parameters of Urban Fiscal Policy: Socioeconomic Change and Political Culture in San Francisco, 1860–1906* (Berkeley: University of California Press, 1986); Terrence J. McDonald and Sally Ward, eds., *The Politics of Urban Fiscal Policy* (Beverly Hills: Sage Publications, 1984); Craig M. Brown and Charles Halaby, "Machine Politics in America, 1870–1945," *Journal of Interdisciplinary History* 17 (1987): 587–612.

10.   Teaford, *Unheralded Triumph*, 175–187; According to Brown and Halaby, "Machine Politics," 597, who studied thirty of the fifty largest American cities, one-fourth of them showed no appreciable machine activity, and forty percent were never under centralized boss control. Of those experiencing machine influence, two-thirds were under factional rather than dominant machines, the latter defined as controlling three successive elections without losing control of both the mayoralty and a city council majority at the same time.

11.   Teaford, *Unheralded Triumph*, 43–54.

	German		Irish Catholic	
	N	%	N	%
All Mayors				
Number	62	52%	58	48%
Times Elected	94	47%	107	53%
Years in Office	261	46%	303	54%
1st and 2nd Generation Mayors				
Number	39	49%	40	51%
Times Elected	58	43%	76	57%
Years in Office	158	44%	198	56%

Table 8.1: Electoral Success by Ethnicity in Fourteen Big Cities

when one includes Protestant Irish, the advantages of Irish over Germans is not overwhelming, about seventy-eight to sixty-two. However, Irish Catholics would appear to be the most appropriate comparison group. Neither language nor religion set the Protestant Irish apart from the dominant culture. Rowland Berthoff's observation about English immigrants would apply equally to Orangemen: They had no second generation; their children were seen as regular Anglo-Protestants.[12]

Because they were more likely to be reelected than Germans, Irish Catholics maintained a slight edge in other indicators of political success. Across the board, Germans made up fifty-two percent of the mayors, but won forty-seven percent of the elections and served for forty-six percent of the time in which one of the two groups headed city hall. If one adopts a narrow definition of ethnicity and looks only at the first and second generations (immigrants and their children), the picture remains quite similar. Taking the totals of Germans and of Irish Catholics, Germans accounted for forty-nine percent of the mayors, compared to forty-three percent of the electoral victories and forty-four percent of the total years in office among one of the two ethnic groups. But despite the slight Irish edge, it is the similarities rather than the contrasts between the two groups that stand out. The predominance of Irish in urban politics, if it existed at all, must have been more pronounced at the level of the foot soldiers than at the head of the columns.[13]

A comparison of the ethnics who held the office of mayor (all males, except Jane Byrne of Chicago) likewise punctures some stereotypes (table 8.2). Although ethnicity becomes increasingly subjective (and some family

12. Rowland T. Berthoff, *British Immigrants in Industrial America, 1790–1950* (Cambridge, MA: Harvard University Press, 1953), 134, 190–195, 210.

13. This is suggested by the limited evidence available in Teaford, *Unheralded Triumph*, 38–39.

	1st & 2nd Gen. Only			All Mayors		
	German	*Sig.*	*Irish*	*German*	*Sig.*	*Irish*
Number of Mayors	39		40	62		58
Year First Elected						
Mean	1896	.05	1908	1904	.01	1920
Median	1900		1906	1909		1919
Age When First Elected						
Mean	49	.31	47	48	.51	47
Median	47		48	46		47
Highest Political Office before Mayor		.02			.01	
None	28%		10%	31%		17%
Alderman	33%		18%	34%		16%
Other Local Office	23%		45%	21%		36%
State Office	15%		20%	13%		22%
National Office	0%		8%	2%		9%
No Political Offices after Mayor	72%	.27	60%	73%	.30	64%
Mean Times Elected	1.5	.08	1.9	1.5	.07	1.8
Mean Years in Office	4.1	.28	5.0	4.2	.15	5.2
One Term Mayors	64%	.14	48%	63%	.15	50%
Highest Level of Education		.02			.03	
Unknown	18%		8%	13%		5%
Primary	18%		15%	16%		14%

Table 8.2: Comparative Profile of Irish Catholic and German Big City Mayors

High School	33%		13%		14%
Professional	18%		50%		50%
College	13%		15%		17%
Type of Elementary Education		.01		.01	
Unknown	28%		33%		29%
Public	36%		28%		31%
Private	33%		8%		9%
Parochial	3%		33%		31%
Ethnicity of Wife		.01		.01	
Unknown or Unmarried	10%		20%		26%
Same as Husband	49%		65%		64%
Other Ethnic	15%		5%		3%
Anglo-American	26%		10%		7%
Confession		(.01)		(.01)	
Unspecified	23%		18%		
Lutheran	21%		18%		
Catholic	8%		21%		100%
Jewish	8%		5%		
German Reformed	3%		2%		
Moravian	3%		2%		
Protestant, Other or Unspec.	36%		35%		
Political Party		.01		.01	
Democrat	31%		37%		91%
Republican	56%		48%		5%
Other	13%		15%		3%

*Significance level (of Cramer's V for crosstabulations)

Table 8.2: Comparative Profile of Irish Catholic and German Big City Mayors (cont.)

trees increasingly mixed) with the passage of time and generations, it proved to be of little consequence whether the analysis encompassed all mayors or was restricted to the first and second generation. Table 8.2 includes all Irish Catholics and Germans who were elected mayor at least once in their own right.

Despite the fact that immigration from Ireland was concentrated earlier in the nineteenth century than that from Germany, Irish Catholics appear to have taken longer than Germans to gain acceptance with the American electorate.[14] The average German mayor took office for the first time around the turn of the century, as compared to 1910 for the average Irishman. Nevertheless, the age at taking office was virtually the same for both groups: The mean and median for Irish were both forty-seven; for Germans the respective figures were forty-eight and forty-six.

A comparative profile does lend some support to the image of the Irish as professional politicians and Germans as outsider "good government" candidates. Despite similar ages, Irish mayors as a rule entered office with somewhat more political experience than their German counterparts. Nearly a third of the German mayors had held no previous public office, but only about one-sixth of the Irish. Similar proportions held for those elected mayor with no previous office higher than alderman. Only fifteen percent of the Germans had risen to state or national office before occupying city hall; the percentage was twice that for the Irish, including eight or nine percent who had held national office. The subsequent careers of former mayors show a similar pattern, though the contrasts are not as extreme. For a majority of both ethnicities, the mayoralty was the last public office they held, but the figure for the Irish was about ten points lower than for Germans, nearly three-fourths of whom retired upon leaving city hall.[15]

---

14. In the aggregate across twenty-five principal American cities, including all of the fourteen under study, the leading immigrant group from 1850 to 1870 was the Irish, followed by the Germans. For the next three decades through 1900, Germans took over the lead, followed by the Irish, who slipped to third place in 1910. According to the 1860 census, in all fourteen cities under study (except for Boston, where Irish came in first and Germans fourth), the Irish and Germans held the two leading positions among the foreign-born. Besides Boston, the Irish came in first in New York, Philadelphia, Pittsburgh, San Francisco, and New Orleans; the Germans held the lead in Chicago, Detroit, Cleveland, St. Louis, Baltimore, Buffalo, Milwaukee, and Cincinnati. Even though the Irish lead faded in later censuses, their early dominance meant they got an early start in producing second and third generations. Such ethnics made their political presence felt even if they did not show up as Irish in the censuses. Niles Carpenter, *Immigrants and Their Children, 1920* (Washington, DC: Government Printing Office, 1927), 385–388.

15. See Teaford, *Unheralded Triumph,* 49–50.

If this suggests greater tendencies toward machine politics on the part of the Irish, additional support is given by their reelection success compared to Germans. Nearly two-thirds of the Germans, but just under half of the Irish, served only a single term. The German average was 1.5 terms; the Irish, 1.8 or 1.9. As for total time in office, Germans averaged just over four years, one year less than the Irish. Boss Plunkitt's characterization "Reformers only Mornin' Glories" who soon fade, immediately comes to mind.[16] Still, one should not exaggerate these contrasts; in fact, none prove to be statistically significant.

Moreover, if machine politics means poorly educated candidates, the profiles of Irish mayors hardly fit the pattern. If anything, they were better educated than the Germans. There were more German than Irish mayors who had not gone beyond primary school, nor can this poor showing of the Germans be the result of missing data. One-third of the Germans, twice as many as the Irish, stopped with high school. The two groups were very close at the college level, but the big contrast was the proportion with professional training (mostly in law), constituting half of all Irish mayors but a quarter or less of the Germans. It should be noted, however, that in the nineteenth century this training was often in the form of reading law rather than attending a professional school, and did not have the status it did in the mid-twentieth century. The Irish lawyers included three who started out as unskilled laborers, and four others who had been in low white-collar jobs. Mayors were often involved in so many enterprises that it was difficult to deal with them systematically, but it does appear that Germans had a stronger tendency toward business in contrast to the Irish gravitation toward law. Among the sixty percent of mayors for whom parental occupational was available, nine Germans and a dozen Irish were of blue-collar origins, all of the German fathers occupying skilled positions but with five Irish unskilled. Also, when one examines the first adult jobs of future mayors, one finds more Irish starting out on the lower rungs. Ten Germans began their careers as manual laborers, only two of them unskilled, compared to nineteen Irish, only five of whom were skilled. This makes the Irish educational achievements appear all the more impressive, though one must remember that many businessmen in the nineteenth century got their start clerking in a family enterprise rather than through any formal schooling.

If the level of Irish education was not lower than that of the Germans, there were some contrasts in the type of elementary education preferred by the two groups, to the extent that this information was available. About one-third of the

16.   William L. Riordon, *Plunkitt of Tammany Hall* (New York: Dutton, 1963), 17.

mayors had attended public schools, slightly more of the Germans and less for the Irish. But of those who had not, Irish overwhelmingly preferred parochial schools. Germans, on the other hand, disproportionately chose private schools, and this despite the network of parochial schools maintained by German Catholics and Lutherans. This is one of several indicators that Irish mayors often came from the heart of their ethnic community, whereas their German counterparts often came from the fringes. Information on spouses was often sketchy, but the manuscript census helped clarify many cases. Fewer than half of the Germans definitely had spouses of the same ethnicity, whereas with the Irish it was close to two-thirds. At least one-fourth of the Germans took Anglo-American wives, but only ten percent or less of the Irish did so despite their linguistic advantages. Nowhere is the high degree of assimilation of German mayors more clearly reflected, however, than in religious confession.

All the Irish mayors in the comparison group were by definition at least nominal Catholics. Of the Germans, however, less than half belonged to confessions rooted in the country of origin. No confession was indicated for about one-fifth of these mayors, perhaps reflecting a transplanted freethinking tradition characteristic of many educated Germans, especially the politically active. More than one-third of the German mayors adhered to Anglo-American confessions, many simply characterized as Protestant. Fewer than half belonged to transplanted confessions with roots in the Fatherland. Catholics and Lutherans ran neck and neck, and there were also three German Jews. One might question to what extent the latter shared a German ethnic identity, particularly in the case of immigrant Adolph Sutro, Populist mayor of San Francisco in the 1890s. But if one examines the profile of second-generation Julius Fleischmann in Cincinnati, his Turnverein membership and affiliation with the Republican Cox machine suggest that a large proportion of his support must have come from (non-Jewish) German Americans. This was even more apparent with another Jewish mayor in the Queen City, German-born Frederick Spiegel, who had edited a German newspaper, chaired a public school committee on the German language, and presided over a number of *Vereine*.[17]

This leaning toward the Republican party was characteristic of German mayors as a whole, though the tendency was not overwhelming. Republicans outnumbered Democrats by about two to one. As expected, Irish Catholic mayors were overwhelmingly Democratic. When one includes Irish Protestants

17. Zane L. Miller, *Boss Cox's Cincinnati: Urban Politics in the Progressive Era* (New York: Oxford University Press, 1968), 173–177, 236–238.

in the equation, it turns out that ethnicity is a strong predictor of party affiliation, but confession is even stronger (table 8.3). The mayors were divided into simple dichotomies: Protestant versus Catholic and Whig-Republican versus Democrat, with those falling outside these categories excluded. Whether the analysis is limited to the first and second generation or includes all mayors of Irish and German descent, the results are very similar. Both gamma (which gives a perfect correlation with just one empty cell) and phi (which produces a perfect correlation only when both diagonal cells are empty) show a strong tendency for German mayors to be Republicans, and Irish, Democrats, but an even stronger tendency for Protestants to be Republicans, and for Catholics to be Democrats. While it is certainly unwarranted to attempt to discern the political loyalties of ethnic groups from the ethnicity of candidates for office, it does suggest that there were contrasting strategies behind running Irish as opposed to German candidates. An Irish candidacy meant a decision to go with one's strength: to exploit the solidarity of the ethnic community, the ninety-five percent Democratic affiliations of Irish Catholics, and the high turnouts produced by big-city machines. German candidacies, especially in the Republican party, often arose out of a different strategy, that of trying to bridge the gap between Anglo-American and ethnic constituencies with candidates who were acceptable to both. Hence the small number of Catholic German mayors and the large number who belonged to Anglo-Protestant denominations. In fact, there was only one Catholic among the dozen first-generation German mayors in the cities examined here, and one of the two Catholics in the second generation was Robert Wagner, Jr., who was neither very German nor very Catholic. The other, Martin Behrmann of New Orleans, had attended a German-language school, but based his political support on a multi-ethnic Catholic coalition. By the third generation, however, Catholics were the leading confession among German mayors with nearly forty percent. Still, it is questionable what this means in terms of German ethnicity; it could simply be a manifestation of the triple melting pot, with these candidates running essentially as Catholics rather than Germans. The same could be said for third-generation Irish who were running not as Irish but as Catholic—or white—candidates.[18]

---

18. A study of the Irish in St. Louis finds that in the second and third generation they "seemed to identify themselves more as Catholics rather than exclusively with their ethnic heritage." Martin G. Towey, "Kerry Patch Revisited: Irish Americans in St. Louis in the Turn of the Century Era," in *From Paddy to Studs*, edited by Timothy J. Meagher (Westport, CT: Greenwood Press, 1986), 154–155.

Kamphoefner

1st and 2nd Generation Mayors	German	Irish	Protestant	Catholic
Democrat	11	37	5	39
Republican/Whig	25	2	16	3
	Phi=.67**	Gamma=.95**	Phi=.72**	Gamma=.96**
All Mayors	German	Irish	Protestant	Catholic
Democrat	22	63	14	63
Republican/Whig	37	13	37	6
	Phi=.47**	Gamma=.78**	Phi=.66**	Gamma=.93**

**=Significant to the .01 level

Table 8.3: Party of Mayors by Ethnicity and Religion

In an attempt to learn more about the factors promoting ethnic success in mayoral races, I assembled a second data set using the fourteen cities covered by the *Biographical Dictionary of American Mayors* as units of observation (table 8.4). German Irish success ratios were calculated on the basis of total number of times elected and total years in the mayor's office (since length of terms varied across time and from city to city); this was done first for the two ethnic groups as a whole and then restricted to mayors of the first and second generations. This success ratio was then set in relationship to the ratio of the two ethnic groups in the population of the respective cities. Initially I used the 1910 census (which fell at about the median year of election of these mayors) to measure ethnic composition based on the first and second generations. As it turned out, however, this measure underestimated Irish voting strength. Irish immigration was concentrated considerably earlier in the nineteenth century; Germans only came to lead in numbers of new arrivals in the 1850s. As early as 1880, second-generation Irish outnumbered the first generation, so that after the turn of the century, there were many more Irish than Germans in the third generation, invisible for census purposes. Thus, I also used 1870 figures on the first generation, which produce a much more favorable estimate of Irish strength relative to German. According to the 1910 census, the mean percentage of German stock across the fourteen cities was eighteen, or more than double the eight percent for Irish. But the 1870 figures show a mean of fifteen percent German born, whereas the Irish come in above twelve percent. I also drew on 1980 figures recording ancestry regardless of generation; this works fairly well for Germans, but with Irish includes the distorting factor of Scotch Irish.[19]

For simplicity's sake, all the officeholding and population figures were calculated as German percentage of German-plus-Irish totals. Measured this way, the average for the fourteen cities was a German share of sixty-eight percent in 1910, but only fifty-four percent in 1870. (One needs to keep in mind, however, that perhaps ten percent of the Irish were Protestant, and by all

---

19. The 1980 ancestry figures were taken from Stanley Lieberson and Mary C. Waters, *From Many Strands: Ethnic and Racial Groups in Contemporary America* (New York: Russell Sage Foundation, 1988), 84–89. These tables include all persons of "single" or "mixed" ancestry, so the percentages add up to more than one hundred. They cover metropolitan areas rather than municipal boundaries, but this is in any case a more accurate reflection of earlier ethnic population makeup. Scotch Irish were coded by the census as being of mixed Scottish and Irish ancestry—see Lieberson and Waters, *Many Strands*, 13–14. The 1870 and 1910 population figures are taken directly from published population figures reflecting city boundaries at the time. For example, Pittsburgh did not in 1870 include Allegheny, while New York in 1870 only consisted of Manhattan, but by 1910 comprised all five boroughs.

	All Mayors German-Irish Ratio		1st and 2nd Generation Mayors German-Irish Ratio	
	Times Elected	Years in Office	Times Elected	Years in Office
German-Irish Ratio, Immigrants, 1870	.77**	.81**	.44	.58*
German-Irish Ratio, Immigrant Stock, 1910	.71**	.72**	.51	.50
German-Irish Ratio, Ethnic Origins, 1980	.66**	.68**	.38	.44

% of Total Years in Office Held by

	Germans		Irish	
	All	1st & 2nd Gen.	All	1st & 2nd Gen.
Immigrant % of City Population, 1870	.70**	.65*	.73**	.69**
Immigrant Stock % of City Population, 1910.	.62*	.51	.73**	.61*
Ethnic Origin % of City Population, 1980	.71**	.52	.44	.17

* = Significant to .05 level.   ** = Significant to .01 level.

Table 8.4: Correlation between Electoral Success and Ethnic Composition of City Population

accounts diametrically opposed to Irish Catholics in their political affiliations. German nationality and ethnicity correspond more closely, notwithstanding some Poles from within Germany and some Germanophones from outside the Reich, who would tend to balance each other out.)

When these German/Irish officeholding ratios are correlated with the population ratios across the fourteen cities, it turns out that ethnic composition is a relatively good predictor of electoral success. Most of the correlation coefficients fall in the .70 range, which means in terms of R^2 that about half of the variation is thus explained. Comparing the various measures of electoral success and population composition, some clear patterns emerge. Stronger correlations result when mayors of all generations are taken into account rather than just those of the first and second generation. Moreover, higher coefficients also result when total years in office is used as the indicator of electoral success rather than times elected. Thus, the indicators one would expect to be most appropriate do in fact produce the strongest correlations. There are also consistent differences in the strength of association depending on which census is used to measure population composition in the cities. The highest correlations come when immigrant population in 1870 is used as the indicator; the 1910 immigrant stock variables produce somewhat weaker associations. The 1980 ethnic origins figures work well with Germans but not with Irish. The best prediction of electoral success comes when the 1870 population ratio is correlated with the ratio of years in office for mayors of all generations, producing a correlation of .81. In other words the ethnic makeup of the cities explains nearly two-thirds of the variation in the ethnic ratio in city hall.[20]

One can also apply a similar technique, but treat the Germans and Irish separately, calculating one group's share of the *total* population in the respective cities and correlating that with the number of years they held office there, as was done in the bottom half of table 8.4.[21] Once again there are some consistent patterns. The 1870 census proves to be a better predictor than 1910; taking all ethnic mayors rather than just the immigrant stock also produces higher coefficients. Comparing the two ethnic groups, Irish success seems to be somewhat more consistently predictable from their share of a city's

---

20. A least-squares estimate based on this regression indicates that when the German/Irish ratio stood at 50:50 in a city, one could expect the Germans to occupy the mayor's office 44.5 percent of the time it was held by one of the two ethnic groups.

21. Actually, one needs to divide the officeholding figure by the number of years "at risk" since some of these cities did not begin electing mayors immediately in 1820 when the directory starts; doing this improves the correlations slightly over using the raw number of years in office.

population than is the case with Germans, but the differences based on 1870 data are practically negligible.

Also interesting is the pattern of the outliers, the cities that did better or worse than one would expect on the basis of their ethnic makeup. The Irish in Boston had an overwhelming advantage, occupying city hall for seventy-two years as compared to just two for the Germans. But this was about what one might expect given the makeup of its electorate. New York, by contrast, had nearly as heavy an Irish population but spent less than half as many years under Irish mayors as Boston. San Francisco, though, had the lowest relative Irish representation. Chicago was the city where the Irish did best in relation to their population and the Germans did worst.

German novelist Friedrich Gerstäcker, in an account of his travels during 1867, was absolutely correct in observing that Germans were nowhere more dominant than in St. Louis, not even in Cincinnati where they were proportionally more numerous. He related the anecdote of a German city controller who said he would have to put a sign outside his door, "English is also spoken here," because the Americans were afraid to come in among so many Germans.[22] In less than ten years, this same controller, immigrant Henry Overstolz, would take over the mayor's office, the first of a number of German Republicans. St. Louis elected more German mayors relative to its population makeup than any other city, followed closely by Buffalo. Both spent more years under German mayors than Milwaukee, the unofficial German capital of the United States, though the German share of their populations was only two-thirds as large.[23]

Still, the routes to electoral success varied in the leading German cities. In St. Louis six German mayors through 1948 were Republican; there was just one German Democrat during the New Deal and another in 1848 before there was a Republican party. In Cincinnati the close association between the Germans and the Republican Cox machine was also apparent. In Buffalo, however, two German Republicans, one of them Catholic, gave way to a string of five German Democrats interrupted by only one Republican in 1930. Milwaukee presents yet another pattern, with the tendency switching from Republicans to Socialists around 1910. So the route to German electoral success could lead

---

22. Friedrich Gerstäcker, *Neue Reisen durch die Vereinigten Staaten, Mexico, Ecuador, Westindien und Venezuela*, vol. 1 (Jena: H. Costenoble, 1868), 130, translation mine.

23. The "expected" time under German mayors was based on a regression with German percentage of the 1870 city population; 1980 ethnic ancestry figures also show St. Louis with the highest positive residuals. *Biographical Dictionary*, 277 and passim.

through various political parties.

What kind of payoffs did the contrasting political strategies of Germans and Irish bring for their ethnic groups? For that matter, what goods did the mayor's office have at its disposal to deliver? Generalizations are difficult, because the structure of city government and the responsibility and power of the mayor's office varied not only from city to city, but also over the course of time in any given city. At all times and places, however, the mayor was the ceremonial head of city government, so the psychic reward of having a fellow ethnic presiding over city hall was everywhere the same. Beyond that, much depended on the time and place, and even the time trends were not entirely uniform. Structural reforms during the second half of the nineteenth century and on into the Progressive era cut back the power of city councils, which often redounded to the mayor's advantage. But the spread of civil service reforms and independent police boards and the increasing professionalization of urban services restricted the competence of the urban executive. At the one extreme under a city-manager system such as that in twentieth-century Cincinnati and for a time in Cleveland, the mayor was—except for ceremonial functions—simply first among equals on the city council. But in other cities, particularly the largest ones, the mayor was a chief executive with veto rights over the city council and extensive appointive powers.[24]

Policing was easily the most politicized governmental function in most big cities, and mayors exerted considerable influence in both the makeup and attitude of police departments. The stereotypical Irish cop has been enshrined as a stock character in American urban folklore. But the predominance of Irish Americans in petty patronage jobs is more than mere legend—it is borne out by census occupational data. Already in 1870, the first time the published census tabulated occupation by ethnicity, the Irish share of governmental employees was more than double what would have resulted had all ethnic groups been uniformly distributed across all occupations. The Irish even outranked natives in this category. Among government officials Irish showed a seemingly modest index of representation, seventy-five, but in fact the English were the only immigrant group that ranked higher. By 1880 the Irish were overrepresented among both government employees and officials, with indexes around 150. It seems, however, that they were largely restricted to low skill positions; for government clerks, the Irish index for both years was in the fifties range. In 1890 the Irish were the highest ranking immigrant group in the category of government officials with an index just over one hundred.

---

24. Teaford, *Unheralded Triumph*, 17–25, 42–46, 172–173.

This apparently brought them large dividends of political patronage in the field of law enforcement: The occupational category of watchmen, police, and detectives shows the Irish with an index of no less than 356, three times that of the English, the next leading immigrant group. In absolute terms, Irish made up about one-fifth of all policemen nationwide at the turn of the century. This Irish bastion persisted for a number of decades. As late as 1950 the census category of firemen, police, sheriffs, and marshals shows first-generation Irish with an index over three hundred, and the second generation exceeding 450, in both cases nearly triple that of any other ethnic group. Needless to say, German Americans did not come anywhere close in most of these categories; not even the English did.[25]

It appears, however, that these political dividends were of dubious value to the Irish, and certainly did not enhance the overall social mobility of this ethnic group. In fact, Thernstrom's study of Boston suggests that it may have done just the opposite. The solid base of the Irish in local government tended to keep them there; winning control of three thousand jobs in the Public Works Department meant seizing one kind of opportunity at the expense of another. A safe, steady job in the police department appears to have conveyed sufficient status for the average Irish Catholic.[26]

If Germans did not gain many low-level government jobs from their position between the political fronts in most municipalities, what did they gain besides psychic gratification through their presence at the head of some city tickets? As a matter of fact, did the modest number of German nominations and elections as big city mayors represent anything beyond mere tokenism? There were two areas of urban policy where German Americans largely got their way, regardless of whether they personally headed city tickets or not: in imposing their value system with regard to alcohol regulations and in placing their mother tongue on the public elementary curriculum in most major cities.

As with the Irish presence on police forces and in minor government positions, the German association with the alcoholic beverage industry, and beer in particular, is an ethnic stereotype with more than just a (barley) grain of truth. In the late nineteenth century Germans were overrepresented among

---

25. Edward P. Hutchinson, *Immigrants and Their Children, 1850–1950* (New York: Wiley, 1956), 81–85, 99–105, 122–128, 220–231. The index is calculated by dividing the proportion of, say, Irish, in a given occupational group by their proportion in the entire labor force, where one hundred equals parity.

26. Stephan Thernstrom, *The Other Bostonians: Poverty and Progress in the American Metropolis, 1880–1970* (Cambridge: Harvard University Press, 1973), 132–133, 160–170.

brewers by a factor of eight or nine, and in 1880 it was nearly ten (an index of 973). Though seldom constituting more than seven percent of the labor force, they made up nearly two-thirds of all people employed in the brewing industry, and this total does not include the second generation. They were also heavily involved in the wholesaling and retailing of alcohol, regularly constituting more than three times their share of saloon keepers and bartenders and peaking out in 1880 with an index of 464: over thirty percent of the occupational total nationwide. In 1870 Germans made up about 3.5 times their share of distillers and of liquor and wine dealers. While the Irish were modestly overrepresented as well in most alcohol-related occupations except brewing, the only branch where they surpassed the Germans was among liquor and wine dealers.[27] Germans appear to have excelled more as producers than as consumers of alcohol; at least their claims of drinking "mäßig, aber regelmäßig" (moderately but regularly) is supported by statistics on alcohol-related disease and arrests.[28] It was as businessmen rather than customers that Germans ran the greatest risk of conflict with alcohol laws.

In the first recorded portrayal of policemen as pigs, cartoonist Thomas Nast in 1874 took aim at Cincinnati police who "do not enforce the laws against the liquor traffic . . . [and] distinguished themselves . . . by arresting forty-three women, who went on the streets to sing and pray." The prominence of the Schwein Kopf Lager Bier Hall in the cartoon left no doubt that Nast's main target was his fellow German Americans, with whom he apparently identified less than with the Anglo-Protestant elite circles he married into.[29]

The Cincinnati incident is symptomatic of broader patterns of cultural clash between German ethnics and the dominant Anglo-American culture involving attitudes toward alcohol and leisure. Typical is the complaint of an 1873 *Atlantic Monthly* article regarding German immigrants: "Wherever they have settled in any numbers, they hold . . . the balance of power, and it would be almost impossible to pass a Maine Liquor Law, or a Sunday Law, or if

---

27. Hutchinson, *Immigrants*, 81–85, 99–105, 122–128.

28. In New York on the eve of the Civil War, Germans had lower rates of conviction for being drunk and disorderly than any other immigrant group; eighty years later, they had among the lowest rates of hospitalization for alcohol-related psychoses in New York State. Richard Stivers, "Historical Meanings of Irish-American Drinking," in *The American Experience with Alcohol: Contrasting Cultural Perspectives*, edited by Linda A. Bennett and Genevieve M. Ames (New York: Plenum Press, 1985), 127–128.

29. Thomas Nast, *Thomas Nast: Cartoons and Illustrations*, edited by Thomas Nast St. Hill (New York: Dover, 1974), 114.

passed, to enforce it. The principle that Christianity is part of the common law is fast disappearing wherever they settle."[30]

Most Germans, not just the Vereinsdeutsche (Club Germans) but the religiously affiliated Kirchendeutsche as well, would have questioned what Christianity had to do with alcohol prohibition. German Catholic periodicals railed against "Puritan fanatics" as vehemently as any freethinking secularists.[31] Until nationwide prohibition was imposed against the background of the First World War (and sometimes even thereafter), German-Americans managed to defend their values at the local level whether or not they controlled city hall.

Of the cities under study here Chicago was the one where Germans came off worst relative to their numbers in competing for the mayor's office—one-term winner Fred Busse stands alone. Even Irish successes in the Windy City remained unspectacular until well into the twentieth century when Ed Kelly and Richard Daley came along.[32] Instead, the scene was dominated by three representatives of the Anglo-Protestant elite: Carter Harrison I and II and "Big Bill" Thompson. Harrison father and son each won five mayoral elections, while Thompson won three four-year terms. Although on opposite sides of the party spectrum, a common characteristic of the Harrisons and Thompson is that all were decidedly "wet." There were other aspects to their appeals to Chicago's largest ethnic group. The elder Harrison had lent his support to German instruction in Chicago's public schools early in the 1880s. His son had studied three years at a German Gymnasium. "Kaiser Bill" Thompson showed outspoken sympathy for neutrality during World War I. It appears that Democrats tried to undermine his ethnic appeal by running a Catholic named Robert Sweitzer as his opponent in two elections. But most Chicago German voters (or Irish in the nineteenth century) were less concerned about ethnic presence at the head of the ticket than with seeing their ethnic values upheld at city hall.[33] One might argue, of course, that the German position on alcohol

---

30. As cited by Wolfgang Helbich, *"Alle Menschen sind dort gleich . . . ": Die deutsche Amerika-Auswanderung im 19. und 20. Jahrhundert* (Düsseldorf: Schwann, 1988), 133.

31. See for example the Louisville *Katholischer Glaubensbote*, 28 April 1866, 3; 5 May 1866, 4; 16 June 1866, 4; 19 January 1867; 4 and 28 December 1870, 4. A similar example in the freethinking Forty-eighter press can be seen in the St. Louis *Anzeiger des Westens*, 27 June 1858.

32. Michael F. Funchion, "The Political and Nationalist Dimensions," in *The Irish in Chicago*, edited by Lawrence J. McCaffrey et al. (Urbana: University of Illinois Press, 1987), 63–67.

33. *Biographical Dictionary*, 151–152, 362; Teaford, *Unheralded Triumph*, 52–53. Harrison came out for the first time in favor of German instruction in 1880 and in 1883 gave a speech to that effect before the German-American Teachers Day. *Chicagoer Arbeiter Zeitung*, 14 August

gained widespread de facto if not always legal recognition in Chicago and other cities because it also received strong support from the Irish. It should be noted, however, that German stakes in the industry were higher, and German beer generally came off better than Irish whiskey as far as alcohol regulation was concerned.

On the issue of German language in the public schools there is no such ambiguity—the Irish were often its most bitter opponents. Of the fourteen cities under consideration here, the only ones that did not offer German instruction in public elementary schools for at least part of the era between the Civil War and World War I were Boston, New Orleans, Philadelphia, and Pittsburgh, all cities in which the Irish outnumbered Germans by a greater or lesser degree.[34] In cities with larger German populations, even the Irish could not always afford to turn a deaf ear: It was under Irish-born mayor James Barry that St. Louis in 1849 arranged to have all city ordinances translated into German. One might have expected German Catholics to oppose German instruction in public schools, which increased both their tax burden and the competition with parochial schools, but this was not always the case. German Catholics were not always Catholic first and German second.[35] The timing of the introduction of German instruction into public school systems such as St. Louis (1864), Chicago (1865), Buffalo (1866), Milwaukee (1867), and Cleveland (1869), often after years of agitation, was hardly coincidental. This was precisely the time when the Republican party was trying to convince German Unionists to "vote as they had shot," and even Catholic veterans were often tempted. Despite the reputation of nativism among Republicans, it was their party which instituted or maintained German instruction in a number of city systems, St. Louis, Cincinnati, and Indianapolis, for example.[36] In Buffalo,

---

1880, 1 August 1883, as translated in the WPA "Chicago Foreign Language Press Survey," microfilm, Roll 12.

34. Selwyn Troen, *The Public and the Schools* (Columbia: University of Missouri Press, 1975), 68–70, 73, 76; Hildegard Binder Johnson, "Adjustment to the United States," in *The Forty-Eighters*, edited by Adolf Zucker (New York: Columbia University Press, 1950), 70; Richard Jensen, *The Winning of the Midwest: Social and Political Conflict, 1888–1896* (Chicago: University of Chicago Press, 1971), 92–122; Bergquist, "German Communities," 15; Heinz Kloss, *The American Bilingual Tradition* (Rowley, MA: Newbury House, 1977), 90–93. See also the Fessler chapter in this anthology.

35. The Louisville *Katholischer Glaubensbote* over two decades consistently supported German instruction in public schools. See 27 July 1870, 4; 18 January 1871, 4; and 9 May 1886, 5. *Biographical Dictionary*, 18.

36. An example of how the school-language issue played into mayoral races is provided in Miller, *Boss*, 235.

however, Republican resistance to German in the schools was apparently a factor in the switch of German allegiance to the Democrats.[37] This shows the advantages of not putting one's eggs all in one partisan basket.

In conclusion, then, so far as the office of mayor in American big cities is concerned, German immigrants and ethnics came off better then Irish Catholics in the first generation, and only slightly worse thereafter. Their electoral chances were greatly improved in cities where Germans made up a large share of the population—an indication that ethnic politics and identity did come into play, just as with the Irish. Moreover, comparative profiles of the Irish and Germans who were elected big city mayors show more similarities than differences. The Irish clearly came off better in terms of low-level patronage jobs. But if one looks at policy outputs, particularly in the realm of cultural issues such as education, language, and alcohol, German Americans were able to wield a considerable amount of influence in urban politics, particularly during the era up to World War I. In short, German-ethnic candidacies for the office of mayor, like much of American-ethnic politics past and present, represented a combination of symbolism and substance.

---

37. Gerber, "Language Maintenance," esp. 47–49.

9

Ethnic Politicians in Congress: German-American Congressmen between Ethnic Group and National Government circa 1880[1]

Willi Paul Adams†

American Civic Culture and German-born Congressmen

Of the members of the United States House of Representatives serving before 1945, forty-three had been born in Germany.[2] For some, the German part of their background still meant something: It was a vital force in their daily existence. Others were "ethnic" politicians in the post-1960 sense of the word: They spoke for and appealed to voters with whom they shared certain elements of their German past and German-American present. Their political behavior allows us to examine the role the American political system played in the integration of German-speaking immigrants. In Lawrence Fuchs's sweeping survey of *Race, Ethnicity, and the Civic Culture*, Germans occupy a prominent position: Many of them took advantage of the opportunities offered by American electoral politics without giving up cultural preferences and the pursuit of various ethnic group interests. Fuchs observed how the inclusive character of American electoral politics made possible at the very least the peaceful coexistence and at most the constructive cooperation of a good number of ethno-culturally diverse groups within one polity.[3]

1.　Note of thanks: Research for this paper was supported by the Woodrow Wilson International Center for Scholars in Washington, DC; the Newberry Library in Chicago; and the Institute for Research in the Humanities at the University of Wisconsin–Madison. Research assistants in Berlin were Kathy S. Alberts and Michael Steinmetz.

2.　Willi Paul Adams, *Ethnic Leadership and the German-born Members of the U.S. House of Representatives, 1862–1945: A Report on Research in Progress* (Berlin: John F. Kennedy-Institut für Nordamerikastudien, Working Paper 88/1996).

3.　See Lawrence H. Fuchs, *The American Kaleidoscope: Race, Ethnicity, and the Civic Culture* (Middletown, CT: Wesleyan University Press, 1990) for information on the Germans, especially 27–30. For a comparative examination of the complex process of "acculturation" focusing on the German and Irish experiences, see the section "Partizipation und politische Akkulturation" in Reinhard R. Doerries, *Iren und Deutsche in der Neuen Welt: Akkulturationsprozesse in der amerikanischen Gesellschaft im späten 19. Jahrhundert* (Stuttgart: Steiner, 1986), 51–65. Doerries stresses the diversity of political opinion and party preferences among German

There is, of course, no denying the obvious differences in quality and degree between the coercion and displacement of the indigenous population, the subjugation of Africans into forced labor, the repression and exploitation of various other racially distinct non-European migrants, and the comparatively smooth absorption of many of the European migrants into an ever-changing European-American mainstream. On the whole, however, after two centuries of massive immigration and after thirteen decades of gradual emancipation of African Americans, we find in the United States—compared to other regions of the world with ethno-culturally diverse populations—more cooperation, peaceful competition, "affirmative action," and convergence than open conflict and territorial separation between ethnically, culturally, and economically defined minority groups and mainstream middle-class society. Compared to the fantasies of racial purity that were acted out with unprecedented cruelty in Central Europe from 1933 to 1945, and compared to the childish invention of national pasts with tight communities of descent neatly located in space and time, we find in the American record, despite an influx of fifty million Europeans, an astonishing degree of national cohesion and a relatively tolerant cultural pluralism. Since 1865, no separatist threat of the kind Québec poses to the Canadian nation today has developed anywhere in the United States. The occasional outbursts of black "nationalism" only demonstrate their function as gestures of radical protest, not as a realistic goal. The divisive multiculturalist politics of group identity during the 1980s seems to have spent its momentum in favor of a more tolerant agenda directed at a *Post-Ethnic America* in which the transethnic common good of the whole nation is kept in full view.[4] The jostling for power and influence continues, as it should, as an integral part of American politics. The Supreme Court's close reading of the Constitution has recently curbed experiments giving preferential treatment to racial minority groups, including those creating congressional districts with a safe majority for one minority group. As a result, left-wing Democrats as well as right-wing Republicans have fewer ethnic minority constituents they have to worry about antagonizing.

---

immigrants. Kathleen Neils Conzen, *Immigrant Milwaukee, 1836–1860: Accommodation and Community in a Frontier City* (Cambridge, MA: Harvard University Press, 1976), 192, finds for pre-1860 Milwaukee: "It was in their political accommodation to urban American life that Milwaukee's Germans developed and maintained a public image of common action."

4.   David Hollinger, *Postethnic America: Beyond Multiculturalism* (New York: Basic Books, 1995); John Higham, *Multiculturalism in Disarray* (Berlin: John F. Kennedy-Institut ür Nordamerikastudien, Working Paper 55/1992).

The civic culture credited by Fuchs with the "ethnic Americanization" (not "Anglo-Americanization") of most European immigrants, was defined in 1963 by political scientists Gabriel Almond and Sidney Verba as the "substantial consensus on the legitimacy of political institutions and the direction and content of public policy" that makes possible democratic government. In the post-1865 American case, this consensus includes "a widespread tolerance of a plurality of interests and belief in their reconcilability, and a widely distributed sense of political competence and mutual trust in the citizenry."[5]

Few citizens could have been more active participants in maintaining and adapting this civic culture than immigrants who became congressmen. In their hometowns, their state capitals, and in Washington, their role, ideally, would have been to mediate between the special interests of their constituencies—ethnic or otherwise—and legislation on the national level that had to reconcile a wide variety of regional, economic, cultural, and other interests. The key question pursued here is to what extent real life approximated the ideal. The political scene on the national level was favorable: The secession of the South had been overcome at great cost, and Congress was the great forum of national reconciliation. Immigrant politicians and journalists sensed that the victorious white Anglo-Saxon majority in the Northern states on the whole was now also ready to welcome representatives of immigrant groups, who since the 1820s had contributed to the growth especially of the Northern and Midwestern states and Missouri.

Two cases have been selected for closer examination: Lorenz Brentano, a Republican from Chicago, who served in Washington from 1877 to 1879 and Peter Victor Deuster, a Democrat from Milwaukee, elected for three terms from 1879 to 1885.[6] Both men were well-known editors of German-language newspapers when they were elected; both were publicly perceived, in Chicago, Milwaukee, and Washington, as ethnically defined politicians with a special

---

5. Quoted in Fuchs, *Kaleidoscope*, 5. Fuchs stated:
    The civic culture was based essentially . . . on three ideas widely held by the founders of the republic, the ideas that constituted the basis of what they called republicanism: first, that ordinary men and women can be trusted to govern themselves through their elected representatives, who are accountable to the people; second, that all who live in the political community (essentially, adult white males at the time) are eligible to participate in public life as equals; and third, that individuals who comport themselves as good citizens of the civic culture are free to differ from each other in religion and in other aspects of their private lives.

6. Additional case studies can be found in Willi Paul Adams, "Ethnic Politicians and American Nationalism during the First World War: Four German-born Members of the U.S. House of Representatives, " *American Studies International* 29 (April 1991): 20–34.

relationship to Germany and German immigrants in the United States. But, as we will see, they differed in terms of other characteristics such as partisan affiliation. The best known German-American politician of this period, Carl Schurz, who represented Missouri in the Senate from 1869 to 1875, makes only a brief appearance here for the sake of contrast. He took part in an acrimonious exchange on the Senate floor in 1874 because he felt insulted by an alleged reference to his being a "foreigner." The fact that this kind of public encounter in Congress was rare, perhaps even unique, is an essential part of the findings of this paper. Since each word is important in this exceptional exchange, it is documented almost verbatim.

Lorenz Brentano, Republican of Chicago, 1877–1879

Lorenz(o) Brentano would have been the first republican prime minister of Baden, had the Prussian army not put down the popular uprising in 1848–1849.[7] Instead, sentenced to imprisonment for life and loss of his property, he fled to Switzerland. From then on, writing and publishing replaced organizing and governing, until Brentano became an ethnic politician, American citizen, and legislator.

In 1850, at age thirty-seven, he crossed the Atlantic together with his wife Caroline Leutz. After failed experiments as a journalist in Pottsville, Pennsylvania, and as a farmer in Kalamazoo, Michigan, the Brentanos moved to Chicago in 1859. He retrained in the law and was admitted to the Illinois bar. Before long, Brentano was editing the Midwest's most influential German-language newspaper, the pro-Republican daily *Illinois Staats-Zeitung*. Later he became its principal proprietor, then sold his share in the newspaper in 1867 for close to $100,000 and invested in real estate. As an independently wealthy

---

7. "Lorenzo" is accepted as his first name in the *Biographical Directory of the American Congress, 1774–1949* (Washington, DC: Government Printing Office), 886. Brentano's radical republican politics during the revolution in Baden in 1848–1849 is mentioned repeatedly in Paul Nolte, *Gemeindebürgertum und Liberalismus in Baden, 1800–1850* (Göttingen: Vandenhoeck & Ruprecht, 1994). His election as mayor of Karlsruhe in January 1849 and again in April 1849 was simply disallowed by the reigning Grand Duke of Baden and his *Staatsministerium*. The lawyer Brentano was no pitchfork-waving rioter. After the Grand Duke's surprising (temporary) flight, Brentano headed an opposition government in May 1849 and set up office in the Karlsruhe city hall as *Präsident* of the provisory government. But Prussia's troops were stronger. By July 1, 1849, Brentano was in exile in Switzerland, justifying his failed brief government in an appeal "An das badische Volk." The *Basler Zeitung* published the essay on July 5 (408).

man, he could afford to spend over three years (1868–1872) as a gentleman scholar and commentator on political affairs in Zurich.[8]

Brentano's active role in the Republican party began in 1854, shortly after the call for the first Republican convention in Jackson, Michigan. An article he wrote explaining the new party's agenda and calling for German-American support received nationwide attention and was later said to have been a significant factor in winning over a substantial segment of the German-American electorate.[9]

When the Southern states began leaving the Union, Brentano immediately took a public stand. Together with ten other German Americans and others, he signed the bipartisan manifesto of January 5, 1861.[10] In 1862, after spending hardly three years in Chicago, Brentano was elected as one of the seven Chicago representatives in the Illinois House of Representatives. From 1863 to 1868 he was elected to Chicago's Board of Education, and during the last year he served as its president. He succeeded in getting the board to include voluntary teaching of lessons in German and German literature; by 1872, thirteen of Chicago's public schools were teaching German.[11] Brentano was an Illinois delegate to the Republican national convention in Baltimore in 1864, and up to the end of his life he boasted of the fact that he had served as secretary of the convention that nominated Lincoln in 1864 to run for his second term. In 1868, Brentano was one of the electors for the Grant ticket.

During his stay in Zurich from 1869 to 1872, Brentano earned the gratitude of the Grant administration when he followed the suggestion of the American ministers in Paris and Switzerland and wrote several widely regarded legal articles in the *Wiener Freie Presse*, *Frankfurter Journal*, and *Augsburger Allgemeine Zeitung*. These supported American claims before an international arbitration commission in Geneva to collect damages from Britain for allowing

---

8.   Heinrici, Max, ed. *Das Buch der Deutschen in Amerika* (Philadelphia: Walther's Buchdruckerei, 1909), 498; obituary in *Der Deutsche Correspondent* [Baltimore], 19 September 1891; obituary in *Illinois Staatszeitung* [hereafter *ISZ*], 18 September 1891. See also Albert Faust, "Brentano, Lorenz," in *Dictionary of American Biography*, vol. 2 (New York: Charles Scribner's Sons, 1958 [1929]), 19.

9.   The article supposedly appeared in the Kalamazoo *Telegraph* in April or May 1854; *The Western Rural*, 20 May 1876, clipping, Brentano Papers, CHS.

10.   Alfred Theodore Andreas, *History of Chicago, from the Earliest Period to the Present Time*, vol. 2 (Chicago: A.T. Andreas Company, 1885), 159.

11.   Hermann Felsenthal, letter to the editor, *ISZ*, 23 October 1876, and article in *ISZ*, 23 September 1891, clippings, Brentano Papers, CHS.

the *Alabama* and other English-built Confederate vessels to raid Northern merchant vessels on the open Atlantic.[12]

Less well known to the American public was Brentano's emotional reaction to the Franco-Prussian War of 1870. In a letter to an old friend in Karlsruhe shortly after the beginning of the war, Brentano gave a classic description of the remnants of loyalty a number of emigrants feel for their home country's victories and defeats in conflicts with other nations. This was all the more surprising for a Forty-eighter who had been driven out of his country by the same hereditary, unaccountable rulers who governed the German states in 1870.

> Although I was deprived of my rights as a German citizen, the inborn love of one's homeland lives on as strongly as ever. I share all your suffering and sorrows in this great and holy struggle, and I equally share your rejoicing over the splendid welfare and victories of the German armies, just as if I still were one of you.

He enclosed five hundred Swiss francs "for the wounded and the sick of your brave army."[13]

The dream of many an emigrant came true in Brentano's case when in 1872 President Grant sent him as the American consul to Dresden, the capital of the kingdom of Saxony. He owed the lucrative appointment, according to the sympathetic *Baltimore Correspondent*, not to frantic office-seeking on his part but to the services which the *Illinois Staats-Zeitung* had rendered to Grant's election campaign.[14]

After three successful years as the official representative of American political and commercial interests in Dresden, Brentano decided to return to Chicago in time to take an active part in the 1876 election campaign. When it became known that Secretary of State Hamilton Fish, who had opposed Brentano's appointment from the beginning, had forced him to resign several months earlier than he had intended to, German-American newspapers

---

12. Obituary in *National-Zeitung*, 18 September 1891, clipping, Brentano Papers, CHS.

13. Lorenz Brentano to Malsch, Zurich, 22 August 1870, Brentano Papers, CHS; my translation. Edelmann, "Verhältnis der Deutschamerikaner."

14. *Tägliche Chicagoer Union*, 19 September 1872, article taken from *Baltimore Correspondent*, clipping, Brentano Papers, CHS. The Brentano file in the Letters of Application and Recommendation collection of the NA, Diplomatic Branch, contains no information on the appointment.

attacked Fish's principle of not sending naturalized citizens as officials back to their country of origin. It was detrimental to American interests, they argued, and they made fun of Brentano's successor for not being able to communicate with the Saxons in their own language.[15]

The ethnic dimension of Brentano's 1876 election campaign was openly discussed, locally as well as nationally. After praising Brentano's qualifications, the *Illinois Staats-Zeitung* referred to the fact that "besides Schleicher, a Democrat from Texas, no German-born citizen has yet been named for the next Congress. Brentano would certainly be a very strong candidate in his district, which is so largely populated by German Americans."[16] The population of the Third District—the city's North side and parts of suburban Cook and Lake counties—was almost half German American. An English-language newspaper claimed that "certainly one half of the Republican voters there are of German parentage."[17] But Brentano encountered strong Irish competition and only secured the nomination on the sixth ballot of the district convention.[18] When all nominations for the November election became known, the *Illinois Staats-Zeitung* reported that in addition to Brentano five German-born candidates were running for the House of Representatives: Salomon Spitzer, Nikolaus Müller and Anton Eickhoff in New York City; Stiastny in New Jersey; and Gustav Schleicher in Texas.[19] The campaign was an unusually bitter one, and ethnic antagonism was exploited to the fullest, especially by the Democratic *Chicago Times*. In its columns the Republican candidate's name was "Herr Brentano," and his understanding of American affairs and especially of Chicago's interests was doubted, as was his very loyalty and ability to speak "the language of the Congress." Substantive issues, such as Brentano's call for civil service reform, were ignored.[20] Brentano received 11,843 votes while his Democratic opponent, Pennsylvania-born John LeMoyne, received 11,435, a result that was considered a "substantial majority" by Chicago standards.[21]

---

15. Lorenz Brentano, letter to the editor of *ISZ*, 22 April 1876, and adjoining clippings, Brentano Papers, CHS.

16. Translation in an unidentified English-language newspaper, possibly the *Chicago Courier*, of 15 September 1876, clipping, Brentano Papers, CHS.

17. Newspaper not identified, 29 September 1876, clipping, Brentano Papers, CHS.

18. Letter to the editor by "German-American," Chicago *Tribune*, 19 September 1876; report on convention in Chicago *Tribune*, 29 September 1876.

19. *ISZ*, 30 October 1876.

20. *Chicago Times*, undated clipping, Brentano Papers, CHS.

21. Unidentified and undated English-language newspaper, clipping, Brentano Papers, CHS.

In his one term in the House of Representatives, Brentano, in addition to pushing local issues, spoke up when German-American relations were dealt with, especially problems faced by naturalized American citizens during visits to Germany.[22] When calls were made to repeal the Bancroft Treaty, a naturalization agreement between the United States and the North German Confederation signed in 1868 but often ignored by German authorities, Brentano warned against its repeal without a better substitute in sight. He was quite capable of patriotic American rhetoric:

> The naturalization treaty concluded on the birthday of George Washington, 22 Febuary 1868, with the North German Confederation, and afterward followed by similar treaties with Bavaria, Württemberg, Hesse Darmstadt, and Baden, was a great triumph of American diplomacy, and will for all time to come shed luster on the name of the great and celebrated statesman and scholar, George Bancroft, who induced the German governments to renounce the principle of indissoluble allegiance and to recognize the principle of the right of voluntary expatriation so repugnant to despotic governments, whose very foundation is their military power.

Brentano explicitly assumed the role of spokesman for German Americans when he added: "I may be permitted to state here from the feeling which I know exists among the German-American portion of the people of the United States, that they would be the last to claim protection for such persons whom they consider citizens of two worlds but true to none."[23]

Bretano's German background was acknowledged in a special way when the House sent him as one of their representatives to Gustav Schleicher's funeral in San Antonio.[24]

At least parts of Chicago's English-language press considered Brentano to be "an accurate exponent of the true sentiments upon political issues of the German-Americans in his district" and presented speeches of his as "an index

---

22. Brentano's resolution concerning the Julius Bäumer case received unanimous approval in the House of Representatives, *Congressional Record*, 45th Congress, 3rd Session, 22.

23. Speech on 24 February 1879, *Congressional Record*, 45th Congress, 3rd Session, Appendix, 161–162.

24. In his memorial address before a special session of the House of Representatives on 17 February 1879, Brentano claimed that Schleicher, because of his love of liberty, would have become a revolutionary Forty-eighter like himself, had he not emigrated shortly before the outbreak of the revolution. *Congressional Record*, 45th Congress, 3rd Session, 1501.

of the sentiments of our German fellow citizens."[25] The role of congressman clearly enhanced and reinforced his role as spokesman of his ethnic group. As an elected representative he had to heed constituent opinion, but as a member of Congress he was also in a better position to shape constituent opinion and to influence public opinion far beyond his district.

Although Brentano was willing to run for re-election in 1878, his district nominated the New York-born and Wisconsin-raised lawyer Hiram Barber, who was elected. After Brentano broke with the *Illinois Staats-Zeitung* in 1879, his former friends reminded him of the power of the press: "You would never have been elected, if the *Illinois Staats-Zeitung* had opposed your candidacy."[26]

Brentano was sixty-five years old when he returned to Chicago in 1879. He wanted to return to Germany as American consul, but his attempts in 1879 and 1881 to be nominated by Presidents Hayes and Garfield failed.[27] Disappointment and anger probably contributed to his break with the Republican party in 1882.[28] Brentano then became an advisor and writer for the *Chicago Demokrat*, and as an independent Democrat he supported Grover Cleveland for the presidency in 1884.[29]

With his strong convictions and sharp pen, Brentano ended up with few friends among organized German Americans. The German Press Club and the Turnvereine refused to send delegations to his funeral in 1891.[30] As a Freethinker, he never enjoyed the political support of Christian churches.[31]

Lorenz Brentano obviously had leadership qualities that were recognized in both the German and American political settings. After his immigration, he went through a decade of adjustment, of learning by trial and error. His first

25. *Chicago Post*, 31 May 1877, clipping, Brentano Papers, CHS.

26. *ISZ*, 6 March 1879.

27. Congressman G. L. Fort to Secretary of State William Evarts, 17 March 1879, Letters of Application and Recommendation, NA, Diplomatic Branch. Louis Schade, the editor of the *Washington Sentinel*, recommended Brentano to Secretary of State James G. Blaine on May 26, 1881, with the argument, among others, that "no German-American has thus far been appointed." Ibid.

28. *Chicago Times*, 2 August 1884, clipping, Brentano Papers, CHS. Schurz and other German Americans also broke with the Republican party in the 1880s in protest against its increasing conservatism.

29. *Chicago Demokrat*, 2 August 1884, clipping, Brentano Papers, CHS; Obituary, *ISZ*, 18 September 1891.

30. Notice in unidentified German-language newspaper, 21 September 1891, clipping, Brentano Papers, CHS.

31. Obituary, *Chicago Times*, 19 September 1891.

attempts as a journalist and as a lawyer in Pennsylvania were failures. The years as a farmer in Michigan may have been intellectually and economically unsatisfactory, but they gave him the time needed to become familiar with the American political scene and to establish contacts with other liberal, reform-minded German immigrants and with the American founders of the Republican Party. This reorientation became the foundation for his second and probably decisive step: to move to one of the urban centers of German immigration and work for one of its flourishing newspapers. When he arrived in Chicago, he was already a leader in search of followers. The newspaper was the only means of communication available to him for reaching potential followers. He did not rise out of ward politics, but his political power from 1861 on derived from his ability to influence German-American voters in and far beyond Chicago. In the words of one of his most persistent critics, the *Chicago Times*: "As a publicist, working almost wholly among American citizens of his own nationality, he acquired notable influence, which was rewarded with honorable public offices."[32] Once he had established himself in American political journalism, his German past enhanced his reputation, at least with the more liberal-minded German Americans. But it also haunted him; the ultra-radicals still blamed him for losing the revolution in Baden. The second institutional pillar of Brentano's leadership was the Republican Party. Spreading and organizing the new political movement among his own ethnic group provided Brentano with a special opportunity for political leadership. The crisis situation of the Civil War, with its intense partisanship and ultimate test of political loyalty, clearly accelerated Brentano's integration into the American political process.

Peter Victor Deuster, Democrat of Milwaukee, 1879–1885

Peter Deuster was sixteen years old in 1847 when he and his Catholic parents moved from a village near Aachen to a farm near Milwaukee. He learned the printing trade, and in 1854 he began editing a newspaper in Port Washington, Wisconsin. He also served as clerk for the circuit court and the land office at this time. In 1856 he moved to the booming city of Milwaukee and coedited the German-language daily *See-Bote*, which, under his proprietorship after 1860, became a strong voice for Catholic opinions and Democratic policies.[33] By 1863 Deuster had made his name, and he was

---

32. Ibid.

33. Conzen, *Immigrant Milwaukee*, 187.

elected to the Wisconsin House of Representatives as a Democrat; in 1870, he successfully ran for the state senate.[34]

In 1878, at the age of forty-seven, Deuster won election to Congress in Wisconsin's Fourth District—comprising Milwaukee, Ozaukee, and Washington counties—with a plurality of only 135 out of 23,530 votes cast.[35] The fact that this made him Wisconsin's first German-born congressman did not go unnoticed in Wisconsin's press, to which, as editor of the Milwaukee *See-Bote*, he was a familiar figure.

In his first term, Deuster served on the standing committees for Commerce and for Expenditures on Public Buildings. In his second term (1881–1883) he moved up to the Foreign Affairs Committee and proudly and actively continued this work through his third term (1883–1885); in addition he joined the select committee on American Shipbuilding.

In debates on the House floor the fact that he represented the heavily German Fourth District was no topic for commentary. The circumstances of the election were only brought up by another Wisconsin representative, Republican George Hazelton of Boscobel, in connection with the all-American issue of an "electioneering fund." Hazelton told Deuster to his face: "The rich men like Mr. Mitchell who own the banks and the railroads, the men who constitute the money power there, are the men who sent you here."[36] Without further clarification, the debate moved on to other points.

In his first full speech before the House, Deuster rejected the coining of a cheaper "light-weight" silver dollar with the familiar set of sound-money arguments. Not a trace of "ethnic" elements in substance or rhetoric is to be found in this professional performance.[37]

A Republican initiative in 1879 to extend the law designed to prevent election fraud in immigrant cities like New York was rejected by Deuster

---

34. On the Germans and other immigrants in Milwaukee politics up to 1860, see Conzen, *Immigrant Milwaukee*, chap. 7. On Deuster's early politics see Frank L. Klement, "Deuster as a Democratic Dissenter During the Civil War: A Case Study of a Copperhead," *Wisconsin Academy of Sciences, Arts and Letters* 55 (1966): 21–38.

35. Deuster was reelected in 1880 with the safe margin of 2,411 because there was no third-party candidate. In 1882 the Fourth District was redrawn to include only the city and county of Milwaukee; Deuster won 9,688 to 8,320. *Wisconsin Blue Book*. The 1880 census for the city and county of Milwaukee reports that thirty-eight thousand of its eighty-three thousand inhabitants had been born in Germany, four thousand in Ireland, two thousand in England and Wales, and over one thousand each in Sweden/Norway and in Canada.

36. *Congressional Record*, 46th Congress, 1st Session, 24 April 1879, 850.

37. *Congressional Record*, 46th Congress, 1st Session, 15 May 1879, 1368–1369.

because its practical consequences would hurt naturalized citizens more than others. Relishing his expertise, Deuster recounted the 1875 case of two naturalized Americans from Prussia who were detained during a visit home. The Prussian police considered their naturalization certificates a forgery, since they knew that the five years residence requirement in the United States could not possibly have been fulfilled by the two emigrants. The American secretary of state, Deuster triumphantly documented, insisted on the certificates' validity and denied the Prussian authorities' competence to second-guess an American naturalization judge. Similarly, he claimed, American election officers were not to second-guess the findings of the immigration court in the same city.[38] Deuster clearly spoke on this topic not to gain an advantage for his particular ethnic group but more generally to forestall a measure that would have expressed distrust in the integrity of immigrants.

A small step in international affairs related to Germany was taken in January 1880 when Deuster introduced a joint resolution to appropriate $20,000 for the American participation in the international fishery exhibition to be held in Berlin in April of that year. Deuster deplored that no preparations had yet been made by the commissioner for Fish and Fisheries to go to Berlin, where "every civilized country will be represented" and where American progress with fish hatching should be displayed to the world. With slight changes, Deuster's proposal passed.[39] Two years later, when he repeated his request, this time for $50,000 for American participation in the fishery exhibition in London in 1883, he was enthusiastic about the success in Berlin. Seven regiments of the German army were now being fed American cod. But even more important, Deuster claimed, was an unforeseen consequence: Hundreds of thousands of visitors from all over Germany and beyond were impressed by what they saw of "the general wealth and abundant resources of the country." Indeed, he reasoned, "examination of the statistics of the emigration from Germany for 1880 indicates a remarkable increase in the number of emigrants during the months following the date of the opening of the Berlin exhibition."[40]

Another obviously "homeland issue" Deuster did not hesitate to address on the floor of the House was humanitarian aid for the victims of a recent

---

38. *Congressional Record*, 46th Congress, 1st Session, 21 April 1879, 652–653.

39. *Congressional Record*, 46th Congress, 2nd Session, 15 January 1880, 345; 4 February, 704–707.

40. *Congressional Record*, 47th Congress, 1st Session, 19 June 1882, Appendix, 401.

flood in the Rhine valley. In January 1883 he had a bill to this effect read and referred to the Committee on Agriculture.[41]

Deuster also became involved in a classic instance of ethnic foreign policy, of immigrants trying to influence American relations with the country they came from. It so happened that the German-Jewish liberal politician Eduard Lasker, on a tour through the United States, died in New York on January 5, 1884. He had been a leader of the National Liberal Party (Nationalliberale Partei) and a member of the Prussian Diet and the Reichstag. As a lawyer defending constitutional civil rights (including those of socialists), he had been a well-known critic of Bismarck. The House of Representatives unanimously resolved on January 9

> that this House has heard with deep regret of the death of the eminent German statesman Edward Lasker. That his loss is not alone to be mourned by the people of his native land, where his firm and constant exposition of and devotion to free and liberal ideas have materially advanced the social, political, and economic condition of those peoples, but by the lovers of liberty throughout the world.[42]

When the American minister in Berlin delivered the letter to Bismarck's office to be passed on to the Reichstag, Bismarck returned it via his ambassador in Washington. This infuriated, among others, Lasker's liberal friends in Germany, and on January 27, 1884, the executive committee of the Liberal Union sent a letter of thanks and wishes for the further development of the friendship between both nations to the House of Representatives. Deuster (and not the Speaker) placed this letter, together with a translation, before the House on February 28, 1884. He used the occasion to criticize the autocratic chancellor, the principle of monarchical government, and Germany's hierarchical society "in which social, and in a great measure, political position is a birthright more than an achievement or reward for merit." Deuster clearly relished the role of mediator on the national stage, not between the two governments, but between the two peoples (that is, the two halves of his own bicultural existence):

---

41. *Congressional Record*, 47th Congress, 2nd Session, 29 January 1883, 1734.

42. *Congressional Record*, 48th Congress, 1st Session, 9 January 1884, 329.

In presenting this communication, in my official place as a member of this body, as a native of Germany, and as an adopted citizen of the United States, I desire to express my earnest conviction that the action of the Liberal Union is a true index of the feelings of united Germany, and that the action of Prince Bismarck will not rise above the dignity of a matter of personal vexation and will in no way affect the kindly relations now existing between the two countries.[43]

Deuster's friend from Oshkosh, German-born Republican Richard Guenther, followed up by deploring that "there seems to exist an impression at present in this country at least among a portion of our citizens, that the people of Germany are hostile toward this country and its institutions." Guenther insisted that Bismarck's rude return of the letter with the Lasker resolution did not reflect the sentiments of the German people; nor did "his autocratic action regarding the prohibition of American products." The letter was referred to the House Foreign Affairs Committee, but not before another member, John Kasson of Des Moines, Iowa, impatient with Deuster's and Guenther's personal foreign relations initiative, had warned that "we have nothing whatever to do with the relations existing between the executive officer of a foreign government and the legislative branch of that government."[44] Only a few weeks later Deuster referred to the Foreign Affairs Committee a request for information from the Secretary of State about attacks in "semi-official newspapers at Berlin" on the American minister.[45]

Almost daily routine for all congressmen was the presentation of constituents' petitions on the clerk's desk (without any accompanying speeches for or against). Deuster received and deposited his share of them; only a few of which can be classified as relating specifically to German Americans as an ethnic group. Obviously close to the newspaper editor's heart were petitions from the Wisconsin Editors and Publishers Association to abolish the duty on type and on material used for making printing paper. He also presented petitions on the same subject from the publishers of *Erziehungsblätter* and the *Freidenker*.[46]

---

43. *Congressional Record*, 48th Congress, 1st Session, 28 February 1884, 1463–1464.

44. *Congressional Record*, 48th Congress, 1st Session, 1464. In July 1884 Kasson was to leave for Berlin as the United States minister to Germany.

45. *Congressional Record*, 48th Congress, 1st Session, 10 March 1884, 1758.

46. *Congressional Record*, 46th Congress, 2nd Session, 4 March 1880, 1332–1333; 8 March, 1395.

Deuster pursued a major lawmaking initiative in April 1880: He submitted a resolution to appoint a special committee to revise the naturalization laws, because "the laws governing the naturalization of persons of foreign birth are illiberal, defective, inadequate, and incomplete and their revision is therefore an urgent necessity."[47] The outspoken resolution was referred to the Committee on the Judiciary—and was never heard of again. Next, Deuster proposed terminating the treaty of naturalization between the United States and the North German Union and concluding a new one with the German Empire that he hoped would secure "more liberal and just provisions respecting the rights of [American] citizens, native born or naturalized," when they visited Germany.[48]

Deuster's next initiative actually led to the Passenger Act of 1882, which replaced the ineffective Passenger Act of 1855. In April 1880 he laid before the House extensive documentation collected by the Commerce Committee on the overcrowded and dangerously unsanitary conditions on many European immigrant ships. His draft law precisely regulated the size of berths, ventilation, and cubic feet per berth, and the number of water closets and cooking ranges; vessels carrying more than fifty passengers other than cabin passengers had to have a "medical practitioner" on board, and two compartments had to be equipped as hospital rooms; explosive compounds and acids were not to be transported on passenger vessels; the master of the vessel was to be held personally responsible and could be fined for violations. On April 18, 1882, the bill was explained to the House by Deuster's Republican colleague Guenther. Deuster himself underlined the urgency of the bill. The port of New York, he reported, had registered 1,561,126 immigrants in the decade 1870 to 1879, and 2,518 had died at sea.[49]

In the 1881 discussion on refunding the national debt by issuing three percent bonds, Deuster, as a member of the Commerce Committee, spoke up in favor of them, using sound economic arguments, without partisan, regional, or ethnic group rhetoric.[50] Similarly, Deuster advocated the establishment of a board of commissioners for interstate commerce to regulate railroad rates—an

---

47. *Congressional Record*, 46th Congress, 2nd Session, 26 April 1880, 2771.

48. *Congressional Record*, 47th Congress, 1st Session, 16 January 1882, 428. A year later, Deuster was still pursuing this objective as a member of the Foreign Affairs Committee, "Naturalization Treaty: Mr. Deuster's Bill," *New York Times*, 30 January 1883, 1.

49. *Congressional Record*, 47th Congress, 1st Session, 18 April 1882, 3012–3023.

50. *Congressional Record*, 46th Congress, 3rd Session, 18 January 1881, Appendix, 32.

idea that was to find majority support six years later with the Interstate Commerce Act of 1887. Deuster in February 1881 spoke knowledgeably of

> the interests of cities like Chicago, Saint Louis, Cincinnati, Milwaukee, Saint Paul, and many other places, where numerous railroad lines compete not only with each other, but with the cheaper water transportation; and where each road, in striving to build up and maintain its own commerce and its commercial supremacy, is often compelled to carry freight to the seaboard for less than a reasonable rate.

Regional economic needs and experience, not ethnic interests, informed Deuster's rhetoric, and he did not hesitate to speak of "my duty as one of the Representatives of the West."[51] He played the same role when he submitted to the House a petition by wholesale lumber dealers in Chicago to admit pine lumber from the Dominion of Canada free of duty. In his supporting speech, he deplored the rapid deforestation of Wisconsin and combined "the immediate interests of my own State" with "a question of great national importance . . . , the frequent warnings that have come of late from all sides against the rapid extinction of our forests." He then summarized the forestry statistics of the 1880 census and painted as alarming a picture of American forests from Maine to the Rocky Mountains as environmental historians looking at the same data a century later could ask for.[52] An issue of more local significance was Deuster's call for a thorough investigation of how the army was (mis-) managing the National Homes for Disabled Volunteer Soldiers, maintained by the federal government. One of these veterans' homes was located in Milwaukee. Since complaints about the inhumane treatment of old sick men by tyrannical officers all across the country had been published, Deuster was interested in distinguishing the good from the bad and clearing the name of "his" institution.[53]

Nationalism and patriotism were the guiding principles, not ethnicity, when Deuster eulogized Godlove Stein Orth, a Republican from Indiana of Pennsylvania German background, who only recently had served with him on the Foreign Affairs Committee. As a "diplomatist" and "statesman," Orth's

---

51. *Congressional Record*, 46th Congress, 22 February 1881, Appendix, 211–213.

52. *Congressional Record*, 47th Congress, 2nd Session, 14 February 1883, 2656–2658.

53. *Congressional Record*, 48th Congress, 1st Session, 26 May 1884, 4519.

ambition had been "to build the greatness of a nation," and he left behind "the traces of a strong mind imprinted upon important acts of legislation, upon national history itself."[54]

When the Chinese Exclusion Act was debated in 1882, Deuster spoke up in favor of excluding unskilled Chinese laborers from immigration. He reproduced the full nativist litany of real and imagined threats to the American economy and society from uncontrolled Chinese immigration. He emphasized at the outset that he considered the question "from the peculiar stand-point of one himself the son of an adopted citizen of this country" and then drew the line between good and bad immigrants:

> This Republic owes its marvelous growth, its wonderful development, its pre-eminence among the nations of our modern times largely to the influx of immigration from the Old World, an immigration totally different from that which found its way to the Pacific coast from Asia. The European immigrant, akin in race to the population of the American colonies which were originally settled by Europeans, became then, and still becomes, an indistinguishable part of our population. He adopts American customs, and, what is more, American ideas and love of personal liberty; he assimilates with and disappears entirely among the native-born, making all that is worth preserving of American life and thought the sacred heritage of his own children. The school-house, the workshop, the avenues of commerce become the scene of this peaceful transformation of kindred elements into a harmonious body that bids fair to establish in due time the most powerful, the most enlightened, the most progressive nation upon the face of the earth. But not so with the Chinese immigration, past, present or future. The Chinaman does not inquire into our liberal ideas as underlying the American system of government; he does not mean to become a willing contributor to the support of our public schools; he has no desire to build a home and raise a family among us, nor would it be desirable, politically, socially, or morally, that he should do so, because he does not change his social and political views so as to conform to the enlarged sphere of thinking afforded him by our system of popular government and social life; even his bones go back to his native country.

---

54. *Congressional Record*, 47th Congress, 2nd Session, 31 January 1883, 1868–1869.

In addition, Deuster repeated the labor unions' argument that cheap Chinese labor will undermine the wages for all labor and "cause starvation among our own laborers." Proponents of the bill liked Deuster's speech so much they yielded him additional time on the floor, since he was "the only adopted citizen who has yet addressed the house on this subject."[55] But there was also opposition to the bill. Charles G. Williams, a Republican lawyer from Janesville, Wisconsin, wanted to keep the gates open for Chinese immigrants and rejected the romanticized view of European immigrants. As a boy, living near the Erie Canal, Williams had seen poor, dirty, and ignorant immigrants from Europe and remembered the names they were given: "Irish and Dutch cattle," "Swede and Swiss and Norwegian hogs." Williams explicitly rejected Deuster's racist pride in European superiority and reminded the House of the ongoing "persecutions [of Jews] in Russia, the conscriptions in Germany, the oppression and tyranny in Ireland."[56]

Deuster also supported the ending of contract labor immigration that immigration legislation had encouraged since 1864. In the discussion leading up to the 1885 (anti-)contract labor law, he clearly took the side of the protectionists to prevent the pauperization of American labor. But he moved to strike from the bill the severe punishments of the master of a vessel for having contract laborers on board. Deuster's Republican colleague Richard Guenther, speaking after him, reminded the House of his earlier vote for the exclusion of Chinese contract laborers and prided himself on his consistency and objectivity: "I am a protectionist, I want to protect American labor against degrading competition. . . . I would vote to exclude my own German countrymen from this country provided they came here with such intentions and under such circumstances as these Chinese did."[57]

Deuster gave his most forceful prolabor speech in April 1884, possibly as part of his last and unsuccessful reelection campaign. Speaking in support of the bill to establish a bureau of labor statistics, he described the relationship between workers, financiers, and congressmen in stark terms: "There is a war between capital and labor, and the legislative power of the Government has been called in as arbiter and peacemaker. . . . The controversy between capital and labor is a momentous one, and its end can not be predicted." He referred to "a recent and gigantic strike" (against the Western Union Telegraph Company) and characterized "the money power" as "the golden aristocracy." He praised

---

55. *Congressional Record*, 47th Congress, 1st Session, 18 March 1882, 2030–2032.

56. *Congressional Record*, 47th Congress, 1st Session, 18 March 1882, 2039.

57. *Congressional Record*, 48th Congress, 1st Session, 19 June 1884, 5364.

as the truly productive forces "the laboring classes, the skilled artisans of the land." To be able to mediate conflicting claims in the future, the government needed to collect data on wages paid in various industries and regions, and on investments made and the emission of "watered" stock by fraudulent boards of directors. Deuster was no socialist. He only rejected schemes like the watering of stock whose effect was "to keep down the laborer and to increase the wealth of the capitalist." He found it unfair that entrepreneurs were protected from competition from European imports, while their workers had to endure "the competition incident to foreign immigration." In the past, the government had helped capital, now it was time for the government to redress the balance by mediating in the interest of labor.[58] There are no ethnic overtones in the whole speech, no mention of labor unions being weakened by ethnic diversity or rivalry, no reference to German precedents or the German-American experience in Wisconsin, or the like.

In December 1882 a bill to erect a new building for the Library of Congress was discussed with some nationalist rhetoric. It was Deuster in the role of the responsible bookkeeper and member of the Committee on Expenditures on Public Buildings who provided the matter-of-fact amendment that a board of experts—including librarians, architects and engineers—be asked to write an exhaustive report taking into account the experience of all major libraries in the country. Other speakers in this debate referred to the National Library in Paris and to the British Museum. Deuster refrained from any reference to German "Kultur."[59]

Creating federal institutions was a natural way to express national pride. Deuster made his contribution in 1884, when he supported a bill to provide $4,000 per year for a new bureau of navigation in the Treasury Department to coordinate "the building up of our merchant marine." He deplored the fact that the American merchant marine was "a midget upon the high seas," although the country had the longest line of seacoast of any nation, and "our mountains, our fields, and our forests contain all the materials necessary to build and equip vessels of all kinds and descriptions." Aware of the fact that "the nations of the earth compete for the world's carrying trade," Deuster advocated strengthening American commercial seapower.[60] This theme was so close to his heart that a few days later he devoted probably his longest speech on the

---

58. *Congressional Record*, 48th Congress, 1st Session, 19 April 1884, Appendix, 489–490.

59. *Congressional Record*, 47th Congress, 2nd Session, 12 December 1882, 224–225.

60. *Congressional Record*, 48th Congress, 1st Session, 21 April 1884, Appendix, 175.

floor of the House in support of a bill encouraging the foreign carrying trade of American vessels. It mandated the repeal of antiquated regulations such as the post-Revolutionary requirement that all the officers of an American vessel be citizens of the United States, and that American consuls in foreign ports be paid a fee by the owners of American merchant ships. Again, Deuster spoke of "our earnest aim to reconquer for our merchant marine the proud position which in former days [before 1861] it held on the high seas." He pointed to the merchant vessels of Great Britain, Germany, France, the Netherlands, Sweden and Norway that now carried a larger share of the world's trade than American ships. He wanted the United States to "enter the contest for the maritime and commercial supremacy of the Atlantic and of the Pacific" and claimed there was a "popular desire for a renewed supremacy of the American flag upon the high seas" that Congress should no longer ignore.[61] Deuster was not calling for pork-barrel legislation; he was not trying to create business for a Milwaukee shipyard. He wanted to boost America's business and power.

Deuster's Germanness was not a taboo. It could even be made fun of on the floor of the House of Representatives. In an admittedly rare scene, on March 24, 1880, when an angry Speaker of the House had the sergeant-at-arms actually round up a dozen members who had left the chamber and undercut the quorum, each culprit had to account for his absence. One schoolboyish excuse after another was brought forth, causing more laughter among the righteous than remorse among the sinners. Before Deuster could answer the Speaker's stern "What excuse have you to offer?" someone moved that "the gentleman from Wisconsin be allowed to speak his native tongue." The minutes record "laughter" and Deuster's reply: "Mr. Speaker, I have no doubt I could offer a better excuse in my native tongue." His non-ethnic explanation for having left his seat caused another wave of "great laughter."[62]

The inevitable beer question came up when the Internal Revenue Act of 1882 was debated. Deuster offered the classic amendment to repeal the tax on fermented liquors, ale, beer, and porter (which in the previous fiscal year had grossed $13.7 million): "These ought to be exempt just as much and for the same reason that you would exempt coffee or tea. These are the beverages of the poor man, and it is conceded all over this broad land, and everywhere

61. *Congressional Record*, 48th Congress, 1st Session, 26 April 1884, 3429–3431.

62. "After I witnessed the minority of this House enacting the celebrated comedy of Shakespeare's "Love's Labor Lost" [*sic*] during the whole afternoon, I felt so drowsy I left and wanted to see my wife." *Congressional Record*, 46th Congress, 2nd Session, 1858–1859.

else, especially in Europe where the test of long experience has demonstrated the fact, that it promotes temperance." Without further debate Deuster's amendment lost by a substantial margin of ninety to sixty-three.[63] Deuster had given his major anti-prohibition speech on March 27, 1884, when he supported a bill to forgo taxing distilled spirits still in warehouse. He had it reprinted, garnered with several pages of statistics, under the title "Does Prohibition Prohibit?" All the continental European immigrant arguments in defense of the normality of drinking are included:

> The tree in the center of the garden [of Eden] was a temptation because it was forbidden. . . . The intemperate use of intoxicants is confined almost exclusively to those reared amid customs which proscribe the social glass. . . . [Drinking alcoholic beverages] has been sanctioned by all nations of the earth since the dawn of time . . . [and] cannot be abrogated or interfered with without invading and endangering the safeguards of personal freedom. . . . You may drive the liquor trade under cover, but it will still flourish.

The accompanying statistics demonstrated the importance of the various taxes raised from the manufacture and sale of alcoholic beverages and of import duties for the federal budget. For the fiscal year ending June 30, 1883, revenue derived from the 115 million gallons produced in or imported into the United States added up to $100,751,344.14.[64]

One argument Deuster did not use was that dry German Americans would lose their ethnic identity. It is as Americans that they have the right to drink what they want. Besides, beer was an American beverage. Deuster taught his co-legislators some American history:

> The Plymouth Pilgrims established a brewery in Massachusetts. They must indeed have been quite fond of beer, as we find in Mourt's *Journal of the Plantation*, published in 1632, that shortly before the landing of the *Mayflower* a consultation was held on board, and that one of the principal reasons for landing as soon as possible was that the stock of beer was nearly exhausted.[65]

---

63. *Congressional Record*, 47th Congress, 1st Session, 24 June 1882, 5321.

64. *Congressional Record*, 48th Congress, 1st Session, 27 March 1884, Appendix, 35–37.

65. *Congressional Record*, 48th Congress, 1st Session, 27 March 1884, 37. Deuster referred the scholars among his colleagues to "the edition by H. M. Dexter, page 39."

Clearly, this is not divisive multiculturalism with one group claiming distinctive, exclusive characteristics that set it apart and preserve its identity. It is, rather, an appeal to a pleasure shared by most humans, a recognition of the all-inclusive anthropological constant of a craving for alcohol. German Americans have the right to drink beer not because they or their forebears came from Germany, but because they are humans living in the freest country in the world. German-American voters, we may assume, were only interested in the *effects* of federal and state laws on their lives, not in the rhetoric that had accompanied their enactment. But the legislators knew that they were most likely to succeed in mediating between ethnic minority group interests and the larger community's priorities—if that was at all necessary—by arguing in terms of "American," "national" values.

A closely related ethno-economic conflict of interests arose in February 1883: an import duty on green and other colored glass bottles. Deuster and his Republican colleague Guenther moved for an amendment of the tariff schedule. They put before the House the calculation made by New York bottle importers in which the price for bottles was given in German marks. The recent import tax increase by the Tariff Commission of two hundred percent on bottles, they demonstrated, would ruin their business. In support of the proposed amendment, Deuster spoke only of the good of the American economy. American bottle makers, he claimed, have so far been able to survive without a prohibitive import duty. At stake now is "a far greater and more important home industry, that of the manufacture of export beer":

> That industry has grown to enormous proportions during the past few years. Our American beer goes to Mexico, South America, Australia, and even to Europe. . . . Our American beer must compete in the foreign markets with the products of England, of Germany, and other countries where these same glass-wares are manufactured cheaply, and to compel them to pay such an exorbitant rate upon bottles would therefore virtually be a blow against our exporting interests, and make that competition abroad difficult, if not cripple it very seriously.[66]

Only a year later, in February 1884, hearings before the Ways and Means Committee closed with American manufacturers of glass bottles describing the precarious existence of their trade and pointing out the low wages paid in

---

66. *Congressional Record*, 47th Congress, 2nd Session, 2 February 1883, 2012.

Europe, especially "in Bremen, the point from which most of the imported bottles come."[67]

In his third term, the immigrant legislator called for an amendment to the United States Constitution. On January 8, 1884, he submitted a text patterned on the negative list of the First Amendment: "Neither the Congress of the United States of America nor the legislature of any State or Territory therein shall enact any laws prohibiting or abridging the manufacture or sale of any article of merchandise composed or prepared in whole or in part of any product of the soil." The Declaration of Independence and American liberty demanded no less: the pursuit of happiness, "individual action and conduct which interferes with no rights of others" needs protection, a mysterious, unnamed "impetus to a complete revolution of the spirit of American institutions" needs to be fended off. Without further debate the clever text in defense of products derived from barley and malt was referred to the Judiciary Committee.[68]

Deuster joined the group of Western congressmen who were no longer satisfied with the Department of Agriculture as President Abraham Lincoln had established it in 1862, and who worked toward increasing its powers until, in 1889, the secretary of agriculture was actually admitted to the cabinet. In May 1882 Deuster introduced a bill to create a powerful "Department of Agriculture and Science" to incorporate all relevant bureaus and other agencies in charge of forestry, mining, statistics, etc., to be headed by a secretary entitled to a seat in the cabinet. Cooperation with various organizations in the states would be close, dry farming methods would be improved, and so on.[69] The great national project, needless to say, had no ethnic component whatsoever.

Deuster, together with Guenther, played an active role in staving off American recognition of an international copyright agreement until 1891. His arguments against the bill, lobbied for by the American Copyright Association, could not have been more chauvinistically American or narrowmindedly in favor of the American reprinting business. To open the debate, Deuster had the Clerk of the House read the February 9, 1884, article "A Scheme to Make Books Dear" from *The Chicago Tribune*. It demanded "free trade in intellectual importations" and chided American authors "who advocate this international copyright on the low ground that they want protection from the competition of foreign authors. . . . There can be no reciprocity between the United States

---

67. "Last of the Public Hearings on the Morrison Bill," *The New York Times*, 23 February 1884, 4.

68. *Congressional Record*, 48th Congress, 1st Session, 8 January 1884, 294.

69. *Congressional Record*, 47th Congress, 1st Session, 8 May 1882, 228–229.

and other nations in the protection of authors. There are scores of foreign authors read in this country to one of ours read abroad."[70] Deuster justified his own objections with a curious mix of exaggerated pride in American culture ("No people read more than the American people, thanks to their free institutions, and thanks, also, to their magnificent free-school system.") and economic anxiety concerning the printing trade well known to Deuster as a newspaper editor: "All the publishers of reprints in the United States, the printers, paper manufacturers, type and stereotype founders, bookbinders, and many thousands of workmen employed in the production of reprinted works, would lose their occupations." Deuster claimed that American publishers were already voluntarily paying European authors for reprinting their works.[71]

Deuster's years in the House of Representatives fell within the cycle of depression in the American economy that lasted from 1873 to 1896. Competition in foreign trade, tariff schedules, and the balance of trade with the leading European exporters—especially Britain, France, and Germany—were, therefore, a constant concern to Deuster on the Commerce Committee and on the Foreign Affairs Committee. As his last major initiative to make American manufacturers more competitive with Europeans, Deuster proposed in May 1884 to permanently forgo any import tax on "any kind of raw material which may in any manner be consumed by the people or by the factories of the United States." His prime exhibit was woolen goods. If only American factories were allowed to import cheap wool from Latin America, they would be able to compete, for instance, with German cloth. But because of the high tariff on wool imported to the United States—up to 150 percent—certain cloths produced in Berlin cost only half of what the American weavers had to charge. German weavers could be supplied with "colonial wools" at a little over half the price American manufacturers had to pay for the raw material. American competitiveness in cotton goods proved, Deuster argued, that when the raw material was available at low cost, American manufacturing know-how and technology was equal to or even superior to that in Europe. American sales in Europe of machinery, tools and other hardware, and firearms was further proof. Deuster rejected the claim made by American manufacturers that the protective tariff also protected the American laborer: "Owing to the tariff the mine-owner of Pennsylvania amasses riches, but not the miner. . . . In farming,

---

70. *Congressional Record*, 48th Congress, 1st Session, 18 February 1884, 1201.

71. Ibid.: "The custom which now obtains with American publishers of publishing new European works from advance sheets, for which they pay the author a remuneration, has heretofore proved sufficient for the purposes for which the passage of an international copyright law is claimed."

which is an unprotected industry, the laborer receives about twice as much, board included, in Wisconsin as in England." Deuster's final appeal to the House of Representatives sounded like an economic Monroe Doctrine:

> We must attribute to our tariff alone the commercial conquest of an immense portion of this continent by European nations, and unless we are now ready to change this tariff so that it will let in free of duty every species of raw material, we will have to continue indefinitely our acknowledgment of a foreign commercial supremacy in a hemisphere where none but an American political and commercial predominance ought to be tolerated.[72]

Deuster lost his reelection bid in 1884, possibly because the vote was split among four candidates. The seat was won with 16,783 to 15,907 votes by Republican State Senator and flour miller Isaac Whitbeck Van Schaick. Deuster went back into the newspaper business. President Cleveland dispatched him as American consul to Krefeld in February 1896. He lost this coveted appointment after McKinley's victory and returned to Milwaukee in October 1897. He died in 1904.[73]

Senator Carl Schurz and the "Foreigner" Episode of 1874

I have found only one instance, so far, of explicitly negative public rhetoric in Congress revolving around the fact that a member was a naturalized citizen. That citizen was the high-strung Carl Schurz. The former American minister to Spain and former brigadier general of volunteers represented Missouri in the Senate from 1869 to 1875. On February 24, 1874, he spoke for three hours against increasing the amount of national bank notes in circulation and against less regulated "free banking" because he feared inflation and fewer European investments. In an extemporaneous reply, Indiana Senator Oliver Morton criticized Schurz for having misapplied book learning. Doctrines of political economy were not eternal and universal truths:

> Doctrines drawn from the experience of old and of small countries are not adapted to a country like ours, that is growing and developing and is now but in its youth. The Senator from Missouri has attempted

---

72. *Congressional Record*, 48th Congress, 1st Session, 2 May 1884, 3704–3709.

73. Obituary in *Milwaukee Sentinel*, 1 January 1905.

to apply those doctrines. He seems not to comprehend the country in which he lives or the times in which he lives. The Senator is what they call in France a *doctrinaire*, a political *littérateur*; he takes his learning from the books.

Morton then answered Schurz's rhetorical question whether to encourage a potential German investor to put his 100,000 marks into American real estate:

If he [Schurz] advises his friend not to send his money here, it only proves that he does not understand this country; he does not comprehend the times in which he lives. If he seriously supposes that this Congress or any member of this Congress is going to propose anything that will endanger a loan of money on the part of any European, he does not understand the country any better than he does that of China, from the history of which he quoted.[74]

The word "foreigner" was not uttered by Morton, and Schurz's status as a naturalized citizen or the country of his birth was not mentioned according to the *Congressional Globe*. Schurz, however, claimed the next day on the floor of the Senate:

Yesterday, when I pronounced opinions different from those of the Senator from Indiana, that gentleman put the 'foreigner' at me, alluding to the fact of my having been born on foreign soil, and concluding that I did not understand this country. I will not inquire whether this was in good taste or not, but I would merely say that I remember the time when I, with others, helped to promote the political interests of the Senator from Indiana, and those who thought like him did not look upon me as a foreigner at all then, and they thought that I understood this country admirably well. But as soon as I happened to differ with his views, he at once discovered that I was not born in this country and do not know anything of its affairs. I think it would be just as well for the foreign-born constituents of the Senator from Indiana to understand that as long as they agree with him he recognizes their full rights of American citizenship, but as soon as they dare to differ with

---

74. *Congressional Globe*, 43rd Congress, 1st Session, 24 February 1874, 1727–1728.

him in politics he will at once let them know that they are foreigners and had better hold their tongues.[75]

In response, Senator Morton explained without apologizing:

When I said I thought the Senator did not understand this country, I did not mean by that to say that all of our foreign-born citizens do not understand this country—no such thing. The Senator has no right to make himself the representative of all our foreign-born citizens that way. I think my friend tried the experiment some two or three years ago of putting himself forward as the representative of citizens of foreign birth, and attempted in that way to lead them out of one party and use them in the formation of a new one. I think this experience was not very satisfactory, and it would hardly be worth his while to try the experiment again.

Schurz came back:

When I say that his allusion to my foreign birth yesterday, in the connection and in the manner in which he made it, was a little offensive, I suppose he cannot find that surprising; not that I am ashamed of the place in which I was born, for surely I am here as a representative of one of the States, and having been sent here by Americans to represent them as an American citizen, enjoying the full right to express my own views, that right ought not to be slighted by any one who is my equal but not my superior, although I happened to be born upon foreign soil.

Senator Morton insisted on the innocence of his remark:

Mr. President, there is a little assumption in the remarks of my friend—but as he makes them good-naturedly I shall receive them in the same way—that I intended to refer to the fact of his foreign birth as an objection, or as an argument against him. Those who know me, and who know my political life, know there can be no foundation for that. Among many of my earliest and most earnest friends in Indiana have been men of foreign birth, and they are today; and I think I may say to

---

75. *Congressional Globe*, 43rd Congress, 1st Session, 24 February 1874, 1771.

my friend, without offense, that I have represented them as truly and I am as good a friend to them today as himself. I spoke of Germany as "his country," because he came from Germany. I did not speak of it or intend to mean that it was his country now. He is an American by adoption, an American by naturalization. But I was referring to the country from which he came, and of which he spoke repeatedly, and of which he often speaks to us. He had just come from that country, and he spoke of it repeatedly, I believe, in his speech; and I referred to it naturally as his country, not meaning to impute to him that he was not faithful to his obligations as an American citizen.

Schurz carried on:

To put an end to this whole controversy, do I understand the Senator from Indiana to say he used that expression only in a Pickwickian sense? If he does that, then I will say that I used mine in a Pickwickian sense, too.

Morton, however, did not want to belittle Schurz's German connection and referred to another, not at all humorous dimension: ethnic foreign policy:

Well, Mr. President, I was not exactly in a Pickwickian mood yesterday. . . . I used the expression very naturally, and in reply to the Senator, who had referred to Germany and referred to his visit there. . . . My friend is partial to his country—I cannot blame him for that—because I remember some two or three years ago my friend arraigned our Government upon this floor for having violated our neutrality with Germany in the sale of arms to France, and insisted that we had been guilty of a breach of international law that was even cause of war.

Schurz interjected:

I did not insist upon anything of the kind.

Morton:

I excuse my friend because of that natural feeling that every man must have for the fatherland.

This arrow shot, Morton ended the exchange with a forced smile: "If he insists that he was speaking in a Pickwickian sense, I will say that I was also."[76]

Perhaps Schurz kept quiet now because he sensed that the former governor of Indiana and seasoned expert in ethnic politics might just be his rhetorical superior.

Conclusions

What can we conclude from these case studies about the interaction of ethnicity, democratic politics, and national government? Brentano and Deuster did not hide their ethnic backgrounds or renounce their ethnic origins or constituents' interests. But they fully accepted the rules of the established political game. They did not go to Washington as ambassadors of an ethnic group or as single-issue advocates. They went to Washington only after they had become thoroughly integrated into their local and state political culture and system. They had learned to identify with territories whose populations were ethnically mixed. Their Americanization had taken place long before they stepped on the train to the capital. They arrived there, like their colleagues, to represent primarily local and regional interests. Because of the settlement patterns, the regional interests of Chicago and Milwaukee were not ethnically monolithic. (The exceptional Mormon territory confirms the rule.) The Congress of hometown boosters was playing an all-American game. The American system of federal government, which was built on loyalty to a particular territory and representation of its interests by simple majority representation with clear-cut responsiblities, served well to integrate an ethnically diverse population politically. (A European-style parliamentary system with stronger nationwide political parties and proportional representation might not have served this purpose as well.)

On the national level, Brentano and Deuster blended into the system and rightly felt fully accepted. It was, no wonder, then, that they both sought one more term in Washington than their party or the voters gave them. Both also contributed to defining American national interests. In doing so, they could

---

76. *Congressional Globe*, 43rd Congress, 1st Session, 25 February 1874, 1774–1775.

be ardent nationalists, for example, when they advocated strengthening the merchant marine or when they made ethnic foreign policy. Increasing the effectiveness of the Bancroft treaty with the German government was a case in point. Especially Deuster as member of the Foreign Affairs Committee did not hesitate to bring his Germany-related expertise and interests into play: Purely political declarations like the Lasker Resolution commending German liberals were rare, while bickering over the import duty on glass bottles (for beer), regulating transatlantic shipping to protect immigrants, and supporting American shipping in its international competition were the more usual subjects of deliberation. Deuster's support of the Chinese Exclusion Bill documents many German Americans' participation in the reigning Euro-American racism that at the time was part of American nationalism.

Fuchs could have pointed out more explicitly that the civic culture underlying the day-to-day functioning of state and national government and administration is vulnerable. Once established, its continued functioning cannot be taken for granted. Civic cultures—as well as economic systems— have deteriorated in the past in the United States and other countries. During the nineteenth century, the political integration of immigrants from all over Europe into one national whole was made possible by electoral politics and a representative government that discouraged sharp ethnic group distinctions and rewarded coalition building to pursue territorially defined interests. What counted was loyalty not to class or race or ethnic group but to place (within a clearly defined federal system of government): This explains a good part of the activities of both the German American and other congressmen during the period of mass immigration between the Civil War and the First World War.

10

The Political and Pedagogical in Bilingual Education: Yesterday and Today

Paul Fessler

F
ew Americans realize that the first large-scale bilingual school system in the United States began over 150 years ago. Or that it was the German language, not Spanish, that received such special treatment in America's public schools. Beginning in the 1840s and continuing through the United States's entry into World War I, German immigrants in cities across the nation received varying degrees of German-language instruction in public schools. Nearly 230,000 students a year studied German in public elementary schools near the close of the nineteenth century.[1] In Cincinnati during the 1840s the city's public schools offered students the option of splitting their schooldays between German- and English-language classes. After the Civil War cities such as Indianapolis, Baltimore, and Cleveland opened similar German-English programs. Other cities such as Milwaukee and Chicago offered German as a subject within a normal elementary curriculum. In more rural settings towns with large German-American populations also had public schools with German-English bilingual programs. When the United States entered World War I against Germany, many Americans viewed German-English bilingual programs as unpatriotic. Even before World War I, however, the popularity of German-language classes had begun to wane. As fewer and fewer German immigrants came to the United States, and as second and third generation German Americans increasingly favored English over German, the demand and funding for these schools had diminished. Nevertheless, German-English programs set an impressive track record for nearly eighty years.

---

1.   Louis Viereck, "German Instruction in American Schools," in *Report of the Commissioner of Education for 1900–1901*, edited by United States Bureau of Education (Washington, DC: Government Printing Office, 1902), 659; John B. Peaslee, "Instruction in German and Its Helpful Influence on Common-School Education as Experienced in the Public Schools of Cincinnati" (Paper delivered at the National German-American Teachers' Association, Chicago, Illinois, 19 July 1889); and Steven L. Schlossman, "Is There an American Tradition of Bilingual Education? German in the Public Elementary Schools, 1840–1919," *American Journal of Education* 91 (February 1983): 139–186.

Besides offering a historical precedent to current bilingual education debates, this story of German-English bilingual instruction highlights how ethnic politics, in addition to pedagogical evidence, has always been a key factor in determining a bilingual curriculum within the public school system. The large, often influential, German vote was up for grabs in cities across America. The German electorate was hardly a cohesive group, with German Lutherans opposing German Catholics opposing freethinkers. This very heterogeneity, however, combined with the size of the German electorate, worked to the advantage of proponents for German language instruction. Often, the German voters represented a block of potential swing voters, giving them leverage with both parties on issues such as bilingual instruction. Since neither party wanted to alienate German voters, German-English bilingual education programs proliferated in the wake of the Civil War and the changing voting patterns of German Americans.[2] As one Milwaukee resident noted, the adoption of German in the public schools was spearheaded by "shrewd politicians who cared neither for the educational value of German nor for the beauty of its literature, but who recognized the . . . strength of the so-called German vote."[3] In a similar vein, a 1906 Cleveland school commission noted that ". . . the reason for the teaching of German in the primary and grammar grades . . . is not educational, but chiefly national and sentimental."[4]

With a few modifications the same questions over political and educational factors are posed in the modern debate over bilingual education. This became apparent in the controversies over ballot referendums attempting to abolish bilingual education that became commonplace beginning in the 1990s. These debates focused not only on the potential educational value of bilingual education programs but also the ethnic politics and identities of linguistic minorities, especially Spanish speakers, in the midst of an English-speaking society and culture. Tying these two eras of bilingual education together in a comparative historical perspective, this paper examines the twin factors of

2.   Walter Kamphoefner, Wolfgang Helbich, and Ulrike Sommer, eds., *News From the Land of Freedom: German Immigrants Write Home* (Ithaca, NY: Cornell University Press, 1991), 19–21; Paul Kleppner, *The Cross of Culture: A Social Analysis of Midwestern Politics, 1850–1900* (New York: Free Press, 1970), 110–118; and Richard Jensen, *The Winning of the Midwest: Social and Political Conflict, 1888–1896* (Chicago: University of Chicago Press, 1971).

3.   Quoted in William J. Reese, *Power and the Promise of School Reform: Grass-roots Movements During the Progressive Era* (Boston: Routledge & Kegan Paul, 1986), 18.

4.   Quoted in Linda Sommerfeld, "An Historical Descriptive Study of the Circumstances that Led to the Elimination of German from the Cleveland Schools, 1860–1918" (Ed.D. diss., Kent State University, 1986), 210–211.

ethnic politics and pedagogical concerns as a factor in developing bilingual education programs in American public schools.

Such comparisons have rarely been considered because defenders of the contemporary bilingual education in the United States tend to ignore German-English bilingual programs. Instead of looking to these German-English programs, education researchers investigate the track records of bilingual education in Sweden, Australia, and Canada to learn lessons from these societies' efforts in bilingual education.[5] Most ignore the long history of bilingual education in America's public schools as a potential subject for comparative study. Of course, there are great differences between the German-English bilingual programs of yesterday and contemporary efforts in the United States. Similar differences, however, do not minimize the value of international comparisons. A historical precedent for bilingual education in America's own past can shed light onto both eras' programs and, perhaps, help moderate the contemporary discourse over bilingual education.

Historical precedent alone, however, does not justify bilingual education. Many will respond that it is just as bad an idea today as it was one hundred years ago. This objection should not be dismissed casually if there is to be legitimate dialogue between two sides debating this issue in contemporary society. It is necessary to move beyond merely identifying a precedent for bilingual education in our nation's past.[6] The nature of this precedent and its value to the contemporary debate must be considered.

What, exactly, does "bilingual education" mean in the United States today? No one can seem to come up with a widely accepted definition.

---

5.   See Christina Bratt Paulston, "Understanding Educational Policies in Multilingual States," *Annals of the AAPSS* 508 (March 1990): 38–47; Rosalie Pedalino Porter, *Forked Tongue: The Politics of Bilingual Education*, 2nd ed. (New Brunswick, NJ: Transaction Publishers, 1996), 85–120; Barry McLaughlin, *Second-Language Acquisition in Childhood*, vol. 2 (Hillsdale, NJ: Lawrence Erlbaum, 1985).

6.   Among the most important of those studies establishing this precedent are Schlossman, "American Tradition of Bilingual Education"; David A. Gerber, "Language Maintenance, Ethnic Group Formation, and Public Schools: Changing Patterns of German Concern, Buffalo, 1837–1874," *Journal of American Ethnic History* (Fall 1984): 31–61; Carolyn Toth, *German-English Bilingual Schools in America: The Cincinnati Tradition in Historical Context* (New York: Peter Lang, 1990), 55–57; Heinz Kloss, *The American Bilingual Tradition* (Rowley, MA: Newbury House Publishers, 1977), 90–91; Joel Perlmann, "Historical Legacies: 1840–1920," *Annals of the AAPSS* 508 (March 1990): 27–37; Walter D. Kamphoefner, "German American Bilingualism: cui malo? Mother Tongue and Socioeconomic Status among the Second Generation in 1940," *International Migration Review* 28 (Winter 1994): 856; Walter D. Kamphoefner, "German Americans: Paradoxes of a 'Model Minority,'" in *Origins and Destinies: Immigration, Race and Ethnicity in America*, edited by Silvia Pedraza and Ruben G. Rumbaut (Belmont, CA: Wadsworth Publishing Company, 1996), 152–160.

Educators employ many different programs and strategies to instruct non-English-speaking students in the United States today. All of the following programs have been termed as bilingual education even if a student's native language is not employed in the program. The most prevalent form of bilingual education is Transitional Bilingual Education (TBE). This program rests upon the hypothesis that non-English-speaking children should first be taught to read and write in their own language. Students then shift these skills to the acquisition of English in later grades. Depending on the teacher, the school, and the state, a wide range of English language instruction is employed in TBE programs. The federal government currently mandates that TBE programs receive a large majority of its funding.[7] Another program currently in operation for Limited English Proficient (LEP) students is English as a Second Language (ESL). In this program LEP students are placed in regular English classrooms but are pulled out of class several times a week for special ESL instruction.[8] "Structured immersion" programs are another option that place LEP students in a separate class where English is normally used, but the curriculum is adjusted in order to ensure comprehension. Within a year it is expected that most students enter fully English classrooms. "Sheltered English" is similar to structured immersion but with greater emphasis on mother-tongue instruction in subjects that require an advanced knowledge of English language and concepts.[9] Certain studies classify all of these programs as bilingual education while other studies consider only TBE programs as such. With so many variations and widespread confusion over terminology it is no wonder that today's debates about bilingual education generate so much turmoil.

7. James Crawford, *Bilingual Education: History, Politics, Theory, and Practice* (Trenton: Crane Publishing Company, 1989), 175; Porter, *Forked Tongue*, 71–77, 307–308; Christine H. Rossell and Keith Baker, *Bilingual Education in Massachusetts: The Emperor Has No Clothes* (Boston: Pioneer Institute, 1996), 3–12, 23–33.

8. The methods used in this program vary widely from school to school. See Crawford, *Bilingual Education*, 177.

9. Depending upon instructors, however, many "Sheltered English" classrooms can be very similar to "structured immersion." The difference in many cases, it appears, is semantic. "Immersion" is anathema to many supporters of bilingual education, while "Sheltered English" sounds gentler and more nurturing. See Rossell and Baker, *Bilingual Education in Massachusetts*, 4; Crawford, *Bilingual Education*, 176–177. For more thorough definitions and explanation of contemporary bilingual education programs, see Crawford, *Bilingual Education*, 175–178; Porter, *Forked Tongue*, 59–84, 121–158; Colman Brez Stein, *Sink or Swim: The Politics of Bilingual Education* (New York: Praeger, 1986), 33–44, 63–70; Rossell and Baker, *Bilingual Education in Massachusetts*, 45–64.

Research studies evaluating these bilingual education programs have been controversial. Most of them focus on the TBE, the most common form of bilingual education in American public schools.[10] Because of faulty research designs and other problems, these evaluations are widely considered inadequate by most participants. Thus, depending on the writer's interpretation of the evaluations, TBE programs have been viewed either as successes or failures. A researcher's definition of success is the most common source of disagreement in these debates.[11] Even defenders of bilingual education are beginning to acknowledge the problems with TBE and its underlying theory of facilitation.[12] Jim Cummins, a Canadian linguist, proposed the idea in 1979. He argues that English-language skills develop best among LEP students who first achieve literacy in their mother tongue. LEP students require five to seven years of native-language instruction in order to learn new concepts. This approach must be used until children are capable of abstract reasoning at approximately eight years of age. Before this stage an LEP student tends to be less able to learn concepts in a second language. Furthermore, according to this theory, an LEP student who is moved prematurely to an all-English class will likely be unable to master both languages.[13]

Amazingly, a number of critics and supporters of TBE do agree on the effectiveness of one type of bilingual education. They concur that two-way bilingual education programs are far superior to all other forms of bilingual

---

10.   Among those studies in support of TBE are D. Ramirez, S. Yuen, D. Ramsey, and D. Pasta, *Final Report: Longitudinal Study of Structured English Immersion Strategy, Early-Exit and Late-Exit Transitional Bilingual Education Programs for Language-Minority Children*, vol. 1 (San Mateo, CA: Aquirre International, 1991); and Virginia Collier and Wayne P. Thomas, *Research Summary of Study in Progress: Language Minority Student Achievement and Program Effectiveness* (Washington, DC: George Mason University, 1995). Studies critical of the above evaluations and TBE programs in general include Christine Rossell, "Nothing Matters? A Critique of the Ramirez, et.al. Longitudinal Study of Instructional Programs for Language-Minority Children," *Bilingual Research Journal* 16 (1992): 159–186; Board of Education of the City of New York, *Educational Progress of Students in Bilingual and ESL Programs: A Longitudinal Study, 1990–1994* (October 1994); and Rossell and Baker, *Bilingual Education in Massachusetts*, 45–65.

11.   Walter G. Secada, "Research, Politics, and Bilingual Education," *Annals of the AAPSS* 508 (March 1990): 81–86; Rossell and Baker, *Bilingual Education in Massachusetts*, 55–59; Crawford, *Bilingual Education*, 87–96; Porter, *Forked Tongue*, 67–69.

12.   Rossell and Baker, *Bilingual Education in Massachusetts*, 45–48; Kenji Hakuta, *Mirror of Language: The Debate on Bilingualism* (New York: Basic Books, 1986), 219; Crawford, *Bilingual Education*, 165–166.

13.   Crawford, *Bilingual Education*, 105–110; Porter, *Forked Tongue*, 69–71.

education.[14] These two-way programs place English-speaking students in the same classroom as non-English-speaking students. In this setting each group learns the other's language as well as their own. This not only avoids the problems of segregated classrooms prevalent in TBE programs, but also promotes harmony and respect among students of both language backgrounds. In addition, English-speaking children benefit from learning another language early in their schooling, rather than relegating language acquisition to a few years in high school. LEP students exit the programs with test scores superior to students in all other programs, including those of native English speakers in English-only classrooms. Likewise, English speakers outperform their peers in regular English classes and become proficient in a second language.[15] As students learn both languages simultaneously, these findings seem to cast further doubt on the validity of the facilitation theory underlying TBE. Though only a relatively small number of these programs exist in the United States, variations on the two-way approach clearly offer the best choice among the various programs used in educating non-English-speaking students.

After stripping away the terminology and educational jargon, the two-way partial immersion program is very similar to the most successful German-English programs established over a hundred years ago. Cincinnati, Cleveland, Indianapolis, and Baltimore offered long-term bilingual programs that most closely parallel the two-way model. These cities' public schools operated bilingual programs where half the school day was taught in English and the other half in German. These German-English programs actively promoted German language maintenance and cultural preservation. At the same time, however, they heavily stressed the mastery of English and initiated English language instruction from the very beginning of a child's formal education. In addition, non-German students enrolled in the German-English bilingual programs in large numbers. Thus, like the two-way immersion program,

---

14. Amy Pyle, "Study Finds Students Fare Best If Taught in Native Language First," *Houston Chronicle* (14 January 1996); Porter, *Forked Tongue*, 154–157, 248–249.

15. One potential drawback to these two-way programs is that they require a substantial number of non-English-speaking and English-speaking students. Some argue that too few English-speaking parents will want to enroll their children in these programs. This would hinder any widespread implementation of the program in the United States. In addition, a large non-English-speaking student body would be required to make it feasible in a school district. Thus, most of the three dozen two-way programs now in existence use Spanish as the second language. Two exceptions are an Arabic-English school in Hamtramck, Michigan, and a Greek-English school in Long Island City, New York. See Crawford, *Bilingual Education*, 168–165; Porter, *Forked Tongue*, 156.

classes included students who were native speakers of German as well as students whose mother tongue was English.

Considering the degree of nativism during this era and the emphasis that historians place on Anglo control of the public school system, this is perhaps the most surprising component of the German-English programs. In Cleveland the enrollment statistics of its German-English program differentiated between children of "German parentage" and of "English parentage" (table 10.1). From 1871 to 1895 students with "English heritage" averaged nearly thirty-five percent of the program's total enrollment. In Cleveland during the early 1870s approximately twenty-five percent of the city's total public school enrollment participated in its German-language program. By 1890 thirty-eight percent of all Cleveland public school students were taking part in the German-English program.[16]

Indianapolis public schools boasted an even stronger presence of non-German children enrolled in its German-language program (table 10.2). Of the 2,460 students enrolled in the German-English program during the 1882–1883 school year, students from "non-German parentage" comprised forty-three percent of the program's total enrollment. Nearly twenty years later, during the 1901–1902 school year, non-German students constituted approximately sixty-five percent of the German-language program's total enrollment. In addition to these non-Germans, African-American students also enrolled in these German language programs. In 1870, twenty-six blacks petitioned Indianapolis to adopt a German-language program in their schools. This petition points to the widespread respect for the German community in Indianapolis. As the Germans' wealth and prominence grew in Indianapolis, Cleveland, and the other cities with bilingual programs, many non-Germans viewed acquisition of German as a wise economic move.[17]

---

16. William Akers, *Cleveland Schools in the Nineteenth Century* (Cleveland: W. M. Bayne Printing House, 1901), 151–152, 161, 168, 185, 189, 193–196, 199–200, 206–207, 209–211, 219, 223–225, 232, 236, 241, 253, 256–257, 273–274, 283, 289–290.

17. Francis Ellis, "German Instruction in the Public Schools of Indianapolis, 1869–1919," *Indiana Magazine of History* 50 (1954): 253, 261, 267. It is likely that some of these numbers in table 10.1 are too high. Second-generation Germans could be labeled as non-German. Also, the school board's *Annual Report* identifies four hundred foreign-born students among those of "non-German parentage," who may have lived in German-speaking regions of countries such as Austria, Hungary, Italy, and Russia. Second-generation German parents with English-language skills could also have been characterized as being from an "English heritage." Even if some second-generation Germans were considered "English," however, the fact that non-German students enrolled in the German-language program demonstrates widespread support and respect for the German language and Cleveland's German community. Toth, *Bilingual*

	German parentage	Non-German Parentage	Total in German Program	Total School Enrollment	German-English as % of Total
1871-1872	2,192 (68%)	1,046 (32%)	3,238	16,647	19%
1874-1875	3,406 (66%)	1,740 (34%)	5,146	19,705	26%
1875-1876	3,798 (68%)	1,751 (32%)	5,549	20,771	27%
1876-1877	4,297 (72%)	1,662 (28%)	5,959	21,659	28%
1877-1878	4,562 (72%)	1,794 (28%)	6,356	22,104	29%
1878-1879	4,868 (70%)	2,051 (30%)	6,919	22,741	30%
1879-1880	5,215 (67%)	2,565 (33%)	7,780	24,262	32%
1880-1881	5,250 (64%)	2,990 (36%)	8,240	24,836	33%
1881-1882	5,763 (65%)	3,066 (35%)	8,829	26,990	33%
1882-1883	6,300 (66%)	3,293 (34%)	9,593	28,519	34%
1883-1884	6,659 (64%)	3,720 (36%)	10,379	30,708	34%
1884-1885	7,416 (62%)	4,511 (38%)	11,927	32,610	37%
1885-1886	7,761 (63%)	4,445 (37%)	12,266	32,814	37%
1886-1887	7,669 (62%)	4,792 (38%)	12,461	33,150	38%
1887-1888	7,929 (60%)	5,290 (40%)	13,219	35,730	37%
1888-1889	8,076 (60%)	5,457 (40%)	13,543	35,963	38%
1889-1890	8,234 (59%)	5,829 (41%)	14,063	37,641	37%
1890-1891	8,651 (62%)	5,279 (38%)	13,930	38,314	36%
1891-1892	8,951 (64%)	5,033 (36%)	13,984	39,813	35%
1892-1893	9,158 (68%)	4,343 (32%)	13,501	41,953	32%
1893-1894	9,649 (69%)	4,429 (31%)	14,078	44,002	32%
1894-1895	9,915 (66%)	5,185 (34%)	15,100	48,576	31%

Table 10.1: Enrollment in German-English Program of Cleveland Public Schools

	Students of German Parentage	Students of Non-German Parentage
1882-1883	1,402 (57%)	1,508 (43%)
1887-1888	1,540 (60%)	1,016 (40%)
1894-1895	1,751 (57%)	1,345 (43%)
1901-1902	2,363 (35%)	4,336 (65%)
1902-1903	2,438 (35%)	4,525 (65%)
1908-1909	2,094 (28%)	5,402 (72%)

Table 10.2: Enrollment in German-English Program of Indianapolis Public Schools

How effective were these programs? In the late nineteenth century Cincinnati school superintendent John Peaslee, a born and bred New England Yankee, testified that bilingual education produced high-quality scholars.[18] He had originally opposed bilingual education when he first arrived in Cincinnati because he assumed spending less class time studying English was harming students in the German program. He was thus amazed when his students from this program excelled in the city's semiannual examinations that were conducted entirely in English. Teachers begged to teach the German-track students because their own annual reviews were tied to the student's exam grades—and the German-track children were the best performing ones in the system. In addition students enrolled in the German-English program were promoted to the intermediate school system more than a year before their peers in the English-only program and scored seventeen percent higher on the high school entrance exams.[19]

Perhaps more importantly, one needs to consider how these bilingual programs, both the German-English and contemporary versions, were

Schools, 79; Heinz Kloss, *Das Volksgruppenrecht in den Vereinigten Staaten von Amerika*, 2 vols. (Essen: Essener Verlagsanstalt, 1940, 1942).

18. Peaslee, "Instruction in German," 9–10.

19. Peaslee, "Instruction in German," 8–9.

introduced and maintained. In rural German enclaves during the nineteenth century German-language classes could be implemented with little or no opposition. In urban areas where Germans were numerous but not absolutely dominant, however, the introduction of German-English programs depended on a more complex set of factors. Though many factors helped German Americans introduce bilingual classes into the public schools, numerical strength was the necessary precondition.[20] German Americans were the largest non-English-speaking immigrant group in nineteenth century America. Even school administrators admitted that the Germans' status as one of the largest taxpayer groups helped their cause for bilingual education.[21] Because of their dominance throughout the cities of the northern United States, politicians paid close attention to their concerns, especially at the local level. Many of these German-speaking immigrants desired to have their native language taught in the public schools. In many cities the German population had reached a "critical mass" by the middle of the nineteenth century. In other words they now had the potential to lobby for bilingual education with a necessarily large and influential voting bloc.

Similarly, Hispanic immigrants are the largest non-English-speaking group in early twenty-first century America. When the bill that eventually became the American Bilingual Education Act of 1968 was introduced in Congress by Texas Senator Ralph Yaborough, it contained provisions to provide bilingual education for Spanish-speaking immigrants, the largest foreign language group in the United States at the time.[22] The dominance of Hispanic voters made many politicians, especially from the Democratic Party, consider their desires and wishes at the local, state, and federal levels. Spanish-speaking immigrant groups had achieved a "critical mass" that brought greater attention to their needs and desires.

Clearly, the impetus for this bill lay in the political influence of the Hispanic districts. This is similar to the electoral dominance of German-Americans decades earlier.[23] Bilingual education was not to remain the private realm of Spanish-speaking immigrants, however. When complaints arose in Congress

---

20. See also Gerber, "Language Maintenance," 31–61; Kloss, *American Bilingual Tradition.*

21. Peaslee, "Instruction in German," 12.

22. Lyons, "Past and Future Directions," 67–68; Crawford, *Bilingual Education*, 32–33. This bill and later law, however, intended only to use mother-tongue instruction to transition children to all English language instruction. Only later did the federal government amend this law to include maintenance bilingual education programs.

23. Crawford, *Bilingual Education*, 32–33.

that the bill targeted only Spanish-speaking immigrants, Hispanic lawmakers, fearful that this provision could kill the bill, backed changes that expanded bilingual education to students of all language backgrounds.[24] As seen above in the discussion on TBE, though, the system still works in favor of Spanish-speaking students and to the disadvantage of other linguistic minorities in the United States. In practice only in the TBE classes for Spanish-speakers do students consistently receive training in their native language.[25] Despite speaking in favor of bilingual programs for all linguistic minorities, Spanish-speaking Americans find themselves dominating the educational system just as German-speaking Americans did during the late nineteenth and early twentieth centuries.

Germans Americans, however, were far less eager to support other language groups' proposals for bilingual education. During the nineteenth century many German Americans who had advocated the use of German in the public schools tended to denounce efforts by other foreign language groups to teach their native languages there too. German Americans emphasized the superiority of the German language in commercial, cultural, and political sectors throughout history. To many German Americans, other European languages, such as Polish or Italian, were clearly inferior and did not have the inherent benefits that German did.[26] The Germans had the necessary political clout and dominance in cities and states to achieve their goals, while other non-English-speaking groups had far less success in implementing bilingual education programs.

In both eras political conflicts have surrounded the decision to use a student's non-English mother tongue in the public schools. In this regard little has changed. The battleground for these debates, however, has shifted. To understand these differences and their impact, the politics surrounding German-English bilingual schools is summarized below, followed by a comparison of them with the contemporary debate.

24. James J. Lyons, "The Past and Future Directions of Federal Bilingual-Education Policy," *Annals of the AAPSS* 508 (March 1990): 32–33.

25. Rossell and Baker, *Bilingual Education in Massachusetts*, 80–102.

26. Peaslee, "Instruction in German," 12–13; Toth, *Bilingual Schools*, 82. There were exceptions. Likely due to German support, Polish and Italian languages were eventually given some recognition in the Milwaukee public schools. Often, however, latent hostility erupted into open conflict. Some ethnic groups, like the Czechs, would attempt to block all non-English-language instruction in the public schools in order to stop the teaching of German. See Jonathan Zimmerman, "Ethnics against Ethnicity: European Immigrants and Foreign-Language Instruction, 1890–1940," *Journal of American History,* 88 (March 2002): 1386–1392.

Though various factions of German Americans frequently bickered among themselves, religious, regional, and political divisions actually strengthened the ethnic group's political clout. Especially after the rise of the Republican Party in the 1850s, the Germans' diverse viewpoints ensured a split in their political affiliation. Whereas most Germans had been Democrats prior to the Civil War, many Germans became solid Republicans during the post-bellum era. Partisan divisions, however, did not erase the common ground that had earlier united most German-speaking Americans. Alcohol and language made for strange bedfellows for the Germans. Ethnic issues such as opposition to prohibition and support for German language instruction overrode most Germans' partisan affiliations. On these issues, Germans could unite against a common threat. If the majority of Germans had been Democrats, however, these ethnic issues would likely have become partisan ones. Republicans would have opposed bilingual education because there was no political reason to support it. Because the Democrats already had the German vote, there would have been little incentive to waste political capital on the issue. It is precisely because the Germans were divided between the Democrats and Republicans that their ethnic demands received immediate attention. Neither political party wanted to lose the powerful German vote, so both parties tried to work with the Germans to address their concerns.

Politicians learned their lessons after the passage of the Bennett Law in Wisconsin and the Edwards Law in Illinois. In 1889 Republican politicians in these two states passed these very similar laws requiring that all children between the ages of eight and fourteen be taught reading, writing, arithmetic, and American history in the English language. These requirements applied not only to public school children but also extended to parochial and private school pupils. In fact, the parochial schools of the German Lutherans were the primary target of these laws. In many of these schools all classes were conducted in German. German Lutherans, previously more associated with the Republican Party, now flocked to the Democratic camp. German freethinkers, Catholics, and Lutherans overcame their differences in order to stand united against the Republicans on this issue. In 1890 the Democrats, with solid German support, easily carried the state elections. Within months both newly elected legislatures repealed the laws. Republicans learned that it was unwise to anger the powerful German-American voting bloc.[27]

---

27. Kloss, *The American Bilingual Tradition*, 68–72. These laws not only united German voters but also unified them with other immigrant groups who had ethnic schools, especially the Poles. See also the Gjerde contribution to this volume.

German Americans had to build on their political influence to convince local interests to create German-English bilingual classes in the public schools. This meant that Germans advocating bilingual education had to build community support to create the bilingual programs. Except in states such as Ohio where German-English programs were required by state law, advocates of bilingual education continually had to prove themselves and their program before the local community. Even if German Americans were gaining increased representation in these political bodies, they were still fighting an educational establishment with assimilationist attitudes. Survival of the German-English programs, therefore, required parental involvement as well as dialogue with local school boards and city councils. Even with electoral clout and the possibility of support from both Democrats and Republicans, the political situation required compromise and dialogue.

In many cases the German community and the public school administration worked together, if with different goals, to implement German-English bilingual education. Many school reformers sought to consolidate popular support for public education during this era. They also believed that the public school curriculum could be an effective agent for the Americanization of immigrant children. It was acceptable to introduce the German language into the public schools primarily because it served their goals. By adopting German language instruction, these reformers enticed many Germans, the largest group of non-English-speaking immigrants in most of these cities during this period, to abandon their private and parochial schools that taught German and to enroll their children in public schools. German-language programs in the public schools, many reformers argued, subjected German-American children previously attending private schools to the Americanizing effects of public education. German-language instruction in the primary grades was acceptable to many of these reformers because assimilationist pressures would be present in other aspects of the public schools. Learning about American culture and the English language, even if only for half of the school day, would promote assimilation.[28]

This local control, however, also meant that these schools' existence was subject to shifts in local politics. The St. Louis public schools' bilingual program suffered as a result of these political shifts. Ethnic rivalries also added

---

28. Sommerfeld, "An Historical Descriptive Study," 94; Edward M. Miggins, "Becoming American: Americanization and the Reform of the Cleveland Public Schools," in *The Birth of Modern Cleveland, 1865–1930*, edited by Thomas F. Campbell and Edward M. Miggins (Cleveland: Western Reserve Historical Society, 1988), 94; Cleveland Board of Education, *Annual Report, 1878*, 61.

to the demise of the St. Louis system. The city's Irish community opposed the preferential treatment that the Germans received in the public schools. When the Democrats took power in the city, the Irish targeted the German-English program.[29] Merely because public-school boosters advocated German instruction in the public schools, one should not conclude that other Anglo-American citizens and other ethnic groups readily accepted German-language instruction. This example demonstrates that one should not romanticize the era of German-English programs or ignore the prevalent nativism of the period. It is equally important to recognize the aspects of compromise and cooperation that resulted from the political debates surrounding the German-English programs. Partisan political battles over German-English programs did occur. However, the Germans' political diversity countered such partisan conflicts and helped temper the political fights.

How does this compare to the current battles over bilingual education in the United States? The political affiliations of the two dominant foreign language groups provide a window into this comparison. German-Americans tended to be more politically diverse than Hispanics have been until recently. During the contemporary bilingual education debate, partisan lines have tended to be clear if not immutable. Even constructive criticism of bilingual education has become a partisan issue. In this charged atmosphere politicians from both parties had little incentive to engage in constructive dialogue or to form a consensus. This political alignment has encouraged both sides to demonize the other on this issue. Hispanics in contemporary America are by far the largest ethnic group benefiting from bilingual education. With the exception of Cuban Americans, however, most Hispanics have been traditionally within the Democratic camp. Further, most supporters of bilingual education consider themselves Democrats. In practice Democrats have taken Hispanic districts for granted while Republicans have overlooked them. In the not too distant past this political alignment made it much easier for Republican politicians to decry bilingual education as being un-American. If Hispanics were solidly behind Democratic candidates, then Republican politicians would not have had to worry about alienating potential voters with this rhetoric.

While this pattern may still prove accurate in some locales, Hispanic voters are increasingly placing their fortunes in the hands of Republican candidates and favoring traditionally Republican themes. Likewise, Republican strategists have begun actively courting this previously neglected voting bloc. In fact, the

---

29. Selwyn K. Troen, *The Public and the Schools: Shaping the St. Louis System, 1838–1920* (Columbia: University of Missouri Press, 1975), 67–68.

image of Hispanic solidarity behind the Democrats has been showing signs of crumbling for some time. Even in 1984 nearly fifty percent of California's Hispanic voters favored the Republican candidate, Ronald Reagan. Especially among more recent immigrants, many Hispanics today tend to favor the themes of social conservatism (pro-life and family values).

Hispanics are also not automatically in favor of bilingual education, at least not the troubled system in California's public schools. During the well publicized ballot initiative, Proposition 227, that sought to outlaw bilingual education in the public schools, nearly forty percent of the state's Hispanic voters chose to end the system. As much as Democratic lobbyists and supporters of bilingual education would like to cast the debate in nativist terms, the proposition's strong support among Hispanics detracts from such charges. Concern over the failure of bilingual programs to educate their children and to prepare them for the American workplace has trumped ethnic and linguistic preservation. This is just one example of the increasing diversification of the Hispanic voting bloc in America.[30]

In fact, this electoral diversification should be viewed as potentially good news for proponents of bilingual education. With Hispanic voters now targeted by both parties, issues vital to Hispanic voters should receive more attention from politicians of all political persuasions. This is similar to the situation one hundred years ago when the politically diverse Germans were able to parlay their ethnic concerns into bipartisan policies. Nationally, the best known beneficiary of this recent trend is President and former Texas governor George W. Bush. With an Hispanic sister-in-law and some knowledge of Spanish, Bush has actively wooed the Hispanic voters in Texas with great success. His position on bilingual education illustrates the power of a diverse Hispanic voting bloc. Bush favors bilingual education as long as the program allows children to master the English language as quickly as possible. Hispanic voters may favor linguistic retention, but they also recognize the vital necessity of English for economic success in the United States. This hybrid stance on bilingual education was missing from the debate within California. While some within the conservative right of the Republican Party oppose Bush's stance on bilingual education as being a "compassionate" and "sensitive" sell-

30. "Enter the Garcia's Own Party," *Economist*, 15 August 1998, 21; Douglas Mitchell et. al, "The Politics of Bilingual Education," *Educational Policy* 13 (Jan.–March 1999): 86–104; Paul Pringle, "Texas Stands by Its Bilingual Education Programs," *Dallas Morning News*, 5 June 1998.

out, demographic and electoral trends favor similar compromises on Hispanic issues across the nation.[31]

The intervention of the federal government is another important difference in the political wars surrounding the German-English programs and the contemporary system. Today's system is built on mandates related to federal funding and pressures from the educational bureaucracy. All languages are now seen as equal and deserving of the same treatment in the public schools. This is much different than during the era of purely local funding when small non-English-speaking groups had little chance of mandating bilingual education. Guidelines and enforcement provided by a governmental body can be a great benefit to these programs. As seen in the 1840 Ohio state law requiring bilingual education, such intervention provides stability for bilingual programs. Cleveland and Cincinnati's German-English programs evolved into the strongest in the nation because these laws assured the school systems of continuity.

The current system of federal funding for bilingual programs, however, has its downside. In accepting such funding school districts are required to follow federal guidelines as to what types of programs to use. Because of federal mandates, the same degree of parental and ethnic community involvement is not required to implement bilingual education programs as was the case in the nineteenth century bilingual battles. In some states, such as Massachusetts, the state government has passed laws mandating particular types of bilingual education regardless of differing local conditions and community opinion.[32] The lack of flexibility tied with the incentive of federal funding encourage many districts to use programs that may not be in the best interest of their LEP student body or in accordance with the wishes of the community and the parents of LEP children. This is not to argue that the federal government should retreat from this issue. Federal oversight helps ensure that nativist sentiments at the local level will not override the educational needs of students. It is true, though, that federal and, in some cases, state intervention have stifled innovation and limited parental control. Because of the often glacial movement of federal and state bureaucracies, these laws should be adjusted to be more responsive to demands for local and parental control of bilingual programs.

As the demise of the St. Louis German-English program over a hundred years ago demonstrates, heated debate and political gamesmanship are nothing

---

31. John O'Sullivan, "Compassion Play" *National Review* (22 February 1999): 22; Pringle, "Texas."

32. Rossell and Baker, *Bilingual Education in Massachusetts*, 12, 20–34.

new in the battle for bilingual education. The polarized political arena and the defensive postures on both sides of the contemporary debate hinder rational discussion on how best to educate non-English-speaking students. In this atmosphere TBE programs are defended as being the best way to proceed, without truly assessing the methods and stated purpose of the program. While TBE is not necessarily harmful, and opponents of bilingual education overstate its detriments, it does not appear that TBE is the best method to move LEP students into English classrooms, especially for non-Spanish-speaking students. If bilingual maintenance is to be the goal of a district's bilingual programs, then the TBE method is not adequate. Rather, two-way partial immersion programs should be given more attention and funding. Nevertheless, the educational establishment persists in retaining funding incentives that support methods not suitable in many school districts. Entrenched interests are less likely to admit problems and move to fix them for fear of allowing an opening to dismantle the entire program. This stifles innovation. As mentioned above, many TBE instructors of non-Spanish speaking children routinely adopt a sheltered English method while still calling it a TBE class in order to comply with the letter of law. Advocates of bilingual education and leaders of minority language groups should not succumb to the fear that drives many of their opponents' nativist attacks. Instead, they should strive to implement an educational system that best serves their children rather than one that serves political gamesmanship and funding fears. Advocates of bilingual education should change the laws requiring TBE and replace them with ones encouraging more innovation. Increasing the number of two-way programs where appropriate would provide a good start.

The historical precedent of German-English programs offers several insights into the current debate about bilingual education. It counters the charge that bilingual education is a new invention catering to the demands of ethnic minorities. Some critics of bilingual education fear that immigrants will not assimilate unless taught exclusively in English. German immigrants during the nineteenth century fought to maintain their mother tongue, yet that did not hinder their integration into American society. Despite impressive German-English programs in urban areas like Cincinnati and Cleveland, language preservation among German Americans did not last. Even within rural German enclaves, bilingual programs were not effective in promoting German-language maintenance. As recent studies have shown, Hispanic Americans are already following the same pattern; second- and third-generation Hispanics in this country are overwhelmingly English-dominant. In other words, bilingual education should not be viewed as a threat that could balkanize American society.[33]

The German-English programs also provide a precedent in American history for the potential long-term success of bilingual education using the two-way partial immersion model. It is extremely unlikely that German-Americans would have campaigned for programs similar to the TBE models supported by many Hispanics, today's largest non-English-speaking group. Although in certain situations German Americans may have been content with at least some foreign-language education, the Cincinnati model or two-way partial immersion would have almost certainly been the preferred method. The two-way partial immersion programs, not TBE, would satisfy linguistic minority parents who want their children to grow up bilingual. The German-English programs produced students who excelled in English without sacrificing their German mother tongue. This should also be the goal of the contemporary bilingual system. Educators should not be content with mere proficiency in the English language. TBE may satisfy some proponents of bilingual education, but it fails to provide quality instruction in either English or the student's native language. The two-way partial immersion technique addresses many of TBE's problems such as segregated classrooms, questionable results, and weak public support. A two-way partial immersion program similar to the German-English system would ensure that non-English-speaking students would master the English language. In addition, programs that produce bilingual citizens pay other dividends in areas such as international trade and tourism to a much greater extent than a century ago. This should embolden educators to increase funding for similar programs across the nation. These two-way programs produce students who surpass those enrolled in classes using only the English language.

The political environment of today's battles over bilingual education has led to extremism on both sides, much as was the case a hundred years ago. This tendency also existed a hundred years ago. But because of enrollment of non-German students in the bilingual classes, support grew for the programs from outside the German-American community. This led many politicians and school board members to refrain from criticizing and attacking the programs regardless of their personal views. More widespread use of two-way partial

---

33. Alejandro Portes and Richard Schauffler, "Language Acquisition and Loss among Children of Immigrants," in *Origins and Destinies*, 432–443; Alejandro Portes and Richard Schauffler, "Language and the Second Generation: Bilingualism Yesterday and Today," *International Migration Review* 28 (Winter 1994): 640–661; Kamphoefner, "German-American Bilingualism."

immersion programs may have the potential for similar broad-based support in contemporary America. Having students whose first language is English as an integral component of the programs would address the criticism that bilingual education is a special interest perk.[34] In addition, these programs would gain important political support from English-speaking parents whose children would attend these programs. Increased popular support through a more diverse student body might help pressure the educational bureaucracy to reform its programs and to allow more room for community debate and decision making. These changes would also help to foster respect among political rivals rather than increased animosity and suspicion. Employing the model of the German-English programs in the form of its contemporary cousin—two-way partial immersion—educators may be able to institute an efficient bilingual education system that could garner broad-based support among all Americans.

---

34. Crawford, *Bilingual Education*, 163–174.

Part IV:

War and National Identity

11

German-Born Union Soldiers: Motivation, Ethnicity, and "Americanization"

Wolfgang Helbich

"*B*ecause the damned Flying Dutchmen are behind me; I would not care for all the Yankees. . . . And in fact, the enemy has incredible respect for the German soldiers, such that even farmers come here from all sides to see the Flying Dutchmen, as they call our German division." So wrote a German from Oldenburg who had immigrated in 1856 at the age of twenty-one and was at that time a sergeant in the German 45th New York Infantry (and by May 1865 a captain), to his parents in Germany in mid-June 1862.[1]

I am particularly fond of this quotation, because in its ingenuous irony and mirror-image quality, it encompasses much of the paradox that has fascinated me for quite some time: How could the strong and often exuberant conviction of the superior martial prowess of German soldiers, from generals on down, expressed by so many German immigrants, coexist throughout the war with the negative and sometimes bitterly scornful opinion that many American-born military men and English-language papers held of the soldierly qualities of German immigrants of all ranks?

The beauty of the quotation is that the author was obviously ignorant of the fact that the term "Flying Dutchmen," which for him evoked pride in the ethnic group's soldierly qualities, was (at that time at least occasionally, and after Chancellorsville quite commonly) an epithet denoting precisely the opposite—not the furiously and irresistibly attacking Germans, but the yellow "Howard's cowards," the "skedaddling Dutch."[2]

This irony is elaborated, though not quite so obviously, by the reference to the admiring Virginia farmers; it was precisely farmers such as these who spread the word about the looting, marauding, murdering "Hessians," which

---

1. August Horstmann, letter fragment "shortly before 16 June 1862"; Wolfgang Helbich, *"Alle Menschen sind dort gleich. . .": Die deutsche Amerika-Auswanderung im 19. und 20. Jahrhundert* (Düsseldorf: Schwann, 1988), 182.

2. See, for example, D. Scott Hartwig, "The Unlucky 11th: The 11th Army Corps on July 1, 1863," *Gettysburg: Historical Articles of Lasting Interest*, 1 January 1990, 33.

was then generalized, by the Confederate press and public, into the enemy image of "foreign mercenary vandals."[3]

And there is even a third irony, or apparently unnoticed contradiction, hidden in the quotation. It is followed almost immediately by an account of the battle of Cross Keys, the salient feature of which was the defeat of the German division caused by the premature attack of the German 8th New York Infantry ordered—clearly in violation of instructions to stay put—by its Austrian-born colonel who was hopelessly drunk.[4]

In this paper I begin discussing the theme of the diametrically opposed images of the Germans in the Union army. I then move on to address some aspects of the German regiments and their contribution to ethnic antagonism in the military and point out what appear to be very significant differences in the motivation to volunteer and fight between German-born and American Union soldiers; consider certain court martial cases as indicators of ethnic relations during the Civil War, and examine how the "Americanization" thesis holds up against the evidence presented.

I

It takes some effort on the part of those of us who have lived through or studied the wars of the twentieth century to imagine large public protest or "indignation" meetings, organized by leading citizens of one ethnicity, taking place in New York City and elsewhere, with the intention of putting pressure on the administration to promote and give more troops to their hero and favorite general and backed by the threat of voter disaffection.[5] But in the almost impenetrable maze of personal ambition, intraethnic and interethnic controversy, intramilitary competition, and political maneuvering that influenced military appointments and military decisions (and vice

---

3. On such clichés in soldiers' letters see James M. McPherson, *What They Fought for, 1861–1865* (Baton Rouge: Louisiana State University Press, 1994), 19; the passage from the Savannah *Republican* quoted in "Our Armies—The Foreign and Native Elements," *The New York Times* [hereinafter *NYT*] 15 November 1864; William L. Nugent, *My Dear Nellie: The Civil War Letters of William L. Nugent to Eleanor Smith Nugent*, edited by William M. Cash and Lucy Somerville Howorth (Jackson: University Press of Mississippi, 1977), 138.

4. Colonel Wutschel was dishonorably discharged on this and other counts, August 23, 1862. War Department reply to an enquiry, December 8, 1924, attached to Muster Rolls, Eighth New York Infantry, NA.

5. "The Sigel Demonstration," *NYT*, 17 January 1862; Jörg Nagler, *Fremont contra Lincoln: Die deutsch-amerikanische Opposition in der Republikanischen Partei während des amerikanischen Bürgerkriegs* (Frankfurt/M.: Lang, 1984), 119–120.

versa), where parts of the "German element" acted in a sectarian, paranoid, and hysterical manner,[6] such an event was far from unique. In its typically condescending posture when dealing with "friendly" ethnics, *The New York Times* granted that "our German friends" had reason for indignation, but also claimed that they showed "a too great impetuosity" and "indulged in language which injures their cause."[7]

It is harder to understand another "indignation meeting" in New York City that took place on June 2, 1863. It aimed at restoring the honor of the German troops. After the battle of Chancellorsville they had become the victims of a vicious press campaign in which the *Times* set the tone with accusations against "the panic-stricken Dutchmen," "the cowardly retreating rascals," "the retreating and cowardly poltroons," who "disgracefully abandoned their positions."[8]

For the speakers at the meeting "nativism" was to blame for these outrageous calumnies, but it is hard to see how such a rally could make hundreds of English-language papers apologize. And of course they did not. Achieving a rehabilitation of the German troops[9] was all the more difficult because not only journalists but also many military men condemned "the Dutch." A captain from Boston who took part in the battle (though in a different area) wrote one day after the event: "And this is all, because the 11th Corps, Sigel's Dutchmen, broke and ran, all of them, at the first shot, as I always knew they would, losing 16 pieces. . . . It is horrible awful. Every man in Sigel's Corps ought to be hauled off the face of the Earth."[10] In a considerably milder, though hardly

---

6.   Even the thoroughly filiopietistic Wilhelm Kaufmann, *Die Deutschen im amerikanischen Bürgerkrieg (Sezessions Krieg 1861–1865)* (Munich, Berlin: Oldenbourg, 1911), manages to contribute to such an impression. The picture becomes clearer by adding such studies as Ella Lonn, *Foreigners in the Union Army and Navy* (Baton Rouge: Louisiana State University Press, 1951); William L. Burton, *Melting Pot Soldiers: The Union's Ethnic Regiments* (Ames: Iowa State University Press, 1988); and especially Nagler's *Fremont contra Lincoln* and Murray M. Horowitz, "Ethnicity and Command: The Civil War Experience," *Military Affairs* 42 (1978): 182–189.

7.   *NYT*, 17 January 1862.

8.   *NYT*, 5 May 1863. On the meeting see Lonn, *Foreigners*, 594–595 and Nagler, *Fremont contra Lincoln*, 119–120.

9.   One hundred and thirty years of historiography would make it appear that their performance under Stonewall Jackson's surprise assault was far from heroic, but by no means as disastrous as the above quotations make it appear.

10.   Henry Livermore Abbot, *Fallen Leaves: The Civil War Letters of Major Henry Livermore Abbott*, edited by Robert Garth Scott (Kent, OH: Kent University Press, 1991), 176. Only slightly less radical was an eyewitness, an artillery officer who tried to advance his battery

sympathetic vein, another New Englander wrote in the fall of 1863:

> The Eleventh Corps has this comparatively easy duty [protecting the railroad], by virtue of their being such excellent skedaddlers in time of battle. Our boys were cruel in their jokes on these fellows, and take every occasion to let them know that their peculiarities are appreciated.[11]

Actually, a German eye-witness, the Assistant Surgeon of the 119th New York Infantry, describes the headlong, chaotic flight of parts of the 11th Corps under Stonewall Jackson's onslaught in much the same terms as American-born officers, and he was so much in the middle of it as to be taken prisoner.[12]

Of course, anti-German feeling was not invented at Chancellorsville. It existed from the beginning to the end of the war, finding expression in a wide spectrum of comments ranging from bitter attacks to good-humored ridicule,[13]

---

against the torrent of fleeing soldiers: "The Eleventh Corps had been routed, and were fleeing to the river like scared sheep. . . . Aghast and terror-stricken heads bare and panting for breath, they pleaded like infants at the mother's breast that we would let them pass to the rear unhindered." Thomas Osborne, *No Middle Ground: Thomas Osborn's Letters from the Field (1862–1864)*, edited by Herb S. Crumb and Katherine Dalle (Hamilton, NY: Edmonston Pub., 1993), 154.

11. Wilbur Fisk, *Hard Marching Every Day: The Civil War Letters of Private Wilbur Fisk, 1861–1865*, edited by Edith and Ruth Rosenblatt (Lawrenceville: University Press Kansas, 1983), 154.

12. Captain Carl Uterhard, M.D., letter to his mother, near Stafford House, VA, 17 May, 1863, excerpts in *Deutsche im Amerikanischen Bürgerkrieg: Briefe von Front und Farm, 1861-1865*, edited by Wolfgang Helbich and Walter D. Kamphoefner (Schöningh: Paderborn, 2002), 219–220. An English translation will be published in 2005.

13. See the quotations given by Bell Irwin Wiley, *The Life of Billy Yank, The Common Soldier of the Union* (Garden City, NY: Doubleday, 1971), 312, and about the "quick tempered and almost ungovernable" Germans of the 103rd New York Infantry, Edward King Wightman, *From Antietam to Fort Fisher, The Civil War Letters of Edward King Wightman, 1862–1865*, edited by Edward G. Longacre (London, Cranbury, NJ: Associated University Presses, 1985), 28, 64, 79, 99, 104, 125. A close study of the 154th New York Infantry, a predominantly native-born regiment serving with the 11th Corps, relates a long list of derogatory comments on the "Dutch" and of ethnic incidents, sometimes serious, as well as the complaint that under German command German units got preferential treatment and American regiments had to suffer—an impression that was echoed by Germans. Private Gottfried Rentschler, 6th Kentucky Infantry, wrote: "If a full company is needed for some easy service, e.g., Provost-Guard, a German company is never taken. If an entire company is required for rough service, e.g., several days or several weeks as Train-Guards, a German company will be ordered whenever possible. As this happens on a company basis, so it happens to individuals in the mixed companies. As a rule, the German has to wade through the mud, while the American walks on the dry road." Mark H. Dunkelman, "Hardtack and Sauerkraut Stew: Ethnic Tensions in the 154th New York Volunteers,

and from hearsay to close professional observation.[14]

German immigrant letter writers reciprocated with regard to both Yankee ethnic character and soldierly qualities.[15] No more than half a dozen letter writers examined for this essay complain about being personally discriminated against, but twice as many describe Americans in the most unflattering terms—uncultured, hypocrites, money-crazed humbugs, swindlers, reckless wasters of human lives. And although the criticism of politicians and corruption is a common theme in American Civil War letters in general, for the sixteen Germans who voiced it, it was the *Americans* who were the villains.[16] And perhaps even more significant was the fact that though freedom, Union, antislavery and the ideals America stood for were praised by a number of letter

Eleventh Corps, during the Civil War," *Yearbook of German-American Studies* 36 (2001): 75 and Joseph R. Reinhart, "Indiana's and Kentucky's German-Americans in the Civil War," March 2000, n.p.: www.geocities.com/inkyger.

It should, however, also be mentioned that almost two-thirds of the approximately fifty editions of letters from American-born participants in the Civil War that I have consulted contained no reference at all to foreign-born soldiers or units, and that one can find an occasional germanophile or Sigel admirer among Anglo-American letter writers. Thus Robert Gould Shaw quotes "Steh ich in finstrer Mitternacht," requests that a German book be sent to him, and attributes the neatness of farms and villages around Newmarket, Virginia, to the many German names to be found there. Robert Gould Shaw, *Blue-Eyed Child of Fortune: The Civil War Letters of Colonel Robert Gould Shaw*, edited by Russell Duncan (Athens: University of Georgia Press, 1992), 87, 150, 195. A Massachusetts abolitionist nurse toward the end of 1862 expressed great confidence in Fremont and Sigel, certainly not because of the latter's ethnicity, but in spite of it. Hannah Ropes, *Civil War Nurse: The Diary and Letters of Hannah Ropes*, edited by John R. Brumgardt (Knoxville: University of Tennessee Press, 1980), 114. (See also 70, 72.)

14. It is at least difficult to attribute entirely to prejudice professional judgments like those of the artillery officer who immediately after Chancellorsville was made chief of artillery of the Eleventh Corps: "I found the batteries in a most deplorable condition and in a state of complete demoralization. . . . I have nowhere seen anything to be compared to these batteries with the exception perhaps of Captain Dilger's battery. . . . These batteries have evidently never had a commander[,] that is, an officer who exercised any control over them." *No Middle Ground*, 143–144.

15. In the following paragraphs as well as later on I refer to a body of German immigrant letters, 1861–1865, written by thirty-six men in the Union army and twenty-three civilians of military age living in the North. While we have letters written by 169 persons (including women, Confederate soldiers, and civilians) in the Bochum Immigrant Letter Collection, I restrict myself to those fifty-nine, since letters from all of them have been published in Wolfgang Helbich, Walter D. Kamphoefner, Ulrike Sommer, eds., *Briefe aus Amerika: Deutsche Auswanderer schreiben aus der Neuen Welt 1830–1930* (Munich: Beck, 1988); Helbich, *Alle Menschen*; and Helbich and Kamphoefner, *Deutsche im Amerikanischen Bürgerkrieg*. Considering the high degree of subjectivity involved in assessing attitudes in an elusive medium like private letters, I prefer giving readers a chance to look at the sources on their own.

16. For good measure five letter writers commented on the Irish in such terms as would have been described as "nativistic" if they had come from Americans.

writers, there is not a single instance where "the American" or an individual Yankee (with the sole exception of Lincoln) was presented as a positive model, let alone admired.

With regard to the martial virtues of the Germans, there is not a word in the letters—no simple reports or corrections or complaints—about the negative public and military opinion in America. If not in the exuberant spirit of the initial quotation, sixteen letter writers (including five civilians) explain that German officers command better, German regiments fight better, German camps are cleaner, German troops are healthier, and finally that Germans are highly respected in the army. As the thirty-one-year-old teacher in Philadelphia who had immigrated in 1857 put it in a letter to his parents in Germany: "It is always the Germans who act most honestly and fight best and the one who fights most courageously of all is the German Major General Sigel."[17]

That this sort of ethnic loyalty and pride was shared by second-generation German Americans, perhaps even more strongly, is spelled out clearly in the Kircher letters.[18] The German-American press (with the exception of certain mavericks such as Karl Heinzen[19]) seems to have fully endorsed Sigel, right or wrong, and praised the superior quality of the German contribution to the war effort in its crusade against "nativism" and "West Point."[20] We still know very little about the views expressed in the press in Germany on this point, but the politically active German Americans, primarily the journalists, must have done a good job of conveying their message to receptive ears. In words quite reminiscent of Sergeant Horstmann's quote at the beginning of this paper, the *Lahrer Hinkender Bote*, a *Volkskalender* representing the least sophisticated elements of the German press, wrote in its 1863 edition: "The Germans . . . have won so much respect from their opponents that whole regiments have

17. Carl Hermanns, 12 April 1862; Helbich and Kamphoefner, *Deutsche im Amerikanischen Bürgerkrieg*, 177. It might be a trifle malicious to add that in a letter of August 5, 1862, he assures his parents that he is safe from conscription since he is not a citizen yet. But if that situation changed, he would rather go back to Germany than fight for swindlers and politicians.

18. Henry A. Kircher, *A German in the Yankee Fatherland: The Civil War Letters of Henry A. Kircher*, edited by Earl J. Hess (Kent, OH: Kent State University Press, 1983), 9, 13–15, 28, 52, 62, 121.

19. Burton, *Melting Pot Soldiers*, 88–89.

20. One precipitating factor leading radical Forty-eighters to promote Fremont as a presidential candidate in 1864 was Lincoln's alleged mistreatment of Sigel. See Nagler, *Fremont contra Lincoln*, 45–46, 56, 95–96, 116.

started to run without firing a shot when they heard the shout 'The Germans are coming, Sigel is coming!'"[21]

Since there were German (and American and Irish) regiments that unquestionably fought well and others that did not, just as there were excellent, mediocre, and incompetent officers from all ethnic groups, the contradictory collective images elevating one's own and disparaging other ethnic groups have less to do with reality than with psychological needs and insecurities heightened by a sense of competition and the constant awareness of cultural difference.

The lowly "Dutch" insisted on believing that they were better soldiers and would thus win the respect of Americans, whereas many of the latter eagerly seized on instances that would prove the clumsy foreigners were inferior to real Yankees. Their respective needs for recognition seem to have been so overwhelming that both sides were blind to this contradiction. Neither ethnics nor Americans may have remained oblivious of the other group's attitudes arising from anxieties and the need to feel superior, but this neither reduced prejudice nor led to any increase in mutual respect. Such collective perceptions would have been less common in American units that included a sizable number of Germans, and more often between American and clearly identifiable German units. In order to explain their role in enhancing ethnic tension in the Union army, some attention will now be given to the "German regiments."

II

A highly educated Yankee officer from Massachusetts and a barely literate German immigrant had roughly the same idea about the formation of (ethnic) regiments. The former characterized the anything-but-fine army as having "a pack of politicians for officers, with their constituents for rank and file," while the German, who never enlisted, found that at the outbreak of the war "there was no other prospect for a worker to make a living other than joining the military; others, who did not have to make a living as workers, saw an opportunity to pose as officers, and so a race started to open up one regiment after the other

21. The German original is: "Die Deutschen . . . haben sich bei ihrem Gegner so in Respekt versetzt, daß bei dem Ruf 'Die Deutschen kommen, Sigel kommt!' schon ganze Regimenter davon gelaufen sind, ohne einen Schuß zu tun." *Lahrer Hinkender Bote* (1863), 253.

in order to make money."[22] These may be biased and one-dimensional views, but we know from the intrigues and antics involved in creating many ethnic regiments and from the biographies of many who volunteered that there is more than a grain of truth in them. But there are other aspects to the formation of ethnic and particularly German regiments.[23]

Much can be said for the impression that German regiments (usually not the numerous German companies within predominantly American regiments)[24] were the logical extension of German clubs or associations in wartime conditions: The Turners and their Turner Regiments demonstrate such a connection most conspicuously. At the same time German regiments had traits of a whole German immigrant community, minus women and children. The language of official business, both spoken and in written orders as preserved in the regimental books, was generally German through mid 1862,[25] though some English orders were interspersed from the beginning, and English expressions for ranks and military technical terms were used throughout.[26]

Many historians have pointed out that the German regiments not only received sauerkraut and sausages but also generous rations of beer. But if warfare did not interfere, they had many more ways of preserving, reinforcing,

---

22. *Blue-Eyed Child*, 168; Christian Häring, 30 August 1863; Helbich and Kamphoefner, *Deutsche im Amerikanischen Bürgerkrieg*, 278.

23. The number of "purely German" volunteer regiments is variously given as thirty-one (Kaufmann, *Die Deutschen*, 184–190), twenty-five (Burton, *Melting Pot Soldiers*, 72–111), and thirty-five (Lonn, *Foreigners*, 666–672). While it seems safe to settle for "some 30," Lonn's count of forty-six "part German" regiments (one third or more) is more problematic. A spot check in the regimental books resulted in three confirmations, but her "half German" 16th Iowa, 24th Indiana, and 74th Ohio turned out to have two and a half companies, 52 men out of 750, and 47 men out of 800, respectively, and the "one third German" 17th Massachusetts listed just two Germans in its Descriptive Book, NA.

24. It was common practice to concentrate Germans (or other ethnics) in one or two companies of a regiment if their numbers were sufficient. Language—difficulty in understanding English—was the most obvious justification for this.

25. In the Order Books of the 35th (reorganized as the 74th) Pennsylvania Infantry, there are no German-language orders after June 1862; for the 52nd New York Infantry, the cut-off date is April 1862; in the 54th New York Infantry, Company D received two company orders in German as late as December 1863; and the 106th Ohio Infantry stopped using German orders in March 1863, but they reappeared, for no obvious reason, in February 1865. Order Books, Regimental Books, NA.

26. This sometimes resulted in sentences such as: "1. Die Zahl der Equipped & unequipped men muß der Gesamtzahl von Present for Duty gleich sein." (The number of equipped & unequipped men must be equal to the total of present for duty.) General Order No. 14, Headquarters, Blenkers Division, 20 February 1862, Order Book 35th/74th Pennsylvania Infantry, Regimental Books, NA.

and sometimes flaunting their German identity. A soldier in an all-German regiment, Sergeant Wilhelm Francksen, described his regiment's quaint housing arrangements that were meant to reflect the German sense of culture and esthetics. A little town, made up of log cabins with fireplaces and chimneys, emerged out of the Virginian wilderness. Some of the cabins were "so sweet and cute that I felt like wrapping one up and sending it to you as a knickknack." In front of the neatly built cabins there was "a porch made of green firs, cedar trees, and wild laurel with red berries, moss, and colored pebbles in front. On the inside everything was arranged cleanly and tastefully: the fireplace, the seats, the small tables."[27] A Mecklenburg-Strelitzer, who had been a sergeant in his country's tiny army and signed up three days after arriving in New York in late August 1861, describes in loving detail how his unit spent the summer and fall of 1863 in Martinsburg, Virginia, and Maryland Hights, Maryland, setting up all the ethnic amenities they desired. They first formed a singing quartet, then constructed a *Turnplatz* for gymnastic exercises, then built a hall adorned with German and American flags, beautifully decorated with all manner of objects and stocked with eight of the best German-American newspapers and magazines as well as the Leipzig *Gartenlaube* and several English (i.e., American) papers. The quartet later expanded into a regular *Gesangverein* that celebrated a *Gesangfest* and, to top it all off, a concert excursion (*Sängerfahrt*) to the battlefield of Antietam, an encounter in which the unit, the 30th Battery of the New York Light Artillery, had participated.[28]

German commanders tried to avoid the impression that their troops were just American soldiers speaking a foreign tongue. They made conscious efforts to build a uniquely German unit identity. Calling Blenker's unit *die deutsche Division* was normal usage; but, whether for the reason assumed here or for personal vanity, General Blenker issued General Order No. 31 on February 9, 1862, informing "all brigades and regiments" that "the designation of the division under my command is not the '5th Division' . . . but 'Blenkers Division' [no apostrophe]; only this designation is to be used in all written records."[29]

27. Letter dated Stafford, Virginia, 1 March 1863; Helbich and Kamphoefner, *Deutsche im Amerikanischen Bürgerkrieg*, 200–201. The regiment was the 26th Wisconsin Infantry.

28. Letter from Wilhelm Albrecht, 22 August 1864; Helbich and Kamphoefner, *Deutsche im Amerikanischen Bürgerkrieg*, 171–174.

29. The German original: "daß die Bezeichnung der unter meinem Kommando stehenden *Division* nicht '5th Division' ist, sondern . . . 'Blenkers Division' heißt und daß bei allen schriftlichen Vorlagen nur diese Bezeichnung zu gebrauchen ist." 35th/74th Pennsylvania Infantry, Order Books, Regimental Books, NA.

More than a year before Chancellorsville, General Blenker remarked that "the venom of the press and others . . . could not prevent all men of my division from keeping their spirits up," and he expresses his thanks "for this good exemplary attitude and proven good spirit of the division."[30] In a brigade order on the eve of Washington's Birthday, Colonel Henry Bohlen as commander of the Third Brigade proclaimed: "The German fighter for the preservation of the freedom and Union that Washington fought for and won will not stand back when tribute is to be paid to his memory."[31] It is hard to estimate the respective proportions of regimental esprit de corps versus German "brotherhood" in a circular signed by the commander of the "German" 45th New York Infantry, Lieutnant Colonel Dobke:

> Official information has been received from Charleston S.C. that two of our brother Officers have sacrified their lives for our adopted country while they were in Rebel prison, deprived of their liberty. Let us mourn their loss and extend our heartful sympathy to the other Officers yet waiting in Rebel prisons for a liberating hand.[32]

In a lighter vein German, or more specifically Forty-eighter or Freethinker identity appears quite clearly in the letter Captain von Hartung of the 74th Pennsylvania Infantry sent to the Rev. George H. Smith, who had applied for the Chaplain's position in the regiment. After mature deliberation, he wrote, the officers had decided "that a call for a chaplain, if made at all, should only be extended to such a divine as could take charge of the german [*sic*]

---

30. The German original: "Gehäßigkeiten der Presse und Personen konnten . . . nicht verhindern, daß alle Männer meiner *Division* ihren guten Geist bewahrten," "Dank für diese gute musterhafte Haltung und bewährten guten Geist . . . der *Division*." General Order No. 13, 21 February 1862, Order Book, Regimental Books 35th/74th Pennsylvania Infantry, NA.

31. The German original: "Der deutsche Kämpfer für die Erhaltung der von Washington erkämpften Freiheit und Union wird nicht zurückstehen, wenn seinem Andenken ein Tribut gezollt werden soll." Brigade Order No. 390, 21 February 1862, 35th/74th Pennsylvania Infantry, Order Books, Regimental Books, NA.

32. They were First Lieutenant Jacob Leidheker, who had died of disease in a hospital in Savannah on September 9, 1864, and Second Lieutenant Otto Gerson, who was said to have been killed by a guard in a military prison in Macon, Georgia, on June 12, 1864. Both had served in the 45th. OAR II, 489, lists only Jacob Leydhecker (as "missing"). But the Compiled Military Service Record of Gerson (NA) clearly indicates his service in Company A, 45th New York Infantry. The commander recommended that all the officers of the 45th wear the badge of mourning for one month. Company H Order Book, 45th New York Infantry Regimental Books, NA.

correspondence of the Rgt as well as its ethics. . . . I regret your patriotic order [*sic*] can not find a sphere of action in our midst."[33]

Innumerable details, from Prussian-looking uniforms (at the beginning of the war) to the use of Prussian drill manuals, from elaborate regimental flags to the singing of German marching (or sentimental) songs could be added to round out the picture of the conscious cultivation and preservation of a specifically German identity in the "Dutch" regiments.

The establishment of such ethnic units met several serious and some frivolous or at least questionable needs. Perhaps the most important one was that the recruits had a poor command of English. But even if they spoke English, many of them preferred being with comrades of a similar cultural background and officers whom they trusted because they were German-speaking—and German. This statement is plausible enough to be acceptable. But how strong such needs were for many can be shown by the experience of some of our letter writers who served in predominantly American regiments.

An immigrant from Baden who had arrived in 1856 wrote from a military hospital in Alexandria in 1862 that not speaking English gave him a lot of trouble. The doctors, he wrote, are all right, but not the orderlies: "If a man can't speak well they let him go to hell." A Saxon who had arrived only in late 1861 and was to die of a wound received at Shiloh just a few months later, added anger to his complaint: "If a sick man is ordered to guard duty, because the doctor cannot understand him, then you have less freedom here than the lowest Secessionist-nigger." And even a soldier as enthusiastic and well adapted as Sergeant Albert Krause mused around Christmas 1864 that he was in a foreign country amid strangers speaking a foreign language, "so that it is like music when occasionally familiar, honest, vigorous German words reach my ears."[34]

As far as close contact or friendship is concerned, even an assistant surgeon with the rank of captain mentions that he associates ("verkehre") only with Germans—German officers, that is. Ordinary German soldiers were in an even less enviable position. One of them explained that "Charles [a German friend] and I live in a rather isolated way. He is almost my only company." And another wrote that after his two German-speaking friends had left he was

---

33. Letter of 22 October 1862, 74th Pennsylvania Infantry, Order Book, Regimental Books, NA.

34. Valentin Beckler, "A German Immigrant in the Union Army: Selected Letters of Valentin Beckler," edited by Robert C. Goodell and P. A. M. Taylor, *Journal of American Studies* 4 (1970): 159. Paul Petasch, letter of 11 December 1861; Albert Krause, letter of 1 December 1864; Helbich and Kamphoefner, *Deutsche im Amerikanischen Bürgerkrieg*, 364, 276. The respective regiments were the 8th New Jersey, 55th Illinois, and 116th New York Infantries.

entirely alone and had very little contact with others. And in what appears to be the most extreme case in our collection of letters, an immigrant with long military service in Germany behind him actually deserted from a regiment he described as composed mainly of Americans and Irish (59th New York Infantry) in order to join a German artillery unit (Battery B, First Battalion, New York Light Artillery). It appears that the language problem tended to recede in American units as time went on, but the cultural distance seems to have remained unchanged. There are more letter writers who express a sense of isolation indirectly, but I consider it more significant that we find very few references to friendship, sympathy, or even occasional associations with Americans. [35]

Other reasons for creating German regiments were less significant or less crucial by comparison. American observers at the beginning of the war had hoped for particularly good fighting units that were composed of men with European military experience, and they expected that immigrants would show a greater eagerness to volunteer if "they have officers of their own nationality."[36] The argument of increasing enlistments also appealed to Germans who were interested in wide German participation in the war: Community leaders saw a chance to demonstrate their importance and to prove their patriotism while German politicians assumed that they could increase their influence through impressive recruitment figures. Still others believed that German bravery could counter and defeat nativism. At the same time German businessmen recognized how much money and publicity could be earned by equipping and servicing German regiments and finally, would-be, or alleged military experts saw a golden opportunity to further their careers and gain honor and affluence. (All of which is not meant to belittle the idealism of many politicians, officers, and recruits.)

It is also quite likely that some German immigrants enlisted in ethnic regiments in order to avoid mixing with Americans "because they feared

---

35. Dr. Carl Uterhard (119th New York Infantry), letter of 27 May 1863; Alphons Richter (56th New York Infantry), letter of 2 March 1863; Gustav Keppler (14th New York Cavalry), letter of 19 November 1864; Wilhelm Albrecht (30 Battery New York Light Artillery), letter of May 1863; Helbich and Kamphoefner, *Deutsche im Amerikanischen Bürgerkrieg*, 222, 164, 250, 167. American-born soldiers fully confirm this impression: "In more than 1,300 surviving letters by members of the 154th, not one instance of friendship with German soldiers was recorded." Dunkelman, "Hardtack and Sauerkraut ," 78.

36. See the emphatic demand for all-German units, "German Regiments," *NYT*, 10 May 1861.

nativist hostility in the ranks."[37] But any hopes of that sort were soon shattered by reality. If anything, the collective blame that fell on the Eleventh Corps may have been harder on the individual soldier than the occassional taunts—or personal isolation—in mixed units. The ethnic regiments, at least the German ones, by their pretensions and conscious efforts to be different, probably did contribute significantly to the upsurge of "anti-Dutch" feeling after Chancellorsville, as William Burton claims.[38]

In view of the "separateness" of German regiments, their deep roots in the German communities, and their constant involvement in day-to-day politicking and election campaigns, with Generals Schurz and Sigel as Republican campaign speakers representing just the tip of an iceberg, is it too far-fetched to see the German units less as American troops who happened to talk and eat differently and more as contingents of an ally fighting side by side with the Americans and under their supreme command? It would be tempting to carry this a little further, for example by pointing out that in some ways they even preferred a different "national" policy, as an ally might, leaning largely toward Forty-eighter positions.[39]

Of course, one cannot go quite that far, but a grain of truth nevertheless remains. My point is that the German regiments were very different from the others, and that because of their separateness, ethnic tensions affected them as a whole, whereas in mixed units ethnicity was more of an individual matter. In both cases, however, the common denominator is cultural differences. I do not believe that the application of the term "nativism" is appropriate for what happened during the war years, and I say this even though the upsurge of political nativism was still in everyone's, especially the immigrants' minds, and the degree of the admixture of "nativism" in party platforms had for many ethnics been the criterion for voting for one party or the other.

At least in the war context it would appear somewhat incongruous to consider the Germans innocent victims of nativism. This was a group who despised the Irish, blackmailed the president for generalships, and won high political elective office, that is, a group with a very solid economic and

---

37. Steven D. Engle, "A Raised Consciousness: Franz Sigel and German Ethnic Identity in the Civil War," *Yearbook of German-American Studies* 34 (1999): 11, and the references in n. 31, p. 17.

38. Burton, *Melting Pot Soldiers*, 101.

39. Even for an analogy to the French Foreign Legion there are some points to be made—the expatriate context, the reasons for enlistment, and the recruiting methods in the second half of the war.

political power base. And prejudice against immigrants, too, was not one-sided—the immigrants fought back, usually quite vigorously. After 1860 they had even more arms at their disposal through their contribution to the war effort than before, when they had been confined to party politics in order to advance their causes.

So rather than using the one-sided term "nativism," I would prefer to speak of pluralistic ethnic competition—for power, for money, for recognition. But of course the players in this game were not equally strong. The Anglo-Americans not only constituted a clear majority and were entrenched in the most important positions of power; the cultural standards they set were well known to all, including those who tried to defend their own, and American values were perceived as a constant challenge to all others.

III

Not only were German regiments noticeably (and often abrasively) different from their American counterparts; so, too, were German-born soldiers, even apart from their cultural peculiarities. If we look beyond the ideological reasons for fighting for their adopted country advanced by German-American leaders and the German-American press—a sense of duty and gratitude, democracy versus aristocracy, and their painful experience with German particularism[40]—to individual motivation for volunteering and fighting, a wide gap seems to open between German and American soldiers.

In a slim volume based on his Fleming Lectures, James M. McPherson set out to show "What They Fought for." Although I have reservations about his methodological approach,[41] I can accept his results as a baseline for comparison

40. Whereas the former two are expressed occasionally by our fifty-nine letter-writers, the theme of fighting for the Union because German *Kleinstaaterei* or being split up in so many mostly small states was so terrible is not mentioned even once.

41. Very briefly: 1. McPherson states that Bell Irvin Wiley, who has probably read more Civil War letters than anyone else (*Billy Yank*), found almost no statements on what the soldiers were fighting for, just before arriving at his own figure of two-thirds who did, without providing any discussion on how this huge discrepancy could be explained. 2. Terms used in the quotations below are never defined, nor the criteria marking the borderline between "simple . . . convictions" and "ideological purposes" explained. 3. Assuming that most of the reading of such a huge volume of material was done by research assistants, printing the instructions given to them would have clarified most of those questions. 4. He never presents a convincing case as to why patriotic utterances should be taken as sincere rather than empty rhetoric, though he does mention the problem. 5. Taking patriotic words out of the context of the letter writer's biography, of the specific communicative situation of letter writing, and of what the writer seemed to want to prove or apologize for and just counting them may lead to grave misinterpretations.

with the German attitudes. McPherson sums up and quantifies the contents of more than ten thousand letters: "Of 562 Union soldiers whose letters or diaries I have read, 67 percent voiced simple but strong patriotic convictions and 40 percent went further, expressing ideological purposes such as liberty and democracy."[42] Breaking these figures down, McPherson finds seventy-eight percent of officers and sixty-one percent of enlisted men expressing patriotism, and forty-nine and thirty-six percent, respectively, advancing ideological themes. In his calculations the foreign-born are included but heavily underrepresented (eight percent of the sample, but twenty-four percent of the Union army). I still use his figures as a basis of comparison with German soldiers, since the foreign-born in his sample will, unless my German letters are entirely misleading, falsify the American-born figures only downward. That is, if McPherson had left the immigrants out entirely, his percentages would most likely have been even higher. Two-thirds of McPherson's Union sample expressed strong patriotism, and four-fifths of the officers did.[43]

Of our German sample of thirty-six men in the Union military, nine were or became officers, five of them in German regiments. Seven of the officers voiced "patriotic" or even "ideological purposes" (four of the seven)[44] or 78 percent—the same proportion as the officers in McPherson's sample. A striking difference appears, however, for the enlisted men. The figure for the Americans was sixty-one (sixty-two) percent; for the Germans, it is eleven percent—three out of twenty-seven.[45] Apparently, German soldiers were far less "patriotic" than their American-born comrades. Such a discrepancy calls for an explantion.

---

42. McPherson, *What They Fought for*, 35.

43. The more comprehensive and somewhat more sophisticated later version of the book, *For Cause and Comrades: Why Men Fought in the Civil War* (New York: Oxford University Press, 1997), widens the base in general to 25,000 or 30,000 letters and diaries (183), and in particular from 562 to 647 Union soldiers and officers, but leaves the percentages largely intact: a very slight increase from sixty-one percent (soldiers) to sixty-two percent, and from seventy-eight percent (officers) to seventy-nine percent.

44. "Ideological": Brucker, Frick, Horstmann, Knoebel; "patriotic": Martens, Richter, Weinrich; indifferent or critical: Boffinger, Uterhard. Here and with the privates (twenty) and non-commissioned officers (seven) I have considered such expressions as fighting for a good cause, preserving the Union, wishing for the abolishment of slavery, defending liberty, or wanting to win the war "patriotic" or, if elaborated, "ideological."

45. Here is a detailed breakdown for the twenty-seven soldiers. "Ideological": Krause; "patriotic": Bullenhaar, Ludwig Kühner; generally positive toward the Union cause, but no expression of patriotism: G. Bauer, Penzler, Treutlein; no relevant remarks, indifferent, or disillusioned: Albrecht, Böpple, Gerstein, Heck, Heinzelmann, Keppler, Krieger, Karl Kühner, Lenz, Miller, Rossi, Ruff, Schorse, Strohsahl, Zimmermann; opposed to the Union cause or essential aspects of it: A. Dupré, Francksen, Hoffmann, Petasch, Schmalzried, Schwarting.

The simplest one would be that it is obvious for men born and raised in America, imbued with American traditions and values, to be more patriotic than foreigners without such a background, knowing little about American history, institutions, or way of life, and possibly caring even less as long as they could improve their standard of living and be rid of government interference. Perhaps they just thought the folks back home were not interested in American ideals, but many of the young men felt the need to apologize for having become a soldier or to demonstrate that they had finally become responsible and mature, and both could be achieved by explaining that they were fighting for venerable ideals. This actually occurred in several cases. Many identified more with Germany than with the Union. As a freshly promoted first lieutenant in an American regiment (56th New York Infantry) wrote in late 1862, he was healthy, full of energy, and ready to fight anytime. "But oh, with how much more feeling would I go into battle if I could draw my saber in the defense of my own Fatherland."[46] And there may have been real or imagined discrimination that made them distrustful of American ideals.

But I see another major reason. Using the letters as well as the biographical information on the writers that we have collected, I have tried to establish their reasons for enlisting. Leaving aside the officers (four of them had clearly idealistic—"patriotic"—reasons for enlisting, the motive of four others is unknown, and the German surgeon who traveled to America in order to gain professional experience is in a category of his own), we are left with twenty-seven enlisted men. Two of them volunteered for idealistic reasons; two were drafted, one of them deserting after four days; two volunteered to evade the draft; and the reasons for enlistment are unknown for eight.[47] Four probably had economic reasons and nine clearly chose the military because they could find no other work or because they found the pay attractive.[48] The case of Gustav Keppler is representative. Debts and the bankruptcy of his employee caused him to join the Union Army, not patriotism: "I did not enlist until I saw no other way out." Or August Strohsahl, who could not find employment on a ship in San Francisco and could get no work on land either, "so I had no

---

46. Alphons Richter, letter of 11 October 1862; Helbich and Kamphoefner, *Deutsche im Amerikanischen Bürgerkrieg*, 163.

47. Krause and Miller; Lenz and the bounty-jumper Schwarting; Gerstein and Ruff; W. Albrecht, Bauer, Bullenhaar, Krieger, Karl Kühner, Penzler, Rossi, Schorse.

48. Francksen, Heck, Heinzelmann, Miller; Böpple, A. Dupré, Hoffmann, Keppler, Petasch, Schmalzried, Strohsahl, Treutlein, Zimmermann.

choice but to become a soldier."[49] If we add the four "probables" and just three of the seven "unknown," thus arriving at sixteen, over half of the soldiers in our sample enlisted either as a last resort or because they considered military wages decent. If one remembers that military service in Germany was a particularly hateful institution among most common people, and that actually two (possibly three) of our letter writers had emigrated mainly to avoid it, it should be clear how very bad off an immigrant had to be in order to take that step. On the grounds of simple plausibility I claim that people who have no alternative to manual labor and who cannot find any work at all, and who also have a very different cultural background and know little about America, would be rather unlikely to write declarations of American patriotism to their families in Germany. Or to put it bluntly: They did not know "what they were fighting for" beyond their pay, their survival, and a vague hope for recognition and advancement in American society.

While we have to abandon the comparison with McPherson's tabulations here, our twenty-three male civilian letter writers, all of military age, seem to confirm the impression left by the German soldiers. None of them reports himself in financial straits or out of a job. Four letter writers remained indifferent, but nine were highly critical of, or flatly opposed to the war and Union policy.[50] On the other hand, five showed pro-Northern sympathies and another five even voiced "patriotic" feelings. This seems to leave us with about as many war supporters as opponents.

While it is entirely unsurprising that critics of the war did their utmost to escape military service, with at least one of them buying a substitute (E. Dupré), there is less consistency in the case of the verbal sympathizer who contrives to avoid conscription on a technicality of residence and another who goes so far as to escape the draft by fleeing to another state. What seems to render the value of these verbal professions even more doubtful is that the other three sympathizers and all five of the verbal patriots flatly refused to volunteer and did their best to evade the draft.[51]

Although the situations of soldiers and civilians are too different to allow direct comparison, the fact that patriotic statements in our civilian sample are

---

49. Letter of 28 July 1864; letter of 4 November 1864; Helbich and Kamphoefner, *Deutsche im Amerikanischen Bürgerkrieg*, 247, 286.

50. O. Albrecht, Buschmann, Leclerc, Odensaß; Boensel, Dünnebacke, E. Dupré, Härring, Hermanns, Monn, Pack, J. Wesslau, K. Wesslau.

51. Klausmeyer, Müller, Herbst, Heubach, Kessler; Augustin, Barthel, Dieden, Klein, Nagel.

unrelated to a personal readiness to risk one's life might provoke some second thoughts about the significance of soldiers' affirmations of patriotism. On the other hand, the civilians' response to the war seems fully understandable. Who would expect the average immigrant embarking on a new, better life to rush to the colors, and foreign ones at that? He may quickly pick up sympathies, opinions, even convictions, but it is a giant step from there to risking one's own life.[52]

It is both complicated and unnecessary to establish the "representativeness" of our thirty-six military letter writers. Looking at McPherson's statistics and my own, it seems clear that some degree of difference could change a couple of percentage points in either direction, but not significantly reduce the astounding factor of five that marks the difference between German-born and American-born enlisted men: "Patriotic feelings" expressed by eleven percent of the former, but sixty-one (sixty-two) percent of the latter. Quite clearly, "patriotism" was an aspect that set German and American soldiers apart. It is impressive if six out of ten American-born enlisted men "knew what they were fighting for"; it may not be surprising, but worth noting that hardly more than one out of ten Germans did.

IV

The impact of ethnic tensions and the incidence of ethnic controversy in the Union army are documented far better than instances of ethnic harmony. This may be so because clashes are more newsworthy, easier to exploit, or more open to emotional identification than bland good feelings. It may also be that there was in fact more strife than understanding.

I am aware of four major types of sources for elucidating the role of ethnicity in the Union Army: newspapers; letters; military orders, reports, and correspondence;[53] and court-martial records. All four have the same

---

52. It might be revealing to look at "the other side of the coin," meaning the German immigrants' view of political and social conditions in Germany. A considerable number of the letter writers considered here also figure in Walter Kamphoefner's "'Auch unser Deutschland muss einmal frei werden:' The Immigrant Civil War Experience as a Mirror on Political Conditions in Germany," in *Transatlantic Images and Perceptions: Germany and America since 1776*, edited by David E. Barclay and Elisabeth Glaser-Schmidt (Cambridge/New York: Cambridge University Press, 1997), 87–107. He also treats the development of immigrant politics and religion on the American side.

53. An example that is both touching and revealing is a letter of 21 October 1861 from Colonel Schimmelfennig, commanding the "entirely German" 35th (later 74th) Pennsylvania Infantry, to Brigadier General Blenker. He explains that his best company, Company A, had been detailed

massive disadvantage that their bulk is so large that a representative sample is extremely difficult to achieve, making quantitative insights almost impossible to reach. Among these sources I find the military court proceedings to be the most fascinating and probably the most reliable material. They are fascinating not only because of the human (and social) interest angle, but also because of the intricacy of the proceedings, making their interpretation difficult.[54] On the other hand, the material from these proceedings is reliable because it is the only source in which two sides—the prosecutor and the defense—are heard, and relevant details are unearthed in cross-examination.

Going through some of these files confirms that whatever interethnic trouble existed, German regiments also suffered from bitter intra-ethnic strife. One case concerned the charge that Captain Krauseneck had misbehaved in battle—hiding from enemy fire behind trees, behind a brick house, and lying on the ground. In his defense Krauseneck claimed that "the Colonel [von Hartung] bears me long time a grudge, and the officers having witnessed against me, had been placed under arrest during my command and wreaking revenge. . . . The actual cause of charges is to keep me out of promotion, now having been my turn."[55] Similarly, Colonel Robert J. Betge, commander of the 168th New York Infantry, confronted with no less than twelve specifications of the charge of "conduct unbecoming an officer and gentleman," discredited the whole list as "fabrications of Lieutenants Volkshausen and Leibuscher"— successfully: a verdict was returned of "not guilty."

---

to Fort Delaware for earth works, and that he wants them to rejoin the regiment: "The Company complains bitterly of the treatment they receive in the Fort, being called the 'Cheese Company' etc. . . . and kept almost constantly employed in making hay, instead of drilling." Letter Books, Regimental Books, 35th/74th Pennsylvania Infantry, NA.

54. Incidentally, a pattern emerges of how the politicization of the war extended even to the municipal level: In many cases an officer's sentence of dishonorable discharge was followed by a petition to the president from residents of his home town for commutation to honorable discharge or at least permission to resign, which was frequently granted. One example is the trial of Captain Krauseneck, 74th Pennsylvania Infantry, with attached documents, 1–3 February 1864, RG 94, box 588 No P–2935 VS 1864, NA.

55. In his twelve-page deposition, the accused pointed out that on September 25, 1862, his regiment refused to follow marching orders because they had not been paid. Brigadier Schimmelfennig appeared, told the commanding officer (Major von Hartung) "you are unable to command the regiment," and rode off. At that moment the major took off his sword and flung it to the ground. All the other officers did the same, making a pile of swords, with the exception of one lieutenant, now captain—the accused—"who tried once more to get his men for the march, but with the words 'throw him out, we won[']t be regulars,'" they refused. He sums up that he was the only officer "who has not disgraced himself." To no avail. The verdict was "guilty," the sentence "dishonorable discharge."

The Betge trial also casts significant light on inter-ethnic relations. In his deposition the accused explained that one Simon, quartermaster of his regiment, had resigned in early October 1861, and that six weeks later Betge was informed that Simon had sold four hundred pairs of shoes, government property, to a German merchant in Washington.[56] He had Simon arrested. The deposition continued:

> Simon had been of great assistance to me in raising the Regiment—he was a German. The German name had already begun to suffer reproach upon those grounds, I was desirous if the Government could be made secure [i.e., be repaid], to stop the prosecution, and thus avoid further Exposures and discredit to the German name.[57]

Ethnic slurs, usually combined with some more substantial violation of the military code, occur in many trials. One of two charges against Private Constantine McJulien of Company C, 119th New York Infantry accused him of "offering violence to his superior," and one specified that he had called a comrade a "son-of-a-bitch," was reprimanded by Second Lieutenant Kolomb, whereupon "he called said Lieutenant Kolomb a damed [*sic*] Dutchman" and picked up a rock. The officer struck him with his sheathed sword, drew it, and the private dropped the rock. The sentence was two months of hard labor without pay.[58]

The numerous proceedings against marauding soldiers offer occasional glimpses into ethnic relations, the multiple uses of "patriotism," and moral standards.[59] Quite frequently, language was mentioned or played a role in trials involving German-speaking soldiers, usually as a more or less complicating factor. Private Frederick Riegel, Company G, 45th New York Infantry, accused

---

56. The buyer was a young merchant from Braunschweig, Emile Dupré, who amassed considerable wealth through selling provisions and luxuries to (mostly German) officers. He was also a prolific writer of letters, selections of which are published in Helbich and Kamphoefner, *Deutsche im Amerikanischen Bürgerkrieg*, 104–123.

57. Betge Court Martial, 23 December 1861—14 February 1862, RG 153, CRR, 4W4–4–3, Case File KKK 407, NA.

58. RG 153, Judge Advocate General: Court Martials, NN 131, NA.

59. It seems worth noting that two privates from a German battery (1st New York Artillery) took along a black servant on an excursion to "steal, plunder, and destroy" in a Virginia farm house (two of them also raped a black woman), and that in their deposition they probably saw an extenuating circumstance in the words "L. P. Trost said now I have found one of them god dam sec. House then he asked for Arms." Trial of 21 July 1862 (Lewis P. Trost, Lewis Sorg, Jeremy M. Spades), RG 153, Court Martial Case Files, KK 206–KK 210, box 349, NA.

of using disrespectful language and incitement to mutiny, may owe his sentence of "not guilty" in part to the testimony of his company's first sergeant: "As for what was said between them, I don't know, as I don't understand German." On the other hand, the prosecutor seems to have wanted to give Private Herman Koester, 27th Pennsylvania Infantry, accused of desertion, a chance when he asked if the Articles of War had been read and explained to the prisoner. But his captain P. A. Mc Aloon stated that this had been done "almost every Sunday . . . both in English and German."[60]

The person who took the minutes of the proceedings, almost always American-born, frequently took delight in being particularly pedantic about recording an immigrant's nonstandard English, like [Question of the accused] "How was you dressed when you ordered Col. Knobelsdorff under arrest[?]" Considerably more significant is the pattern that in cases involving both Americans and Germans, the witnesses almost always took the side of their ethnic compatriot.[61]

The rather complicated court martial proceedings against Colonel Charles Knobelsdorff, 44th Illinois Infantry, offer another example of this, but they are even more revealing in several other respects. Though there was conflicting testimony on a number of details, the basic facts that occasioned the trial are quite clear. On August 7, 1862, Captain Charles M. Barnett, Battery I, 2nd Illinois Artillery, had ordered Private Andrew Hogan of this battery to be gagged with a piece of wood and hung up by his hands for striking a superior.[62] Several hundred soldiers—from Barnett's battery as well as from Knobelsdorff's 44th whose camp was directly adjoining—thereupon assembled and demanded that the man be untied, threatening violence unless he was.

---

60. Riegel Court Martial, 26 July 1862, printed version in General Orders No 15, Headquarters First Corps, Army of Virginia [Commander: Major General F. Sigel] and original, RG 153. Koester Trial, same date, printed and original, General Orders No 15, Headquarters First Corps, Army of Virginia, NA. For two other instances of the role of language in court martial proceedings, see Catherine Catalfamo, "The Thorny Rose: The Americanization of an Urban, Immigrant, Working Class Regiment in the Civil War: A Social History of Garibaldi Guard: 1861–1864," (Diss. phil., University of Texas, August 1989), 128–135.

61. One example is the case presented by Catalfamo, "Thorny Rose," 130–131. There are many others.

62. Knobelsdorff claimed that Barnett was "accustomed to punish his men by tieing [sic] them up in a most cruel manner." (Report to General Granger, 7 August.) He also stated that in Hogan's case this was done "in a most cruel and inhuman manner, thereby endangering the life of said soldier." ("Charges and Specifications against Barnett," preferred by Knobelsdorff, undated, but mentioned as forthcoming in the Report of 7 August.)

Barnett then sent for Knobelsdorff—to disperse the men of his regiment, he said, whereas the colonel claimed that he sent "to me for assistance to quell the riot." When Knobelsdorff arrived, the men from his regiment cheered; then he ordered them to go to their quarters and directed Barnett to untie the man. This the captain refused to do, claiming his unit was detached from the brigade, and he was therefore not under the colonel's command, nor did the latter have a right to disperse the men from the battery; Knobelsdorff claimed that Captain Barnett did so "in a loud and violent manner . . . before the assembled crowd." An artillery lieutenant finally untied Hogan, an armed guard took him to the guard house of the 44th, and the men dispersed.

On the same day Knobelsdorff reported the incident to General Granger, the division commander, demanding Barnett's arrest. The latter chose to press charges against Knobelsdorff. In the trial, which was demanded by General Granger, the incident supplied the basis for two charges—"aiding and abetting mutiny and sedition" and "conduct prejudicial to good order and military discipline," with the following specifications: forcing the captain to untie the prisoner, dispersing the men of Barnett's battery against his protests, allowing the men from the regiment to enter the artillery camp, not dispersing them promptly, and taking away the prisoner.[63]

---

63. There were two other charges against Knobelsdorff. "Conduct unbecoming an officer and a gentleman" was still directly connected with the Hogan affair: On August 9 the colonel asked Captain Barnett to take the prisoner back in his care, which Barnett refused, unless by order of General Granger. On August 10 Knobelsdorff requested such an order from the general, writing that he had put him in the 44th Illinois Guard House "at the request of Capt. Barnett." This phrase was charged to be "false and wholly untrue." With regard to this charge and specification seven members of the court of nine officers plus the judge advocate, including the only general (Stanley) and the only German, Colonel Friedrich Schaefer of the Second Wisconsin Infantry, expressed their belief that the accused had acted under a misapprehension rather than with intention to state the untruth, and recommended him to the "favorable consideration of the receiving officer." The other charge, with two specifications, was "disobedience of orders." One instance was still related to the above. In an excited quarrel between the general and the colonel, both of whom claimed to be sick and felt that the other wanted to humiliate him in front of numerous witnesses, Granger placed Knobelsdorff under arrest and ordered him to remove his tent to the encampment of the provost marshall. This he refused to do, but he did assert that he would consider himself under arrest before walking off. The general called, then ordered him back, but Knobelsdorff countered that if he wanted to give him an order, he should put his sword on: "I am an officer."

The other specification concerned Sergeant John Weppert and Private John O'Neil of Company K in Knobelsdorff's regiment. The colonel received an order from the general: "The above named men to be confined and charges preferred against them" (3 August). Four days later Knobelsdorff replied that Granger should order the officer who arrested them to prefer charges against them. He continued: "As I am informed Sergt. John Weppert has been punished already by your order by tying him to a tree for six hours."

In the interrogation there were some revealing questions and answers—the latter all given by Captain Barnett. The court inquired about Hogan: "Was he a German?" Answer: "No, an Irishman." Asked whether "there had been any previous difficulty between you and the accused?" Barnett replied no, not recently, "but there had been difficulty." Knobelsdorff asked if Hogan had been court-martialed before being tied up; he had not. The accused also wanted to get a reply from the captain to "Did you not say 'we are now under another General who will fix you!'" Answer: "I said 'we are now under another General. I will appeal to him.'" The previous general had been Franz Sigel.[64] The sentence read that Knobelsdorff "be dismissed the service of the United States." General Rosecranz found

> in the testimony before the Court evidence of a disposition on the part of Col. Knobelsdorf to make his own feelings the standard of duty. As such a disposition is wholly inconsistent with the duties of a soldier the Genl commanding approves the findings and sentence subject to the confirmation the [*sic*] Department Commander.

It all looks like a classic case of West Point[65] versus foreign officer,[66] and it probably was. The majority of the court pleaded extenuating circumstances on one charge; one of the insubordination specifications involving stolen sheep appears fairly ridiculous, and the other was clearly brought about by Knobelsdorff's exasperation that he and not Barnett had been put under arrest. The untying of Hogan rather obviously resulted from a humane impulse against cruel punishment (and without a trial at that). Thus it is hard to find justification for cashiering an officer who had considerable experience and merits and was popular with the men of his regiment unless, that is, regulations were narrowly and rigidly applied to put an end to a long-smoldering conflict, for whose existence there are clear indications, and to leave no doubt that

---

64. Frederick H. Dyer, ed., *Compendium of the War of the Rebellion* (Dayton, OH: Morningside Bookshop, 1978), 478, 541. In his plea to the Court, the accused pointedly stated that "for the last eight months I have been in command of different Brigades under Generals Sigel & Asboth" and that he was confident of "having always enjoyed the confidence and respect of my superiors." Brigadier General Alexander Asboth was an immigrant (1851) from Hungary. Ezra J. Warner, *Generals in Blue: Lives of the Union Commanders* (Baton Rouge: Louisiana State University Press, 1964), 11.

65. Gordon Granger graduated with the class of 1845, William Rosecranz in 1842. Warner, *Generals in Blue*, 181, 410.

66. Von Knobelsdorff had been a Prussian officer. Kaufmann, *Die Deutschen*, 520.

American professional military standards took precedence over European or Forty-eighter humane considerations.

V

Peter Klein, a young coal miner from the Saar region who had plied his trade in Pennsylvania for a while but now applied his skills to goldmining in California, evinced clearly patriotic feelings enhanced by personal identification with the Union cause:

> The war or rather the rebellion was started by the slave owners, to overthrow the free constitution of the country and to set up a government by the nobility. These slave owners . . . now want to enslave the free white workers, so that the black workers don't take the whites as an example and want to be free too. . . . And we, free men and honest workers, we don't want to put up with that and want to keep the good and free constitution. And with God's help we will win.

But he continued:

> For us Germans, this war is very good, for since the Germans have shown themselves to be the keenest defenders of the Constitution, and provide entire regiments of the best and bravest soldiers and officers, they're starting to earn the respect of the native Americans. Now the Americans don't make fun of us anymore since they know that we are the mainstay of their country and their freedom.[67]

In other words: a just and noble war with an extra dividend for the brave Germans.

---

67. He must have picked up all that in conversation, for he was at least a functional illiterate who always found a compatriot to pen his letters. Letter of 18 August 1861. Walter D. Kamphoefner, Wolfgang Helbich, and Ulrike Sommer, eds., *News from the Land of Freedom: German Immigrants Write Home* (Ithaca: Cornell University Press, 1991), 402–403. For the German original see Helbich, Kamphoefner, and Sommer, *Briefe*, 381.

In a similar vein *The New York Times* explained that German immigrants

find themselves again in the old contest which has so long been waging in Europe—the struggle between a privileged aristocracy and those who defend the rights of man. . . . These experiences of the noble patriotism of our foreign-born citizens, during this revolution, have scattered many presumptuous theories. . . . All 'nativism'—all proscription of foreigners is forever broken up.[68]

Fifteen months later, the *Times* combined an implicit apology for its defamation of the 11th Corps at Chancellorsville with an elaboration on the demise of nativism:

One of the grand results of this war is to be the assimilation of all American blood, from whatever source. . . . [The immigrants'] active service under the flag of the Union, their fighting side by side with the descendants of those who laid the foundation of the Republic, will do more to Americanize them and their children than could have been effected in a whole generation of peaceful living. . . . The war will prove itself a wonderful school for instilling American ideas, sentiments, sympathies, and convictions, and for unlearning a great deal that has been brought over from the old world by those immigrants both to their and to our disadvantage.[69]

Many historians have taken for granted that the hopes of the immigrant in California and the expectations of the journalists on the East Coast were fulfilled. Even a scholar as knowledgeable and measured as John Higham got carried away: "The war completed the ruin of organized nativism by absorbing xenophobes and immigrants in a common cause. Now the foreigner had a new prestige; he was a comrade at arms. The clash that alienated sections reconciled their component nationalities."[70]

Are Higham and *The New York Times* correct? Should the war be seen as an accelerated melting pot, as a blast furnace that burned out nativism, as a

---

68. "The German Loyalists," *NYT*, 16 March 1862.

69. "The Germans in Hooker's Battles—The National Spirit of Our Adopted Citizens," *NYT*, 4 June 1863.

70. John Higham, *Strangers in the Land: Patterns of American Nativism, 1860–1925* (New York: Atheneum, 1963), 13.

firestorm of blood and iron that cleansed the nation of ethnic tensions, or a mighty agent of "Americanization"? Any answer, of course, largely depends on definitions.

A number of points may be conceded right away. Political nativism as known in the 1850s declined drastically—though hardly because of the common fighting experience. Tens of thousands of ethnic soldiers who served in American regiments must have had a better command of English at the end of their term than at the beginning, and all immigrants in uniform undoubtedly learned about American ways—though one could assume that such an acculturation might have occurred just as rapidly in civilian life and would probably have been more comprehensive. On the other hand, if the Civil War is seen as part of the secular effort to educate workers for industrial work discipline, and if one can at least partly agree with a statement like ". . . the whole concept of assimilation/Americanization has been at heart merely a subterfuge for the initiation of new working classes, particularly immigrant, into the American system of class stratification based upon the needs of corporate capitalism,"[71] then it would seem that being subjected to military discipline might in fact accelerate that process.

On the other hand, one may safely state that a general fraternization across ethnic lines simply did not take place in the Union army. While inter-ethnic friction was ruled out within purely ethnic regiments, soldiers suffered both from collective discrimination and from individual prejudice in their frequent contacts with neighboring units of different backgrounds. And in the American or mixed regiments in which at least four out of five immigrant soldiers served, instances of tension along ethnic lines abounded, well documented in the literature as well as in the sources used in this paper. Precious few examples of the opposite can be found—of benign neglect of cultural differences, tolerance of, good fellowship with, or even admiration for soldiers or officers with a different background.

But even apart from ethnic incidents or tension, whether poking fun at "the Dutch" or griping about the Yankees, it appears that the pattern of behavior in the military was remarkably similar to that of civilian life: Ethnicity played a minor role at work and in daily routine; in the army these were drills, target practice, marching, picket duty, and parades, to mention just a few that constituted a soldier's "job." But when it came to social life—whom to cook and eat with, whom to befriend and whom to visit (German officers had an

---

71. Catalfamo, "Thorny Rose," 11.

uncanny way of finding German families even in enemy country), whom to sing or talk about home with—there was an automatic clustering of soldiers of the same ethnicity, even if such clusters (often reduced by preferences of class and education) comprised only two or three individuals. And these clusters seemed more often than not to be exclusive in the sense that social contacts with outsiders were very limited or non-existent. Thus, patterns of prewar behavior seem to have continued during the war, and after the war as well, and there is no plausible reason why they should not have. Military "work" was one thing; reflecting on the horrors of war and sharing one's innermost feelings belonged to the sphere of the ethnic ingroup.

In this respect, the war produced little or no change, and it is difficult to imagine how such a change could have come about. In fact, one can make a good case for an exacerbation of ethnic tensions, that the war experience made the gap between Germans and Americans greater than it had been in peacetime. [72] But "Americanization" could mean several other things—increased identification with the United States, a loosening of the ties to the German-American community, decreased identification with Germany, and increased acceptance of ethnics by the dominant society. Unfortunately, we do not have the means to measure such processes. But the wave of Teutonic patriotism that carried away almost the entire German-American community in 1870–1871—or should one say "the triumph of the national team that made every member of the community feel more important and more respected"?—makes one wonder about the bond-cutting effect of the Civil War.[73] Similarly, there are few indications of veterans being estranged from their ethnic communities—except, of course, in such cases as that of George Hansen,

---

72. Christian B. Keller, "Germans in Civil War-era Pennsylvania: Ethnic Identity and the Problem of Americanization," (Ph.D. diss., Penn State University, 2001), passim; Engle, "Raised Consciousness," 9, 11. Yet Engle, with a rather broad construction of "assimilation," considers the heightened awareness of ethnicity and greater ethnic mobilization as a major assimilationist step in that Germans "were claiming a bigger slice of the American pie" or "acting effectively in the public sphere" (2, 9–11).

73. It is almost unnecessary to mention that such undisputedly successful German Civil War officers as August Willich volunteered (unsuccessfully) for service in the Franco-Prussian War (Burton, *Melting Pot Soldiers*, 84), or that one of our letter writers (a private in an American regiment) expressed his ardent wish that he might be able to fight the French as a German soldier (Karl Friedrich Kühner, letter of 22 October 1870, see Helbich and Kamphoefner, *Deutsche im Amerikanischen Bürgerkrieg*, 349).

when the local community was rural, Catholic, traditional, and stubbornly opposed to the war.[74]

Of our letter writers, the one who had perhaps the most successful postwar career (beginning as a technical draftsman and a sergeant in a mixed regiment and later elected city engineer of the booming city of Buffalo in the 1880s) was not only a member of the veterans' organization Grand Army of the Republic (GAR) but also of numerous German-American organizations. He obviously saw no conflict between his American social, business, and political life and his active role in the German community: On the contrary, his activities in ethnic institutions almost certainly promoted his citywide success. But perhaps more to the point is the pride and satisfaction he expressed when some German-American cultural event garnered respect or even admiration from Americans.[75] Is this not reminiscent of the military valor that supposedly earned respect for the Germans? In any case it appears reasonable to assume that when such recognition is very much appreciated, it must have been quite rare.[76]

What makes the whole question of the discrimination against, or lack of respect for Germans during and after the Civil War so strange, is that educated opinion in periodicals with a national circulation was perhaps condescending, but generally very positive about the qualities of German immigrants—before, during, and after the war.[77] This would seem to reduce the discrimination of Germans during the war largely to irrational reactions, psychological needs, and probably most importantly, resentment of cultural differences.

One criterion to measure the degree of how much these were reduced (and American patriotism fostered) during the war would appear to be GAR membership. But only at first sight. We know that ethnic soldiers including Germans were underrepresented, but not by how much.[78] We also know that

---

74. Kathleen Conzen, "Immigrant Religion and the Public Sphere: The German Catholic Milieu in America," in this volume.

75. Albert Krause, letter of 22 July 1883, see Helbich and Kamphoefner, *Deutsche im Amerikanischen Bürgerkrieg*, 277.

76. The theme of respect on the basis of ethnic achievement is widespread in German immigrant letters of the last third of the nineteenth century.

77. See the excerpts from *Christian Examiner* (1851), *North American Review* (1856), *Atlantic Monthly* (1867, 1873, 1896) in Helbich, *Alle Menschen*, 126–136.

78. Stuart McConnell, *Glorious Contentment: The Grand Army of the Republic, 1865–1900* (Chapel Hill, London: University of North Carolina Press, 1992), 71, 222.

numerous posts were predominantly German.[79] What we do not know is how many German veterans did not join because they felt discriminated against, because they did not feel at ease in an American organization, or because they simply did not care. (After all, by 1890 only about one-third of surviving veterans were GAR members.)[80] We know that three (possibly more) of our letter writers joined the GAR—an officer in a German regiment, a sergeant in a mixed one, and a private in an American regiment.

A final look at our thirty-six military letter writers might make the discussion of "Americanization" more concrete. Nine of them died of their wounds or from disease, and three were permanently crippled. Of the twenty-four who survived the war with their health more or less intact, two were elected into their state legislatures, Indiana and Missouri, though Dr. Brucker of Troy, Indiana, had already served there before becoming a surgeon. Six veterans became farmers (as most of them had been before the war); six worked in the retail trade, as craftsmen or as professionals (Brucker and Krause); and Dr. Uterhard returned to Germany (to use his battlefield experience there in the wars of 1866 and 1870–1871), and of the fate of four we know nothing. For most of the above who had more or less prosperous and at least respectable careers after the war, it can be said that they did not start something new after mustering out but had already trained for or practiced their postwar occupation before enlisting. It is not obvious but cannot be discounted that the "Americanization" experience of wartime service was helpful in their civilian careers. Seven others seem to have gained nothing whatsoever from "Americanization," however that may be defined. They—five privates in American and German units, but also two officers in American regiments—were never able to organize their lives and did not escape poverty and social marginality.[81] Of course, one cannot simply discount individual circumstances or differences in ability and ambition, but the fact that the American Dream remained an empty promise for almost one-third of the men in our sample should at least caution against considering the "Americanization" of immigrant veterans a generally successful introduction into mainstream America.

Virtually all aspects discussed in this paper could be presented, analyzed, and interpreted in far more detail. The large bodies of sources mentioned as well as an awe-inspiring mass of printed material might be consulted

---

79. McConnell, *Contentment*, 55.

80. McConnell, *Contentment*, 54.

81. Boffinger, Gerstein (?), Heck, Heinzelmann, Richter, Rossi, Treutlein.

and incorporated. This would probably confirm the impressions I have tried to convey, but even a massive amount of further work would still result in just that—impressions. The nature of the themes I have dealt with simply does not allow clear-cut proof, convincing quantification, or meaningful generalization.

What I have tried to do instead is to offer some glimpses at the role of (mainly German) ethnicity in the Civil War, which is the result of my attempt to understand how some fifty German immigrants, whose letters have been preserved, experienced the Civil War of their "adopted country." For the thirty-six soldiers in particular, their motives for volunteering and fighting, their unshakable faith in the superiority of the German military and its chance to gain "acceptance" by feats of arms, the role of their cultural background in their military and social lives, the degree of their identification with American patriotism were my major points of departure.

My strongest impression gained in this less than systematic process is that ethnicity in various forms, no doubt often based on hearsay prejudice, but mainly in the shape of perceived, experienced, and mostly resented cultural differences, played a major and often underestimated role in the U.S. military. Since I found no indication that it decreased toward the end of the war, I cannot help but wonder about the meaning of the famous "Americanization" that is supposed to have taken place. As a matter of fact, there are indications that for some immigrants the reverse may have occurred, at least as far as patriotism and identification with America are concerned.

Friedrich Schmalzried had spent twelve years in the United States, close to several relatives in a German-American milieu in rural Michigan, when he enlisted in the predominantly American First Michigan Cavalry in August 1861. During his first year of service, his letters sounded quite happy about his work, his pay, and the respect he enjoyed among his comrades. But in early 1863 he seemed to have changed his mind:

> If I am lucky enough to get home, I will perhaps go to Germany. I do not want to become a Yankee, for it is not a very proud name to be a Yankee. They do not have many good sides. . . . My horse is black and has three white trammels. He will be six years next spring. . . . I like him because he is German through and through and does not love the

Yankees either. When one gets too close to him, he kicks him with his long hind legs.[82]

---

82.   Friedrich Schmalzried, letter of 31 January 1863; for the German original see Helbich and Kamphoefner, *Deutsche im Amerikanischen Bürgerkrieg*, 154. Five months later the writer died of disease in Mount Pleasant Military Hospital, Washington, DC.

12

Reviving Ethnic Identity: Foreign Office, Reichswehr, and German Americans during the Weimar Republic

Michael Wala

When the First World War ended in 1918, there were not that many people still alive who had lived through the Civil War. Nonetheless, the supposedly outstanding military service by German Americans during that conflict ranged high in the self-image of Americans of German descent as proof of their willingness to sacrifice for their adopted country. It had become an accepted and highly respectable part of their German-American heritage. However, German-American associations, the *Vereine*, had in the intervening period mostly worked to preserve an ethnic consciousness based more on a shared cultural heritage than on a common military or political background. These sociocultural organizations helped counter the increasing de-ethnicization consequent to the loss of language skills among second and third generation German Americans. They served to preserve ethnic German culture and identity, and, additionally, were often perceived as the nucleus of political representation for the ethnic group as a whole.[1] When the United States entered World War I in 1917, the links binding many German Americans to Imperial Germany were severed. Most of the once flourishing German *Vereinswesen* did not survive the war structurally intact, despite some claims to the contrary.[2] And the military skills of German Americans, once proudly displayed as an asset that helped preserve the Union, now were likely to be perceived as part of their militaristic German heritage, a German trait

---

1. See Reinhard R. Doerries, *Iren und Deutsche in der Neuen Welt: Akkulturationsprozesse in der amerikanischen Gesellschaft im späten 19. Jahrhundert* (Stuttgart: Steiner, 1986), 201, 203 and Reinhard R. Doerries, "Organization and Ethnicity: The German-American Experience," *Amerikastudien* 33 (1988): 313. The number of German-American organizations before 1917 was quite large. The 1916/1917 issue of the directory of German-American organizations published by the German American Directory Publishing Company, Milwaukee, Wisconsin, contains more than three hundred pages of listings.

2. See, for example, Theodore Huebner, *The Germans in America* (New York: Chilton, 1962), 153.

that supposedly had drawn the country into a conflict that had cost tens of thousands of American lives.

The United States had been a rather "reluctant belligerent" in World War I, being forced by German decisions to enter a war it did not really want to fight. Nonetheless, the United States and Germany had not been bitter, unrelenting enemies, and after the war the United States had no particular motivation to prevent Germany from regaining its economic, political, and military potential in Europe. On the contrary, American policy makers were interested in a viable, politically stable, democratic, and capitalist Germany in a region they believed to be threatened by Bolshevism. As the economically and politically most powerful nation emerging from the battlefields of Europe, the United States was thus soon perceived by German politicians and officials as the only potential ally for their ambitions to bring about a quick political and economic rehabilitation.

The terms of the Treaty of Versailles drastically curtailed the new republic's freedom of action, checking its aspirations for a swift restoration as an important power. Thus, revision of Versailles became of pivotal importance for German foreign policy and soon was almost an obsession among many politicians and officers of the German Foreign Office, the Auswärtiges Amt. Every strategy that would help Germany reach this goal was scrutinized, every potential resource contemplated. The German foreign office paid tribute to the changed situation after World War I not only in its political strategies but also in its structural setup. During the Schülersche Reform in 1920,[3] a new department—the Abteilung für Deutschtum im Ausland und kulturelle Angelegenheiten (Department for Ethnic Germans Abroad and Cultural Affairs)—was established, designed to compensate for the traditional means of international representation (particularly the army and navy) unavailable to Germany because of Versailles. The Culture Department, as it was soon called, was to promote German art and science abroad, foster academic exchange, and support German schools in foreign countries. Its main task, however, was to help strengthen the ties of German emigrants and their offspring to the "fatherland."[4]

---

3.   See Kurt Doß, *Das Auswärtige Amt im Übergang vom Kaiserreich zur Weimarer Republik: Die Schülersche Reform* (Düsseldorf: Droste, 1977).

4.   For the establishment of Abteilung VI, Kulturpolitik see Kurt Düwell, *Deutschlands auswärtige Kulturpolitik, 1918–1932: Grundlinien und Dokumente* (Köln: Böhlau, 1976) and Manfred Abelein, *Die Kulturpolitik des Deutschen Reiches und der Bundesrepublik Deutschland: Ihre verfassungsgeschichtliche Entwicklung und ihre verfassungsrechtlichen Probleme* (Köln:

It was no coincidence that this task also fell to what remained of Germany's military forces. The Wehrgesetz (Defense Law) of March 23, 1921, charged the Reichsmarine with "preserving the bonds between Germans and their descendants abroad and their brethren in Germany" in the event that German navy vessels would visit foreign harbors.[5] When in the mid-1920s German training cruisers again began to fly the German flag across the seven seas, Reichswehr and Auswärtiges Amt cooperated closely to plan the ships' journeys. Despite constant animosities between diplomats and the Reichswehr during the Weimar period, the navy was open even to last-minute requests by the Auswärtiges Amt for calls on harbors where it believed a visit of a German man-of-war would strengthen the German community or support the goals of German diplomacy.[6] Because these voyages were more of a political than military nature, it did not matter much that the German navy only had small, old vessels such as the *Berlin* and the *Hamburg*, until the cruiser *Emden* was put into service in 1925 and the *Karlsruhe* was commissioned in 1929.[7]

Westdeutscher Verlag, 1968), 113–130. The scholarly literature on German-American cultural diplomacy and cultural relations during the Weimar period is somewhat disappointing. See, for example, Wolfgang Dexheimer, "Die deutsch-amerikanischen Kulturbeziehungen seit den zwanziger Jahren," in *Deutsche auswärtige Kulturpolitik seit 1871: Geschichte und Struktur,* edited by Kurt Düwell and Werner Link (Köln: Böhlau, 1981), 126–140. One of the few solidly based studies is Franziska von Ungern-Sternberg, *Kulturpolitik zwischen den Kontinenten, Deutschland und Amerika: Das Germanische Museum in Cambridge/Mass.* (Köln: Böhlau, 1994).

5. See Rolf Güth, *Die Marine des deutschen Reiches 1919–1939* (Frankfurt/M.: Bernard und Graefe, 1972), 50. This and all subsequent German quotes were translated by the author.

6. Before the cruiser *Emden* sailed for North America in the winter of 1928–1929, for example, the German Foreign Office asked the navy to include not only stops in Charleston, South Carolina, and Philadelphia, Pennsylvania, but as late as November 1928 it also requested visits to Galveston and Houston, Texas. Davidsen (Auswärtiges Amt [AA]) to Ges. Rat Schlimpert, 9 November 1928, Abtlg. II F–M (Militär u. Marine), "Akten betreffend: Auslandsreise des Kreuzers Emden 1926/1928 Berichte," vol. 2, R 33448, Politisches Archiv (PA) AA; Marineleitung to AA, 28 May 1929, ibid. See also the correspondence in 1924–1925 about the cruiser *Berlin's* possible stops at Veracruz, Mexico—because it was thought that the diplomatic relations between Germany and Mexico might profit from a visit; Chef der Marineleitung to Reichskanzlei, 18 October 1924, Reichskanzlei, "Akten betreffend Reichswehr," vol. 1, R43I/601, Bundesarchiv Potsdam (BA–P). See also the quite positive report by Paul Wülfing von Ditten, the *Berlin's* commandant, Abschrift, "Bericht über den Aufenthalt des Kreuzers 'Berlin' in San Juan [de Guatemala] vom 14. bis 17. II. 1925," "Geheim!" dated 23 February 1925, Po 14c, "Auslandsreisen deutscher Kriegsschiffe," Botschaft Washington, Nr. 1169 (BoWa and number), PA–AA.

7. Jost Dülffer, *Weimar, Hitler und die Marine: Reichspolitik und Flottenbau, 1920–1939* (Düsseldorf: Droste, 1973), 60–62; Werner Rahn, *Reichsmarine und Landesverteidigung 1919–1928: Konzeption und Führung der Marine in der Weimarer Republik* (München: Bernard

The United States was an obvious target for such efforts by Culture Department and Reichswehr because the large number of Americans of German descent seemed to constitute a major asset in this strategy. Between 1820 and 1914 more than five and a half million Germans had left their homes for the United States, and in 1910 close to eight million Americans—almost eight percent of the American population—claimed to be first or second generation German Americans.[8] This, in combination with longstanding academic links between the two nations, seemed to provide an extraordinary lever to influence public and elite opinion in favor of Germany.

The bungled attempts to utilize German Americans to such ends during World War I were not forgotten in Berlin. Nonetheless, the Foreign Office requested that the German consulates and the embassy in Washington, DC, report on the condition of the German-American communities almost immediately after Germany and the United States had re-established diplomatic relations in the summer of 1921.[9] The diplomats were asked to evaluate the prospects for propaganda and to suggest ways to revive German-American ethnic identity. What seemed to many officials in Berlin to be an acceptable and straightforward proposal was emphatically rejected by most German diplomats in the field. They argued that the German-American community's

---

und Graefe, 1976), 164–171; Güth, *Die Marine des deutschen Reiches*, 72–78. Admiral Paul Behnke—recalled from retirement—was made chief of the navy in 1920 and reinstituted the journeys of training vessels to foreign countries after 1922. The papers of Behnke are in the Bundesarchiv-Militärarchiv (BA–MA). For information on individual ships see Jürgen Rohwer, "Baudaten der von 1921 bis zum 31.8.1939 für die deutsche Reichs- und Kriegsmarine in Auftrag gegebenen Kriegsschiffe," appendix in Dülffer, *Weimar, Hitler und die Marine*, 570–587.

8.   The numbers are based on U.S. Census data; U.S. Department of Commerce, *Historical Statistics of the United States*, 9, 116–117. La Vern J. Rippley suggests in "Ameliorated Americanization: The Effect of World War I on German-Americans in the 1920s," vol. 2, 228 [in *America and the Germans: An Assessment of a Three-Hundert Year History*, edited by Frank Trommler and Joesph McVeigh (Philadelphia: University of Pennsylvania Press, 1985)], that after 1917 a negative attitude toward German ancestry may have led many German Americans to deny their ethnic roots. This *may* be the reason why the numbers of Americans claiming to be of German birth or descent dropped from 7.981 million in 1910 to 7.032 million in 1920. It would not explain, however, why the number of Irish Americans dropped from 4.1 million to 3.1 million between 1920 and 1930, a much steeper decline.

9.   The Foreign Office had started to look into the issue of propaganda even earlier. When in October 1920 outside demands on Foreign Minister Simons pressed for active work among the German Americans, Foreign Office personnel stated in a memorandum that the issue was being discussed, but that a decision on a program had not yet been reached. They made it clear, however, that uncoordinated propaganda was potentially dangerous. Major a. D. Guerke, E. A. Niemayer, Dr. Carl Arnold to Simons, 28 October 1920, Abtlg. III, "Akten betreffend: Deutschtum in den Vereinigten Staaten von Amerika," vol. 1, R 80287, PA–AA; Gronow and Erckert, "Aufzeichnung," dated 3 November 1920, ibid.

direct influence on domestic politics was rather insignificant, a condition that was even more obvious in the area of foreign relations. This was not likely to change within the very near future, not even through overt propaganda efforts. In a March 1922 memorandum, the German consul general in Chicago, Rudolf Steinbach, argued that the German-American community should nonetheless be cultivated. This would help to foster a generally positive attitude toward postwar Germany. Outright support for Weimar Germany could be expected only after German Americans had regained their self-respect. This should not be promoted by propaganda, however, but rather by more subtle attempts to rekindle their pride in their ancestry.[10] After World War I, many *Vereine* had ceased to exist, their membership scattered, German Houses deserted. Attempts by prominent German Americans to revive prewar organizations or to establish similar ones anew succeeded only in a few cases. Most efforts to create larger associations intended to focus the political voice of German-Americans did not succeed and were, in fact, regarded as potentially dangerous by Weimar diplomats.[11]

In 1919 when the Steuben Society of America was established in New York, its founders believed that it was necessary to set up their organization as a secret society. This indicates how precarious it was to revive German-American political organizations during this period.[12] A year earlier in Chicago, the German-American Citizens' League (Deutsch-Amerikanischer

---

10. [Dr. Rudolf Oskar] Steinbach [Consul General Chicago] to Botschaft Washington, 21 March 1922, Nachrichten-Abteilung, "Akten betreffend: Maßnahmen zur Hebung des deutschen Ansehens in den Vereinigten Staaten," P 16, vol. 1, R 121325, PA–AA. Consul General Lang, who was chargé from August 1921 until Ambassador Otto Wiedfeldt arrived in 1922, was even more cautious. He could not invite prominent German Americans to the embassy because the furniture did not arrive from Germany until the spring of 1922, but he declined to meet with them in public places, preferring to forego the chance to make important contacts rather than run the risk of attracting unwanted attention; see Generalkonsul Lang to AA, 20 April 1922, Po 2, vol. 1, Archive of the German Embassy at Washington, DC, filmed by the American Historical Association, microfilm T 290, reel 2, National Archives (NA). For a short biography see Frank Lambach, *Our Men in Washington: From the First Prussian Minister Resident to the Ambassadors of the Federal Republic of Germany* ([Bonn: Auswärtiges Amt,] 1976).

11. Barbara Wiedemann-Citera, *Die Auswirkungen des Ersten Weltkrieges auf die Deutsch-Amerikaner im Spiegel der New Yorker Staatszeitung, der New Yorker Volkszeitung und der New York Times, 1914–1926* (Frankfurt/M.: Lang, 1993), writes that this process was completed in 1926 (173). It seems that it had actually only begun at that time and was still not finished when Hitler's rise to power and the consequent decline of German-American relations again shattered all hopes for a revival of German America.

12. Frederick C. Luebke, *Germans in the New World* (Urbana/Chicago: University of Illinois Press, 1990), 58.

Bürgerbund) had been formed openly, developing out of the remnants of the Chicago chapter of the German National Alliance (Deutscher National-Bund), an organization prohibited during the war. An umbrella organization for 130 local groups, the Citizens' League had about twenty-five thousand members and, as the German consul general in Chicago, Dr. Sethe, put it in 1922, controlled about fifty thousand votes. According to Sethe, the organization was spreading, branching out into the Midwest and into New York, where the notorious George Sylvester Viereck headed the state chapter.[13] The League and the Steuben Society had different ambitions, which were reflected in their different language and membership policies: Whereas the League used German as its lingua franca and was also open to recent immigrants who had just applied for American citizenship, the Steuben Society used English as its language and admitted only American citizens as members.[14]

German diplomats were uneasy about these developments almost as soon as diplomatic relations were re-established. In an October 1922 report on the attitude in the United States toward Germany, the German embassy warned against the creation of "bloc movements" of German Americans such as the Citizens' League. It was understandable, the report stated, that German Americans would want to establish groups similar to those that had existed before World War I. Attention attracted by such openly pro-German organizations, however, endangered the trend in public and elite opinion toward a more sympathetic view of Germany.[15] German diplomats preferred

---

13. George Sylvester Viereck had been deeply involved in German propaganda activities during World War I, through the Press Office in New York, and he had published the magazine *The Fatherland* and other papers. See Reinhard R. Doerries, *Imperial Challenge: Ambassador Count Bernstorff and German-American Relations, 1908–1917* (Chapel Hill: University of North Carolina Press, 1989), 41–42, 52. For more information on Viereck see Niel M. Johnson, *George Sylvester Viereck: German-American Propagandist* (Urbana, IL: University of Illinois Press, 1972) and Elmer Gortz, *Odyssey of a Barbarian: The Biography of George Sylvester Viereck* (Buffalo: Prometheus Books, 1978).

14. In 1932 R. F. Leyendecker told the audience at the Erster National-Kongress der Amerikaner Deutschen Stammes that the Steuben Society's founders intended "to arouse citizens of German descent to a greater sense of their civic and political duties and rights"; R. F. Leyendecker, "The Steuben Society of America," in *Erster National-Kongress der Amerikaner Deutschen Stammes: Sitzungsberichte und Erläuterungen* (New York: Deutsch-Amerikanische Konferenz von Gross-New York, n.d. [1932]), 89. Sethe to AA, 5 August 1922, Abtlg. VI, "Akten betreffend: Die Förderung des Deutschtums im Ausland in den Vereinigten Staaten von Nordamerika," vol. 1, R 60104, PA–AA.

15. [Legationssekretär Baron] L. Plessen, ["Stimmung in den Vereinigten Staaten gegenüber Deutschland,"] 18 October 1922, attached to Otto Wiedfeldt to AA, 18 October 1922, Po 2, vol. 1, T 290, reel 2.

German-American organizations to work as essentially American organizations within the political system and society. Most of them would have agreed wholeheartedly with the statement made in an article in the *Monatshefte für deutsche Sprache und Pädagogik* by Heinrich Maurer, a professor of German Literature at Lewis College, Chicago: "We have to live for America . . . to be German for America and not for ourselves."[16]

All of Weimar Germany's ambassadors to the United States, Otto Wiedfeldt, Ago von Maltzan, and Friedrich von Prittwitz und Gaffron, favored this course.[17] In March 1923 when the pressure mounted from Germany to increase propaganda and to educate the American public on the problems of reparations and the Ruhr, Wiedfeldt warned that any form of propaganda was likely to be counterproductive. American criticism of foreign propaganda had just recently increased because of the establishment of an "Information Bureau" in the United States by the French government. "We could not but make a greater mistake than do something similar," Wiedfeldt cautioned the Foreign Office. Informal contacts with the American press and with members of the social and political elite would serve the goals of German foreign policy much better.[18]

During his service in Washington, Wiedfeldt mostly confined his contacts to what he perceived as "influential people" and did not pay particular attention to the larger German-American community.[19] This changed after his successor, Maltzan, took over. In the summer of 1925, after only a few months in office,

---

16. Heinrich Maurer, "Der Kampf um das Deutschtum in Amerika in seiner kulturgeschichtlichen Bedeutung," *Monatshefte für deutsche Sprache und Pädagogik* (yearbook 1922): 36–37, 51.

17. On Otto Wiedfeldt, the first German ambassador after World War I, see Ernst Schröder, *Otto Wiedfeldt* (Essen: Fredebeul und Koenen, 1964) and Ernst Schröder, *Otto Wiedfeldt als Politiker und Botschafter der Weimarer Republik* (Essen: Fredebeul und Koenen, 1971). Adolf Georg Otto von Maltzan Freiherr zu Wartenberg und Penzlin was ambassador from 1925 until September 1927, when he died in an airplane accident in Germany. See Gustav Stresemann, "Botschafter Ago von Maltzan zum Gedenken," *Europäische Gespräche* 5 (November 1927): 573–578. For Prittwitz, who was the only German diplomat to resign in 1933, see his memoirs, *Zwischen Petersburg und Washington: Ein Diplomatenleben* (München: Isar Verlag, 1952) and Michael Wala, *Weimar und Amerika: Botschafter Friedrich von Prittwitz und Gaffron und die deutsch-amerikanischen Beziehungen von 1927 bis 1933* (Stuttgart: Steiner, 2001).

18. Wiedfeldt to AA, 15 March 1923, Po 2, T 290, reel 2; and also in Wiedfeldt to AA, 29 April 1923, Nachrichten Abteilung, "Akten betreffend: Propaganda fremder Staaten 'Vereinigte Staaten,'" vol. 1, R 121427, PA–AA.

19. Wiedfeldt did not travel as much as Maltzan and later Prittwitz, but when he went to Detroit to visit the Ford Motor Company, he paid a visit to the prominent German American K. E. Schmidt and made an effort to meet with about thirty influential German Americans; Wiedfeldt to AA, 13 June 1923, Po2, vol. 1, T 290, reel 2.

Maltzan requested reports from the German consulates in Chicago, Seattle, and San Francisco on German-American communities.[20] The message of these reports forwarded to the Foreign Office was clear: Propaganda was not only useless but very dangerous. Most German Americans were "first and foremost Americans now and forever," but they could be encouraged to remain friends of Germany and supporters of German Kultur. The cultural ties of German Americans to Germany should be strengthened through occasional visits of German representatives, through academic exchanges, and by close contacts with the German-American press. Immediate political gains could not be attained from such efforts, but they would pay off in the long run by creating a generally more positive attitude toward Germany.[21] In Berlin, Dr. Sievers of the Kulturabteilung was thankful for the clear and straightforward analyses Maltzan had sent. They contained nothing particularly new for the Foreign Office, he wrote, but were very valuable because they shattered a number of illusions still being held by many in Germany.[22]

Despite occasional pressure to conduct more propaganda and to activate the German Americans for immediate political goals, the Foreign Office and its representatives in the United States kept to this policy until 1933. Both Maltzan and his successor Prittwitz were anxious to stay in close contact particularly with the German language press on the East Coast.[23] Here, as well as in the larger cities throughout the nation, this was the daily fare of consulates and embassy officials, but the diplomats also paid attention to smaller communities. Maltzan visited various parts of the United States,[24] and his

20. Maltzan, "Inhalt: Deutschtum in Amerika," to AA, 30 January 1926, Abtlg. VI, "Akten betreffend: Die Förderung des Deutschtums in den Vereinigt. St. v. N.A.," vol. 2, R 60105, PA–AA; and attached reports from Vice Consul Leitner, Chicago, dated 27 August 1925; Consul General Ziegler, Chicago, dated 21 September 1925; Legationsrat Frohwein, Seattle, dated 7 October 1925; and Consul Kraske, dated 10 October 1925; ibid.

21. Consul Frohwein used the quote from a German-American newspaper published in Seattle to illustrate what he believed to be the attitude of the vast majority of German Americans; Frohwein to Deutsche Botschaft, 7 October 1925, R 60105, PA–AA.

22. Vorlegender Legationsrat Dr. Sievers, "Aufzeichnung," 12 August 1926, R 60105, PA–AA.

23. In his memoirs Prittwitz claims to have had a close relationship with the Ridder family who published the *New Yorker Staatszeitung*; Prittwitz, *Zwischen Petersburg und Washington*, 216. In 1925 more than two hundred German-language newspapers and periodicals existed in the United States, thirteen of which were located in New York City; Düwell, *Auswärtige Kulturpolitik*, 119–120.

24. Simon, "Inhalt: Dienstreise von General-Konsul Dr. Simon," to AA, 25 June 1928, R 80145, PA–AA.

successor continued what he had begun on a larger scale, repeatedly traveling not only to the Midwest but also to the South and the Far West. Prittwitz discussed this with the Foreign Office and with Stresemann in December 1927 before leaving for his new post, and even President Hindenburg concurred on the importance of German Americans first and foremost as Americans.[25]

With this policy in mind Prittwitz traveled to Chicago and Milwaukee in January 1929 to make contact with the regional "centers" of German America.[26] Two months later he visited parts of the South. In New Orleans—as in Jacksonville, Florida, and other cities in the South—the German-American community had just begun to reorganize. The German House had been reopened only shortly before the ambassador arrived. However, compared with the situation before World War I, there were noticeable changes. The German American Club of Jacksonville, for example, which had had a large clubhouse before the war, now reopened in a much smaller building, and membership was still quite small. During his journey Prittwitz met many Americans of German descent, he reported to Berlin, who were proud of their heritage, an indication that the "war-time psychosis seems to be spent."[27] Prittwitz's evaluation of the German-American community, nonetheless, was scathing:

> Despite extraordinarily good results in the area of athletics and music, the major part of the German-American community has not been able to elevate its meetings beyond beer drinking and social chit-chat over coffee. The support of German art and literature, which should have been of major interest, has been seriously neglected. It is an irony of fate, that the major source of support for German culture has shifted to the American universities."[28]

---

25. Prittwitz, *Zwischen Petersburg und Washington*, 214–217.

26. In Chicago he talked to members of the Germania Club, the Chicago Club, the Midday Club, and the Commercial Club. He also went on the air at a local radio station. In Milwaukee he addressed the Deutsche Vereinigung. See Prittwitz to AA, 29 December 1928, Personalia Nr. 138, "v. Prittwitz u. Gaffron," vol. 3, PA–AA; Prittwitz, "Botschafterbesuch in Chicago und Milwaukee," to AA, 12 February 1929, R 80145, PA–AA; "Redenverzeichnis," n.d., Papers of Friedrich Wilhelm von Prittwitz und Gaffron (NL Prittwitz), box 002, #1B, inventory no. I–138, Konrad-Adenauer-Stiftung, St. Augustin (KAS).

27. Prittwitz, "Inhalt: Südenreise," to AA, 30 April 1929, AA, Länderabteilung III, Verkehrswesen 12, Ver. Staaten v. Amerika, vol. 1, "Reiseberichte," 46965, BA–P.

28. Prittwitz to Bülow, 20 May 1930, R 29474, PA–AA; Prittwitz, "Reise nach Minnesota und Iowa," to AA, 3 February 1931, Personalia Nr. 138, "v. Prittwitz u. Gaffron," vol. 3, PA–AA; and "Anlage 1," ibid.; "Redenverzeichnis," n.d., 002/2, NL Prittwitz/KAS; Prittwitz, "Inhalt:

Thus, when Anton Erkelenz, a member of the German Reichstag, proposed to establish a Vereinigung Carl Schurz that would address this issue, his proposal was warmly welcomed. The organization—with financial backing from the industrialist Robert Bosch and a number of other prominent Germans—was to promote German spirit, culture, science and art, traditions, and language, particularly among second and third generation German Americans.[29] Starting with a discussion Erkelenz had with Ambassador Maltzan in Washington, the Auswärtiges Amt had been involved in every step of the initial planing and it also helped to set up the Vereinigung's agenda.[30] Foreign office officials tried to avoid the impression that the organization was a propaganda tool, and for this reason, for example, they refrained from sending a delegate to the organizational meeting in mid-May 1926. This did not prevent them—despite an agreement that it should "under no circumstances" receive more than five thousand Reichsmarks to cover initial costs—from making substantial contributions to finance the Vereinigung Carl Schurz for programs such as inviting a number of German-American journalists to Germany in 1927.[31]

The same strategy of unofficial cooperation and financial support was used with organizations in charge of academic exchanges. The German Academic Exchange Service (Deutscher Akademischer Austauschdienst or DAAD) had begun its work in 1924 with twelve scholarships to the United States, a number that increased to forty-eight by the academic year. Cooperating with

Nordwestreise," to AA, 31 May 1931, Abtlg. III, "Akten betreffend: Politische Beziehungen der Vereinigten Staaten zu Deutschland," vol. 18, R 80150, PA–AA.

29. [Erkelenz,] "Zur Pflege deutschen Geisteslebens in den Vereinigten Staaten: Deutsch-amerikanische Vereinigung Karl Schurz," n.d. [18 January 1926], Abtlg. III, "Akten betreffend: Deutschtum in den Ver. Staaten von Amerika," vol. 1, R 80287, PA–AA.

30. Erkelenz to Maltzan, 11 January 1926, Abtl. III, "Akten betreffend: Politische und kulturelle Propaganda," vol. 6, R 80298, PA–AA; Maltzan to Erkelenz, 27 March 1926, Abtl. III, "Akten betreffend: Politische und kulturelle Propaganda," vol. 6, R 80298, PA–AA.

31. [Walter de Haas, Ministerialdirektor, AA] to Ministerialdirektor Heilborn, 1 February 1926, R 80298, PA–AA; Vorlegender Legationsrat Graf Podewils to Heilborn, 14 May 1926, R 60105, PA–AA. On the financial contributions—twenty-five thousand Reichsmarks in 1927 and in 1928, twenty-thousand in 1929, and fifteen for 1930 and 1931—see Vorlegender Legationsrat Karl Alexander Fuehr, "Aufzeichnung betr. die Vereinigung Carl Schurz," dated 18 February 1931, Abtl. III, "Akten betreffend: Politische und kulturelle Propaganda—Vereinigung Carl Schurz," vol. 1, R 80327, PA–AA; de Haas to Reichsministerium des Inneren [which donated fifteen thousand Reichsmarks in 1928], 23 July 1928, Abtlg. III, "Akten betreffend: Deutschtum in den Vereinigten Staaten v. Am.," vol. 2, R 80288, PA–AA. Erkelenz et al. to Reichsaußenminister Stresemann, 12 November 1926, R 80298, PA–AA. Erkelenz proposed to invite ten German-American journalists.

the Institute of International Education in the American German Student Exchange, the DAAD helped forty-nine Americans be accepted by German institutions that same year.[32] Even though the organization may have "put itself at the service of the official cultural policy," as its managing director Anton Morsbach declared in 1930, it is unlikely that the Foreign Office reached its goal of having fifty percent of students visiting German universities be German Americans; the American partners conducted their selection process quite independently.[33]

What probably did more to revive German-American interest in Germany than a purely academic exchange was the Amerika-Werkstudenten-Dienst (America Working Student Service), established in 1925. By 1933 about five hundred German students a year went to the United States to work in companies and on farms, and many enjoyed frequent contact with German Americans. The students were enthusiastic about their experiences in America, but they were also aware that they may have had acquired a taste for personal freedom, teamwork, and egalitarian social manners that would not be appreciated in their native Germany. At a meeting initiated by industrialist Carl Duisberg in 1928, one of the students warned the assembled employers that returnees employed at their company might give them a pat on the shoulder exclaiming: "Man, am I happy to be working for you!" But, the speaker reassured his listeners, there was no real reason to worry, because "the young man will soon learn again to click his heels and to take off his hat."[34]

32. Institute of International Education, *The American German Student Exchange: Six Years of Progress* (New York: IIE, n.d. [1929]), 1. The academic exchange with the United States was quite clearly the most important aspect of the Exchange Service. It was not until 1926 that it started an academic exchange with Great Britain and 1928 with France, and even then the numbers for these countries remained well below those for the United States. See Hans Freytag, "Über deutsche Kulturpolitik im Ausland," *Deutsche Rundschau* 55 (August 1929): 97–109; Düwell, *Auswärtige Kulturpolitik*, 175; Abelein, *Kulturpolitik*, 124–125.

33. Frohwein to Deutsche Botschaft, 7 October 1925, R 60105, PA–AA; "Bericht des Oberregierungsrates a.D. Dr. Morsbach über seine Reisen nach Amerika, Januar–Mai 1929; März–Juli 1930," 2, Abtlg. VI, "Akten betreffend: Studentenaustausch. Nordamerika.," vol. 1, R 64236, PA–AA.

34. The Amerika-Werkstudenten-Dienst later developed into the Carl-Duisberg-Gesellschaft. See Georg Schreiber, "Die Amerika-Werkstudenten: Ein Geleitwort," *Studentenwerk* 2 (July 1928): 130–135 and Helmut Hemscheidt, "Wirtschaftsfrieden in der amerikanischen Industrie?" *Studentenwerk* 2 (July 1928): 136–140. The quotation is from "Welt der Amerika-Werkstudenten." On the lasting impression of their experience see Herbert Krippendorff, "1926–1962: Zwei Generationen Amerika-Praktikanten," *Der Auslandskurier* 3 (1962): 9–10.

The German representatives were full of praise for the academic exchange programs,[35] but in reviving German-American ethnic identity their real work was with the representatives of German-American organizations. In this the diplomats in the United States were helped after 1926 by the Reichsmarine and visits by navy vessels such as the cruiser *Hamburg* under the command of Captain Otto Groos. Leaving Wilhelmshaven in February 1926, the *Hamburg* was to stop at the West Indies, cross through the Panama Canal, and visit ports in Latin America before steaming to Los Angeles for the first visit of a German navy ship to the United States after World War I.[36]

For the local German-American community the *Hamburg* was an obvious attraction, not only because it established a link to the Old Country, but also because the ship offered its visitors an attraction that was unavailable to them in the entire United States: beer. Drinking beer had always been a part of the German cultural heritage in America, and Prohibition had been a great burden for the German-American community. It was no wonder then that the Citizens' League organized in Chicago in 1918 had as one of its foremost goals the repeal of the Nineteenth Amendment to the Constitution.[37]

When the *Hamburg's* sailors went ahead and sold this beverage banned in the United States for a "buck a bottle," it may have been enjoyed by many a visitor, but it did not go unnoticed by the authorities. The Department of State demanded an explanation from the ambassador, and the press, even in Germany, reported the incident. Carl von Ossietzky, editor of the paper *Montag Morgen*, had a poem published that depicted the sailors of the *Hamburg* as drunkards waving beer bottles while escorting their concubines through Hollywood;

---

35. See, for example, Prittwitz, *Zwischen Petersburg und Washington*, 194.

36. The *"Reiseplan* des Kreuzers 'Hamburg' 1926/27," n.d., can be found in R43I/601, BA–P. Here, Los Angeles, California, was the only stop on the American mainland mentioned before the ship was to leave for Honolulu, Hawaii. The altered plan, with San Francisco as an additional stop, dated February 15, 1926, is located in Office of the Adjutant General, Central Files, AG 355.11 Germany (3–6–26), Record Group (RG) 407, NA. It had been submitted by the German ambassador to the Department of State and then forwarded to the War Department. See Department of State to Secretary of War, 6 March 1926, 862.3311/153, Department of State, Decimal Files, RG 59, NA. All visits of foreign ships to Latin American harbors were closely monitored by the American military or naval attachés in those countries. For such a reaction to the *Hamburg's* visit to San José de Guatemala, see Gwynn, "Subject: Propaganda: Visit of the German Cruiser 'Hamburg,'" G–2 Report, dated 30 April 1926, Records of the War Department, General and Special Staff, Military Intelligence Division, document 2257–B–68/1 (MID and document number), Record Group (RG) 165, NA.

37. Sethe to Auswärtiges Amt, 5 August 1922, R 60104, PA–AA.

"Sling," the famous Weimar court reporter for the *Vossische Zeitung*, wondered if a German warship should really become a "Stehbierhalle," a cheap bar.[38]

Captain Groos was probably quite relieved when he steamed for Honolulu on June 8, 1926, where he was greeted enthusiastically by the local German-American community. Weeks before the ship arrived, prominent German-Americans had established a welcome committee to set up a program for the officers and enlisted men during the almost three weeks the *Hamburg* was to stay. The sailors could use the streetcars for free, had access to the Army Service Club, and could attend a dance every Saturday, where suitable dance partners were provided "under proper chaperonage," as the local intelligence officer of the U.S. Army, Captain H. Compton Jones, reported to Washington. On Independence Day, sailors from the *Hamburg*, much to the dismay of Jones, even took part in the parade—under arms and in a goose step. The effect of this visit on the German-American community was quite noticeable, he wrote: The German language, which had hardly been used in public after the war, was again heard frequently on the streets of Honolulu. When the arrival of the cruiser *Emden* was announced in 1929, this even led to the revival of the German Club that had been dormant since 1917, the first such re-establishment of a German-American organization on the Hawaiian Islands after the war. The *Emden's* captain even initiated the establishment of a Deutscher Verein that was to serve all German-American organizations.[39]

38. [Maltzan,] "Notiz: Zu dem Erlass II F 2229 vom 18. August 1926," n.d., BoWa 1169, PA–AA; Maltzan to Secretary of State Kellogg, 1 June 1926, BoWa 1169, PA–AA. "Sling" is Paul Schlesinger who wrote on February 11, 1927, about the court hearings on the poem. See Ruth Greuner, ed. *Sling: "Der Fassadenkletterer vom 'Kaiserhof'": Berliner Kriminalfälle aus den zwanziger Jahren* (Berlin: Arani, 1990), 272–273, 343, note 50. During the hearings a representative of the German navy claimed that undercover agents had provoked the incident. Ossietzky and Erich Weinert, the author of the poem, were sentenced to a five hundred Mark fine. See "Ein neuer Beleidigungsprozeß um den Kreuzer 'Hamburg.' Der Amerikabesuch des Schulschiffes," *Preußische Kreuz Zeitung*, 10 February 1927; a clipping of the article is in BoWa 1169, PA–AA.

39. Captain H. Compton Jones, Acting Chief of Staff (AcofS), G–2, Headquarters Hawaiian Quarters, "Subject: Report on the visit of the German Cruiser Hamburg to Hawaiian waters," to ACofS, G–2, War Department, 16 July 1926, MID 2257–B–68/3. Major Casey Hayes, ACofS, G–2, Headquarters Hawaiian Quarters, "Subject: Visit of German Cruiser 'Emden,'" to ACofS, G–2, War Department, 26 August 1929, MID 2257–B–89/7. On an earlier visit to American waters the *Emden* had been to Sitka in Alaska and to Seattle, Washington. The *Emden's* captain had learned from the experience of the *Hamburg* and kept alcoholic beverages under lock and key when his ship visited American harbors. See Foerster, "Bericht des Kreuzers 'Emden' über den Aufenthalt in Seattle vom 21. Juli bis 5. August 1927," 10–11, n.d., Po 14c II, "1926–29, Kreuzer Emden," BoWa 1170/I, PA–AA. [Lothar] v[on] Arnauld [de la Perière], *"Geheim!, Bericht* des Kreuzers 'Emden' über den Aufenthalt in Honolulu vom 16.VIII.–23.VIII. 1929,"

Consul General Hentig was enthusiastic about the effect the cruiser had when it stopped in San Diego, California, during its return journey to Germany. Probably with a bit of self-serving exaggeration, Hentig reported to the Auswärtiges Amt that it had been of pivotal importance for the German-American community in Southern California. Americans of German descent had been awakened to a national consciousness and a new feeling of self-respect. They were starting to enroll their children in German language classes again, and a number of educational institutions began reintroducing such classes.[40]

But such visits were not always successful. When the *Emden* stopped in New Orleans, Louisiana, in March 1930, not only did the crew encounter German-American communists who tried to distribute pamphlets, but the ship's captain, Lothar von Arnauld de la Perière, was also confronted with Louisiana's notorious governor, Huey P. Long. When von Arnauld, in full dress uniform and accompanied by German Consul Rolf L. Jaeger, made his courtesy visit to Long after his ship had docked on Sunday morning, the governor opened the door dressed in green silk pajamas, blue slippers, and a red and blue bathrobe. Appalled, the captain threatened to leave New Orleans immediately if Long did not apologize. This, the governor did the next day when he visited the *Emden*. When Long left, he was rewarded with a twenty-one-gun salute.[41]

He may have intended to ridicule the German navy, but Long's insult probably helped to unite the German-American community. Consul Jaeger reported that the visit had been of particular importance to the German Americans in his district. After years of hesitation they had re-established a Deutsches Haus in the fall of 1928. Visits by Maltzan and Prittwitz had helped increase ethnic identity among German Americans, but many had still been reluctant to acknowledge their background. The sight of German navy cadets and officers in the streets of New Orleans and the warm welcome given to them

---

4, Abtlg. II F–M (Militär u. Marine), "Akten betreffend: Auslandsreise des Kreuzers 'Emden' II 1926/1928 Berichte," vol. 2, R 33452, PA–AA.

40. Hentig to AA, 16 September 1929, R 33452, PA–AA.

41. Jaeger to Botschaft Washington, 5 March 1930, BoWa 1170/I, PA–AA. See also "German Officer Insulted by Gov. Long's Pajamas," *St. Louis Post Dispatch*, 4 March 1930, clipping in BoWa 1170/I, PA–AA. A copy of the leaflet of the Communist Party of the U.S.A., "An die Matrosen des Kreuzers 'Emden'!" asking them to join their comrades in the American navy to fight against the imperialist war, can be found in BoWa 1170/I, PA–AA.

by the citizens of the city had done much for the self-respect of the German element.[42]

It seems that all these efforts by the German Foreign Office and the Reichswehr had some impact on German-American communities throughout the United States. Clubs and other sociocultural organizations were revitalized and many German Americans became willing or even eager to express interest in their ethnic and cultural heritage. That official German efforts were conducted very cautiously helped to foster a favorable view of Germany during the Weimar period. Whether the revitalization of German-American ethnic identity ever translated into a direct political advantage for Germany is doubtful. When in October 1932 the First National Congress of Americans of German Descent was held in New York City, some officials from the German Foreign Office greeted this effort enthusiastically as a starting point for crystallizing the political voice of the German-American community. They believed that it was a result of their own efforts, and saw the meeting as an indication of the potential future impact of German Americans in the American political arena. The published minutes of the meeting, however, show little to support this expectation.[43] Whatever small potential this meeting might have had in terms of promoting cultural relations and academic exchange, any revitalization of German-American ethnic identity became irrelevant when news of antidemocratic practices and antisemitic policies in Germany reached the United States in early 1933.

All of the ambassadors, Wiedfeldt, Maltzan, and Prittwitz, had cautioned those in Germany who called for an increase in propaganda and attempts to utilize Americans of German descent, warning that this could only be counterproductive. After Prittwitz resigned from his post in March 1933 and Hans Luther succeeded him in Washington, this changed, despite Luther's suggestion that the careful cultivation of German Americans should be continued along the lines developed by his predecessors. For example, the German consul general in New York, Otto Kiep—who had hoped to become

---

42. Jaeger to AA, 13 March 1930, 6–7, Abtlg. II F–M (Militär u. Marine), "Akten betreffend: Auslandsreise des Kreuzers 'Emden III' 1930 und Berichte," vol. 1, R 33453 PA–AA. Reichswehr officers—a number of whom were stationed with the U.S. Army for one-year stints after 1929—experienced the same warm welcome from German-American communities. Like the visits of German navy vessels, their contacts with German Americans often served as a catalyst for renewed interest in German Americans' ethnic ties. See the many documents and reports in Oberkommando des Heeres, Generalstab des Heeres (RH 2) Nr. 1821 and RH 2 Nr. 1822, BA–MA.

43. The minutes and speeches of the meeting are published in *Erster Nationalkongress*.

Maltzan's successor in 1927—suggested to the Foreign Office that increased propaganda would help generate understanding for the "new Germany." Funded with more than thirty thousand dollars for a six-month period, Kiep went ahead and planned a number of propaganda activities, including a newspaper entitled *Germany Today* and the publication of pamphlets and books. His most trusted adviser was none other than George Sylvester Viereck. The press and public opinion in the United States reacted almost immediately, and Kiep was recalled to Germany within a matter of weeks. Despite the warnings that the Foreign Office had received from Wiedfeldt, Maltzan, Prittwitz, and even Luther, propaganda among German Americans was intensified. These efforts were now mainly directed and organized by the Deutsches Ausland-Institut in Stuttgart. No lessons had been drawn from the World War I period, and German Americans were again perceived as a monolithic bloc that could be utilized by Germany to keep the United States neutral in the unfolding European conflict.[44]

During the Weimar period, all German ambassadors, having learned from the botched German propaganda efforts in the United States during World War I, shied away from open and aggressive propaganda among German Americans, and they withstood massive and repeated pressure from Berlin to mount propaganda efforts in the United States. They perceived German Americans as a possibly valuable asset in the bilateral relations between the United States and Germany—if handled carefully. Certainly, reports by diplomats about their successes have to be taken with a grain of salt. But in this

---

44. Otto Kiep, *Mein Lebensweg, 1886–1944: Aufzeichnungen während der Haft* (München: n.p., 1982), 122, 144, 154. Kiep wrote these memoirs while he was in jail because of his involvement in the attempted coup of July 1944. He was executed in 1944 in Plötzensee. AA to Reichsministerium für Volksaufklärung und Propaganda, z. Hd. v. Herrn Staatssekretär Funk, 14 August 1933, Abtlg. III, "Akten betreffend: Politische und kulturelle Propaganda in den Vereinigten Staaten von Amerika," vol. 15, R 80307, PA–AA. Already in this letter the AA cautioned that more than thirty thousand dollars would be needed if all of Kiep's ideas were to be implemented. Kiep was retired from active duty on 28 August 1933; see Abtlg. IB, "Akten betreffend: Otto Karl Kiep," Geldakten, Nr. 417G, vol. 1, PA–AA. For German propaganda in the United States after 1933 see Cornelia Wilhelm, *Bewegung oder Verein? Nationalsozialistische Volkstumspolitik in den USA* (Stuttgart: Steiner, 1998) and her essay "Von der Volksgeschichte zur Volkstumspolitik: Heinz Kloss und die volkspolitische Mobilisation des Deutschamerikanertums 1933–1945," in *Gesellschaft und Diplomatie im transatlantischen Kontext: Festschrift für Reinhard R. Doerries zum 65. Geburtstag*, edited by Michael Wala, (Stuttgart: Steiner, 1999), 181-204. Older works include Klaus Kipphan, *Deutsche Propaganda in den Vereinigten Staaten, 1933–1945* (Heidelberg: C. Winter, 1971); Arthur L. Smith, *The Deutschtum of Nazi Germany in the United States* (The Hague: M. Niejhoff, 1965); Sander A. Diamond, *The Nazi Movement in the United States, 1924–1941* (Ithaca/London: Cornell University Press, 1974).

case, the reports written by consuls in San Diego, San Francisco, Los Angeles, and New Orleans relate positive but also negative information and events, and the diplomats give a large measure of credit to the German navy. This, I would argue, indicates a higher degree of accuracy than might be expected otherwise.

If the attempts by the Foreign Office and Reichswehr were successful, as this episode from the interwar period shows quite clearly, ethnic identity is not only shaped by endogenous factors emanating from the ethnic group itself or by its interaction with other ethnic groups and the dominant society. External interests, in this case the interests of the former home country, may come into play and need to be taken into account as well.

Index

Catholicism, German 9–10, 274
  communication channels of 83–85
  continuing ties to Germany of 80
  historiography of 79–80, 85
  influence of German theology on 37–38
  influences on immigration of 83–91
  religious ideology of 85–86
  varieties within 86
Cecilian Society 103
Census, United States 150
  under enumeration in 191–192
Censuses of Agriculture, United States 149
Center Party (Germany) 86
Chain migration 30–34, 63
Chancellorsville, Battle of 295, 297–298, 319
Chevalier, Michel 119–120
Chicago
  acceptance of Jews in 53, 55, 57
  Anglo political dominance in 240
  bilingual education in 241, 273
  disunity of German community in 54–55
  German Catholics in 89
  German community in 53, 334
  German Jews in 46, 49, 50–57, 60–63, 65–68
  local politics in 236
  social separation of Jews in 56
Chicago Demokrat 251
Chicago Tribune 57
Children, Anglo-American
  European critiques of 131–132
Chinese Exclusion Act (1882) 259, 272
Chinese immigrants 259–260
Chosen people
  American and German concepts of 6–7
Christ Episcopal Church (Alexandria, VA) 201–203, 206 n.
Church and state, separation of 7–9, 50, 65
Church associations 11–14, 17

Church membership
  effect on political engagement of 200–201, 203–204
  relationship with social status of 201–202
Church of the Immaculate Conception (Newport, KY) 188
Cincinnati 24, 26, 182, 187
  bilingual education in 241, 278, 281, 288–290
  ethnic conflict in 239
  German Catholics in 89
  German Jews in 49, 230
  German political dominance in 236
  nativist riots in 188
City government
  exaggeration of machine politics in 224
  myth of Irish predominance in 224, 225, 228
Civil War
  antisemitism in 59–60
  ethnic competition in 296–297, 307–308
  German-American participation in 295–326
  German Jewish support for 57–59, 68
Cleveland
  bilingual education in 241, 273, 278–279, 288–289
Cleveland, Grover 267
Cohen, Naomi 44–45
Commerce Act (1887) 258
Community formation
  effects of cultural differences on 18–19
Conewago (PA) 88
Confession
  effects on political affiliation of 230–231
Congregationalists 9
Conservative Party 208–209
Conzen, Kathleen Neils 34, 221
Cooperstown (NY) 218

Hamtramck (MI)
bilingual education in 278 n.
Hanover, Kingdom of
emigration from 19
immigrants from 26
Hansen, George 321–322
Harnack, Adolf 4
Harrison, Carter I 240
Harrison, Carter II 240
Hauke, Fredericke 210
Havemeyer, William F. 223
Hayman, R. D. 190
Haymarket Affair 69–70, 72–73, 109
Hazelton, George 253
Hebrew Benevolent Society 185
Hecker, Friedrich 58
Heinzen, Karl 300
Henni, John Martin 84, 93, 95, 98–100,
102, 106
Hentig (German Consul General) 339
Hetsch, J. J. 187
Higham, John 5, 319
Hincks, Francis 209
Hirsch, Emil 56, 68
Hispanics
assimilation of 289
growing political diversity among
286–287
political importance of 282
social conservatism of 287
support for bilingual education
among 282–283
Historical Climatology Network (HCN)
149–150
Hoan, Daniel 224 n.
Hogan, Andrew 315, 317
Horner, Henry 53
Horstmann, August 295, 300
House of Representatives
German-born members of 243
Huston, Reeve 174
Identity, ethnic 44, 46, 48, 230, 302–
305
Ignatiev, Noel 181

Illinois Staats-Zeitung (Chicago) 53,
55–57, 246, 248–249, 251
Immigrant aid societies 13–14
Immigrant churches
European aid to 11
importance of 26–27
support of European seminaries by
12
ties to European churches of 11–12
Immigrants, Dutch Reformed
religious disputes among 39 n.
Immigration, German Catholic
economic dimension of 83
religious dimensions of 81–82
settlement patterns in 81
Immigration
causes of 25–26
linkage to religion of 3–5
Independent Order of True Sisters 56
Indianapolis
bilingual education in 241, 273,
278–279
Institute of International Education 336
Internal Revenue Act (1882) 262
Ireland, John 8, 14
Irish Americans 7–8
historiography of 177–178
machine politics and 228–229
political engagement of 181, 236
support for Democratic Party by
181, 206–207, 213–214
Irish Catholic Colonization Society 13
Irish Catholics 4
importance of 7
political activities in Québec of 179
Irish immigrants
associational activities of 173, 177
historiography of in Canada 178–
179
opposition to bilingual education
among 241, 286
political dominance of 177
political engagement of 174, 176,
178, 194–195, 199–200, 202, 207–
208, 214